MW00464974

Secrets Revealed of
America's Greatest Cocktails

The Hottest Spirits, Coolest Drinks, and Freshest Places

Robert Plotkin

1987

Tucson, AZ - 2007

www.GreatAmericanCocktails.com

Other Books by Robert Plotkin

1001 Questions Every Bartender and Lounge Lizard Should Know How to Answer (2005)
Beverage Operator's Survival Guide (2005)
The Original Guide to American Cocktails and Drinks — 5th Edition (2004)
The Original Pocket Guide to American Cocktails and Drinks (2004)
The Professional Bartender's Training Manual — 3rd Edition (2002)
Drinks For All Ages — The Original Guide to Alcohol-Free Beverages and Drinks (2002)
Caribe Rum — The Original Guide to Caribbean Rum and Drinks (2001)
Successful Beverage Management — Proven Strategies for the On-Premise Operator (2000)
¡Toma! Margaritas! The Original Guide to Margaritas and Tequila (1999)
Preventing Internal Theft: A Bar Owner's Guide — 2nd Edition (1998)
Increasing Bar Sales — Creative Twists to Bigger Profits (1997)
Reducing Bar Costs: A Survival Guide for the '90s (1993)
501 Questions Every Bartender Should Know How to Answer (1993)
The Professional Guide to Bartending: The Encyclopedia of American Mixology (1991)
The Intervention Handbook: The Legal Aspects of Serving Alcohol — 2nd Edition (1990)

Published by: **BarMedia**
P.O. Box 14486
Tucson, Arizona 85732-4486
520.747.8131
www.BarMedia.com

Copyright 2007 BarMedia
All Rights Reserved
Printed in Canada

Book Design
Katie Alter

Production and Editing
Carol Plotkin
Sarah Dilks
Jocelyn Nelson

Photography
Erik Hinote
Cover photo taken at Janos Restaurant and J BAR, Tucson, AZ

All Rights Reserved. No part of this book may be reproduced or transmitted in any form or by any means, electronic or mechanical, including photocopying, recording, or by any information storage retrieval system without written permission of the author, except for inclusion of a brief quotation(s) in a review. No liability is assumed with respect to the use of the information herein. The information in this book is true and correct to the best of our knowledge. It is offered with no guarantees on the part of the authors or BarMedia. The authors and publishers disclaim all liability in connection with use of this book.

ISBN 10 0-945562-35-7
ISBN 13 978-0-945562-35-1

To Katie Marie Alter,

Through the years you've remained the bedrock of our efforts.
For that and much more, this book of ours is dedicated to you.

Table of Contents

The author and editors of this book strongly advocate responsibility and moderation in the consumption and service of alcohol. The information contained herein is intended to assist in the responsible service of alcohol with the understanding that certification from an alcohol-awareness program is highly beneficial. Responsibility falls on each individual who serves alcohol. Whether at home or a commercial operation, serve conscientiously and responsibly.

Furthermore, we would like to advance the following:

☑ A strong drink is not necessarily a good drink. Increasing a drink's liquor portion increases its alcoholic potency. Over-portioning alcohol is a liability-laden practice.

☑ Not all drinks are created equally. A Martini served straight up is more potent than one served on the rocks. Alcohol is soluble in water and will increase the rate at which ice melts. As a result, the melting ice will dilute the drink's alcohol, rendering it slightly less potent.

☑ Similarly, a blended drink is less potent than one served on the rocks. Blending a drink with ice makes it more diluted. In most instances, the principal ingredient in a blended drink is water (the ice).

☑ Neat drinks are prepared directly into the glass in which they are served. They are undiluted and high in alcohol concentration. Care should be taken with respect to their service.

☑ Shooters and layered cordials are conventionally consumed in one swallow, thereby increasing the rate at which the alcohol is absorbed into a person's bloodstream. Increased rate of consumption tends to accelerate intoxication.

☑ A double, contains 2 times the liquor of a standard drink and is more than twice as potent as two prepared regularly. A double will profoundly impact intoxication. Conversely, a tall drink, one prepared in a tall glass with significantly more mix, is less potent than the same drink prepared in the regular manner.

Serve Responsibly • Drink Responsibly

The first secret to making exceptional cocktails is gaining an appreciation of their ephemeral nature. The zeal and exuberance of these drinks are short-lived. They are optimally consumed shortly after leaving the mixing tin, making them more like moments of time meant to be savored in sips.

Cocktails also have the somewhat magical capacity to elicit smiles from their recipients. They're raised in toast and can immediately satisfy and invigorate. When expertly prepared these drinks are things of beauty, arguably making them works of art that appeal to all of our senses. Ever sip on a Gauguin?

Shaken or stirred, cocktails have been a part of our society for more than two centuries and for more than 200 years there have been people passionate about the art and craft of preparing cocktails. For many, the process is more intoxicating than what the drinks contain. It's rather a heady role playing the alchemist. Ultimately, crafting an amazing cocktail is an exacting science involving drops, dashes and dollops, the combining of dissimilar ingredients, such that in the end, the sum becomes more than its parts.

Secret number two behind the art of making drinks, sensational cocktails can only result from using sensational products. Premium spirits and fresh ingredients are at the heart of every great drink. A familiar theme in this book will be that committing top-shelf spirits and liqueurs to mixed drinks isn't sacrilege, it's an act of creative genius.

This book is a practitioner's guide on making exquisite cocktails. Its secrets, which really amount to tips, suggestions and accrued insights, apply equally to professionals and social hosts. The recipes portrayed in this book are a creative collection derived from scores of mixologists currently in residence at our country's finest lounges, bars and restaurants. It offers a look at how America's best and brightest mixologists interpret the classics, from the Martini, Margarita and Manhattan to the Cosmo, Mojito and Daiquiri. If you love great cocktails, you've come to the right place.

Our book is predicated on the implacable belief that life is too short to drink a bad cocktail. Inspiration is typically the essential difference between a great drink and one that's merely adequate. Ask a mixologist about how they created their fabulous cocktail and the secret to its success is inevitably the last innovation attempted. Each will attest to having experienced rapture upon first tasting their final version, a eureka moment in which it's realized that you've achieved in the glass that which you had envisioned in your mind. Creation is complete.

The third secret behind making great drinks deals with sessionability, a word used to describe a cocktail that your guests can enjoy throughout an evening without it becoming tiring, overbearing, or otherwise unsuitable. Creating a sessionable drink is more challenging than it may initially seem. Cocktails lacking character and dimension are a bore and guaranteed to send people packing. On the other hand, cocktails with excessive amounts of flavor will quickly over-power the palate and rankle the sensibilities like an accordion. Achieving balance between characteristics such as tart, sweet, savory and acidic is the primary mission and mixologist's stock and trade.

The fourth secret has to do with the most unheralded potable in all of mixology, water. Through contact with ice, water becomes an essential ingredient in cocktails and mixed drinks. Its purpose is to lower the drink's temperature and allow the ingredients to meld and harmonize. The quality of the ice and therefore water will assuredly impact the taste of the finished drink, so choose carefully.

Mastering effervescence is another drink making secret. Adding a fine spritz to a drink is a marvelous thing, a centuries old practice. Mere carbonation is passé, now it's about adding quality effervescence. Spritz helps achieve all-important balance between the various elements in a cocktail. It enhances a drink's mouth feel, and most importantly, effervescence energizes a libation, transforming it from flat to teeming with vibrancy and pizzazz.

One thing you can do to immediately improve your drink making abilities is to look beyond using artificially charged water. Conventional club soda can hardly compare to the effervescence of natural sparkling waters, source derived products like San Pellegrino, or Perrier. These famous waters have an abundance of fine bubbles and mild acidity that invigorates a cocktail.

The final secret is incorporating in your repertoire the time-honored skill of muddling. Beyond its theatrical appeal, muddling is a marvelous way of injecting cocktails with the succulence and flavor of fresh ingredients. The enduring popularity of Old Fashioneds and Mojitos can largely be credited to the process of muddling.

If nothing else, this book pays homage to the liberating concept that there exist no limits on what can be shaken, mixed, or blended behind the bar, as long as the result is magic. If you can imagine it, you can make it. *Salud!*

Robert Plotkin
Tucson, Arizona

GreatAmericanCocktails.com

Visit **www.GreatAmericanCocktails.com** for continually updated information and bonus material that will keep your mixology skills perpetually sharp. The web site is the first of its kind! It's a companion to this wonderful book that gives you access with your own VIP password to our ever-growing site, all FREE of cost when you own the book! There will be new drinks and new spirits as well as new featured places added as they come to market, so you'll be the first to know about the hottest new trends and how to make the most of them.

VIP Access to information only found on the web site!

- Drink Preparation Instruction
- Glassware Information and Images
- Additional Fabulous Drink Recipes
- Insightful comments from our Mixology Mates
- Download Bonus Material
- Leave a comment on a recipe or read comments from others

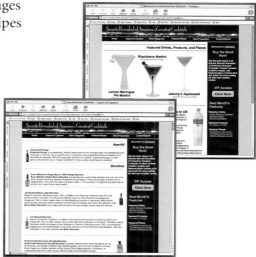

VIP Access

User Name: VIP
Password: 119364896

Visit often for new updates and features
www.GreatAmericanCocktails.com

Our Mission Statement

Through our products and web sites, our mission is to bring people enjoyment and pleasure from their libations, while encouraging responsible social behavior. We believe it's okay to enjoy life and also accept some responsibility for the well-being of our planet. To that effort, we donate 100% of the sales proceeds of select items each month from GreatAmericanCocktails.com to organizations that promote sustainability and judiciousness. We continue to explore ways to grow our company while staying within guidelines that allow us to expand our progressive values and promote positive social change. Visit our web site to see our donation recipients' listings and how we are continuing to grow philanthropically.

America's Favorite Spirits

America's Favorite Spirits

America's Favorite Places

Chapter One

An American Original
The Martini

In January 1934, President Franklin D. Roosevelt signed the constitutional amendment ending Prohibition in the United States. Afterwards, he promptly made a pitcher of icy cold Martinis for all those present in the oval office. Such is the place the cocktail holds in American society.

These are heady times for cocktails in general and Martinis specifically. The American born libation is once again the undisputed king of cocktails, atop the list of drinks that every bar and aspiring mixologist must excel at making. A trademark Martini doesn't have to be elaborate, just well conceived and skillfully executed.

Although its exact origin is still a matter of conjecture, most drink historians believe that the Martini is over a century old and its likely creator was the inimitable Professor Jerry Thomas, widely considered the founder of American mixology. In 1887, he was the first to publish a tome on the subject, *The Bon Vivant's Companion or How To Mix Drinks*. In his book he includes a recipe for the Martinez Cocktail, a libation made with Old Tom Gin (a sweetened version of gin), vermouth, a few dashes of Maraschino liqueur and bitters. Later reprints of the book refer to this drink as the *"Classic Martini."*

While tracking down the origins of this most famous cocktail may be interesting, the more pertinent question is what has the Martini become? The reason for its relevancy is the explosive growth of Martini variations, many of which bear little resemblance to the original recipe. Traditionalists contend that regardless of their burgeoning popularity, cocktails sporting such ingredients as cream, cordials, juice and confections cannot be presumed to be Martinis. Others suggest that changing drinking habits have naturally led to an evolving definition of what sort of libation can be called a Martini.

Before tackling the question, practitioners need to identify the Martini's underlying mechanics. The cocktail's universal appeal can be attributed to the magical marriage of French (dry) vermouth and liquor. As an aperitif wine, the vermouth softens the backbone of the gin or vodka, rendering the cocktail incalculably smooth and sublime.

The other significant element of the cocktail's anatomy is the garnish, which traditionally is a speared pair of green olives. Certainly the olives give the drink an elegant and finished appearance, but they are more than mere window dressing. The olives imbue the cocktail with a salty, briny flavor.

So, in essence, the Martini can be said to be the combination of vermouth, gin (or vodka) and green olives. But, as mixologists know all too well, the Martini is a highly individualized drink. Vary the ratio of vermouth to the gin and the resulting cocktail will taste markedly different. Certainly changing the base liquor from gin to vodka will a have a pronounced effect, as will serving the drink on the rocks versus the more traditional straight up. Even substituting pimento stuffed green olives for ones stuffed with garlic or bleu cheese will dramatically alter the taste of the drink.

If change and individuality are at the heart of the Martini's mystique, then where does one impose creative limitations? In other words, when is the drink so severely altered that it stops bearing resemblance to a Martini and begins to more resemble something entirely different?

Purists typically balk at the inclusion of any ingredient in a Martini other than the vermouth, liquor and a garnish. They'll suggest that if you want to be creative, get a box of Crayons, but don't mess with perfection. While their point is well taken, change is an inexorable force and the Martini is not immune to its effects.

Plymouth™ Gin

Plymouth Gin deserves its status as the world's finest light spirit, this according to the judges at the San Francisco World Spirits Competition. It is fundamentally different from other super-premium brands. This marvelously delicious spirit could well be called the gin that launched a thousand ships. The landmark brand has a long, storied history with the British Royal Navy, in fact it is distilled a short distance from the naval base at Plymouth, England.

Distinguished Plymouth Gin continues to be made where it originated over 200 years ago, at England's oldest, continuously operating distillery, the Black Friars Distillery. The venerable brand is distilled in a large copper alembic still using pure grain spirits, soft Dartmoor water and an infusion of seven, hand selected botanicals.

A quick sniff is all that's necessary to explain Plymouth Gin's enduring popularity. It has an expansive, citrus and juniper bouquet and a seamlessly smooth body. The gin immediately fills the mouth with the exuberant flavors of juniper, coriander, orange and lemon. The gin finishes long and is brimming with flavor.

Exceedingly dry and highly aromatic, it's little wonder why the BBC consistently names Plymouth as England's finest gin. It should be noted that in 1896 the first published recipe for the Martini called for the use of Plymouth Gin and remains an ideal brand to choose when creating a signature Martini.

Come see why Plymouth Gin is still the daily issue to officers in the British Royal Navy.

In the 1950s and '60s, the Martini underwent significant changes as it became increasingly more popular to order Martinis dry or extra dry, which in parlance means to use exceedingly little vermouth. During the same time frame, vodka began to supplant gin as the spirit of choice in Martinis. So, does a cocktail prepared with a few drops of dry vermouth and two or more shots of vodka still qualify the resulting cocktail as a Martini?

That remains a contentious point. In the 1948 seminal work by David Embury entitled, *The Fine Art of Mixing Drinks*, the famed master mixologist asserts that using less than one part of vermouth to seven parts English gin disqualifies the drink's status as a Martini. However, with the popularity of extra dry Martinis — which typically is nothing more than chilled gin or vodka with olives — the conventional definition of what is and what isn't a Martini has steadily undergone change.

What if you replace standard issue vermouth with an equally appealing aperitif wine, such as Lillet or Dubonnet? Is it still a Martini? Again, the answer will vary with each respondent. For example, in the Ian Fleming spy thriller *Casino Royale*, James Bond ordered a dry Martini, "served in a deep champagne goblet and made with three measures of Gordon's (gin), one of vodka, half a measure of Kina Lillet. Shake it very well until it's ice-cold, and then add a large, thin slice of lemon peel." This famous version is now referred to as the **Vesper**, or the **007 Martini**. Not only does James Bond obviously prefer Lillet to vermouth, he splits the base liquor between gin and vodka, which to this day is somewhat unconventional. Would you brave telling James Bond that his cocktail wasn't a Martini?

As this chapter will reveal, the nation's finest mixologists have been tweaking the Martini into glorious new incarnations. While some of these drinks may bear similarities to other cocktail styles; one can still see the genetic footprint of the Martini in their formulation. Is it possible to be overly enthusiastic and lead a Martini too far off the path? Perhaps, but why dally in the theoretical? If the cocktail looks and tastes delicious and you're holding the glass, does it really matter?

Secrets Revealed of America's Greatest Martinis

What's better than divulging secrets? Nothing, especially when they're secrets on making the best Martinis in town. Ah, but a word of caution about our friend, the Martini. It is the most often returned drink at any bar. Use too much vermouth and the drink will get returned. Not enough and it'll come back. Shaken, not shaken, too watery, not sufficiently chilled and the Martini will be coming back. Yeah, they're that touchy. The only viable precaution is to make certain you clearly hear the guest's drink order and prepare the cocktail like you were working with nitroglycerin. Here then are some of the best kept secrets behind America's greatest Martinis.

• **Shaking vs Stirring Martinis** — In the day, if you shook a Martini you were said to have "bruised" the poor drink because of its cloudy appearance. The cloudiness results when a Martini prepared with a significant proportion of vermouth is shaken, thus rendering it extremely cold. Slight cloudiness aside, a shaken Martini is still imminently healthy and robust.

Nevertheless, violently agitating a cocktail comprised solely of a spirit and aperitif wine might be construed as overkill. While shaking a drink will quickly render it cold, the practice will also highly aerate the cocktail and cause more ice to melt, thereby risking over-dilution. Stirring the cocktail takes a little longer to achieve the desired serving temperature, but it is generally presumed a more civilized approach. With deference to James Bond, most Martini aficionados prefer that the cocktail be treated more gently.

So, what's really important when mixing a classic Martini? The primary objective is dropping the temperature of the ingredients to serving temperature. While only the genuinely obsessed would bother sticking a thermometer into the drink to ensure that it is sufficiently chilled, the proper serving temperature for a Martini is around 37-38°F.

Thoroughly mixing the various ingredients into a homogenous cocktail is next on the list. Distilled spirits have specific gravities lighter

Van Gogh® Double Espresso Vodka

Ultra-premium Van Gogh Flavored Vodkas are handcrafted in small batches at the Dirkzwager Distillery in Holland. The entire line is based on infusing a blend of premium grains and purified water with amazing flavors. None better typify their top-shelf status in the flavor community than *Van Gogh Double Espresso Vodka*, an extraordinary, caffeine enriched vodka with more taste than it knows what to do with.

This singular release has an intriguing burnished, coppery brown appearance and a wafting bouquet of freshly brewed coffee. The medium-weight vodka tingles on entry as it immediately fills the mouth with the warm flavor of espresso. Its persistence of flavor is remarkable. This Double Espresso vodka needs to be sampled neat to be fully appreciated. Baristas are going to love it.

Van Gogh Oranje Vodka has a floral bouquet and the sensational taste of Spanish Valencia and Mediterranean blood oranges, while *Van Gogh Citroen Vodka* has a light, appealing bouquet and vibrant palate of peeled citrus. If you're into chocolate, be prepared to be wowed by *Van Gogh Dutch Chocolate*. Every molecule in this vodka screams of life-sustaining Dutch chocolate.

The famed line also includes *Van Gogh Melon, Mango, Coconut, Vanilla, Black Cherry, Mojito Mint, Pomegranate, Espresso, Raspberry, Pineapple, Wild Appel and Original Vodkas*. The entire family of flavored vodkas is indispensable behind the bar. With a simple flick of the wrist, you can add robust flavor to any cocktail without adding the slightest trace of sweetness.

than water, while ingredients such as fortified wines and liqueurs are heavier than water. The gentle act of stirring is sufficient to mix the various ingredients into solution.

The last and rarely acknowledged purpose behind stirring is to add a healthy measure of water to the cocktail. It is the unheralded member of Team Martini. The water seamlessly melds with spirits and modifiers. It softens the blend and further dulls the edge of the liquor. For that reason it's advisable to only use quality ice made from spring or mineral water. The taste of the water will play a part in the finished cocktail.

• **Creative Vermouth-ing** — As mentioned, vermouth is what renders the Martini gloriously smooth. It is also the ingredient whose use requires the most care. Vermouth is typically produced in two distinctively different styles — French and Italian, which are also known as dry and sweet vermouth respectively. It is the dry, French vermouth that is the featured performer in the Martini.

French vermouth is made from a blend of light, Picpoul and Clairette varietal wines, which are aged 2-3 years in oak casks that are exposed to the elements to accelerate maturation. After aging, the wines are infused with botanicals and fortified with spirits to 18% alcohol by volume. Most premium vermouths have a complex floral and fruity bouquet and a dry, mouth-filling palate laced with spice and citrus.

Over the course of the last century the trend was to use increasingly less vermouth in the cocktail, thereby making a progressively drier Martini. Early versions of the drink called for 3 parts gin and 1 part vermouth (3:1), however, over time, the 7:1 dry Martini became the accepted norm. It's said Winston Churchill made his Martinis by pouring gin into a pitcher and glancing briefly at a bottle of vermouth across the room, which by definition is the epitome of an Extra Dry Martini.

Today, however, a steadily growing number of mixologists are reverting to the classic style of using more vermouth when preparing Martinis. This trend comes with a caveat. Vermouth is a complex, sophisticated wine, one that is difficult and laborious to make. Suffice to say, the better the vermouth, the better the resulting Martini.

• **The Fortified Difference** — A time proven avenue for creating delectable signature Martinis is to substitute one of a number of aperitifs for vermouth. There is a natural affinity between spirits and fortified wines. These wines — venerable products such as Lillet and Dubonnet, Fino sherry, Oloroso port, Madeira — are imbued with tremendous flavors and lavishly textured bodies, making them incomparable ingredients in Martinis. Today's practitioners are continuing to explore and redefine the boundaries of this magical pairing.

The list of viable candidates must surely start with Dubonnet and Lillet. Both are French aperitif wines fortified with grape spirits and flavored with proprietary blends of herbs, spices and fruit. They are unsurpassed in Martinis and add greatly to the cocktail's exuberance.

Next would be Iberian greats Sherry and Port. Sherry is a fortified wine produced in Jerez de la Frontera, the famed wine growing region in southern Spain. Of the two styles, dry delicate Fino Sherry is most frequently used instead of vermouth to invigorate Martinis. The Fino Sherry admirably highlights the distinguishing characteristics of each and every one of the botanicals in gin.

Ports are fortified wines made primarily from red wine grapes cultivated in the Upper Duoro Valley of northern Portugal. The style most often recruited for use in making cocktails is Tawny Port, which is a blend of older wines, pale in color with a distinctive amber edge. While Ports are most often paired with whiskeys, it is not unusual to see it featured with super-premium gin or vodka in a Martini.

No reason to stop there. Pineau des Charentes is a fortified wine made from Bordeaux grape varieties and young Cognac brandies. It is elegant, flavorful and ideally suited as a modifier in Martinis. The same can be said about Madeira, a typically sweet, fortified wine made in Portugal and Marsala, an amber fortified wine from Sicily. With such a diverse cast of aperitifs to choose from, one wonders if there are enough days in the week for fully exploring the possibilities.

• **Raising the Bar** — The sustained popularity of super-premium gins and vodkas has strapped a booster to the Martini boom. While some may see committing the world's finest spirits to cocktails a sacrilege, others see it as an act of creative genius. As was the case with vermouth, the better the liquor, the better the Martini. The cocktail's uncomplicated and unfettered structure makes it an ideal vehicle for showcasing the enhanced character and unsurpassed quality of top-shelf spirits. Flavored vodkas are also frequently recruited for use in signature Martinis. They offer flavor without sweetness, which in many recipes is advantageous.

Why limit your Martinis to just gin or vodka though? Tequila and rum perform beautifully in these cocktails. For example, the **Black Tie Martini** features Appleton Estate Jamaica Rum, while **Fidel's Martini** is made with a blend of Cruzan Banana Rum and Stolichnaya Vodka. The **Crystal Pearlessence Martini** is constructed with vodka and a healthy splash of VSOP Cognac and the **Paisley Martini** is made with gin, dry vermouth and a dash of Scotch whisky.

• **Infused and Enthused** — Infusion jars are unrivaled at creating singularly brilliant spirits that the competition can't duplicate.

32° Luxe Lounge

📪 *The Quarter* at the Tropicana Casino and Resort
2801 Pacific Avenue
Atlantic City, NJ 08401

☎ 609.572.0032

▶▶◀ www.32lounge.com

✉ info@32lounge.com

Impeccably swank **32° Luxe Lounge** is a veritable feast for the senses. It caters to discerning twenty and thirty somethings and those seeking a Continental experience. The place has a high voltage thrum, alive with music and the din of champagne bottles being opened and people sipping cocktails. The interior design is drenched in European chic. It is nightlife at its finest.

A quick tour tells the story. The fashionable lounge has a plush, intimate feel with demure lighting and a pulsating hip-hop beat. The bill of fare is strictly first class. Champagne by the glass, classic cocktails, an expansive wine selection, plus a back bar loaded with top-shelf offerings.

The availability of bottle service allows invited guests in the VIP seating section to enjoy cocktails of their own design. The lounge provides the mixers and garnishes, everything the guest needs to act as their own host. The European style service fits the place like a glove. Private liquor cabinets — each rented by the year — allow VIP guests to store bottles under lock and key for future visits.

Those seated around the bar are under the expert care of a masterful staff of professionals. Specialties of the house often contain the iridescent glow of red or blue. Everything in the lounge shimmers, gleams or somehow catches your eye and admiration. One of the signatures of the house is the *Lemon Meringue Pie Martini*, an icy blend of Ketel One Citroen, Stoli Vanil and lime juice served in a chilled cocktail glass rimmed with crushed graham crackers. Whatever you choose to sip, be prepared to be wowed. And you can bring your Euros. —RP

Lemon Meringue Pie Martini
Drink recipe on pg 20

When you create a winning infusion, there's only one place to get it. You can turn virtually any spirit into something extraordinary by infusing it with everything from kiwis, melons and pepper tovanilla, cucumbers and sun dried tomatoes.Steeping spirits is straightforward and uncomplicated. The process involves marinating fresh fruit, among other things, in large, airtight containers filled with spirits. Several days to a week later, the fruit will infuse the chosen spirit with flavor, color, aroma and loads of appealingcharacter. Consider promoting a signature Martini made with lemon-infused gin, pepper-steeped tequila, vanilla and cherry-infused rum or pineapple vodka. The possibilities are endless.

- **Modifier Bonanza** — A splash or two of a liqueur contributes four invaluable things to a Martini. It adds a blast of flavor, texture and heft to the body, a welcome touch of sweetness and gives the cocktail an alluring hue. When Lauren Dunsworth of Lola's first combined a measure of DeKuyper Sour Apple Pucker and Ketel One Vodka to create the *Lola's Apple Martini*, a new wave of Martinis were born. Soon Kahlúa was enlisted for use in the *Café Nuttini*, Godiva in the *Chocolate Martini* and Frangelico in the *Nutcracker Martini*. Chambord, Grand Manier and Blue Curaçao are also popularly featured in specialty Martinis.

Bak's Zubrówka® Bison Grass Vodka

Long revered by enthusiasts and aficionados, Zubrówka is a traditional Polish vodka flavored with bison grass, which is indigenous exclusively to Eastern Poland. For years this spectacular spirit was unavailable in the States. Its importation was long delayed because of a trace element in the grass — coumarin — resulted in the vodka being banned in America.

Well, worry not, and welcome the long awaited arrival of *Bak's Zubrówka Bison Grass Vodka*. Produced at the Polmos Bielsko Distillery, the vodka is triple-distilled in column stills from potatoes and artesian well water. It is then infused with the essential oils of the bison grass before being filtered through charcoal and oak chips. It is bottled at 82 proof.

Bak's Zubrówka is coumarin-free and a dead ringer for the traditional infused version. The bottle even contains a long, slender blade of bison grass. The vodka has a pale yellow hue, a soft, lightweight body and a generous bouquet of fresh, grassy and floral aromas. The palate is loaded with spicy, sweet flavors that gradually fade into a warm and relaxed finish.

The bison grass in the Zubrówka is said to give one vitality and strength. Others insist that it has aphrodisiac properties. Whatever the motivation, this vodka is an experience not to be missed. It is a genuine treat to drink in conventional manner, but it deserves to be first sampled neat. Zubrówka is an authentic and superbly delicious vodka.

Inspired modifiers are not limited to liqueurs, however. For instance, add an effervescent dose of champagne in your Martini, or heat things up with a few dashes of jalapeño juice. Splash in fresh lime juice, or use any one of the many flavored syrups on the market. There are no boundaries on creativity.

• **A Muddled Affair** — The Mojito and Old Fashion are illustrative of how to best incorporate fresh ingredients on a per cocktail basis. In their preparation ingredients such as cut limes, oranges or fresh mint sprigs are muddled, thus releasing their succulence and essential oils. Sugar is added to balance out the acidic pith. The cocktail is then ready to receive the spirits and various modifiers that make it a singular creation.

Increasingly mixologists are reaching for the bar muddler when constructing their specialty Martinis. Examples abound, such as the ***Berry Basil***, a signature at 33 Restaurant & Lounge, which features muddled fresh blackberries and basil, or the ***Cote d'Azur***, a specialty Martini at Brasserie JO, in which muddled English cucumbers and finely chopped parsley are used to modify Lillet and Ketel One Citroen. The application of the century old drink making technique has elevated craft Martinis to fresh new heights.

• **Improving on Perfection** — Garnishing a Martini isn't an obligation or act of embellishment; it's a creative opportunity. In a cocktail consisting of little more than a spirit and aperitif wine, the garnish essentially becomes another source of flavor and dimension. Pimento stuffed olives do not circumscribe the garnishing possibilities. This point cannot be stressed enough. Embrace the freedom and live a little. Consider your options, a partial list includes prosciutto stuffed olives, speared lychees, orange zest spirals, anchovy-wrapped olives, fresh picked strawberries, bleu cheese stuffed olives, spearmint sprigs, kiwi slices, pickled green tomatoes, sliced cucumbers, and watermelon spears. A thoroughly engaging garnish ensures that the Martini will be as visually appealing as it is delicious.

• **Enhanced Presentation** — The final act of the performance entails the cocktail's presentation. One of the more inventive cocktails devised is the ***Smoked Martini*** made with super-premium gin. The twist is this — while the drink is chilling in the mixing glass, the bartender lights a cedar strip, blows out the fire and allows the fragrant smoke to swirl up inside an inverted chilled snifter. The effect is dramatic. The theatrics are engaging and imbue the cocktail with a captivating smoky flavor.

A more traditional approach is to present the guest with a large chilled cocktail glass and a tray with the ingredients needed to build a Martini perfectly suited to his or her own personal preferences. A small water carafe resting in a larger, iced glass is filled with chilled liquor; another carafe contains the vermouth. There are small compartments with condiments such as olives, onions and lemon twists. It's an elegant presentation that nearly eliminates any possibility of the Martini being returned due to bartender error.

Make every Martini you serve a work of art. Involve others in your efforts of devising a signature Martini or two. Once the winners have been selected, don't keep them a secret. Great Martinis are meant to be shared.

"Steeping spirits is straightforward and uncomplicated."

Stolichnaya® Elit Vodka

Stolichnaya Elit Vodka is the flagship of the brand's world-class range. It will undoubtedly become the standard bearer for what sociologists call the "pursuit of small indulgences," a megatrend in which we are all a bit more receptive to periodically sampling the good life. And that's just what Stolichnaya Elit is — a slice of the good life.

This most appropriately named spirit is distilled in small batches using select winter wheat and pristine glacier water. But the secret to this amazing distilled spirit is something called "freeze filtration," a technique devised in the days of the czars. Vodka was placed in barrels subjected to the terrible cold weather. Impurities in the vodka slowly gravitated to the wooden staves where they would become frozen and fall out of solution. Later the essentially pure vodka would be poured out through an opening in the bottom of the barrel.

Your first taste of Stoli Elit may well surprise you. It has a seamless, feather-weight body and an impeccably clean, flavorful character completely devoid of harshness. The vodka gradually warms the mouth and then quickly dissipates into a relaxed finish.

Here's a vodka that begs to be sampled neat, or with a slight chill. Stolichnaya Elit will make believers out of those who doubt that vodka is a standalone performer. Most mixologists will naturally opt to use it as the featured attraction in a gourmet Martini, Cosmopolitan and other vodka-based cocktails. It will make any drink that much better.

007 Martini
a.k.a. Vesper
Excerpted from The Original Guide to
American Cocktails and Drinks- 6th Edition
Cocktail glass, chilled
Pour ingredients into an iced mixing glass
1 1/2 oz. Gin
1/2 oz. Vodka
1/2 oz. Lillet Blanc
Shake and strain
Garnish with a lemon twist
Pour ingredients into the iced mixing glass. Stir gently and strain contents into a chilled cocktail glass. Garnish with a lemon twist.

Ancho Caramel Cranapple Martini
Specialty of J BAR
Created by Patrick Harrington, Linda Zubel
Cocktail glass, chilled painted with a thin
   ribbon of ancho caramel sauce*
Pour ingredients into an iced mixing glass
1 1/2 oz. Vox Green Apple Vodka
2 oz. cranberry juice
Shake and strain
Garnish with a sliced green apple drizzled
   with ancho caramel sauce*
Paint a thin ribbon of chilled ancho caramel sauce around the inside of a chilled cocktail glass. Pour ingredients into the iced mixing glass. Shake thoroughly and strain contents into the prepared cocktail glass. Garnish with a sliced green apple drizzled with ancho caramel sauce.
*Ancho Caramel Sauce Recipe - pg 317

Asian Pear and Ginger Martini
Specialty of Jade Bar
Created by Greg Portsche
Cocktail glass, chilled
Pour ingredients into an iced mixing glass
2 oz. Ketel One Citroen Vodka
1/2 oz. Granny Smith Sour Apple Schnapps
1/2 oz. Hiram Walker Peach Schnapps
1/2 oz. ginger simple syrup*
Shake and strain
Garnish with a pear chip
Pour ingredients into the iced mixing glass. Shake thoroughly and strain contents into a chilled cocktail glass. Garnish with a pear chip.
*Ginger Simple Syrup Recipe - pg 320

Black Tie Martini
Excerpted from The Original Guide to
American Cocktails and Drinks- 6th Edition
Cocktail glass, chilled
Pour ingredients into an iced mixing glass
2 oz. Appleton Estate Extra Jamaica Rum
1/4 oz. Dry Vermouth
Stir and strain
Garnish with black olives
Pour ingredients into the iced mixing glass. Stir gently and strain contents into a chilled cocktail glass. Garnish with 2 black olives.

Blackberry Martini
Specialty of 33 Restaurant & Lounge
Created by Ari Bialikamien
Cocktail glass, chilled
Pour ingredients into an empty mixing glass
Splash simple syrup
Handful of fresh ripe blackberries
Muddle contents
Add ice
1 oz. Belvedere Pomarancza Vodka
1/2 oz. Lillet Blanc
Splash Rose's Lime Juice
Shake and strain
Garnish with a fresh blackberry on a skewer
Pour simple syrup and blackberries into the empty mixing glass. Muddle and add ice. Pour in the vodka, Lillet and Rose's Lime Juice. Shake thoroughly and strain contents into a chilled cocktail glass. Garnish with a fresh blackberry on a skewer.

Blonde Ambition

Specialty of Backstreet Café
Created by Sean Beck
Cocktail glass, chilled
Pour ingredients into an iced mixing glass
1 3/4 oz. Grey Goose L'Orange Vodka
1/4 oz. Cointreau
Splash fresh lime juice
1/2 oz. white cranberry juice
1 oz. fresh tangerine juice
Shake and strain
Garnish with 4 dried cranberries
Pour ingredients into the iced mixing glass. Shake thoroughly and strain the contents into a chilled cocktail glass. Garnish with 4 dried cranberries dropped into the bottom of the glass.

Café Nuttini Martini

Excerpted from The Original Guide to American Cocktails and Drinks- 6th Edition
Cocktail glass, chilled
Pour ingredients into an iced mixing glass
2 oz. Vodka
1/2 oz. Kahlúa
1/2 oz. Disaronno Amaretto
Stir and strain
Garnish with an orange twist
Pour ingredients into the iced mixing glass. Stir gently and strain contents into a chilled cocktail glass. Garnish with an orange twist.

Cantaloupe Martini

Specialty of Jade Bar
Created bye Greg Portsche, Michelle French
Cocktail glass, chilled
Pour ingredients into an iced mixing glass
2 oz. Ketel One Vodka
2 oz. Watermelon Liqueur
Splash fresh lime juice
Splash fresh orange juice
Shake and strain
Garnish with a fresh cantaloupe melon ball
Pour ingredients into the iced mixing glass. Shake thoroughly and strain contents into a chilled cocktail glass. Garnish with a fresh cantaloupe melon ball.

Cappuccinitini

Specialty of Jade Bar
Created by Greg Portsche
Cocktail glass, chilled
Pour ingredients into an iced mixing glass
1 1/2 oz. Stoli Vanil Vodka
1 1/2 oz. Godiva Cappuccino Liqueur
2 oz. Fonte's Espresso Reserve Blend
Shake and strain
Garnish with 3 chocolate covered coffee beans
Pour ingredients into the iced mixing glass. Shake thoroughly and strain contents into a chilled cocktail glass. Garnish with 3 chocolate covered coffee beans.

Chai Latte Martini

Specialty of 33 Restaurant & Lounge
Created by Jenn Harvey
Cocktail glass, chilled
Pour ingredients into an iced mixing glass
2 oz. Chai Tea Infused Rum*
1/2 oz. Disaronno Amaretto
1/2 oz. simple syrup
1/2 oz. cream
Shake and strain
Pour ingredients into the iced mixing glass. Shake thoroughly and strain contents into a chilled cocktail glass.
*Chai Tea Infused Rum
Steep rum with 3 bags of chai tea for at least one day; if made with loose tea, strain before serving.

Chai Tea Martini

Specialty of The Original McCormick & Schmick's
Created by Geoff V. Helzer
Cocktail glass, chilled
Pour ingredients into an iced mixing glass
1 1/4 oz. Ketel One Vodka
Splash half & half
2 oz. Tazo Chai Tea
Shake and strain
Garnish with an orange twist
Pour ingredients into the iced mixing glass. Shake thoroughly and strain contents into a chilled cocktail glass. Garnish with an orange twist.

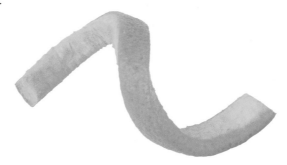

33 Restaurant & Lounge

33 Stanhope Street
Boston, MA 02116
☎ 617.572.3311
▶▶ www.33restaurant.com
✉ AskUs@33Restaurant.com

Born from the fusion of an up-and-coming eatery and a hot, trendy club, **33 Restaurant & Lounge** is a vital, invigorating destination venue, a tempting blend of impeccably prepared cuisine served in a high energy environment. The atmosphere is alluring and electric, the crowd young and urbane. For those in Boston looking for a cutting edge revival of dinner and dancing, 33 is decidedly the place.

While the merging of an upscale restaurant and high volume club is not necessarily new, what's laudable is how seamlessly 33 transitions from one concept to the other. It operates much like the beating halves of a heart. The wafting aromas from the kitchen are inescapable in the lounge and the restaurant taps its feet to the bass and downbeat of the lounge.

The pulse of the place is the bar. Their signature cocktails are luxurious and singular in design with a vitality that can only be obtained through craftsmanship and a reliance on nothing but the freshest ingredients. The qualitative difference is appreciable. One of 33's most requested specialties is the **Blackberry Martini,** a delectable cocktail made with Belvedere Pomarancza Vodka, Lillet Blanc and muddled ripe blackberries. It's tart and flavorful. Another popular favorite is the **Amber Sidecar,** an inspired blend of Macallan Amber Liqueur, Cointreau and a bevy of muddled fresh fruits all of which are served over ice.

The food end of the equation is equally inventive. Executive chef Anthony Dawodu offers his guests contemporary American cuisine and a menu loaded with fresh seafood, homemade pastas, and New England specialties all delicious and beautifully presented. Vegetarians will love it here. Correction, anyone rhythmically breathing will love it here. —RP

Blackberry Martini
Drink recipe on pg 11

Chocolate Martini

Excerpted from The Original Guide to
American Cocktails and Drinks- 6th Edition
Cocktail glass, chilled
Pour ingredients into an iced mixing glass
1 3/4 oz. Van Gogh Dutch Chocolate Vodka
3/4 oz. Van Gogh Vanilla Vodka
1/2 oz. Godiva Chocolate Liqueur
Stir and strain
Garnish with a lemon twist
Pour ingredients into the iced mixing glass. Stir
gently and strain contents into a chilled cocktail
glass. Garnish with a lemon twist.

Colossal Shrimptini

Specialty of Oyster Restaurant & Nightclub
Created by Gary Griffin
Cocktail glass, chilled
Pour ingredients into an iced mixing glass
2 oz. Absolut Peppar Vodka
1/4 oz. Dry Vermouth
1 colossal shrimp
Shake and strain
Dash Tabasco Pepper Sauce
Garnish with a skewered shrimp
Pour ingredients into the iced mixing glass.
Shake thoroughly and strain contents into a
chilled cocktail glass. Add a dash of Tabasco and
garnish with the colossal shrimp used in preparing
the drink.

"Make every Martini you serve a work of art."

Vox® Vodka

If you're searching for a sophisticated vodka to call your own, look no further than *Vox Vodka* from the Netherlands. This pristine, ultra-premium spirit was bred for a chilled cocktail glass and the unhurried time to enjoy it.

The vodka is meticulously produced from 100% wheat selected for its mild taste. It is distilled five times and painstakingly filtered through screens made of inert material to achieve essential purity. Even the demineralized water used in production is filtered repeatedly to remove all traces of color, taste and odor.

Ultra-premium Vox Vodka has single-handedly turned neutral into something strikingly beautiful. It has brilliant clarity, a nearly weightless body, an impeccably clean palate and a cool, crisp finish. The 80-proof vodka is appropriately packaged in a striking, sculpted bottle made of Austrian glass. It's a class act from the first sip to its clean finish.

In 2003 the distillery launched *Vox Raspberry Vodka*. This all-world vodka has a sultry body, a generous, true to fruit bouquet, and a full, rounded palate that fills the mouth with the flavor of sun drenched fruit. The vodka tapers off without burn or unwanted heat, leaving behind the lingering flavor of fresh raspberries. The whole experience is exquisite.

The successful range now also includes *Vox Green Apple Vodka*, a tangy, tart and lightweight spirit primed and ready for any cocktail related assignment. In fact, the entire range of Vox vodkas exist in a universe of unlimited creative possibilities.

Cote d'Azur

Specialty of Brasserie JO
Created by David Johnston
Cocktail glass, chilled
Pour ingredients into an empty mixing glass
1 inch slice English cucumber
1 oz. finely chopped fresh parsley
Splash fresh lemon juice
$1/2$ oz. simple syrup
Muddle contents
Add ice
2 $1/2$ oz. Ketel One Citroen Vodka
$1/2$ oz. Lillet Blanc
Shake and strain
Place the cucumber, parsley, syrup and juice into the empty mixing glass. Muddle and add ice. Pour in the vodka and Lillet. Shake thoroughly and strain contents into a chilled cocktail glass.

Creole Watermelon

Specialty Cyrus
Created by Scott Beattie
Cocktail glass, chilled
Pour ingredients into an empty mixing glass
$1/3$ mixing glass full of cubed watermelon
2 Fresno chili rings*
$1/2$ oz. fresh lime juice
Muddle contents
Add ice
1 $1/2$ oz. Hangar One Straight Vodka
Shake and strain
Garnish with a watermelon triangle
   sprinkled with lime juice, a sprinkle of
   kosher salt, ground pepper and chili powder.
Fill the empty mixing glass a third full with cubed watermelon, add chili rings and lime juice. Muddle and add ice. Pour in the vodka. Shake thoroughly and strain contents into a chilled cocktail glass. Garnish with a seasoned watermelon triangle.
NOTE: *For the watermelon triangles make sure to remove rind and seeds.*
*Fresno Chili Rings Preparation - pg 319

Crystal Pearlessence Martini

Excerpted from The Original Guide to
American Cocktails and Drinks- 6th Edition
Cocktail glass, chilled
Pour ingredients into an iced mixing glass
3 oz. Pearl Vodka
$3/4$ oz. VSOP Cognac
Stir and strain
Garnish with a lemon twist
Pour ingredients into the iced mixing glass. Stir gently and strain contents into a chilled cocktail glass. Garnish with a lemon twist.

Cucumber Martini

Specialty of 33 Restaurant & Lounge
Created by Pej Martarjem
Salt rimmed cocktail glass, chilled
Place ingredients into an empty mixing glass
4-5 thin cucumber slices
Splash fresh lime juice
Muddle contents
Add ice
2 oz. Absolut Citron Vodka
1 oz. Cointreau
Dash Tabasco Pepper Sauce
Shake and strain
Place the cucumber slices and lime juice into the empty mixing glass. Muddle and add ice. Pour in the remaining ingredients. Shake thoroughly and strain contents into a salt rimmed, chilled cocktail glass.

Dry Martini

Excerpted from The Original Guide to
American Cocktails and Drinks- 6th Edition
Cocktail glass, chilled
Pour ingredients into an iced mixing glass
3 oz. Gin
$1/4$ oz. Dry Vermouth
Stir and strain
Garnish with 2 olives
Pour ingredients into the iced mixing glass. Stir gently and strain contents into a chilled cocktail glass. Garnish with 2 olives.

En Fuego

Specialty of Indigo Eurasian Cuisine
Created by Tim Skelton, Jason Castle
Salt rimmed house specialty glass, chilled
Pour ingredients into an iced mixing glass
3 $1/2$ oz. Ketel One Citroen Vodka
2 dashes Tabasco Green Pepper Sauce
$1/2$ oz. pepperoncini juice
Shake and strain
Garnish with a skewered olive and pepperoncini
Pour ingredients into the iced mixing glass. Shake thoroughly and strain contents into a salt rimmed, chilled house specialty glass. Garnish with a skewered olive and pepperoncini.

Espressotini

Specialty of Savoy
Created by Mickey Loomis, Jamie Allred
Cocktail glass, chilled, painted with a thin
  ribbon of caramel syrup
Pour ingredients into an iced mixing glass
1 1/2 oz. Stoli Vanil Vodka
1 oz. Baileys Irish Cream
1/4 oz. Frangelico
1 oz. espresso
Shake and strain
Garnish with a chocolate covered
  biscotti stir stick
Paint a thin ribbon of caramel syrup around the
inside of a chilled cocktail glass. Pour ingredients
into the iced mixing glass. Shake thoroughly
and strain contents into the prepared cocktail
glass. Garnish with a chocolate covered biscotti
stir stick.

Extra Dry Martini

Excerpted from The Original Guide to
American Cocktails and Drinks- 6th Edition
Cocktail glass, chilled
Pour ingredients into an iced mixing glass
3 oz. Gin
2-3 drops Dry Vermouth
Stir and strain
Garnish with 2 olives
Pour ingredients into the iced mixing glass. Stir
gently and strain contents into a chilled cocktail
glass. Garnish with 2 olives.

"The better the liquor,
the better the Martini."

Ultimat® Vodka

When Pablo Picasso was asked what three things astonished him most, his answer was, "the blues, cubism and Polish vodka." One of the finest and most innovative Polish spirits to cross our borders is *Ultimat Vodka*. A few sips of this brilliantly flavored vodka and you'll understand why Picasso was astonished.

Ultimat Vodka is crafted at the Polmos distillery in Bielsko-Biala, Poland. It is made from a distinctive mash comprised of 70% potato, and 15% of wheat and rye. Each constituent ingredient contributes to the finished product's bouquet and taste profile. The vodka is then meticulously filtered to remove all trace impurities and then bottled at 80-proof.

This is a luxurious, flavor imbued spirit. Even sampled at room temperature the vodka is completely devoid of excess heat and imparts a lively, semisweet bouquet. It has an oily textured, silky smooth body and a marvelously flavorful palate. Perhaps its best quality is a long, relaxed finish.

The brand has undergone growth of late. *Ultimat Black Cherry Flavored Vodka* is made from Ultimat Vodka macerated with fresh cherries. It's crystal clear, medium-weight with a prominent aroma of cherry blossoms. The vodka rolls over the palate filling the mouth with the dry and thoroughly satisfying flavor of black cherries and spice.

Also new to the range is *Ultimat Chocolate Vanilla Flavored Vodka*. True to its name, the vodka is an unfettered blend of chocolate and vanilla, one ideally suited for use in drink making.

Fidel's Martini

Excerpted from The Original Guide to
American Cocktails and Drinks- 6th Edition
Cocktail glass, chilled
Pour ingredients into an iced mixing glass
3 oz. Stolichnaya Vodka
1 oz. Banana Rum
Stir and strain
Garnish with a banana slice
Pour ingredients into the iced mixing glass. Stir
gently and strain contents into a chilled cocktail
glass. Garnish with a banana slice.

Gingertini

Specialty of Bar Masa
Created by Mike Vacheresse
Cocktail glass, chilled
Pour ingredients into an empty mixing glass
4 slices fresh ginger, quarter size
Muddle contents
Add ice
3 oz. Chopin Vodka
1/2 oz. Plum Wine
Shake and strain
Place ginger pieces into the empty mixing glass.
Muddle and add ice. Pour in the vodka and
wine. Shake thoroughly and strain contents into
a chilled cocktail glass.

Grand Melon Martini

Specialty of Stone Rose Lounge
Created by Jeff Isaacson
Cocktail glass, chilled
Pour ingredients into an iced mixing glass
2 1/2 oz. Bacardi Grand Melon Rum
1/2 oz. Cointreau
Splash pineapple juice
Shake and strain
Garnish with a small watermelon triangle
Pour ingredients into the iced mixing glass.
Shake thoroughly and strain contents into a
chilled cocktail glass. Garnish with a small
watermelon triangle.

Grapefruit and Basil Martini

Specialty of Jade Bar
Created by Greg Portsche
Cocktail glass, chilled
Pour ingredients into an empty mixing glass
5 fresh basil leaves
3 dashes lemongrass simple syrup*
Muddle contents
Add ice
3 oz. Ketel One Citroen Vodka
1/2 oz. fresh grapefruit juice
Shake and strain
Garnish with a fresh basil leaf
Place basil leaves and lemongrass syrup into
the empty mixing glass. Muddle and add
ice. Pour in the remaining ingredients. Shake
thoroughly and strain contents into a chilled
cocktail glass. Garnish with a fresh basil leaf.
*Lemongrass Simple Syrup Recipe - pg 321

Green Tea Martini

Specialty of Michael's Kitchen
Created by Michael's staff
Cocktail glass, chilled
Pour ingredients into an iced mixing glass
1 1/2 oz. Grey Goose Le Citron Vodka
1 1/2 oz. ZEN Green Tea Liqueur
Splash fresh lemon juice
Shake and strain
Garnish with a lemon wedge
Pour ingredients into the iced mixing glass. Shake
thoroughly and strain contents into a chilled
cocktail glass. Garnish with a lemon wedge.

Greenteani

Specialty of Savoy
Created by Eric Scheffer, Ricky Shriner
Cocktail glass, chilled
Pour ingredients into an iced mixing glass
2 1/2 oz. Ketel One Vodka
1 oz. green tea simple syrup*
Splash grapefruit juice
Shake and strain
Garnish with a fresh mint leaf
Pour ingredients into the iced mixing glass. Shake
thoroughly and strain contents into a chilled
cocktail glass. Garnish with a fresh mint leaf.
*Green Tea Simple Syrup Recipe - pg 320

Holly & Mistletoe Martini

Specialty of The Original McCormick & Schmick's
Created by Geoff V. Helzer
Cocktail glass, chilled
Pour ingredients into an iced mixing glass
1 1/4 oz. Stoli Vanil Vodka
1/4 oz. Godiva White Chocolate Liqueur
Splash seedless raspberry puree
Shake and strain
Garnish with a fresh mint leaf
Pour ingredients into the iced mixing glass. Shake thoroughly and strain contents into a chilled cocktail glass. Garnish with a fresh mint leaf.

Kaffir Key Lime Martini

Specialty of Rosemary's Restaurant
Created by Michael Shetler, Bernice Matola
Crushed graham cracker rimmed
   cocktail glass, chilled
Pour ingredients into an iced mixing glass
1 1/2 oz. KeKe Beach Cream Liqueur
1 1/4 oz. Stoli Vanil Vodka
3/4 oz. Hangar One Kaffir Lime Vodka
1/2 oz. Licor 43 Cuarenta y Tres
Splash fresh lime juice
1/2 oz. heavy cream
Shake and strain
Garnish with a lime wheel
Pour ingredients into the iced mixing glass. Shake thoroughly and strain contents into a crushed graham cracker rimmed, chilled cocktail glass. Garnish with a lime wheel.

Key Lime Martini

Specialty of Jade Bar
Created by Greg Portsche
Crushed graham cracker rimmed
   cocktail glass, chilled
Pour ingredients into an iced mixing glass
2 oz. Bacardi Limón Rum
1/2 oz. Midori
Splash cream
Splash Rose's Lime Juice
Shake and strain
Garnish with a lime wheel
Pour ingredients into the iced mixing glass. Shake thoroughly and strain contents into a crushed graham cracker rimmed, chilled cocktail glass. Garnish with a lime wheel.

Kiwitini, 33 Restaurant's

Specialty of 33 Restaurant & Lounge
Created by Jenn Harvey
Cocktail glass, chilled
Pour ingredients into an empty mixing glass
1 peeled, sliced kiwi
1/2 oz. lemongrass simple syrup*
Muddle contents
Add ice
2 oz. 42 Below Feijoa Vodka
Splash Rose's Lime Juice
Shake and strain
Garnish with a fresh kiwi slice
Place the peeled, sliced kiwi and lemongrass syrup into the empty mixing glass. Muddle and add ice. Pour in the remaining ingredients. Shake thoroughly and strain contents into a chilled cocktail glass. Garnish with a kiwi slice.
*Lemongrass Simple Syrup Recipe - pg 321

Kiwitini, Lola's

Specialty of Lola's
Created by Loren Dunsworth, Hayley Sinclair
Cocktail glass, chilled
Pour ingredients into an iced mixing glass
1 1/2 oz. 42 Below Kiwifruit Vodka
1 1/2 oz. fresh kiwi juice
Splash pineapple juice
Shake and strain
Garnish with a fresh kiwi slice
Pour ingredients into the iced mixing glass. Shake thoroughly and strain contents into a chilled cocktail glass. Garnish with a fresh kiwi slice.

Lemon Basil Martini

Specialty of Stone Rose Lounge
Created by Jeff Isaacson
Cocktail glass, chilled
Pour ingredients into an iced mixing glass
2 oz. Grey Goose Vodka
1/2 oz. Triple Sec
2 fresh basil leaves, torn
2 sugar packets
2 oz. fresh lemon juice
Shake and strain
Garnish with a lemon wheel
Pour ingredients into the iced mixing glass. Shake thoroughly and strain contents into a chilled cocktail glass. Garnish with a lemon wheel.

Absinthe Brasserie & Bar

⌂ **398 Hayes Street**
   San Francisco, CA 94102
☎ **415.551.1590**
▶▶ **www.absinthe.com**
✉ **comments@ absinthe.com**

The ambience at **Absinthe Brasserie & Bar** drips with romance, making it an ideal destination for those seeking atmosphere, conviviality and the flavor of Provence. The name alone is evocative of mystery and forbidden fruit. It refers to the laudanum-like elixir popular at the turn of the last century, a potent, narcotic-tinged liqueur whose production was eventually banned. Want a break from the ordinary? Here's your ticket.

A quick spin around the place and the reasons for its extraordinary allure become immediately evident. The décor is traditional brasserie from its pressed tin ceilings, French rattan café chairs and copper tabletops, mica sconces, soft lighting and vintage Absinthe art. It has an authentic South of France feel, with both informal and formal dining areas, plus a lavish private dining room complete with its own staff, bar and separate entrance.

The ambience in the lounge is lively and the bar is well stocked and capably manned. Absinthe's featured cocktails are balanced, classically structured and thoroughly delicious. Martini aficionados will be especially delighted with a cocktail called *Smoke on the Water*. The signature drink is made with Hangar One Straight Vodka laced with peaty Laphroaig Single Malt Scotch. Also hovering in the superb range is *Jonny's Appleseed*, a cocktail comprised of *hors d'age* calvados, homemade apple syrup and finished with rosé champagne.

The Brasserie caters to the pre-opera crowd and late night diners. The upscale cuisine is brimming with fresh seafood selections and classic French specialties. On the menu there are ten types of fresh oysters, any one of which they'll combine with Bloody Mary sauce and premium vodka to make an *Absinthe Oyster Shooter*. Factor in that the Absinthe Brasserie & Bar fare is reasonably priced and your evening should be complete. —RP

Jonny's Appleseed
Drink recipe on pg 242

Lemon Drop Martini

Specialty of Stone Rose Lounge
Created by Jeff Isaacson
Sugar rimmed cocktail glass, chilled
Pour ingredients into an iced mixing glass
2 1/2 oz. Ciroc Vodka
1/2 oz. simple syrup
2 oz. fresh lemon juice
Shake and strain
Garnish with a lemon wedge
Pour ingredients into the iced mixing glass. Shake thoroughly and strain contents into a sugar rimmed, chilled cocktail glass. Garnish with a lemon wedge.

Lemon Meringue Pie Martini

Specialty of 32° Luxe Lounge
Created by Terry Kilgariff, Orlando Rivera
Crushed graham cracker rimmed cocktail glass, chilled
Pour ingredients into an iced mixing glass
1 1/4 oz. Ketel One Citroen Vodka
3/4 oz. Vanilla Vodka
Splash Rose's Lime Juice
3 oz. fresh lemon sour mix
Shake and strain
Garnish with a lemon twist
Pour ingredients into the iced mixing glass. Shake thoroughly and strain contents into a crushed graham cracker rimmed, chilled cocktail glass. Garnish with a lemon twist.

"Increasingly mixologists are reaching for the bar muddler when constructing their specialty Martinis."

Bafferts® Gin

If you're in the market for a spirit that marches to the beat of a different drummer, then look no further than **Bafferts Gin**, a spry, marvelously twisted gin with a unique outlook on life. Instead of aiming to wow the senses with a voluminous bouquet and energized palate, the maker's took an altogether singular approach.

Introduced in 2000, Bafferts Gin is the creation of Hayman Distillers of London. It is crafted with a base of premium, column-distilled grain spirits. During the final distillation, the gin is infused with a mixture of botanicals, the fewest of any other premium gin. Therein lies the twist. Bafferts is a light, delicately flavored gin, which as their marketing suggests, makes it a spirit vodka enthusiasts will thoroughly enjoy.

Bafferts has pristine clarity and a trim, light-weight body. The bouquet is a refined offering of juniper and hints of citrus zest, while the palate presents mere hints of the principle botanical flavors. Subtle as they are, the flavors add a delightful dimension to the crisp and understated finish. The overall effect is irresistible.

Bafferts Mint Gin has a charm of its own. It is generously aromatic with a supple, medium-weight body and a layered palate of elegant, mouth filling flavors. Pity someone hasn't thought of pairing the taste of fresh mint with gin before this, because it's a brilliantly seductive combination.

lly's Martini
specialty of Tommy's Mexican Restaurant
created by Jacques Bezuidenhout, Charles Vexenat
cktail glass, chilled
ur ingredients into an empty mixing glass
sh agave simple syrup*
...sh orange bitters
2 grapefruit twists
Muddle contents
Add ice
2 oz. El Tesoro Platinum Tequila
1/2 oz. Lillet Blanc
Stir and strain
Garnish with a grapefruit twist
Pour the agave syrup, orange bitters and grapefruit twists into the empty mixing glass. Muddle and add ice. Pour in the remaining ingredients. Stir thoroughly and strain contents into a chilled cocktail glass. Garnish with a grapefruit twist.
*Agave Simple Syrup Recipe - pg 317

Lola's Apple Martini, The Original ✳
Specialty of Lola's
Created by Adam Karstens, Loren Dunsworth
Cocktail glass, chilled
Pour ingredients into an iced mixing glass
1 1/2 oz. Ketel One Vodka
1 1/2 oz. DeKuyper Pucker Sour Apple Schnapps
Splash fresh lemon sour mix
Shake and strain
Garnish with a floating Granny Smith
   apple slice
Pour ingredients into the iced mixing glass. Shake thoroughly and strain contents into a chilled cocktail glass. Garnish with a floating Granny Smith apple slice
NOTE: Soak apple slices in ice and lemon to keep fresh.

Lucky Cat Martini
Specialty of P.F. Chang's China Bistro
Created by P.F. Chang's Staff
Cocktail glass, chilled
Pour ingredients into an iced mixing glass
2 oz. Smirnoff Vanilla Vodka
1 oz. pineapple juice
Shake and strain
Sink 1/2 oz. Chambord
Garnish with a pineapple leaf spear
   and fresh pineapple slice
Pour ingredients into the iced mixing glass. Shake thoroughly and strain contents into a chilled cocktail glass. Sink Chambord and garnish with a pineapple leaf spear and fresh pineapple slice.

Lychee Martini
Specialty of Indigo Eurasian Cuisine
Created by Joe Felix, Jason Castle
House specialty glass, ice
Pour ingredients into an iced mixing glass
3 oz. SKYY Vodka
4 oz. lychee juice
Shake and strain
Garnish with 3 lychee on wooden skewer
Pour ingredients into the iced mixing glass. Shake thoroughly and strain contents into an iced house specialty glass. Garnish with 3 lychee on a wooden skewer.

Marilyn Monroe Martini
Specialty of Oyster Restaurant & Nightclub
Created by Thom Greco
Cocktail glass, chilled
Pour ingredients into an iced mixing glass
1 oz. Stoli Strasberi Vodka
Shake and strain
Fill with champagne
Garnish with a fresh strawberry
Pour Stoli Strasberi Vodka into the iced mixing glass. Shake thoroughly and strain contents into a chilled cocktail glass. Fill with champagne and garnish with a fresh strawberry.

Classic Martini
Excerpted from The Original Guide to American Cocktails and Drinks- 6th Edition
Cocktail glass, chilled
Pour ingredients into an iced mixing glass
3 oz. Gin
1/2 oz. Dry Vermouth
Stir and Strain
Garnish with two olives
Pour ingredients into the iced mixing glass. Stir gently and strain contents into a chilled cocktail glass. Garnish with two olives.

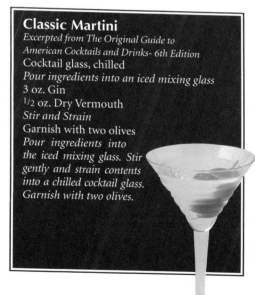

Martini JO

Specialty of Brasserie JO
Created by Chef Jean Joho
Cocktail glass, chilled
Pour ingredients into an iced mixing glass
3 1/2 oz. Grey Goose Vodka
1/4 oz. Lillet Rouge
Shake and strain
Garnish with an orange twist
Pour ingredients into the iced mixing glass.
Shake thoroughly and strain contents into a
chilled cocktail glass. Garnish with an orange
twist, zesting it over the glass.

Northwest Raspberry Martini

Specialty of The Original McCormick & Schmick's
Created by Geoff V. Helzer
Sugar rimmed cocktail glass, chilled
Pour ingredients into an empty mixing glass
1 1/2 oz. fresh lemon juice
3 sugar cubes
Muddle contents
Add ice
1 1/2 oz. Stolichnaya Vodka
1/4 oz. DeKuyper Triple Sec
Splash cranberry juice
Splash seedless raspberry puree
Shake and strain
Pour the lemon juice and sugar cubes into the
empty mixing glass. Muddle and add ice. Pour
in the remaining ingredients. Shake thoroughly
and strain contents into a sugar rimmed, chilled
cocktail glass.

"Garnishing a Martini isn't an
obligation or act of embellishment;
it's a creative opportunity."

Rhum Barbancourt Estate Réserve

Rhum Barbancourt was founded in 1862 by Frenchman Dupré Barbancourt. His ambition was to apply the techniques that he had learned making cognac to the rhum making process, and few spirits better illustrate the dream than ***Rhum Barbancourt Estate Réserve***.

This revered spirit is made from fresh cane juice that is fermented for three days and double-distilled, first in a single column still and then in a copper alembic still. The final distillate is diluted with purified rainwater prior to being aged in the Domaine's chais for a minimum of 15 years in Limousin oak barrels. It is then bottled at 86-proof.

The Estate Réserve is a luxurious, sophisticated rhum, once the private reserve of the Barbancourt distillery. It has a medium-weight body, seamlessly smooth texture and a pronounced bouquet of warm, toasty aromas. The palate of this rhum is exceptional, brimming with chocolate, honey and toffee flavors that linger impressively long before eventually tapering off into an elegant, nuance laced finish.

The august range also includes five-star ***Rhum Barbancourt Réserve Spéciale***. It is aged a minimum of 8 years in French oak vats. It has tremendous complexity and a character full of charm and sophistication, making it ideal for use in signature cocktails. ***Rhum Barbancourt Three-Star*** is light, delicate and aged for four years, and recently released ***Rhum Barbancourt Pango*** is a blend of pineapple, mango and Haitian spices.

Now & Zen

Specialty of Marcus' Martini Heaven
Created by Marcus' Staff
Cocktail glass, chilled
Pour ingredients into an iced mixing glass
2 oz. Yazi Ginger Vodka
1/4 oz. ZEN Green Tea Liqueur
Shake and strain
Garnish with a lemon twist
Pour ingredients into the iced mixing glass. Shake thoroughly and strain contents into a chilled cocktail glass. Garnish with a lemon twist.

Nutcracker Martini

Excerpted from The Original Guide to
American Cocktails and Drinks- 6th Edition
Cocktail glass, chilled
Pour ingredients into an iced mixing glass
2 1/2 oz. Vodka
1/2 oz. Frangelico
Stir and strain
Garnish with a lemon twist
Pour ingredients into the iced mixing glass. Stir gently and strain contents into a chilled cocktail glass. Garnish with a lemon twist.

Nuts & Chocolate

Specialty of The Original McCormick & Schmick's
Created by Geoff V. Helzer
Chocolate syrup and crushed hazelnut
 rimmed cocktail glass, chilled
Pour ingredients into an iced mixing glass
1 1/4 oz. Stoli Vanil Vodka
1/4 oz. Frangelico
Shake and strain
Garnish with a cherry
Pour ingredients into the iced mixing glass. Shake thoroughly and strain contents into a chocolate syrup and crushed hazelnut rimmed, chilled cocktail glass. Garnish with a cherry on the rim of the glass.

OP-M Original

Specialty of Rosemary's Restaurant
Created by Michael Shetler
Cocktail glass, chilled
Pour ingredients into an iced mixing glass
3 oz. Absolut Citron Vodka
1 oz. Cointreau
1 oz. OP Aquavit
Shake and strain
Float with Chambord
Garnish with an orange twist
Pour the Absolut Citron Vodka, Cointreau and OP Aquavit into the iced mixing glass. Shake thoroughly and strain contents into a chilled cocktail glass. Float the Chambord. Garnish with an orange twist.

Orange Twist

Specialty of Courtright's Restaurant
Created by Marco Recio
Cocktail glass, chilled
Pour ingredients into an iced mixing glass
2 oz. Charbay Blood Orange Vodka
1 oz. Lillet Blanc
Shake and strain
Garnish with a blood orange slice
 and lemon twist
Pour ingredients into the iced mixing glass. Shake thoroughly and strain contents into a chilled cocktail glass. Garnish with a blood orange slice and lemon twist.

Paisley Martini

Excerpted from The Original Guide to
American Cocktails and Drinks- 6th Edition
Cocktail glass, chilled
Pour ingredients into an iced mixing glass
2 oz. Gin
1/2 oz. Scotch Whisky
1/2 oz. Dry Vermouth
Stir and strain
Garnish with a lemon twist
Pour ingredients into the iced mixing glass. Stir gently and strain contents into a chilled cocktail glass. Garnish with a lemon twist.

PB & J

Specialty of Marcus' Martini Heaven
Created by Marcus' Staff
Cocktail glass, chilled
Pour ingredients into an iced mixing glass
1 1/2 oz. Vodka
3/4 oz. Frangelico
3/4 oz. Chambord
Shake and strain
Garnish with a lemon twist
Pour ingredients into the iced mixing glass. Shake thoroughly and strain contents into a chilled cocktail glass. Garnish with a lemon twist.

Peach Martini

Specialty of The Mission Inn Hotel & Spa
Created by Brooke Crothers
Cocktail glass, chilled
Pour ingredients into an iced mixing glass
2 1/2 oz. DeKuyper Peachtree Schnapps
1 1/4 oz. Stoli Persik Vodka
1/2 oz. fresh orange juice
Shake and strain
Float with Champagne
Garnish with an orange slice
Pour the schnapps, vodka and orange juice into the iced mixing glass. Shake thoroughly and strain contents into a chilled cocktail glass. Float the champagne. Garnish with an orange slice.

Pear Perfect

Specialty of Bar Masa
Created by Mike Vacheresse
Cocktail glass, chilled
Pour ingredients into an iced mixing glass
1 1/2 oz. Iichiko Shochu
1 oz. Otokoyama Sake
1 oz. fresh pear mix*
Shake and strain
Pour ingredients into the iced mixing glass. Shake thoroughly and strain contents into a chilled cocktail glass.
*Fresh Pear Mix Recipe - pg 319

Pepper Martini

Specialty of Michael's Kitchen
Created by Michael's staff
Cocktail glass, chilled
Pour ingredients into an iced mixing glass
1 1/2 oz. Pepper-Infused Frïs Vodka*
1 1/2 oz. Frïs Vodka
Stir and strain
Garnish with two olives
Pour ingredients into the iced mixing glass. Stir thoroughly and strain contents into a chilled cocktail glass. Garnish with two olives.
*Pepper-Infused Frïs Vodka Recipe - pg 321

Pineau Sour Martini

Specialty of Brasserie JO
Created by David Johnston
Cocktail glass, chilled
Pour ingredients into an iced mixing glass
1 1/2 oz. Cîroc Vodka
1 oz. Dor Pineau des Charentes
1 oz. fresh lemon sour mix
Shake and strain
Garnish with a peeled grape
Pour ingredients into the iced mixing glass. Shake thoroughly and strain contents into a chilled cocktail glass. Garnish with a peeled grape.

Pomegranate Martini

Specialty of Michael's Kitchen
Created by Michael's staff
Cocktail glass, chilled
Pour ingredients into an iced mixing glass
1 1/2 oz. Frïs Vodka
1 oz. PAMA Pomegranate Liqueur
1 oz. fresh grapefruit juice
Shake and strain
Garnish with multicolored Swedish Fish
Pour ingredients into the iced mixing glass. Shake thoroughly and strain contents into a chilled cocktail glass. Garnish with multicolored Swedish Fish.

Pumpkin Martini

Specialty of Lola's
Created by Loren Dunsworth
Nutmeg rimmed cocktail glass, chilled
Pour ingredients into an iced mixing glass
3 oz. Absolut Vanilia Vodka
Pinch of nutmeg
Splash half & half
2 heaping tbsp. pumpkin/chai mix*
Shake and strain
Pour ingredients into the iced mixing glass. Shake thoroughly and strain contents into a nutmeg rimmed, chilled cocktail glass.
*Pumpkin/Chai Mix Recipe - pg 321

Rosietini

Specialty of Rosemary's Restaurant
Created by Michael Shetler
Cocktail glass, chilled
Pour ingredients into an iced mixing glass
4 oz. Rosemary's Infused SKYY Vodka
1/2 oz. Cointreau
1/4 oz. Dry Vermouth
Shake and strain
Garnish with goat cheese stuffed olives
  on a rosemary sprig
Pour ingredients into the iced mixing glass. Shake thoroughly and strain contents into a chilled cocktail glass. Garnish with two goat cheese stuffed olives skewered on a rosemary sprig.
*Rosemary's Infused SKYY Vodka
     Recipe - pg 322

Backstreet Café

✉ **1103 S. Shepherd Drive**
Houston, TX 77019
☎ **713.521.2239**
▶️ **www.backstreetcafe.net**
✉ **tracy@backstreetcafe.net**

L ocated off the beaten path, **Backstreet Café** is a rare treat, a classy American bistro ensconced in a charming, two story, Deco era house with intimate dining rooms and front and back patio seating. For those who enjoy relaxed al fresco dining, magnificent views and sumptuous fare — and who doesn't? — Houston's Backstreet Café is a slice of the good life.

Mind you this is not your run of the mill, world-class restaurant. The grounds are lush with flowers, shrubbery, vine covered trellises and a spreading camphor tree whose canopy shades the back patio. The downstairs dining room features a large, marble top bar and cozy banquette seating. French doors divide the dining rooms

giving the entire place a warm and private feel. Fireplaces, crank out casement windows and a solarium round out the architectural features.

Particularly captivating is the Café's inventive repertoire of signature drinks, all of which showcase fresh, seasonal ingredients. A case in point is the **Wild Berry Mimosa,** a luscious cocktail made with fresh blueberries, raspberries, blackberries, strawberries, lime juice and Roederer Estate Brut Champagne. It's elegant and sublime. So too are **Blonde Ambition**, a creative variation of the Cosmo sporting fresh lime, white cranberry and tangerine juice, and the **Anjou Pear Mojito**, a specialty made with light rum, a splash of Calvados, mint and Anjou pear puree.

Backstreet Café's award winning menu is the brainchild of executive chef Hugo Ortega. Its New American Bistro fare highlights freshness and originality with a wide assortment of ingredients, from Asian noodles and Indian tandoori techniques to Native American grains and fresh seasonal vegetables, all with a strong American accent.

In a city with a diverse and thriving restaurant community, the Backstreet Café is Houston's equivalent to Nirvana. Kudos. —RP

Blonde Ambition
Drink recipe on pg 12

Royal Plum

Specialty of Bar Masa
Created by Mike Vacheresse
Cocktail glass, chilled
Pour ingredients into an empty mixing glass
1 soft, ripe plum, quartered
1 tsp. sugar
Muddle contents
Add ice
2 oz. Ketel One Vodka
1/4 oz. Churchill's Tawny Porto Ten Years Old
Shake and strain
Place plums and sugar in the empty mixing glass. Muddle and add ice. Pour in the remaining ingredients. Shake thoroughly and strain contents into a chilled cocktail glass.

Ruby Red Pom Pom

Specialty of Rickshaw Far East Bistro & Bambú Lounge
Created by Angie Chang
House specialty glass, ice
Build in glass
1 1/2 oz. Charbay Ruby Red Grapefruit Vodka
1 oz. PAMA Pomegranate Liqueur
Splash fresh grapefruit juice
1 oz. fresh lemon sour mix
Garnish with a lemon wheel
Pour ingredients into the iced house specialty glass in the order listed. Garnish with a lemon wheel.

"There are no boundaries on creativity."

Ketel One® Vodka

Ketel One Vodka is a popular phenomenon centuries in the making. The super-premium brand can trace its origin to 1691, when the Nolet family built a distillery in Schiedam, Holland. For 10 generations, the family has been distilling the finest handcrafted spirits using the techniques and recipes perfected by the patriarch and his successors.

Ketel One Vodka is made according to strict quality standards. It is distilled in small batches entirely from select wheat. The final distillation occurs in centuries old, alembic copper pot stills. After distillation, the vodka is rested in tile-lined tanks to allow the spirit to become fully integrated.

Ketel One drinks like a handcrafted vodka. It has pristine clarity and a gloriously round, flawlessly textured body. The vodka's subtle yet pleasing bouquet is laced with the aromas of citrus and toasted grain. The pleasure continues as the vodka fills the mouth with layers of sweet and spicy flavors that last long into the elegant finish.

Like its world-class sibling, ***Ketel One Citroen Vodka*** is elegant and essentially flawless. The vodka is crystal clear and has a wafting bouquet of tree ripened limes and lemons. The zesty palate is endowed with a refreshing, true to fruit citrus flavor that persists well into the relaxed and lingering finish. From stem to stern, this is an unsurpassed treat for the senses.

The Ketel One siblings are exemplary vodkas that know no creative limitations.

Sake Martini

Specialty of Indigo Eurasian Cuisine
Created by Tim Skelton, Jason Castle
Cocktail glass, chilled
Pour ingredients into an iced mixing glass
2 1/2 oz. Gekkeikan Sake
1 1/2 oz. SKYY Vodka
Splash ginger-infused water
Shake and strain
Garnish with a cucumber sliver and
  pickled ginger on wooden skewer
Pour ingredients into the iced mixing glass. Shake thoroughly and strain contents into a chilled cocktail glass. Garnish with a cucumber sliver and a piece of pickled ginger on a wooden skewer.

Scarlet Martini

Specialty of 33 Restaurant & Lounge
Created by Jenn Harvey
Cocktail glass, chilled
Pour ingredients into an iced mixing glass
1 1/2 oz. Stoli Persik Vodka
1 oz. lemongrass simple syrup*
1/2 oz. blood orange puree
Shake and strain
Garnish with an orange slice
Pour ingredients into the iced mixing glass. Shake thoroughly and strain contents into a chilled cocktail glass. Garnish with an orange slice.
*Lemongrass Simple Syrup Recipe - pg 321

Sexual Healing

Specialty of Shanghai 1930
Created by Shanghai's staff
Cocktail glass, chilled
Pour ingredients into an iced mixing glass
1 1/2 oz. Vodka
1 oz. Lillet Blanc
1/2 oz. Grand Marnier
1 oz. lychee syrup
Shake and strain
Garnish with a cherry and fresh lychee slice
Pour ingredients into the iced mixing glass. Shake thoroughly and strain contents into a chilled cocktail glass. Garnish with a cherry and a fresh lychee slice.

Shochu Sunrise

Specialty of Bar Masa
Created by Mike Vacheresse
Cocktail glass, chilled
Pour ingredients into an iced mixing glass
1 oz. Torikai Shochu
1/2 oz. Cointreau
1 oz. fresh tangerine juice
Shake and strain
Sink with 1 oz. fresh pomegranate juice
Pour the Torikai Shochu, Cointreau and tangerine juice into the iced mixing glass. Shake thoroughly and strain contents into a chilled cocktail glass. Sink the pomegranate juice to mimic a sunrise.

Silk Martini

Specialty of BarMedia
Robert Plotkin and staff
Cocktail glass, chilled
Pour ingredients into an empty mixing glass
1/2 oz. Limoncello
Swirl Limoncello inside the mixing glass
 coating the inside
Discard excess and add ice
2 1/2 oz. Silk Vodka
Stir and strain
Garnish with a lemon spiral twist
Pour limoncello into the empty mixing glass. Swirl thoroughly, coating the inside of the glass. Discard the excess and add ice. Pour in the vodka, stir and strain into a chilled cocktail glass. Garnish with a lemon spiral twist.

Smoke on the Water

Specialty of Absinthe Brasserie & Bar
Created by Jonny Raglin
Cocktail glass, chilled, coated with
   Laphhroaig 10-Year-old Single
   Islay Malt Scotch
Pour ingredients into an iced mixing glass
4 oz. Hangar One Straight Vodka
Shake and strain
1/4 oz. Laphhroaig 10-Year-old Single Islay
   Malt Scotch (*to coat inside of cocktail glass*)
Garnish with an olive and onion
Pour Hangar One Straight Vodka into the iced mixing glass. Shake thoroughly and strain contents into a chilled cocktail glass that has been coated with the Laphhroaig Scotch. Garnish with an olive and onion.

Smoked Martini

Excerpted from The Original Guide to
American Cocktails and Drinks- 6th Edition
Cocktail glass, chilled
Pour ingredients into an iced mixing glass
2 1/2 oz. Tanqueray Gin
1/2 oz. Laphhroaig 10-Year-old Single
   Islay Malt Scotch
Stir and strain
Garnish with a lemon twist
Pour ingredients into the iced mixing glass. Stir gently and strain contents into a chilled cocktail glass. Garnish with a lemon twist.

"Great Martinis are meant to be shared."

Blue Ice™ American Vodka

Blue Ice American Vodka is one of only a handful of genuinely extraordinary vodkas distilled in America. This world-class spirit is handcrafted at the Silver Creek Distillery in Rigby, Idaho, the only distiller of potato spirits in the United States. In fact, they avoid working with grains all too common in vodka production — rye, wheat, corn, barley or oats. Being from Idaho, that makes sense.

Situated by the slopes of the Grand Tetons, Silver Creek Distillery crafts spirits as pristine as its surroundings. Blue Ice Vodka is an excellent example. It is quadruple-distilled entirely from Idaho Russet Burbank potatoes. The all-important spring water used in production is drawn from a 200-foot deep aquifer fed by the Snake River. The vodka is rigorously filtered five times through charcoal, lava rock garnet, travertine and a submicron filter rendering it essentially pure. The vodka is all natural, additive free and bottled at 80-proof.

In its brief existence, Blue Ice has risen up to the ranks of the world's finest vodkas and is a match for the famed potato spirits of Eastern Europe. It has crystalline clarity, a light, supple body slightly oily in texture. The bouquet is crisp and refreshing with notes of herbs and citrus. Its delicate palate of soft, slightly sweet flavors immediately expands in the mouth and lingers throughout the cool, medium length finish.

Blue Ice Vodka is a solid performer and an ideal selection for use in cocktails. To fully appreciate how superb the vodka is, however, sample it straight, or with a slight chill.

Sour Apple Martini

Specialty of Courtright's Restaurant
Created by Marco Recio
Cinnamon sugar rimmed
  cocktail glass, chilled
Pour ingredients into an empty mixing glass
2 slices Granny Smith apple
Muddle contents
Add ice
1 1/2 oz. Stolichnaya Vodka
1/2 oz. DeKuyper Pucker Sour Apple Schnapps
Splash sweet 'n' sour
Splash pineapple juice
Shake and strain
Place apple slices into the empty mixing glass.
Muddle and add ice. Pour in the remaining
ingredients. Shake thoroughly and strain
contents into a cinnamon sugar rimmed, chilled
cocktail glass.

Speeding Bullet

Specialty of Courtright's Restaurant
Created by Marco Recio
Cocktail glass, chilled
Pour ingredients into an iced mixing glass
2 oz. Hendrick's Gin
1/2 oz. Dewar's Scotch Whisky
Shake and strain
Garnish with cornichon, cocktail onion
  and bleu cheese stuffed olive
Pour ingredients into the iced mixing glass.
Shake thoroughly and strain contents into a
chilled cocktail glass. Garnish with a cornichon,
cocktail onion and a blue cheese stuffed olive.

The Star F*!ker Martini

Specialty of Lola's
Created by Loren Dunsworth, Greg Huebner
Oversized cocktail glass, chilled
Pour ingredients into an iced mixing glass
1 1/2 oz. Ketel One Vodka
1 1/2 oz. DeKuyper Pucker Sour Apple Schnapps
Splash cranberry juice
Shake and strain
Float with Red Bull Energy Drink
Garnish with a fresh star fruit slice
Pour the vodka, schnapps and cranberry juice
into the iced mixing glass. Shake thoroughly and
strain contents into an oversized, chilled cocktail
glass. Float the Red Bull Energy Drink and
garnish with a fresh star fruit slice.

The Starlight 200

Specialty of Harry Denton's Starlight Room
Created by Jacques Bezuidenhout
Cocktail glass, chilled
Pour ingredients into an iced mixing glass
1 1/2 oz. Plymouth Gin
3/4 oz. Leacock's Rainwater Madeira
1/2 oz. Warre's OTIMA 10 Year Old Tawny Port
Dash of Angostura Aromatic Bitters
Stir and strain
Garnish with an orange spiral twist
Pour ingredients into the iced mixing glass.
Stir thoroughly and strain contents into a chilled
cocktail glass. Garnish with an orange spiral twist.

Strawberry Lemonade Martini

Specialty of 32° Luxe Lounge
Created by Terry Kilgariff, Orlando Rivera
Sugar rimmed cocktail glass, chilled
Pour ingredients into an iced mixing glass
1 1/4 oz. Ketel One Citroen Vodka
3/4 oz. Stoli Strasberi Vodka
1/4 oz. Triple Sec
Splash grenadine
Splash Rose's Lime Juice
3 oz. fresh lemon sour mix
Shake and strain
Garnish with a fresh strawberry
Pour ingredients into the iced mixing glass. Shake
thoroughly and strain contents into a sugar
rimmed, chilled cocktail glass. Garnish with a fresh
strawberry.

Strawberry Martini

Specialty of Savoy
Created by Brandon Craft, James Ducas
Sugar rimmed cocktail glass, chilled
Pour ingredients into an empty mixing glass
1 tsp. sugar
3 fresh strawberries
Muddle contents
Add ice
2 1/2 oz. Stolichnaya Vodka
1/2 oz. Crème de Cassis
1/2 oz. fresh lime juice
Shake and strain
Garnish with a fresh strawberry
Place strawberries and sugar into the empty mixing glass. Muddle and add ice. Pour in the remaining ingredients. Shake thoroughly and strain contents into a sugar rimmed, chilled cocktail glass. Garnish with a fresh strawberry.

Teddy Roosevelt Martini

Specialty of The Mission Inn Hotel & Spa
Created by Brooke Crothers
Cocktail glass, chilled
Pour ingredients into an iced mixing glass
2 oz. No. TEN by Tanqueray
3/4 oz. Grand Marnier
3/4 oz. Dubonnet Rouge
Shake and strain
Garnish with a lemon and orange twist
Pour ingredients into the iced mixing glass. Shake thoroughly and strain contents into a chilled cocktail glass. Garnish with a lemon and orange twist.

Thai Martini

Specialty of The Original McCormick & Schmick's
Created by Geoff V. Helzer
Cocktail glass, chilled
Pour ingredients into an empty mixing glass
Splash pineapple juice
1 sugar cube
Muddle contents
Add ice
1 1/4 oz. Stolichnaya Vodka
1/4 oz. DeKuyper Pucker Island Blue Schnapps
Shake and strain
Float with 1/2 oz. Chiao Kuo Basil Seed
   Drink with honey
Garnish with a cherry
Pour the pineapple juice and sugar cube into the empty mixing glass. Muddle and add ice. Pour in the vodka and schnapps. Shake thoroughly and strain contents into a chilled cocktail glass. Float the Chiao Kuo Basil Seed Drink. Garnish with a cherry on the rim of the glass.

West POM Beach Pomegranate Martini

Specialty of Joe's Seafood, Prime Steak & Stone Crab
Created by Dan Barringer, Mike Rotolo
Cocktail glass, chilled
Pour ingredients into an iced mixing glass
1 1/2 oz. Effen Vodka
1/2 oz. simple syrup
1 oz. white cranberry juice
2 oz. POM Pomegranate Juice
Shake and strain
Garnish with a lemon twist
Pour ingredients into the iced mixing glass. Shake thoroughly and strain contents into a chilled cocktail glass. Garnish with a fresh lemon twist.

Zentini

Specialty of Savoy
Created by Eric Scheffer, Ricky Shriner
Cocktail glass, chilled
Pour ingredients into an iced mixing glass
3 oz. Nanbu Bijin Southern Beauty Sake
1/2 oz. Triple Sec
Splash fresh lime juice
Shake and strain
Garnish with 3 drops of Midori
   in center of glass
Pour the sake, triple sec and lime juice into the iced mixing glass. Shake thoroughly and strain contents into a chilled cocktail glass. Garnish with 3 drops of Midori in the center of the glass.

Chapter Two

A Grassroots Phenomenon
The Margarita

There is a thin line between fact and fiction, a line often obscured with the passage of time. Such is the case surrounding the origin of the *Margarita*, which occurred somewhere during a fifteen year span between the mid-1930s and the late '40s. Some versions claim the place of origin as the United States, others Mexico. Weeding through the conflicting accounts made for some interesting detective work. It's a good story.

The year was 1948 and times in the U.S. were good. The war had ended three years before and the country was experiencing a prolonged period of prosperity. For the rich and famous, Acapulco was an irresistible playground. San Antonio native Margarita Sames and her husband Bill owned a villa near the Flamingo Hotel in Acapulco, Mexico.

The couple lived in Acapulco for part of the year along with a close circle of friends that consisted of Fred MacMurray, Lana Turner, Nicky Hilton, next door neighbor John Wayne, Joe Drown, owner of the Hotel Bel-Air, and restaurateur Shelton McHenrie, owner of the Tail o' the Cock restaurant in Los Angeles.

The group was practically inseparable. The Sames house was the setting for many raucous affairs that sometimes lasted days on end. They reveled in the laid back attitude of Acapulco, spending their nights playing by the pool and eating lunch around sunset.

Shortly before Christmas that year, Margarita Sames was challenged by several ranking members of the team to devise a new and exciting cocktail, something to break up their regimen of beer and Bloody Marys. Her initial attempts were loudly and unanimously rejected. Undaunted, Margarita went back to work.

Having grown up in France, Sames was fond of Cointreau, and after spending years vacationing in Mexico, she had developed an appreciation for tequila. She mixed the two together along with some fresh lime juice. She tried different formulations; some came out too sweet, some too tart. Then she hit on what she thought was the perfect blend — one part Cointreau, three parts tequila and one part lime juice. Knowing that most people drank tequila preceded by a lick of salt, Sames chose to garnish her cocktail with a rim of coarse salt.

She brought out a tray of champagne glasses brimming with her new creation. The group enthusiastically proclaimed the cocktail a triumph. It quickly became the group's signature cocktail, the main course and featured attraction that Christmas and New Year's Eve.

Sames credited the proliferation of the drink to her friends. John Wayne, Fred MacMurray and Lana Turner returned to Hollywood and started spreading the word at their favorite haunts. Nicky Hilton began promoting the cocktail at the Acapulco Hilton, as did Joe Drown at the Hotel Bel-Aire. The swank and fashionable Tail o' the Cock restaurant near Los Angeles may likely have been where many Americans first sampled the Margarita.

In the years following, Margarita Sames continued serving her cocktail at parties and private gatherings. She spent many afternoons sipping Margaritas with Eleanor Roosevelt, and legendary baseball manager John McGraw, a lifelong friend of the Sames and the Margarita.

In 1993, her friends threw Margarita Sames an 82nd birthday party that lasted five days. The drink of choice...well, you can just imagine.

The Margarita has enjoyed far more than its allotted fifteen minutes of fame. In fact, after climbing into the limelight in the 1970s, the drink has

Jose Cuervo® Tradicional® Reposado Tequila

There is no name more famous in the tequila world than Jose Cuervo. But did you know that there were two Jose Cuervos? Jose Antonio de Cuervo is widely acknowledged as the first person to ever produce what would eventually become known as tequila. In 1795, his son — Jose Maria Guadalupe Cuervo — was granted the first license to commercially produce tequila from King Carlos IV of Spain. The brand has remained internationally renowned for two centuries. Few products better illustrate why the distillery has achieved preeminence than *Jose Cuervo Tradicional Reposado Tequila*.

Made in the town of Tequila at the Jose Cuervo distillery — La Rojeña — Tradicional is handcrafted entirely from mature blue agaves. The harvested piñas are steamed in clay ovens prior to being pressed and fermented. The tequila is double-distilled and then aged in white oak casks for 6 months. It is bottled at 80-proof.

A sip or two is all it takes for Tradicional Reposado to reveal why it's the best selling 100% agave tequila in Mexico. The straw colored tequila has a medium–weight body with a generous bouquet of oak and herbaceous aromas. The palate features the flavors of herbs, caramel and vanilla, all of which last long into the warm, spicy finish.

Most enthusiasts don't know that Jose Cuervo Tradicional is actually a vintage dated tequila. The lower label on the bottle pictured above contains the phrase "210 años," which means that it was produced in 2005.

continually ranked among the most frequently requested cocktails in America. A devastating tequila shortage in the '90s and subsequent price hikes notwithstanding, the Margarita rage has persevered.

The Evolution Continues

So what exactly is a Margarita? Ask a hundred bartenders and you may well get 100 slightly different answers. Sure they'd say that it contains tequila, triple sec and lime juice. But how much of each ingredient? What kind of fresh sour mix do you use — lime or lemon? The truth is that despite the Margarita's enormous popularity there is little consensus as to its recipe.

There are five essential truths about Margaritas that with few exceptions should be considered inviolate. The first of these is that the cocktail is built on a foundation of lime juice, not lemon as is often the case, which means that using standard, lemon-based sweet 'n' sour is incorrect. As will be discussed later, a fresh lime sour mix is concocted largely the same way as a fresh lemon juice sweet 'n' sour. If trapped behind the bar with nothing but a bottle of sour mix and an order for a Margarita, squeeze the juice from four lime wedges into the mixing glass (which equals roughly 3/4 ounce of fresh juice) and add an equal amount of the sweet 'n' sour. The result will be a balanced mix upon which to build the cocktail, one with a lime-forward character.

Second, the concept of Margaritas and tequila are inseparable. Creative spin offs aside, such as the *Sake Margarita*, the cocktail is made with tequila. Although this may sound a bit obvious, there are several important considerations.

There are agave-derived spirits on the market that are not tequila. Their only reason for existing is to offer an inexpensive alternative to tequila. Trust that these products once again prove that you get what you pay for. These products are prohibited from claiming to be a tequila, but to be sure read the label to make sure that it has the CRT mark and an NOM designation. The CRT — Consejo Regulador del Tequila — is the regulatory council of distillers established in 1994 to safeguard standards of the tequila industry. The four digit NOM number appears on every label of tequila. NOM is an acronym for Norma Oficial Mexicana, a set of laws that establish standards of quality for the production of tequila. An NOM number is assigned to an individual distillery, signifying that the brand of tequila was made by that distiller alone.

The third immutable truth about Margaritas involves balance. There are four flavor elements in the cocktail that must be balanced on the palate, namely sweet, tart, the taste of the tequila and the flavor of the orange modifier. Vary too far toward any one extreme and you're headed for trouble. Balance in this instance means being able to taste all four about equally.

The fourth is that Margaritas need to be vigorously shaken, anything less is problematic. The purpose behind energetically shaking the drink is three-fold. The action thoroughly integrates the ingredients, properly chills the drink and introduces a modicum of water into the mix. The enhanced production value alone of enthusiastically shaking the cocktail makes the exertion worthwhile.

Finally, the garnish on a Margarita is a fresh lime wedge. It is a most functional embellishment, one that allows a guest the option of squeezing more fresh lime juice into the drink. While lime wheels are attractive and in keeping with the theme, they're not designed for extracting the juice they contain. Using both a lime wheel and lime wedge in combination is a clever compromise between form and function.

Secrets Revealed of America's Greatest Margaritas

As is the case with the Martini, every great bar needs to perfect the recipe for a truly sensational Margarita. It's simply too popular of a cocktail not to. Perhaps a fresh, homemade sour mix will define your Margarita, or the combination of a super-premium tequila and ultra-sophisticated modifier, like Grand Marnier Cuveé

Scorpion™ Mezcal Gran Reserva Añejo 7 Year Old

Scorpion Mezcal Gran Reserva Añejo 7 Year Old is sultry, sophisticated and attention grabbing, a must for any self-respecting back bar.

Skillfully crafted in Oaxaca, Mexico, super-premium Scorpion is a 100% agave mezcal. Two varieties of agaves are used to create the brand's singular characteristics. Instead of chemicals or additives, naturally occurring yeasts are used to precipitate fermentation. The entire range of Scorpion Mezcals are made in alembic stills, distilled in small batches and aged in charred, oak barrels. As for the FDA approved, scorpion exoskeleton inside the bottle, it's a harmless observer.

The flagship of the Scorpion range is the triple-distilled, Añejo Gran Reserva Mezcal 7 Year Old. It has the look of extremely old bourbon and a completely captivating bouquet marked with the aromas of vanilla, black cherries, baking spices and peaty smoke. The oily, medium-weight body delivers a semisweet array of flavors, including maple, caramel, vanilla and a lingering dose of smoke on the finish. The limited edition mezcal is bottled at 80-proof.

The Scorpion range includes three other añejo mezcals; the *Scorpion Mezcal Gran Reserva Añejo 5 Year Old*; the twice-distilled 3-year añejo, and an añejo aged a minimum of a year in oak. *Scorpion Reposado* is aged in oak for up to 11 months, while the *Scorpion Silver Mezcal* is bottled fresh from the still — unaged and unaffected by wood.

de Cent-Cinquantenaire. Regardless of the particulars, perfecting the Margarita is a requisite step to attracting a following.

The Margarita knows no creative boundaries. It's versatile and can adopt an impressive array of flavors. At the risk of stripping the creative process of its mystery and inspirational genius, there is a formula to engineering a gourmet, high performance Margarita. It involves tweaking one or more of the ingredients. Learning how these elements affect the dynamics of the finished Margarita is at the heart of the creative process. Here then are the best kept secrets behind America's greatest Margaritas.

• **Casting a Tequila** — Not all tequilas are created equally, which means that at the onset several qualitative decisions need to be made. The first involves whether to feature a mixto or 100% agave tequila in your Margarita.

Mixtos (mees-toh) are the principle type of tequila imported into the United States. They are made from a blend containing a legal minimum 51% agave and other, non-agave sugars. These sugars are added to the aguamiel and water mixture during fermentation. Mixtos are typically distilled in technologically advanced column stills, which produce lighter bodied, more highly rectified spirits.

While mixtos tequilas are made from blends, and therefore frequently inexpensive, it is a mistake to categorically dismiss them as low quality. The best selling brands of tequila in the world are mixtos. They are exuberant, lively spirits with an edgy, vibrant quality that distinguishes them from other light spirits.

The premium counterparts to mixtos are 100% agave tequilas. As the name would imply, these pure tequilas are made entirely out of blue agave. The result is a spirit of incomparable quality. The production of 100% agave tequilas is closely scrutinized by the government to ensure that stringent quality standards are maintained. Seals are affixed to the opening of the barrels to certify when the tequila was barreled and to guarantee that nothing was added during aging. By law, a brand must state that it is a 100% blue agave tequila on its front label. These ultra-premium tequilas rank among some of the finest spirits in the world.

The second qualitative decision is which style of tequila to use in your Margarita. Unaged silver (blanco) tequila is often featured in the cocktail, not because of its relatively lower cost, but because it adds a vitality to the Margarita that the aged, more reserved tequila doesn't quite manage. Gold tequila — joven abocado — is produced by adding caramel coloring and flavor additives to silver tequila, giving it an amber/golden hue and a touch of sweetness, or wood/oak flavor.

Reposado (rested) tequila is aged in wood for a minimum of two months, although most remain in the oak four to eight months. It is the best selling style of tequila in Mexico. Reposado is matured just long enough for its character to soften, while leaving the inherent quality of the agave unaffected by the tannins in the wood. Reposado tequila is often as spicy and herbaceous as a blanco tequila, but with the added richness of the oak. It strikes a true balance between the fresh, spirited character of a blanco tequila and the mellow refinement of an añejo.

Añejo tequila must be aged a minimum of one year in casks 600 liters or smaller, with most aged in 180 liter, oak barrels. The smaller barrels impart more wood character to the tequila. Most distillers mature their tequila in barrels previously used to age bourbon. The oak imparts less tannin into the tequila imbuing it with a subtle brandy character. Añejo tequilas are typically smooth and luxurious. They are characteristically aromatic with a broad, well-rounded flavor and a long, lingering finish.

The final consideration is what quality of tequila to use in your Margarita. As will be a consistent theme in this book, the better the liquor, the better the finished cocktail will taste. So don't hesitate committing a super-premium tequila to a Margarita. A growing phenomenon is to create a Margarita made with ultra-premium tequila, which are those costing more than $100 per 750ml. When looking to devise a top-shelf Margarita choose a recipe that adequately showcases the tequila. The recipe should have a minimum of ingredients that may obscure the enhanced quality of the tequila. Also to best accentuate the flavor of the tequila, the cocktail should be served straight up rather than on the rocks, or blended.

- **A Split Decision** — Where's it written that you can only use one style or brand of tequila in your signature Margaritas? The objective behind splitting the tequila base in the drink is to give it more character by pairing two or more complementary styles of tequila. For example, the *Three Amigos Margarita* is made with equal parts of Sauza Conmemorativo Añejo and Hornitos Reposado tequilas, and finished with a float of Sauza Tres Generaciones Añejo. Each tequila contributes greatly to the cocktail's flavor and alluring presentation. Another recipe that illustrates the technique is the *El Conquistador Margarita*, which thrives on a split base of El Tesoro Platinum and Añejo tequilas.

Splitting the cocktail's foundation has expanded into several creative avenues. One is to pair the tequila in the drink with equal parts of such character-laded spirits as flavored vodkas and flavored rums. Another is to couple the tequila with a lesser amount of another spirit altogether, such as brandy (*Dirty Margarita*), gin (*Margarita Britannia*), or bourbon (*Kentucky Margarita*).

- **Infused and Peppered** — When looking to craft a signature Margarita, consider building the cocktail on a base of infused tequila. Mixologists are infusing spirits with everything from kiwis, melons and pineapples to ginger, peppers and sun dried tomatoes. It's a straightforward and uncomplicated process involving steeping the spirit of choice with a variety of fresh fruit, spices, or vegetables in large, airtight containers. Several days later the tequila will have been infused with flavors, color, aroma and loads of appealing character. The *Pepper-Tequila*

Bar Masa

📫 **10 Columbus Circle,
4th floor Time Warner Center
New York, NY 10019**

☎ **212.823.9800**

▶▶ **www.masanyc.com**

✉ **info@masanyc.com**

It's easy to get these two acclaimed restaurants confused. Both Masa and neighboring **Bar Masa** are hidden away on the fourth floor of the Time Warner Center on Columbus Circle. Both serve their guests the same world-class sushi and seafood, a bill of fare meticulously prepared by Master Chef Masa Takayama. The revered sushi virtuoso performs his wizardry nightly at Masa, holding court and personally enthralling the small group of guests seated in the restaurant. While both offer incomparable dining experiences, Masa is the one that'll cost you a month's salary for the opportunity.

The slightly more affordable Bar Masa features an equally intimate and serene setting. The restaurant seats 13 at the bar and 26 in the lounge. No reservations are accepted. Although the decor of the long, windowless dining room is somewhat

austere, the effect is quieting and tranquil. Appropriately, the bar, with its magnificent Bubinga wood top, is the focal point of the room as it is where the restaurant's sensational cocktails are devised.

The chef's mastery of fresh ingredients carries over to Bar Masa, where the signature cocktails have been brilliantly devised with an exotic flair. It is the precision and attention to detail that makes their drinks so intriguing. As examples, the Bar Masa *Gingertini* is a magnificent blend of muddled fresh ginger, a splash of plum wine and a bracer of Chopin Vodka, while the savory *Royal Plum* is made with muddled plums, Churchill's Tawny Porto and Ketel One Vodka.

As one would expect, much of Bar Masa's drink repertoire showcases the talents of spirits from the Pacific Rim. Perhaps the finest is appropriately named the *Pear Perfect*, an elegant cocktail made with Iichiko Shochu, Otokoyama Sake and fresh pear juice.

Sit back, sip and marvel. Bar Masa is an elegant slice of the good life. —RP

Royal Plum
Drink recipe on pg 26

Infusion is made by steeping tequila with jalapeño peppers, a serrano chili and an assortment of green, red, and yellow bell peppers for color. After two to three days it becomes pepper-infused tequila, which in turn provides the heating element for several intriguing Margaritas, including the *Cajun Margarita*, *Sonoran Spittoon Margarita* and *Margarita Picosita*. The *Lime-Tequila Infusion* is made by steeping tequila with limes, oranges and simple syrup.

The *Summer Shades Margarita* is a popular infusion prepared with cantaloupe, pineapples, strawberries and peaches steeped with Blue Curaçao, Midori and gold tequila. After several days the infusion should have a light, fruit bouquet, a pale turquoise color and a delightfully fresh flavor. Mix the infusion with an equivalent amount of lime sour mix and shake in an iced mixing glass prior to serving.

- **The Triple Play** — The modifier is an essential ingredient in a cocktail. Its role is to soften the edge of the liquor while complementing the spirit's natural flavor. It should never dominate a recipe, rather act in a supporting role, giving the cocktail dimension and personality. The orange modifier

Imported GranGala® Triple Orange Liqueur

The Stock Distillery has been producing world-class brandies in Italy for well over a century. While famous throughout Europe, the firm has yet to become a household name in the United States. That will certainly change as increasingly more Americans discover the sophisticated pleasures of award-winning *Imported GranGala Triple Orange Liqueur.*

This skillfully crafted liqueur is made in Trieste, Italy from a blend of hand selected oranges from Sicily and mature, barrel-aged VSOP brandy. It is then aged further to ensure that the various constituent elements have fully integrated. It is bottled at 80-proof.

The craftsmen at the Stock Distillery have graced GranGala with a fetching bronze color and smoothly textured, medium-weight body. The liqueur has an expansive bouquet loaded with the aroma of fresh oranges and delicate notes of almonds and brandy. The lush, semisweet palate features exuberant orange and lemon flavors and a healthy measure of sumptuous brandy. The liqueur sports a warm, flavorful finish.

The natural inclination is to serve an exuberant and sophisticated product such as GranGala in a heated snifter or on the rocks. While certainly a popular way to enjoy it, the liqueur enjoys many uses behind the bar. The most noteworthy application for GranGala is as a modifier in a wide range of specialty Margaritas, where its brandy base and zesty orange flavor make it an ideal substitute for triple sec.

in the Margarita is intended to seamlessly meld the tequila and lime juice base into a well balanced cocktail.

Triple sec is a clear, relatively inexpensive orange-flavored liqueur. The best advice governing its use is to select the most premium brand within reach. As one might anticipate, there is a wide range of quality among the various brands of triple sec on the market. The most important selection criteria are a brilliant orange flavor and a clean, crisp finish. An inferior triple sec can negate much of your creative efforts. Another often relied upon cordial is Blue Curaçao, an orange-flavored liqueur slightly sweeter than triple sec and beloved for its luminous blue color.

When preparing a super-premium Margarita, Cointreau is an extremely popular choice as the modifier. The French liqueur is unsurpassed in the role. Cointreau is crystal clear, highly aromatic and imbued with a vibrant orange palate. The advantage to using Cointreau in a signature Margarita is that the liqueur will augment the cocktail's bouquet and taste profile, but won't alter its color.

Another popular, super-premium modifier is Grand Marnier. While Cointreau and Grand Marnier are both premium orange liqueurs, the latter is formulated with a cognac base. Modifying a premium Margarita with Grand Marnier will slightly alter the cocktail's color and introduce the flavor of brandy and sweet, succulent oranges. Other super-premium liqueurs in this class include Italian GranGala and Extase from France. Each is an orange, brandy-based liqueur with a proven track record of performing brilliantly in Margaritas.

When preparing top-shelf Margaritas a creative option is to split the modifier by using equal parts of both Cointreau and Grand Marnier. Several sterling examples of recipes modified by both liqueurs include the *Margarita Primero Clase*, *Triple Gold Margarita* and the *Margarita la Perseverancia*.

• **The Liqueurs Have It** — Liqueurs run the gamut of flavors, colors and cost, making them excellent modifiers. Pick a flavor and there's likely a liqueur that matches it. In fact, liqueurs are frequently relied upon for enhancing the flavor and texture of specialty Margaritas.

Several brands of liqueurs have risen far beyond the call of duty. Proven Margarita performers include the French black raspberry liqueur Chambord, the Japanese honeydew liqueur Midori, the Italian almond liqueur Disaronno Amaretto, American made PAMA Pomegranate Liqueur, Mexican herbal liqueur Damiana and Agavero, a Mexican liqueur flavored with blue agave.

Several recipes combine more than one liqueur to achieve the desired taste profile. For example, the *Margarita Azul* is prepared using both Disaronno Amaretto and Blue Curaçao, while the *Rio Grande Margarita* is made with Tia Maria and

Frangelico. Rarely will adding a splash of a liqueur do anything but jazz up a Margarita.

- **Scratch Mix Artistry** — The underlying foundation of the Margarita and source of the cocktail's vibrancy is the base sour mix. Its quality and creative composition greatly affects the finished cocktail. Part of the secret to making a world-class Margarita mix lies in selecting high quality, great tasting limes. But much of the artistry comes into play in the proportions used. Most scratch recipes call for 3 parts lime juice to 1 part of simple syrup (3:1). If the resulting mix is deemed too tart, shift the proportions closer toward 2:1.

It should be noted that many a great fresh lime sour mix has been crafted using a slightly larger cast of performers. An added splash or two of fresh orange, lemon or grapefruit juice is a proven way to add more dimension and pizzazz to the mix.

A few tips about juicing limes. Fruit at room temperature yields more juice than chilled fruit. Avoid getting the bitter white pith of the lime into the juice. While pulp in orange or grapefruit juice is a cache of quality, lime and lemon juice needs to be strained before use.

Gran Patrón® Platinum Tequila

Those who find themselves with a few extra dollars in their pocket and a palpable thirst for a classy spirit should invest in a bottle of **Gran Patrón Platinum Tequila**. The ultra-premium silver tequila is richly textured and imminently satisfying. Patrón is the bestselling brand of 100% agave tequila and the release of Gran Patrón Platinum will likely solidify their preeminence.

There are several significant things that distinguish this incomparable tequila from all others. Legally tequila must be distilled at least twice. In order to achieve a lighter bodied, more brilliant spirit the tequila is distilled a third time. In addition it is distilled in an alembic still. The second twist is that a portion of each batch is aged briefly in American oak barrels prior to being blended back. The ultra-premium silver tequila carries a retail price of $160 per 750ml.

Technical explanations aside, all one really needs to know about Gran Patrón Platinum is evident once the tequila hits the glass. This triple-distilled marvel has pristine clarity, satiny texture and a medium-weight body. The bouquet is somewhat muted, but it does eventually yield aromas of black pepper and citrus. The initial attack is warm — not hot — and the tequila immediately fills the mouth with spicy, peppery flavors. The finish is perhaps best described as luxurious.

Gran Patrón Platinum is a tequila created with a snifter in mind. Afford it a few minutes to breathe and fully oxygenate. Your patience will be generously rewarded.

Pouring freshly squeezed juice through a cheesecloth (chinois), or strainer will do the trick.

A sour mix made using fresh lime juice needs to be refrigerated. While only a guideline, most fresh juices won't keep much more than 24 hours before needing to be discarded.

• **A Sweet Difference** — Simple syrup is a workhorse behind the bar and crucial to making a delicious fresh sour mix. It is made with equal parts of boiling water and sugar. Its advantage when making cocktails is that unlike granulated sugar, simple syrup will immediately go into solution. The sour mix at Tommy's Mexican Restaurant in San Francisco is sweetened with agave syrup, which is made using equal parts of agave nectar, bottled water and simple syrup. The mixture is heated slowly until all of the components have fully integrated. The agave syrup is one reason why the Margaritas at the famed tequilaria taste singularly delicious.

• **Base Modifiers** — Welcome to one of the poorest kept secrets in mixology, namely that Margaritas taste great when blended with fruit. Devising a fresh fruit puree to add to the cocktail requires little more effort than plugging in the blender. Use sour mix, simple syrup or fresh lime juice to adjust the balance of the fruit puree, preventing it from becoming overly sweet or too acidic and tart.

Consider alternative base modifiers such as jellied cranberry sauce, prickly pear marmalade, Bartlett pears, or applesauce. The realm of possibilities is bounded only by your imagination.

• **Putting on a Game Face** — Before unleashing a signature Margarita make sure that it looks as fabulous as it tastes. That process begins with the ritual of rimming the glass with salt. Affixing the salt is best accomplished by wetting the outside of the rim with lime juice and then dipping the glass into a saucer of kosher salt. The benefit being the salt won't adhere to the inside of the glass where it would quickly dissolve into the Margarita.

In this day and age consider salting only half the rim. This will allow all guests to receive a well-dressed Margarita while affording them the opportunity of moderating how much salt they consume. If given the time, salt the Margarita glasses in advance, allowing the lime juice and salt combination to harden. This will alleviate the messy problem of salt falling off the rim of the glass.

There are recipes that call for a sugared rim, typically fruit Margaritas, or recipes on the sweeter side. In the past, one was limited to using conventional granulated sugar on the rim. Now there are a number of brands of colored and flavored sugars, not to mention raw, or brown sugar. Another option is using powdered lemonade mix on the rim. It has a sweet lemon flavor and an attractive color. For an entirely different presentation, rim the edge of a glass first with grenadine before dipping it into powdered lemonade mix.

• **Coup de Grace** — The final touch to any noteworthy Margarita is the garnish. The classic garnish for the cocktail is a lime wedge, which permits people to add a delightful blast of fresh lime juice to the drink, should they choose to do so. As mentioned before, lime wheels are attractive, but not functional.

There are two mistakes people make when garnishing a Margarita. The first is outfitting the cocktail with a puny lime wedge. Why garnish the cocktail with an inadequate sliver of fruit? What people want is a hefty lime wedge that they can get their hands on to squeeze the fresh juice into their drink.

The second mistake is just dropping the lime wedge into the drink. Do bartenders really expect a guest to fish the lime out of the drink with their fingers? Or what about a bartender who first squeezes the lime wedge before dropping it into the drink. Now there's a crushed piece of fruit staring up at the guest. The appropriate move is to hook the lime wedge on the rim of the glass and allow the guest to do with the garnish as they see fit.

One last piece of advice regarding the process of creating a world-class Margarita. Years of experience suggest, begin by concocting a delicious and imminently refreshing base sour mix. If it's well balanced it will taste sensational by itself. Then add in the tequila and modifier. It should be a smooth, interesting journey from there.

Blue Mesa Grill

✉ **5100 Beltline**
Addison, TX 75240
☎ **972.934.0165**
▶▶ **www.bluemesagrill.com**
✉ **info@bluemesagrill.com**

Blue Mesa Grill is an impeccably devised place where Dallas nightlife meets the starry altitudes of Taos. The popular tequila bar and Southwestern restaurant has the pervasive feel of Santa Fe, an affect that stays with you until walking back into the hot and humid Dallas night. What attracts its lively urbane clientele to the Blue Mesa is its dedication to promoting great tequilas and a tempting, irresistible array of bold, Southwestern dishes. The phrase "best of all worlds" comes to mind.

Blue Mesa hops with vitality and energy from open to close, the principal source of which emanates from behind its elegant bar. The interior features polished

concrete floors, modern, minimal decor and colors of the New Mexico desert. Although the view from the restaurant's bank of windows is extraordinary, the place to be is at the bar. The bartenders are gracious and want little more than for you to discover the tequila of your dreams and couple the experience with a one of a kind Sonoran dish.

Not surprisingly, the cocktail of choice at the Blue Mesa Grill is the Margarita. Few places make them better. The owners and bartenders have made careers of twisting and tweaking the cocktail to new, delicious heights. An ideal example of their handiwork is the award winning *Dirty Margarita*, a lavishly flavored cocktail made with Herradura Reposado, a splash of brandy, caramelized simple syrup , sweet 'n' sour and fresh lime juice. A great night to check out Blue Mesa is at one of their famed "Second Tuesday" parties, when on the second Tuesday of each month they introduce a new brand of tequila, offer intriguing tasting flights and a selection of gourmet Margaritas.

The owners, Liz and Jim Baron, now have five Blue Mesa Grills scattered around the Dallas/Fort Worth area. All are bona fide gems. —RP

Dirty Margarita
Drink recipe on pg 47

The Ambassador

Specialty of The World Bar
Created by Kenneth McClure
Cocktail glass, chilled
Pour ingredients into an iced mixing glass
2 oz. Stoli Razberi Vodka
1/2 oz. Grand Marnier
1/2 oz. fresh lemon juice
1/2 oz. fresh lime juice
1/2 oz. simple syrup
Shake and strain
1/2 oz. Blue Curaçao
Garnish with an orange twist
Pour all ingredients except for the Blue Curaçao into the iced mixing glass. Shake thoroughly. Pour the Blue Curaçao into the bottom of the chilled cocktail glass and add the strained contents. Garnish with an orange twist.

Besito

Specialty of Tommy's Mexican Restaurant
Created by Jacques Bezuidenhout
Bucket glass, ice
Pour ingredients into an iced mixing glass
1 1/2 oz. Corazón Tequila Reposado
1/2 oz. Marie Brizard Triple Sec
1/4 oz. agave nectar
3/4 oz. fresh lemon juice
1 oz. apricot puree
Shake and strain
Top with sparkling wine
Garnish with a lemon twist
Pour ingredients into the iced mixing glass. Shake thoroughly and strain contents into an iced bucket glass. Top with sparkling wine and garnish with a lemon twist.

"The Margarita knows no
creative boundaries."

Casa Noble® Crystal 100% Agave Tequila

The entire range of Casa Noble 100% Agave Tequilas is worthy of grand cru status. For people who are looking for tequilas that will gently seduce their senses, here's the ticket. Across the board, these artisan tequilas are a sophisticated treat that deserve their day in a snifter.

Casa Noble Tequilas are made using mature agaves slow baked in stone ovens and then spontaneously fermented. The natural yeast lends an intriguing flavor to the finished spirit. Breaking from tradition, all of the Casa Noble tequilas are triple-distilled in alembic stills.

Sophisticated *Casa Noble Crystal 100% Agave Tequila* is a superb spirit with a sleek, velvety body and an engaging bouquet. The palate features a balanced offering of floral and spice and the finish is long and relaxed.

The distillery also produces *Casa Noble Reposado*, one that strikes a true balance between the fresh, spirited character of the Casa Noble Silver Tequila and the mellow refinement of their limited reserve añejo. The reposado is aged 364 days, just long enough to soften its character, while leaving the inherent quality of the agave unaffected by the tannins in the wood.

Casa Noble Añejo Limited Reserve is a regal añejo tequila extended aged in French white oak casks rather than ex-bourbon barrels. Made in limited quantities, the Casa Noble Añejo has a silky texture, a spicy palate and a slightly sweet, smoky finish.

The Billionaire

Specialty of The Mission Inn Hotel & Spa
Created by Mission Inn's staff
Salt rimmed cocktail glass, chilled
Pour ingredients into an iced mixing glass
1 1/4 oz. Casa Noble Añejo Tequila
1/4 oz. Grand Marnier Cuvée
    du Cent-Cinquantenaire
1-2 dashes Del Maguey Tobala Mezcal
2 1/2 oz. fresh lime sour mix
Shake and strain
Garnish with a lime wedge
Pour ingredients into the iced mixing glass. Shake thoroughly and strain contents into a salt rimmed, chilled cocktail glass. Garnish with a lime wedge.

Black Dog Margarita

Specialty of Hard Rock-Las Vegas
Created by Brad Bateman
Tall house specialty glass, ice
Pour ingredients into an iced mixing glass
1 1/4 oz. Jose Cuervo Black Medallion Tequila
1/2 oz. Blue Curaçao
1 oz. cranberry juice
3 oz. fresh lime sour mix
Shake and strain
Float with 1/2 oz. Chambord
Pour the tequila, Blue Curaçao, cranberry juice and sour mix into the iced mixing glass. Shake thoroughly and strain contents into an iced, tall house specialty glass. Float with Chambord.

Cactus Rose

Specialty of The Mission Inn Hotel & Spa
Created by Mission Inn's staff
Sugar rimmed house specialty glass, chilled
Pour ingredients into an iced blender canister
1 1/4 oz. Sauza Extra Gold Tequila
1/4 oz. Grand Marnier
1/4 oz. Chambord
1 oz. cranberry juice
2 1/2 oz. fresh lime sour mix
Blend ingredients
Garnish with a lime wedge
Pour ingredients into the iced blender canister. Blend thoroughly and pour contents into a sugar rimmed, chilled house specialty glass. Garnish with a lime wedge.

Cajun Margarita

Excerpted from The Original Guide to
Margaritas and Tequila
Salt and pepper rimmed cocktail glass, chilled
Pour ingredients into an iced mixing glass
1 1/4 oz. Pepper Infused Silver Tequila*
1-2 dashes Tabasco Pepper Sauce
1-2 dashes jalapeño pepper juice
2 oz. fresh lime sour mix
Shake and strain
Garnish with a small jalapeño pepper
    and lime wedge
Pour ingredients into the iced mixing glass. Shake thoroughly and strain contents into a salt and pepper rimmed, chilled cocktail glass. Garnish with a jalapeño pepper and lime wedge.
*Pepper-Infused Silver Tequila Recipe - pg 321

Citrus Burst Margarita

Specialty of The Refectory Restaurant & Bistro
Created by Julie Mulisano, Alex Reger
Salt rimmed cocktail glass, chilled
Pour ingredients into an iced mixing glass
1 1/2 oz. Herradura Silver Tequila
1/2 oz. Patrón Citrónge Orange Liqueur
1/2 oz. fresh lemon juice
1/2 oz. fresh lime juice
1/2 oz. fresh orange juice
2 oz. fresh lime sour mix
Shake and strain
Splash 1 oz. lemon-lime soda
Pour the tequila, Citrónge, juices and sour mix into the iced mixing glass. Shake thoroughly and strain contents into a salt rimmed, chilled cocktail glass. Splash with lemon-lime soda.

Coconut Margarita

Specialty of Blue Mesa Grill
Created by Tres Whitley
Shaved coconut rimmed,
    tall house specialty glass, chilled
Pour ingredients into an iced blender canister
2 oz. Cazadores Blanco Tequila
1/2 oz. Triple Sec
2 oz. sweet 'n' sour
2 oz. Coco López Cream of Coconut
Blend ingredients
Garnish with a cherry
Pour ingredients into the iced blender canister. Blend thoroughly until thick and smooth in consistency. Pour contents into a shaved coconut rimmed, chilled tall house specialty glass. Garnish with a cherry.

Coconut-Pineapple Margarita
Specialty of The Mission Inn Hotel & Spa
Created by Brooke Crothers, Victoria Constantino
Sugar rimmed house specialty glass, ice
Pour ingredients into an iced mixing glass
1 1/4 oz. Pineapple Infused Tequila*
1 1/2 oz. Coco Lopez Cream of Coconut
2 1/2 oz. fresh lime sour mix
2 1/2 oz. pineapple juice
Shake and strain
Garnish with a pineapple slice
Pour ingredients into the iced mixing glass. Shake thoroughly and strain contents into a sugar rimmed, iced house specialty glass. Garnish with a pineapple slice.
*Pineapple-Infused Tequila Recipe - pg 321

Cranberry Habanero Margarita
Specialty of J BAR
Created by Patrick Harrington, Steve Draheim
Margarita glass, chilled
Pour ingredients into an iced blender canister
1 1/2 oz. Sauza Extra Gold Tequila
3/4 oz. Grand Marnier
3/4 oz. simple syrup
3/4 oz. fresh lime juice
1/4 cup J BAR Cranberry Habanero Chutney*
Blend ingredients
Pour ingredients into the iced blender canister. Blend thoroughly and pour contents into a chilled Margarita glass.
*J BAR Cranberry Habanero
   Chutney Recipe - pg 321

> "Before unleashing a signature Margarita make sure that it looks as fabulous as it tastes."

Jose Cuervo® Reserva de la Familia®

Clear some space on the top-shelf for ultra-premium *Jose Cuervo Reserva de la Familia Tequila*, or better yet build another shelf. First introduced in 1995 to celebrate the distillery's 200th anniversary, this magnificent, vintage-dated tequila is a museum quality specimen and will likely redefine your concept of luxury living.

As the name would imply, this highly sought after tequila was once the private domain of the descendants of Jose Maria Guadalupe Cuervo. Reserva de la Familia is a mature, well-rested 100% agave tequila crafted from the finest stocks of añejos in the Jose Cuervo cellars. The blend is comprised of tequilas that have been aged in both new charred French and American oak barrels. Typifying its artisan nature, the limited edition spirit is bottled, labeled, numbered and sealed in wax by hand. The reserve añejo is bottled at 80-proof.

You can tell you're in for a special treat the moment this elegant tequila hits your glass. The 2005 vintage has a deep, lustrous, amber color and a supple, medium-weight body. Minutes after it is poured the tequila releases its full bouquet, one laced with the aromas of flora, ripe fruit and oaky vanilla. As it rolls over the palate the tequila fills the mouth with a savory and spicy array of flavors, and then gradually subsides into a cognac-like finish.

Reserva de la Familia is a highly prized tequila, one that could only have been created by Jose Cuervo. Welcome to the good life. *Salud!*

Dirty Margarita

Specialty of Blue Mesa Grill
Created by Jim Baron
House specialty glass, chilled
Pour ingredients into an iced mixing glass
2 oz. Herradura Reposado Tequila
1/2 oz. Christian Brothers VS Brandy
1 oz. fresh lime juice
2 oz. sweet 'n' sour
2 oz. caramelized simple syrup
Shake and strain
Garnish with a lime wheel
Pour ingredients into the iced mixing glass. Shake thoroughly and strain contents into a chilled house specialty glass. Garnish with a lime wheel.

Drunk Apple

Specialty of The Spanish Kitchen
Created by Lorena Segura
House specialty glass, chilled
Pour ingredients into an iced mixing glass
1 1/2 oz. Sauza Blanco Tequila
1 1/2 oz. DeKuyper Pucker Sour Apple Schnapps
Splash sweet 'n' sour
Shake and strain
Garnish with a lime wedge and apple wheel
Pour ingredients into the iced mixing glass. Shake thoroughly and strain contents into a chilled house specialty glass. Garnish with a lime wedge and apple wheel.

El Conquistador Margarita

Excerpted from The Original Guide to American Cocktails and Drinks- 6th Edition
Salt rimmed house specialty glass, ice
Pour ingredients into an iced mixing glass
3/4 oz. Sauza Conmemorativo Añejo Tequila
3/4 oz. Sauza Hornitos Reposado Tequila
1/2 oz. Chambord
1/2 oz. Grand Marnier
1/2 oz. Rose's Lime Juice
1 1/2 oz. fresh lime sour mix
1 1/2 oz. pineapple juice
Shake and strain
Garnish with a lime wedge
Pour ingredients into the iced mixing glass. Shake thoroughly and strain contents into a salt rimmed, iced house specialty glass. Garnish with a lime wedge.

El Corazon

Specialty of Nacional 27
Created by Adam Seger
Kosher salt and Tellicherry peppercorn
    rimmed cocktail glass, chilled
Pour ingredients into an iced mixing glass
2 oz. Corzo Silver Tequila
1 1/2 oz. passion fruit puree
1 oz. POM Pomegranate Juice
1 oz. fresh lemon sour mix
Shake and strain
Pour ingredients into the iced mixing glass. Shake thoroughly and strain contents into a salt and pepper rimmed, chilled cocktail glass.

Escalade Margarita

Specialty of Yard House
Created by Kip Snider
Sugar rimmed pint glass, ice
Pour ingredients into an iced mixing glass
1 1/2 oz. 1800 Silver Tequila
1/2 oz. Cointreau
1/2 oz. fresh lime juice
1/2 oz. fresh orange juice
1/2 oz. Rose's Lime Juice
5 oz. sweet 'n' sour
Shake and strain
Float with 1/2 oz. HPNOTIQ
Pour tequila, Cointreau, juices, and sweet 'n' sour into the iced mixing glass. Shake thoroughly and strain contents into a sugar rimmed, iced pint glass and float with HPNOTIQ.

Espresso Margarita

Specialty of Stone Rose Lounge
Created by Jeff Isaacson
Cocktail glass, chilled
Pour ingredients into an iced mixing glass
1 oz. Patrón Silver Tequila
1 oz. Patrón XO Café Coffee Liqueur
1 oz. White Crème de Cacao
Shake and strain
Pour ingredients into the iced mixing glass. Shake thoroughly and strain contents into a chilled cocktail glass.

Exotic Rita
Specialty of Hard Rock Cafe- New York
Created by Hard Rock's staff
Salt rimmed Margarita glass, ice
Pour ingredients into an iced mixing glass
1 1/2 oz. Patrón Silver Tequila
1/2 oz. Cointreau
3/4 oz. Monin Pomegranate Syrup
3 oz. Hard Rock Cafe's Margarita Mix
Shake and strain
Garnish with a lime wheel
Pour ingredients into the iced mixing glass. Shake thoroughly and strain contents into a salt rimmed, chilled Margarita glass. Garnish with a lime wheel.

Fuzzy Orange Margarita
Specialty of Dave & Buster's
Created by D&B Mixologists in Dallas, TX
House specialty glass, ice
Pour ingredients into an iced mixing glass
1 1/4 oz. Patrón Silver Tequila
1/2 oz. DeKuyper Peachtree Schnapps
3/4 oz. Monin Blood Orange Syrup
3 oz. fresh lime sour mix
Shake and strain
Garnish with a lime wheel and orange flag
Pour ingredients into the iced mixing glass. Shake thoroughly and strain contents into an iced house specialty glass. Garnish with a lime wheel and orange flag.

Ginger Rita
Specialty of 33 Restaurant & Lounge
Created by Jenn Harvey
Sugar rimmed Margarita glass, ice
Pour ingredients into an iced mixing glass
1 1/2 oz. Ginger Infused Tequila*
1/2 oz. Cointreau
1/2 oz. Rose's Lime Juice
1/2 oz. orange juice
1/2 oz. fresh lime sour mix
Shake and strain
Pour ingredients into the iced mixing glass. Shake thoroughly and strain contents into a sugar rimmed, iced Margarita glass.
*Ginger Infused Tequila Recipe
Steep peeled and sliced fresh ginger in a liter bottle of tequila for one week.

J BAR Pineapple Margarita
Specialty of J BAR
Created by Stewart Startt
Margarita glass, chilled
Pour ingredients into an iced blender canister
1 1/2 oz. Sauza Extra Gold Tequila
1 oz. fresh lime juice
2 oz. simple syrup
1/2 cup fresh pineapple, cubed
Blend ingredients
Garnish with a pineapple wedge
Pour ingredients into the iced blender canister. Blend thoroughly and pour contents into a chilled Margarita glass. Garnish with a fresh pineapple wedge.

Kentucky Margarita
Excerpted from The Original Guide to American Cocktails and Drinks- 6th Edition
Cocktail glass, chilled
Pour ingredients into an iced mixing glass
1 1/4 oz. Maker's Mark Bourbon
1/2 oz. Grand Marnier
Splash fresh lime juice
1 1/2 oz. fresh lime sour mix
Shake and strain
Garnish with a lime wedge
Pour ingredients into the iced mixing glass. Shake thoroughly and strain contents into a chilled cocktail glass. Garnish with a lime wedge.

La Baja Noche
Specialty of The Mission Inn Hotel & Spa
Created by Elizabeth Skrzynecky
Sugar rimmed house specialty glass, chilled
Pour ingredients into an iced mixing glass
1 1/4 oz. Sauza Extra Gold Tequila
3/4 oz. Chambord
1/4 oz. Cointreau
1 1/4 oz. fresh lime sour mix
1 1/4 oz. fresh orange juice
Shake and strain
Garnish with a lime wedge
Pour ingredients into the iced mixing glass. Shake thoroughly and strain contents into a sugar rimmed, chilled house specialty glass. Garnish with a lime wedge.

Bookmarks

Rooftop Lounge at the Library Hotel
299 Madison Ave.
New York, NY 10017
☎ 212.204.5498
▶▶ www.hospitalityholdings.com
✉ info@hospitalityholdings.com

Perched atop the Library Hotel 14 floors above the sidewalks of Manhattan is one of the city's genuinely special destination venues — Bookmarks. The classically fashioned lounge lives and breathes in rarified fresh air, a condition that seems to set the tone for the entire experience. Its wrap around terrace offers guests spectacular 360-degree cityscape views, open expanses of sky above and a sumptuous lineup of exquisitely crafted cocktails. Those looking for a respite from the chaotic and jarring should put Bookmarks on their speed dial.

The rooftop lounge features a glass enclosed greenhouse, wooden deck, wicker deck furniture and stone railings. Weathered brickwork, a working fireplace and tables piled high with the works of Dylan Thomas and Walt Whitman are a few of the many unusual touches. The ambience is relaxed, stylish and thoroughly first rate; the clientele, largely off-the-clock execs and the well heeled nature loving crowd.

The highly acclaimed specialty of the house and principal bill of fare is the cocktail. It is an art form that they have embraced and worked to near perfection. Perhaps inspired by the Italian Riviera, the *Limonsecco* is a cocktail featuring Pallini Limoncello, SKYY Citrus Vodka and topped with glorious sparkling Prosecco.

Another effervescent signature is the *Blueberry Fizz*, a highly sophisticated blend of muddled blueberries, lime juice and simple syrup finished with Grand Marnier and a generous fill of Moët & Chandon Champagne. *The Inferno* is an innovative specialty clearly intended to be enjoyed in the fresh open air. It's a sensational cocktail made with Belvedere Vodka, Campari, chocolate liqueur and a few dashes of Tabasco. The ingredients are shaken and served in a tall iced glass with a fill of soda.

Bookmarks is the real deal, a bona fide Gotham attraction. Great drinks and plenty of atmosphere. —RP

The Inferno
Drink recipe on pg 305

La Rosa

Specialty of Tommy's Mexican Restaurant
Created by Jacques Bezuidenhout
Margarita glass, chilled
Pour ingredients into an iced mixing glass
1 1/2 oz. Corzo Silver Tequila
3/4 oz. Briottet Crème de Mûre
Dash agave nectar
1/2 oz. fresh lime juice
3/4 oz. freshly brewed hibiscus tea, cooled
Shake and strain
Garnish with a small lime wheel
Pour ingredients into the iced mixing glass. Shake thoroughly and strain contents into a chilled Margarita glass. Garnish with a small lime wheel.

Lavender Margarita

Specialty of Stone Rose Lounge
Created by Jeff Isaacson
Cocktail glass, chilled
Pour ingredients into an iced mixing glass
2 1/2 oz. Don Julio Blanco Tequila
1 oz. Parfait d'Amour
1/2 oz. fresh lime juice
1/2 oz. simple syrup
Shake and strain
Garnish with a lime wedge
Pour ingredients into the iced mixing glass. Shake thoroughly and strain contents into a chilled cocktail glass. Garnish with a lime wedge.

> "A lime wheel and lime wedge
> in combination is a clever compromise
> between form and function."

Corazón Tequila® de Agave Añejo

America's fascination with 100% agave tequilas borders on the phenomenal and rest assured that *Corazón Tequila de Agave Añejo* will only serve to fuel the trend. For those who are looking for a lush, elegant tequila to sip and enjoy, pull up a snifter and sample this handcrafted gem.

Corazón Tequila is distilled in the highlands of Arandas, which is widely considered to be among the most prestigious growing regions in Jalisco. The Corazón range of tequilas is produced entirely on the sprawling Destiladora San Nicholas Estate using traditional, century old methods. The tequilas are made from mature, estate grown agaves. After harvesting, the hand cultivated agaves are steam cooked in stainless steel ovens, slowly fermented and double-distilled in the estate's stainless steel pot stills. The results are highly sophisticated spirits worthy of top-shelf status.

Corazón Tequila Añejo is aged for a minimum of 2 years in small, Canadian oak barrels. Its supple, medium-weight body has a velvet-like texture and an alluring floral and fruit bouquet. The tequila is exceedingly delicious; its palate generously imbued with the rich flavors of spice, black pepper and oaky vanilla. If you enjoy long, flavorful and sultry finishes, this luxurious, skillfully crafted tequila is for you.

Corazón Tequila Añejo is most appropriately served in a snifter, although it seems to thrive when featured in a ultra-premium Margarita. The 80-proof tequila is packaged in a striking hand blown decanter, a perfect presentation for an impressive, elegant spirit.

Mango Rita
Specialty of Blue Mesa Grill
Created by Sergio Perales
House specialty glass, ice
Pour ingredients into an iced mixing glass
1 1/4 oz. El Tesoro Reposado Tequila
3/4 oz. Grand Marnier
1/2 oz. orange juice
1/2 oz. sweet 'n' sour
1 oz. fresh lime juice
1 oz. Jumex Mango Juice
Shake and strain
Pour ingredients into the iced mixing glass. Shake thoroughly and strain contents into an iced house specialty glass.

The Original Margarita
a.k.a Margarita Sames' Margarita
Excerpted from The Original Guide to Margaritas and Tequila
Salt rimmed cocktail glass, chilled
Pour ingredients into an iced mixing glass
1 1/2 oz. Silver Tequila
1/2 oz. Cointreau
1/2 oz. fresh lime juice
Shake and strain
Garnish with a lime wedge
Pour ingredients into the iced mixing glass. Shake thoroughly and strain contents into a salt rimmed, chilled cocktail glass. Garnish with a lime wedge.

Margarita Azul
Excerpted from The Original Guide to American Cocktails and Drinks- 6th Edition
Salt rimmed house specialty glass, chilled
Pour ingredients into an iced mixing glass
1 1/4 oz. Tarantula Azul
1/2 oz. Disaronno Amaretto
1/2 oz. Blue Curaçao
1/2 oz. fresh lime juice
1 1/2 oz. fresh lime sour mix
Shake and strain
Garnish with a lime wedge
Pour ingredients into the iced mixing glass. Shake thoroughly and strain contents into a salt rimmed, chilled house specialty glass. Garnish with a lime wedge.

Margarita Britannia
Excerpted from The Original Guide to American Cocktails and Drinks- 6th Edition
Cocktail glass, chilled
Pour ingredients into an iced mixing glass
3/4 oz. Sauza Tres Generaciones Plata Tequila
3/4 oz. Beefeater London Dry Gin
1/2 oz. Grand Marnier
1 1/2 oz. fresh lime sour mix
Shake and strain
Garnish with a lime wedge
Pour ingredients into the iced mixing glass. Shake thoroughly and strain contents into a chilled cocktail glass. Garnish with a lime wedge.

Margarita de Jamaica
Specialty of Nacional 27
Created by Adam Seger
Hibiscus sugar* rimmed cocktail glass, chilled
Pour ingredients into an iced mixing glass
2 oz. 1800 Silver Tequila
3/4 oz. Cointreau
1 oz. fresh lime juice
1 1/2 oz. hibiscus infusion*
Shake and strain
Pour ingredients into the iced mixing glass. Shake thoroughly and strain contents into a hibiscus sugar rimmed, chilled cocktail glass.
*Hibiscus-Infusion Recipe - pg 320
*Hibiscus Sugar Rim Recipe
Finely chop dried hibiscus flowers and mix with an equal amount superfine bar sugar.

Margarita La Perserverancia
Excerpted from The Original Guide to American Cocktails and Drinks- 6th Edition
Salt rimmed cocktail glass, chilled
Pour ingredients into an iced mixing glass
1 1/4 oz. Sauza Tres Generaciones Añejo Tequila
3/4 oz. Cointreau
1 1/2 oz. fresh lime sour mix
Shake and strain
Garnish with a lime wedge
Pour ingredients into the iced mixing glass. Shake thoroughly and strain contents into a salt rimmed, chilled cocktail glass. Garnish with a lime wedge.

Margarita Primero Clase

Excerpted from The Original Guide to
American Cocktails and Drinks- 6th Edition
Salt rimmed house specialty glass, chilled
Pour ingredients into an iced mixing glass
1 ³/4 oz. El Tesoro Añejo Tequila
³/4 oz. El Tesoro Paradiso Tequila
³/4 oz. Cointreau
2 oz. fresh lime sour mix
Shake and strain
Garnish with a lime wedge
Pour ingredients into the iced mixing glass.
Shake thoroughly and strain contents into a salt
rimmed, chilled house specialty glass. Garnish
with a lime wedge.

Millionaire Margarita

Specialty of Blue Mesa Grill
Created by Tres Whitley
Cocktail glass, chilled
Pour ingredients into an iced mixing glass
1 ³/4 oz. Jose Cuervo Reserva de la
    Familia Añejo Tequila
³/4 oz. Grand Marnier Cuvée du Centenaire
2 oz. sweet 'n' sour
Shake and strain
Garnish with a lime wheel
Pour ingredients into the iced mixing glass. Shake
thoroughly and strain contents into a chilled
cocktail glass. Garnish with a lime wheel.

"The final touch to any
noteworthy Margarita
is the garnish."

El Tesoro® Tequila

Renowned El Tesoro de Don Felipe 100% agave tequilas are handmade at a small distillery named La Alteña located high in the Los Altos Mountains. There the Camarena family makes tequila the same way they have for over 70 years, using methods long since abandoned by other distillers as too expensive or labor intensive. The range of small batch, alembic distilled tequilas is anchored by the altogether remarkable **El Tesoro Tequila**.

The silver tequila is bottled within 24 hours of distillation — unfiltered and unaltered, exactly as it came out of the still. Definitely sample this spirit neat. It is highly aromatic, and loaded with robust character and clean, crisp peppery flavors.

The distillery also makes **El Tesoro Reposado Tequila**, an elegant and supremely smooth tequila barrel-aged between 6 and 9 months. The patriarch of the line is the inimitable **El Tesoro Añejo**, which is matured for 2 to 3 years in small, oak bourbon barrels. It has a deep, satisfying bouquet, an exceptionally rich, well-rounded flavor and a long, lingering finish.

El Tesoro Paradiso Tequila is an innovative style of tequila. It is a 5-year-old añejo, handcrafted from a blend of El Tesoro tequilas that are further aged in French oak barrels previously used to age A. de Fussigny Cognac. Paradiso strikes a sublime balance between the elegance of cognac and the sultry character of tequila, both of which are deeply imbued in its bouquet, body, flavor and finish.

The Millionaire

Specialty of The Mission Inn Hotel & Spa
Created by Mission Inn's staff
Salt rimmed cocktail glass, chilled
Pour ingredients into an iced mixing glass
1 1/4 oz. Casa Noble Reposado Tequila
1/2 oz. Grand Marnier Cuvée du Centenaire
2 1/2 oz. fresh lime sour mix
Shake and strain
Garnish with a lime wedge
Pour ingredients into the iced mixing glass. Shake thoroughly and strain contents into a salt rimmed, chilled cocktail glass. Garnish with a lime wedge.

Paradise Found

Specialty of Mosaic Restaurant
Created by Stephanie Kozicki, Matt Rinn
Salt rimmed cocktail glass, chilled
Pour ingredients into an iced mixing glass
1 1/2 oz. El Tesoro Paradiso Tequila
1 oz. Grand Marnier Cuvée du Centenaire
1/2 oz. fresh lemon sour mix
1/2 oz. fresh key lime juice
1 oz. mandarin orange puree
Shake and strain
Garnish with a fresh mandarin orange wedge
Pour ingredients into the iced mixing glass. Shake thoroughly and strain contents into a salt rimmed, chilled cocktail glass. Garnish with a fresh mandarin orange wedge.

Passion Pulse

Specialty of Rio/iBaR Lounge
Created by Francesco Lafranconi
Cocktail glass, chilled
Pour ingredients into an iced mixing glass
1 1/2 oz. Patrón Silver Tequila
1 oz. Grand Marnier
1 oz. RémyRed Red Berry Infusion
3/4 oz. passion fruit coulis
1 oz. fresh lime sour mix
Dash Angostura Aromatic Bitters
Shake and strain
Garnish with a lemon twist
    and fresh ground nutmeg
Pour ingredients into the iced mixing glass. Shake thoroughly and strain contents into a chilled cocktail glass. Garnish with a lemon twist and fresh ground nutmeg.

Peach Margarita

Specialty of The Mission Inn Hotel & Spa
Created by Brooke Crothers, Alan Lee
Sugar rimmed house specialty glass, chilled
Pour ingredients into an iced blender canister
1 1/4 oz. Silver Tequila
1 1/4 oz. Jet Extreme Peach Smoothie Mix
3/4 oz. orange juice
3 peach slices
1 3/4 oz. simple syrup
2 1/2 oz. fresh lime sour mix
Blend ingredients
Garnish with a fresh peach slice
Pour ingredients into the iced blender canister. Blend thoroughly and pour contents into a sugar rimmed, chilled house specialty glass. Garnish with a fresh peach slice.

Picosita Margarita

Excerpted from The Original Guide to American Cocktails and Drinks- 6th Edition
Salt and pepper rimmed house specialty glass, ice
Pour ingredients into an iced mixing glass
3/4 oz. Silver Tequila
3/4 oz. Pepper Infused Silver Tequila*
1/2 oz. Triple Sec
1/2 oz. Rose's Lime Juice
1 3/4 oz. fresh lime sour mix
Shake and strain
Garnish with a lime wedge
    and small jalapeño pepper
Pour ingredients into the iced mixing glass. Shake thoroughly and strain contents into a salt and pepper rimmed, iced house specialty glass. Garnish with a lime wedge and small jalapeño pepper.
*Pepper-Infused Silver Tequila Recipe - pg 321

Pineapple Margarita

Specialty of Stone Rose Lounge
Created by Jeff Isaacson
Cocktail glass, chilled
Pour ingredients into an iced mixing glass
2 oz. Gran Centenario Plata Tequila
1 oz. Cointreau
2 oz. pineapple juice
Shake and strain
Garnish with 3 speared pineapple cubes
Pour ingredients into the iced mixing glass. Shake thoroughly and strain contents into a chilled cocktail glass. Garnish with 3 speared pineapple cubes.

Red Rocker

Specialty of Hard Rock Cafe-New York
Created by Hard Rock's staff
Margarita glass, ice
Pour ingredients into an iced mixing glass
1 1/2 oz. Cabo Wabo Reposado Tequila
1/2 oz. Disaronno Amaretto
1 oz. Hard Rock Cafe's Margarita Mix
2 oz. cranberry juice
Shake and strain
Garnish with an orange slice
Pour ingredients into the iced mixing glass. Shake thoroughly and strain contents into an iced Margarita glass. Garnish with an orange slice.

Rio Grande Margarita

Excerpted from The Original Guide to American Cocktails and Drinks- 6th Edition
Salt rimmed house specialty glass, ice
Pour ingredients into an iced mixing glass
3/4 oz. Sol Dios Añejo Tequila
3/4 oz. Tia Maria
3/4 oz. Triple Sec
1 1/2 oz. orange juice
1 1/2 oz. fresh lime sour mix
Shake and strain
Garnish with a lime wedge
Pour ingredients into the iced mixing glass. Shake thoroughly and strain contents into a salt rimmed, iced house specialty glass. Garnish with a lime wedge.

Sake Margarita

Excerpted from The Original Guide to American Cocktails and Drinks- 6th Edition
Salt rimmed cocktail glass, chilled
Pour ingredients into an iced mixing glass
1 1/4 oz. Sake
3/4 oz. Grand Marnier
1/2 oz. Rose's Lime Juice
2 oz. fresh lime sour mix
Shake and strain
Garnish with a lime wheel
Pour ingredients into the iced mixing glass. Shake thoroughly and strain contents into a salt rimmed, chilled cocktail glass. Garnish with a lime wheel.

Bourbon Street & Voodoo Lounge

314 Main Street
Cedar Falls, IA 50613

319.266.5255

www.barmuda.com/bourbon
street/index.php

Bourbon Street Restaurant & the Voodoo Lounge are exactly what the heartland is looking for. They're like the Peace Corps spreading the good word of the French Quarter to the bedrock of Cedar Falls, Iowa. Plates of steamy jambalaya and shrimp Creole, tall, icy Hurricanes, live New Orleans jazz and the promise of good times only serve to seal the deal.

Bourbon Street Restaurant is housed in a historic, two story brick building on the city's revitalized Main Street. The ambience of the place is enthralling. A 13 foot

oak tree dominates the dining room; its canopy lends the space an airy, courtyard quality reminiscent of the French Quarter. The upscale casual restaurant offers a Cajun, Creole and American South menu loaded with New Orleans' standouts and clever twists on local favorites, most notably a divine Cajun pork tenderloin.

Whereas the cuisine will sustain your body, the Voodoo Lounge upstairs will revitalize your spirit. It's a recreation of the New Orleans' experience, authentic right down to the humidity. The decor is a classy ensemble of black leather sofas and love seats, antique bronze chandeliers and vintage pressed tin ceiling. The bartenders are top notch, the back bar expansive and the bar's roster of signature drinks is inspired.

Among their libations of note is the *New Orleans Hurricane*, a magnificent rum based drink that helped put the French Quarter on the map. If you're in the mood for something more combustible, sample the Voodoo's altogether delicious *Ragin' Cajun Bloody Mary*. It's a creative masterpiece, a life altering blend of spices, sauces and Absolut Peppar Vodka.

As they say in New Orleans, let the good time roll! —RP

Ragin' Cajun Bloody Mary
Drink recipe on pg 191

Silver Yuzu Margarita

Specialty of Rosemary's Restaurant
Created by Michael Shetler, Francesco LaFranconi
Cocktail glass, chilled
Pour ingredients into an iced mixing glass
1 1/2 oz. Patrón Silver Tequila
1/4 oz. Cointreau
1/2 oz. yuzu juice concentrate
1/2 oz. fresh lemon sour mix
1/2 oz. fresh lime juice
1/2 oz. agave nectar
1 egg white (pasteurized)
Shake and strain
Garnish with a lime wheel
Pour ingredients into the iced mixing glass. Shake thoroughly and strain contents into a chilled cocktail glass. Garnish with a lime wheel.

Sonoran Spittoon Margarita

Excerpted from The Original Guide to
American Cocktails and Drinks- 6th Edition
Salt and pepper rimmed cocktail glass, chilled
Pour ingredients into an iced mixing glass
1 1/4 oz. Pepper Infused Silver Tequila*
1/2 oz. Triple Sec
1/2 oz. Rose's Lime Juice
1 1/2 oz. fresh lime sour mix
Shake and strain
Garnish with a lime wedge
    and small jalapeño pepper
Pour ingredients into the iced mixing glass. Shake thoroughly and strain contents into a salt and pepper rimmed, chilled cocktail glass. Garnish with a lime wedge and small jalapeño pepper.
*Pepper-Infused Silver Tequila Recipe - pg 321

> "The Margarita has enjoyed far
> more than its allotted
> fifteen minutes of fame."

Partida® Añejo 100% Blue Agave Tequila

The Partida family estate is on 5,000 acres outside of Amatitan, Mexico. Its rich, red volcanic soil is ideal for cultivating the blue agave and the microclimate perfectly attuned to the crafting of tequila. While the entire range of Partida tequilas is highly esteemed, the *Partida Añejo 100% Agave Tequila* seems to command the most attention.

Super-premium Partida tequilas are made from mature, estate grown blue agaves. The piñas are slow baked, slowly fermented and double-distilled in pot stills. The *Partida Blanco 100% Blue Agave Tequila* is bottled fresh from the still, with the remainder of the run transferred to new French oak barrels for aging.

Partida Añejo Tequila is too magnificent to share with friends. It's matured for a minimum of 18 months in oak barrels previously used to age Jack Daniels. During aging the tequila acquires an alluring copper hue and a generous bouquet of ripe red fruit, honey and cocoa aromas. About the moment it washes over your palate you'll realize that you're in the presence of greatness. The tequila has a lushly textured, satiny smooth body and waves of pastry like flavors. The memorable finish is top notch.

Partida Reposado 100% Blue Agave Tequila is aged in oak barrels for a minimum of six months. The tequila has an amber hue, a light-weight, supple body and a slightly sweet bouquet. The palate is a layered affair of delicious vanilla, spice and almonds. Unaged *Partida Blanco* is a sleek, aromatic tequila with a vibrant blend of floral, herbs and citrus.

Sorberita

Specialty of Backstreet Café
Created by Sean Beck
Citrus-infused, salt rimmed
      cocktail glass, chilled
Pour ingredients into an empty mixing glass
1 1/2 oz. Herradura Silver Tequila
1/2 oz. Cointreau
1/2 oz. fresh lime juice
2 oz. scoop lemon sorbet
2 oz. scoop strawberry sorbet
Muddle contents
Add ice
Shake and strain
Garnish with a strawberry
Pour ingredients into the empty mixing glass. Muddle and add ice. Shake thoroughly and strain contents into a citrus-infused, salt rimmed, chilled cocktail glass. Garnish with a fresh strawberry dropped into the bottom of the glass.

Sour Peach Margarita

Specialty of Blue Mesa Grill
Created by Robert Estrada
House specialty glass, ice
Pour ingredients into an iced mixing glass
1 oz. El Tesoro Reposado Tequila
1/2 oz. DeKuyper Peachtree Schnapps
1/2 oz. Triple Sec
1/2 oz. sweet 'n' sour
2 oz. fresh lime juice
Shake and strain
Garnish with a fresh peach slice
Pour ingredients into the iced mixing glass. Shake thoroughly and strain contents into an iced house specialty glass. Garnish with a fresh peach slice.

Summer Shades Margarita

Excerpted from The Original Guide to
American Cocktails and Drinks- 6th Edition
Cocktail glass, chilled
Pour ingredients into an iced mixing glass
2 oz. Fruit Infused Sauza Extra Gold Tequila*
2 oz. fresh lime sour mix
Shake and strain
Garnish with a lime wedge
Pour ingredients into the iced mixing glass. Shake thoroughly and strain contents into a chilled cocktail glass. Garnish with a lime wedge.
*Fruit-Infused Sauza Extra Gold
      Tequila Recipe - pg 319

Three Amigos Margarita

Excerpted from The Original Guide to
American Cocktails and Drinks- 6th Edition
Salt rimmed house specialty glass, ice
Pour ingredients into an iced mixing glass
3/4 oz. Sauza Conmemorativo Añejo Tequila
3/4 oz. Sauza Hornitos Reposado Tequila
1/2 oz. Cointreau
1/2 oz. Rose's Lime Juice
1 oz. lemon-lime soda
1 1/4 oz. fresh lime sour mix
Shake and strain
Float with 3/4 oz. Sauza Tres Generaciones
      Añejo Tequila
Garnish with a lime wedge
Pour tequilas, Cointreau, Rose's Lime Juice, lemon-lime soda, and fresh lime sour mix into the iced mixing glass. Shake thoroughly and strain contents into a salt rimmed, iced house specialty glass. Float the Sauza Tres Generaciones Añejo Tequila. Garnish with a lime wedge.

Tommy's Margarita

Specialty of Tommy's Mexican Restaurant
Created by Julio Bermejo
Half salt rimmed bucket glass, ice
Pour ingredients into an iced mixing glass
2 oz. Herradura Silver Tequila
1 oz. fresh lime juice
3/4 oz. agave nectar
Shake and strain
Pour ingredients into the iced mixing glass. Shake thoroughly and strain contents into a half salt rimmed, iced bucket glass.

Triple Gold Margarita

Excerpted from The Original Guide to
American Cocktails and Drinks- 6th Edition
Salt rimmed house specialty glass, chilled
Pour ingredients into an iced mixing glass
3/4 oz. Sauza Tres Generaciones Añejo Tequila
3/4 oz. Sauza Conmemorativo Añejo Tequila
1/2 oz. Cointreau
1 1/2 oz. fresh lime sour mix
Shake and strain
Float with 3/4 oz. Goldschläger
Garnish with a lime wedge
Pour tequilas, Cointreau, and fresh lime sour mix into the iced mixing glass. Shake thoroughly and strain contents into a salt rimmed, chilled house specialty glass. Float the Goldschläger. Garnish with a lime wedge.

Yucatan Mezcal Margarita

Specialty of The Spanish Kitchen
Created by Danny Rodriguez
Salt rimmed house specialty glass, ice
Pour ingredients into an iced mixing glass
1 1/2 oz. Mezcal Divino with Pear
2 oz. papaya nectar
2 oz. guava nectar
1 oz. Coco López Cream of Coconut
Shake and strain
Garnish with a lime wedge
Pour ingredients into the iced mixing glass. Shake thoroughly and strain contents into a salt rimmed, iced house specialty glass. Garnish with a lime wedge.

"The underlying foundation of
the Margarita and source of
the cocktail's vibrancy is
the base sour mix."

Cabo Wabo™ Reposado 100% Agave Azul Tequila

For countless legions of tequila aficionados, the center of the known universe is Cabo San Lucas in Baja California Sur, Mexico. It is there that you'll find the famed Cabo Wabo Cantina, namesake and birthplace of all world *Cabo Wabo Reposado 100% Agave Azul Tequila*. No other brand of super-premium tequila is so closely associated with the image of fun and sun as Cabo Wabo. It's a world-class spirit with a laid back attitude.

The brand has generated considerable excitement in its brief, yet accolade-filled life. Created in 1996 by ex-Van Halen rocker Sammy Hagar, the Cabo Wabo Tequilas are distilled at Agaveros Unidos de Amatitán in Jalisco. They are traditionally crafted tequilas — mature agaves slowly baked in wood-fired adobe ovens and double-distilled in copper pot stills. The *Cabo Wabo Blanco 100% Agave Azul Tequila* is bottled directly from the still. The reposado is aged in both French and American oak barrels for 4-6 months, while the tequila destined to become *Cabo Wabo Añejo 100% Agave Azul Tequila* will mature in wood for a minimum of a year.

Cabo Wabo Reposado is worth the fuss. The tequila has a glorious hue, a firm, medium-weight body and aromatic notes of vanilla, caramel and light citrus. Its palate is a nuanced affair of black pepper, oily nuts and caramel flavors. Great finish, great tequila.

The Blanco is a delightful spirit — floral, slightly fruity with an undercurrent of spice and pepper. Cabo Wabo Añejo is aromatic, flavorful and marvelously refined. It's a masterpiece.

Chapter Three

Toast of the Town
The Manhattan

It must have been one heck of a party. As the story goes, during the presidential race of 1876, New York socialite and heiress Jenny Jerome held a campaign function for candidate Samuel Tilden at the famed Manhattan Club. Miss Jerome, soon to become Lady Randolph Churchill and mother of Winston, requested a special cocktail be created for the event.

What the staff devised consisted of rye whiskey, Angostura Bitters and Italian (sweet) vermouth. Like a spark to tinder, the cocktail swept through New York society. The drink that we now know as the **Manhattan** literally became the toast of the town. It's said that financial mogul J. P. Morgan drank the cocktail every day at the end of trading on Wall Street.

The secret to the Manhattan's enduring popularity can be attributed to the natural affinity between spirits and fortified wines. These wines — venerable products such as Sherry, port, vermouth and Madeira — are imbued with tremendous flavors and lavishly textured bodies, making them incomparable ingredients in cocktails. The annals of mixology are replete with classic drink recipes that marry fortified wines and spirits and today's practitioners are continuing to explore and redefine the boundaries of this magical pairing.

The explanation for this compatibility lies in how fortified wines are crafted. Back in the days of sailing ships, sending wines across the oceans required vintners to add spirits to their wines to enable them to withstand the rigors of long sea voyages. The spirit, typically a grape distillate, raised the wine's alcohol level from 13% to upwards of 20%. Out of necessity was born an entirely new and delightful genus of potables, namely fortified wines. Using fortified wines in cocktails is a resurgent "lost art." Incorporating vermouths, Sherries and ports into cocktails add tremendous body, depth of flavor and complexity to the drinks.

Vermouth is the most frequently relied upon fortified wine behind American bars. It is flavored with aromatic herbs and spices according to closely guarded trade recipes. Sweet vermouth — often referred to as Italian vermouth — is typically made from Apulia and Moscato di Canelli grapes. After 1-2 years of aging, the wines are blended, filtered and fortified with distilled spirits. Dry (French) vermouth is made from light, thin-skinned Picpoul and Clairette grapes. The wines are aged 2-3 years in oak casks that are exposed to the elements to accelerate maturation. After aging, the wines are infused with botanicals and fortified with spirits.

There are principally three versions of the Manhattan. The namesake version is made with Italian (sweet) vermouth, bourbon or blended whiskey, and a maraschino cherry garnish. The classic proportions are 3 parts whiskey to 1 part vermouth. The **Dry Manhattan** is made by substituting French (dry) vermouth for sweet, and is garnished with either a lemon twist, or pimento-stuffed green olives. The **Perfect Manhattan** — or **Medium Manhattan** — is prepared using about a quarter of an ounce of each type of vermouth, and garnished with a lemon twist. Should a guest request their Manhattan "sweet," add a splash of maraschino cherry juice.

These days it is all too common for a Manhattan to be made without bitters, which is a pity because it's a highly recommended ingredient. Bitters add a marvelous aroma and flavor to the cocktail, such that without it the drink seems a bit lost. Before proceeding in earnest making your own bitters, consider working first with one or more of the four franchise players in the bitters world, namely Angostura, Regans' Orange Bitters #6, Peychaud's and Fee's Peach or Mint Bitters.

Two other popular variations on the theme are the **Brandy Manhattan** and the **Southern Comfort Manhattan**. The Brandy

Maker's Mark® Bourbon Whisky

Maker's Mark Bourbon Whisky is an exquisite small batch whiskey that well deserves its iconic status. A principal player in bourbon's phenomenal resurgence, the distinctive, red wax-dipped bottle has secured its place on top-shelves across the country and is one of the most recognizable whiskeys in the world.

Maker's Mark is crafted at the Star Hill Distillery in Loretto, Kentucky, which is among the smallest distilleries in the state and on the registry of National Historic Landmarks. The brand is one of only a few bourbons to include wheat instead of rye in its mash bill, which also includes corn, barley malt and a sour mash component. The whiskey is made with a yeast strain that is purported to be the oldest in Kentucky. For all intents and purposes, the hugely successful brand is a handmade product.

Maker's Mark Bourbon, 90-proof, has a soft, supple body and a captivating bouquet of honey, vanilla, spices and fruit. The color is rich with the red hue of aged wood. The palate is loaded with the satisfying flavors of caramel, butter and notes of toasty oak. The whiskey has a relaxed and slightly smoky finish.

Here's a world-class whiskey that doesn't cost a week's paycheck. While its captivating array of flavors and aromas come alive with a splash of spring water, Maker's Mark is unsurpassed in a Manhattan or any other bourbon based assignment.

Manhattan is concocted using sweet vermouth, the Dry Brandy Manhattan with dry vermouth and the **Perfect Brandy Manhattan** is made with both vermouths. The Southern Comfort Manhattan is prepared using dry vermouth instead of the sweet, this to create a more balanced cocktail.

The classic **Rob Roy** is the name given to a Manhattan made with Scotch whisky. The **Dry Rob Roy** is made by substituting dry vermouth for sweet. The **Perfect Rob Roy**, or **Affinity Cocktail**, is prepared with about a ¼ oz. of each type of vermouth and garnished with a lemon twist.

There are several popular variations on the Rob Roy theme, each an excellent method of promoting single malts. The **Highland Fling** is a super-premium Rob Roy featuring a 12-year old Highland single malt. Another option on the Rob Roy is to replace the sweet vermouth with equal parts of Dubonnet Rouge and tawny port and then adding in a measure of single malt Scotch.

Secrets Revealed of America's Greatest Manhattans

The Manhattan's revival has everything to do with the drink itself. It is about as suave and delectable as a cocktail gets. It's smooth, aromatic, and has a thoroughly satisfying flavor. Unlike the Martini, which is more of an acquired taste, the Manhattan possesses a nearly universal appeal and don't require enduring a learning curve to appreciate. While a relatively straightforward concoction, there are a sufficient number of components in the drink to devise genuinely singular and innovative signature Manhattans. Learning how to tweak these various elements is at the heart of the creative process.

While it's true that few cocktails will transcend the popularity of the Martini, it's equally true that few cocktails will ever taste better than a well-chilled Manhattan. The choice is yours — follow the crowd, or find soul-satisfying bliss? Here then are the best kept secrets behind America's greatest Manhattans.

• **Stirred or Shaken?** — The decision whether to stir or shake a Manhattan is not as clear-cut as is with the Martini. Traditionally, a cocktail constructed only of an aperitif or fortified wine and a distilled spirit would be stirred gently in the mixing glass until the ingredients have reached serving temperature. As is the case of the Martini, the proper serving temperature for a Manhattan is around 37-38°F. The basic ingredients are sufficiently close in specific gravity as to not require shaking to ensure that they fully integrate.

But vigorously shaking a Manhattan is gaining acceptance, possibly because the principal ingredient is bourbon, a stalwart and hardy spirit that thrives when shaken. Bourbon's deep rich color prevents any semblance of "bruising," an affliction associated with a shaken Martini. Another consideration is that shaking a Manhattan will result in a bit more water going into the cocktail, not a bad thing when working with whiskeys.

• **Uptown Vermouth** — Mastering the Manhattan requires the use of high quality vermouth. As mentioned in the Martini* chapter, there are perceptible differences in quality between the various brands of vermouth. While it may be inexpensive, vermouth is a complex aperitif wine, one that is difficult and laborious to make well. Suffice to say, the better the vermouth, the better the resulting Manhattan.

When in doubt, fall back to the time-tested brands, such as Italian Martini & Rossi, Cinzano, Stock, and French Noilly Prat. They are immeasurably better than the rest of the field, and have a marked impact on the quality of the finished drink. Taking shortcuts with a cocktail like the Manhattan invariably nicks the final product.

Another option also now exists. There are a number of finely crafted vermouths being made at American vineyards rocketing up the charts. A leading example is Vya Preferred California Sweet Vermouth made by winemaker Andrew Quady of Madera. It is an impeccable vermouth, a blend of Orange Muscat, French Colombard and Valdepenas varietal wines that are infused with herbs, spices, flowers, and citrus. Port is added to the blend

Glenmorangie® Single Highland Malt Scotch Whisky

Located in the northern Highlands, the Glenmorangie Distillery was established in 1843 at the site of a former brewery. Today, the renowned distillery only produces single malts and the anchor of their portfolio is the revered *Glenmorangie Single Highland Rare Malt Scotch Whisky*.

Perennially ranked among Scotland's best selling single malts, Glenmorangie 10-year old is a magnificent dram, one that typifies why single malts are all the rage. The whisky is crafted using lightly peated malt and mineral rich water from the nearby Tarlogie Springs. It is distilled in large, uniquely designed pot stills and aged in air-dried, freshly charred casks made from American mountain oak barrels.

Glenmorangie 10 Year Old Single Malt may well be one of the most accessible whiskies ever made, with a broad bouquet and a delicious palate graced with honeyed and lively citrus flavors. The malt's finish is like a pleasant dream.

Being the ultimate innovator, Glenmorangie has released a glorious array of intriguing, 12-year old single malts finished for up to 2 years in a second, different wood. These distinctively wonderful whiskies include *Port Wood Finish* (port pipes), *Madeira Wood Finish* (Malmsey Madeira drums), *Sherry Wood Finish* (Oloroso sherry casks) and *Burgundy Wood Finish* (Burgundy barrels). *Slainte!*

giving the vermouth a velvety texture and beautiful tawny hue, both of which contribute greatly to a Manhattan.

• **The Aperitif Difference** — One of the appeals of the Manhattan, like the Martini, is that it accommodates a great deal of creative latitude. When exploring just how versatile the cocktail is, consider substituting another type of aperitif wine for the vermouth. An excellent jumping off point is using one of the two grand dames of the category, Dubonnet and Lillet. Both brands are available in two styles — rouge and blanc. Ideally suited for use in signature Manhattans, the rouge version is made on a base of premium red wine and infused with a proprietary blend of herbs, spices and peels. The wine is fortified with grape spirits to an elevated strength of 19% alcohol by volume.

Those with adventure in their soul may want to try substituting the vermouth with Pineau des Charentes in their next specialty Manhattan. Pineau des Charentes is a French aperitif made from a blend of unfermented grape must and Cognac brandy. Most varieties of Pineau are crafted from the grapes Ugni Blanc, Folle Blanche, and Colombard, with occasional Sémillon, Sauvignon Blanc and Montils. The mixture is aged for at least 18 months in oak barrels. Pineau seems created specifically with the Manhattan in mind. Its natural sweetness is expertly balanced by the acidity and the increased percentage of alcohol.

• **Fortified Options** — Fortunately for the Manhattan adoring public, there are more fortified wines that can be drafted into service. In fact, the roster of possible contestants includes some of the biggest, most famous names in aperitif wines.

Port is a fortified wine made primarily from red wine grapes cultivated in the Upper Duoro Valley district of northern Portugal. Most are shipped from the city of Oporto, located at the mouth of the Duoro River. Ruby ports are made from a blend of young wines from different vintages, while tawny port is a blend of older wines, pale in color with a distinctive amber edge.

Port is a sensational replacement for sweet vermouth in a Manhattan. On the whole they have supple, velvety textured bodies, wafting, fruit-laced bouquets and ideally balanced, flavor laden palates. It is especially well-suited for pairing with whiskeys and brandies. For example, at Harry Denton's in San Francisco, the signature of the house is the *Angels' Share*, a decadent combination of Louis XIII de Rémy Martin Cognac, Domaine Charbay Nostalgie Black Walnut Liqueur, Porto Rocha 20 Year Old Port and a splash of Chartreuse V.E.P. Liqueur. The *Port of Manhattan* is a specialty cocktail made with tawny port and a splash of Chambord, both of which ideally accentuate the woody, smoky character of the featured bourbon.

Sherry is another stellar fortified wine tailor-made for use in gourmet Manhattans. It is produced in the district of Jerez de la Frontera, the famed wine-growing region in southern Spain between Cadiz and Seville. They are typically made from Palomino grapes. There are principally two styles of Sherry, Fino, which is dry and delicate, and Oloroso, which is fuller-bodied and semisweet.

Illustrating Sherry's versatility is the **Spanish Manhattan**, an elegant cocktail made with Fino Sherry instead of vermouth. The nutty character of the Sherry makes it perfectly cast in a supporting role. Harry Denton's also features the **Heavenly Dram**, a classy offering featuring The Macallan Fine Oak 25 Year Old Single Malt Scotch, Pedro Ximanez Sherry, lemon juice and honey syrup.

Madeira is a celebrated fortified wine often featured as a modifier in specialty Manhattans. While considered a sweet dessert wine, there are dry styles of Madeira as well. Made in Portugal, the wine is blended and aged in Soleras, similar to how Sherries are produced. Madeiras are typically fortified with grape spirits, or brandy.

• **Tapping the Spirit World** — There are numerous reasons to promote top-shelf Manhattans, not the least of which is the axiom that the better the whiskey, the better the resulting Manhattan.

One of the objectives when devising a signature Manhattan is to present a specific brand of bourbon in a creative vehicle that best enhances its characteristics. For example, the **Italian Manhattan** does a superb job showcasing Maker's Mark Bourbon. This small batch whiskey is highly aromatic and an ideal candidate for use in a gourmet cocktail. The recipe substitutes Disaronno Amaretto and several dashes of cherry juice for the sweet vermouth. The nutty almond flavor of the amaretto highlights the smoky, caramel flavors in the whiskey.

Nowhere is it written that you are confined to only using bourbon in your specialty Manhattans. Lacing a whiskey or brandy with a fortified wine is a model for success and it has spawned numerous variations made with an array of different spirits. One example is the **Quebec Manhattan**, which is made with Canadian whisky, dry vermouth and several dashes each of Amer Picon and maraschino liqueur.

An early variation of the cocktail is the **Prohibition Manhattan**. It is made with rye whiskey, sweet vermouth and orange bitters. The **Irish Manhattan** is constructed using Irish whiskey, sweet vermouth and a healthy dose of bitters.

• **Modifying with Liqueurs** — An innovative way to alter the character and personality of a Manhattan is to modify it with a liqueur. Mixology is replete with successful examples. The **New Orleans Manhattan** is made by first swirling the inside of the chilled cocktail glass with Frangelico. The excess is discarded and then the Manhattan is poured in. The Frangelico adds a delightful nutty aroma and flavor to the cocktail.

The **Satin Manhattan** is a chic cocktail made with sweet vermouth, Grand Marnier and whiskey, while the **Blue Grass Blues Manhattan** is a blend of dry vermouth, Blue Curaçao, bitters and bourbon. Other liqueur options include using Chambord to make a **Raspberry**

Brasserie JO

📬 **59 W. Hubbard Street**
   Chicago, IL 60610
☎ **312.595.0800**
▶▶ **www.brasseriejo.com**
✉ **brasseriejo@leye.com**

Welcome to a slice of heaven Parisian-style. **Brasserie JO** is a lively, airy eatery with a '40s French feel. It is an authentic brasserie in every way — robust cuisine with an Alsatian flair, handcrafted beers, affordable wines and a vibrant, joyful environment. If you're looking to loosen up and embrace life for a night, Brasserie JO is your type of place.

Located downtown on the Chicago River, the brasserie exudes style and elegance all without pretense. The traditional decor features high vaulted ceilings, white tablecloths, cherry wood tables, polished brass accents, a heavy wood revolving door and dog friendly patio seating. The restaurant's private wine rooms and banquet facilities rank as some of Chicago's most desirable and highly sought after real estate.

The 220-seat Brasserie JO was the 1996 winner of the James Beard Award for "Best New Restaurant" in the U.S. It reflects the talents and personality of world-renowned chef/proprietor Jean Joho. His expansive menu of updated French classics are simply presented and impeccably executed. The desserts are all immense and divinely inspired.

The lounge is dominated by a 20-foot zinc bar and a large train station clock on the back bar. The atmosphere is upbeat and high energy. The brasserie offers a marvelous array of specialty drinks, including the *Carabao Daiquiri*, a delectable cocktail made with 10 Cane Rum, mango puree and fresh lime juice. Another universally appealing libation is the *Cote D'Azur*, a blend of Ketel One Citroen Vodka, Lillet Blanc, muddled cucumber, parsley, lemon juice and sugar. *Magnifique!*

Brasserie JO is a sophisticated oasis in the Windy City. Everyday French never tasted so good. —RP

Carabao Daiquiri
Drink recipe on pg 127

Manhattan, Benedictine D. O. M. in the *Preakness Manhattan*, Kirschwasser for a *Danish Manhattan* and *Yellow Chartreuse* in the *Biscayne Manhattan*.

- **Muddled Results** — As generations of Old Fashioned enthusiasts will attest, bourbon and muddled fruit taste sublime. In the pursuit of a genuinely delicious Manhattan, don't overlook the creative option of muddling fruit such as oranges, lemons, cherries, peaches, apricots and tangerines and adding it to the cocktail. The selected fruit should be placed into an empty mixing glass, muddled, and then

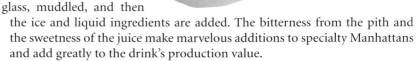

the ice and liquid ingredients are added. The bitterness from the pith and the sweetness of the juice make marvelous additions to specialty Manhattans and add greatly to the drink's production value.

Evan Williams® Single Barrel 1997 Vintage Bourbon

Evan Williams Single Barrel 1997 Vintage Bourbon is a spectacular, world-class whiskey, the only one of its kind. As such there are several remarkable things about it. First, the bourbon is drawn from a single barrel, and when the cask is emptied, that's it. The whiskey in a neighboring cask may be similar, but it won't be an exact match. Second, the whiskey is vintage dated, marking a slice of life that can never be duplicated. Each year's vintage has a flavor profile that is distinct from the previous releases. Last and certainly not least, it is an incredible value when compared to similarly amazing whiskeys.

Made by Heaven Hill in Bardstown, Kentucky, this intriguing bourbon was distilled and barreled in the autumn of 1997. After resting for nine years in charred oak casks, the critically acclaimed whiskey is drawn straight from the barrel and diluted to 86.6-proof. Each label is marked with the exact date the bourbon was placed in oak and bottled.

The 1997 vintage of Evan Williams Single Barrel again offers enthusiasts a veritable extravaganza for the senses. It is endowed with a deep, mahogany color and a voluminous bouquet of vanilla, cocoa, pipe tobacco and candied fruit. The satiny palate is a lavish affair, a dry, puckery offering of ripe cherries, cereal grains and fruit. The finish is like an extended paid vacation — delightful to the last moment.

This remarkable bourbon is a "must-have" for any top-shelf. Take a sip and you'll see why whiskey aficionados have snapped up the previous 11 vintages.

• **Ending Credits** — The garnish on a Manhattan is a stemmed maraschino cherry. When devising a specialty Manhattan however, creative latitude goes with the territory. Make sure that the garnish you choose complements the taste and enhances the appearance of the cocktail. Possibilities include Amarena cherries, brandied cherries, an orange wedge, lemon or orange twist spiral.

Little did the staff at the Manhattan Club realize the revolution that they were fomenting when first they laced rye whiskey with vermouth. More than a century later, mixologists are still following suit and crafting timeless classics by pairing spirits with delicate fortified wines in the form of gourmet Manhattans. *Vive la révolution!*

Angel's Share

Specialty of Harry Denton's Starlight Room
Created by Jacques Bezuidenhout
Brandy snifter, heated
Pour ingredients into an empty mixing glass
1 1/4 oz. Louis XIII de Rémy Martin Cognac
3/4 oz. Domaine Charbay Nostalgie
   Black Walnut Liqueur
1/2 oz. Porto Rocha 20 year old Port
Stir and strain
Garnish with a lemon spiral twist
Pour ingredients into the empty mixing glass. Stir lightly. Pour contents into the heated snifter. Garnish with a lemon spiral twist.

The Bee's Knees

Specialty of Savoy
Created by Eric Scheffer, Ricky Shriner
Cocktail glass, chilled
Pour ingredients into an iced mixing glass
3 oz. Knob Creek Bourbon
1/2 oz. Limoncello
Drop of honey
Shake and strain
Garnish with a lemon twist
Pour ingredients into the iced mixing glass. Shake thoroughly and strain contents into a chilled cocktail glass. Garnish with a lemon twist.

"The better the whiskey,
the better the resulting cocktail."

The Dalmore® Highland Single Malt Scotch Whisky

Founded in 1839 by Alexander Matheson, The Dalmore Distillery is located in the northern Highlands in Alness, Scotland about 20 miles north of Inverness. Despite not being a household brand, its highly acclaimed malts have made it one of the most esteemed distilleries in the famous whisky producing regions. That reputation is represented most ably by *The Dalmore Highland Single Malt Scotch Whisky*.

A marvelous dram for after dinner, the malt is double-distilled in copper pot stills and aged for a minimum of 12 years principally in American white oak, with roughly one third having been matured in Sherry wood casks. The mahogany colored whisky is imbued with a wafting, Sherry laced nose and a lush, satiny textured body. Its palate is slightly spicy with lively citrus notes. The finish is long and memorable.

The Dalmore 21 Year Old Highland Single Malt Scotch Whisky is a rare and delectable find. The whisky is comprised almost exclusively of malt aged in American oak, with only 3% having been aged in Sherry casks. It is an impeccably balanced whisky loaded with tantalizing nuances.

The Dalmore Single Highland Cigar Malt Scotch Whisky is comprised of a higher percentage of whiskies aged in Olorosso Sherry barrels, lending the finished malt a dry, full, velvety textured body, waves of spice and citrus aromas and ample Sherry notes on the extended finish. The overall effect is sensational.

Big Apple Cobbler

Specialty of The Campbell Apartment
Created by Mark Grossich
Pilsner glass, ice
Pour ingredients into an iced mixing glass
1 oz. Jack Daniels Tennessee Whiskey
1 oz. Berentzen Apfel
Dash Angostura Aromatic Bitters
Shake and strain
Fill with ginger ale
Garnish with a red apple slice
Pour ingredients into the iced mixing glass. Shake thoroughly and strain contents into an iced pilsner glass. Fill with ginger ale and garnish with a red apple slice.

Biscayne Manhattan

Excerpted from The Original Guide to
American Cocktails and Drinks- 6th Edition
Cocktail glass, chilled
Pour ingredients into an iced mixing glass
1 1/2 oz. Bourbon
1/2 oz. Triple Sec
1/2 oz. Sweet Vermouth
3 dashes B&B Liqueur
Stir and strain
Garnish with a lemon twist
Pour ingredients into the iced mixing glass. Stir thoroughly and strain contents into a chilled cocktail glass. Garnish with a lemon twist.

Bitter Rob

Specialty of Rosemary's Restaurant
Created by Michael Shetler
Bucket glass, ice
Build in glass
1 1/2 oz. Campari
1/2 oz. Lillet Blanc
Dash orange bitters
Splash orange juice
1/2 oz. agave nectar
Top with club soda
Stir ingredients
Garnish with an orange twist
Pour ingredients into the iced bucket glass in the order listed. Stir gently and garnish with an orange twist.

Blue Grass Blues Manhattan

Excerpted from The Original Guide to
American Cocktails and Drinks- 6th Edition
Cocktail glass, chilled
Pour ingredients into an iced mixing glass
1 1/2 oz. Woodford Reserve Bourbon
1/2 oz. Dry Vermouth
1/4 oz. Blue Curaçao
3 dashes Angostura Aromatic Bitters
Stir and strain
Garnish with a lemon twist
Pour ingredients into the iced mixing glass. Stir thoroughly and strain contents into a chilled cocktail glass. Garnish with a lemon twist.

Bob-tailed Nag

Specialty of Absinthe Brasserie & Bar
Created by Jonny Raglin
Cocktail glass, chilled
Pour ingredients into an iced mixing glass
2 oz. Michter's US 1 Unblended
    American Whiskey
1/2 oz. Barolo Chinato Cocchi
2 dashes Fee's Mint Bitters
Stir and strain
Garnish with a lemon twist
Pour ingredients into the iced mixing glass. Stir thoroughly and strain contents into a chilled cocktail glass. Garnish with a lemon twist.

Brandy Manhattan

Excerpted from The Original Guide to
American Cocktails and Drinks- 6th Edition
Cocktail glass, chilled
Pour ingredients into an iced mixing glass
3 oz. Brandy
1 oz. Sweet Vermouth
2-3 dashes Angostura Aromatic Bitters
Stir and strain
Garnish with an orange slice and cherry
Pour ingredients into the iced mixing glass. Stir thoroughly and strain contents into a chilled cocktail glass. Garnish with an orange slice and a cherry.

Caballito

Specialty of Cuba Libre Restaurant & Rum Bar
Created by Cuba Libre's staff
Cocktail glass, chilled
Pour ingredients into an iced mixing glass
2 oz. Cuba Libre Dark Rum
1/4 oz. Sweet Vermouth
Splash guarapa
Splash fresh lime juice
Shake and strain
Garnish with a mint sprig
Pour ingredients into the iced mixing glass. Shake thoroughly and strain contents into a chilled cocktail glass. Garnish with a mint sprig.

Clermont Manhattan

Specialty of Cyrus
Created by Scott Beattie
Cocktail glass, chilled
Pour ingredients into an iced mixing glass
2 oz. Vanilla Bean & Citrus Peel-
    Infused Bourbon*
1/2 oz. Sweet Vermouth
3 dashes Angostura Aromatic Bitters
Stir and strain
Garnish with 3 Amarena cherries
Pour ingredients into the iced mixing glass. Stir thoroughly and strain contents into a chilled cocktail glass. Garnish with three Amarena cherries.
*Vanilla Bean & Citrus Peel-Infused
    Bourbon Recipe - pg. 322

Cunningham

Specialty of Harry Denton's Starlight Room
Created by Marco Dionysos
Cocktail glass, chilled
Pour ingredients into an iced mixing glass
1 1/2 oz. Johnnie Walker Black Label Scotch
1/4 oz. Benedictine
1/4 oz. Cherry Heering
1/2 oz. fresh lemon juice
1/2 oz. fresh blood orange juice
Shake and strain
Garnish with brandied cherries
    and a flamed orange twist
Pour ingredients into the iced mixing glass. Shake thoroughly and strain contents into a chilled cocktail glass. Garnish with three brandied cherries and a flamed orange twist.
CAUTION! Extreme care must be used whenever flame is used in or near an alcohol drink.

Danish Manhattan

Excerpted from The Original Guide to American Cocktails and Drinks- 6th Edition
Cocktail glass, chilled
Pour ingredients into an iced mixing glass
1 1/2 oz. Bourbon
1/4 oz. Kirschwasser
1/4 oz. Peter Heering Cherry Heering
Stir and strain
Garnish with a lemon twist
Pour ingredients into the iced mixing glass. Stir thoroughly and strain contents into a chilled cocktail glass. Garnish with a lemon twist.

Dry Brandy Manhattan

Excerpted from The Original Guide to American Cocktails and Drinks- 6th Edition
Cocktail glass, chilled
Pour ingredients into an iced mixing glass
3 oz. Brandy
1/2 oz. Dry Vermouth
1 dash Angostura Aromatic Bitters
Stir and strain
Garnish with a lemon twist
Pour ingredients into the iced mixing glass. Stir thoroughly and strain contents into a chilled cocktail glass. Garnish with a lemon twist.

Brûlée the Dessert Experience

⌖ *The Quarter* at the Tropicana Casino and Resort
2801 Pacific Avenue
Atlantic City, NJ 08401
☎ 609.344.4900
▶ www.bruleedesserts.com
✉ info@bruleedesserts.com

Brûlée the Dessert Experience is a fashionable nightspot designed specifically for the pleasure center in your brain to get out and live a little. Its magnificent 3 course desserts have all the attraction of a celestial body. This is a glimpse into the good life not to be missed.

Brûlée is located in the Cuban inspired *Quarter*, a dining, entertainment and retail complex at the Tropicana Casino and Resort in Atlantic City. The interior is impeccable. The dining room features an atrium like ceiling awash in light, color and crystalline reflections. The effect is nearly as dazzling as the cuisine. It is a memorable setting for an unforgettable culinary treat.

Executive Chef Jemal Edwards is the creative *tour-de-force* behind the Brûlée line-up of pastries, confections and delectables. All of Brûlée's desserts are served in a classic three course French style, beginning with the *Amuse Sucrée*, a sorbet first course, the *Entrée*, or main dessert selection and *Petits Fours*, or the cookie and truffle finale. Dessert captains perform tableside, ably flambéing and assembling the more elaborate of offerings.

The liquid side of the Brûlée experience is equally impressive and altogether irresistible. The bar's top-shelf sports Sherries, vintage ports and rare cognacs, old malts and the crème de la crème of liqueurs. Each dessert on the menu is accompanied by a spot on appropriate beverage recommendation. Brûlée's signature drinks are well devised and satisfying. The *Blueberry Amaretto Sour* is an especially delightful companion for the decadent Chocolate Jubilation, a celebration of chocolate cake, caramel and banana ice cream, whereas the *Café Brûlée* is the thing to sip while enjoying the Chef's selection of chocolates. *Bon appetit!* —RP

Blueberry Amaretto Sour
Drink recipe on pg 164

Dry Manhattan

Excerpted from The Original Guide to
American Cocktails and Drinks- 6th Edition
Cocktail glass, chilled
Pour ingredients into an iced mixing glass
3 oz. Bourbon
1/2 oz. Dry Vermouth
1 dash Angostura Aromatic Bitters
Stir and strain
Garnish with a lemon twist
Pour ingredients into the iced mixing glass. Stir
thoroughly and strain contents into a chilled
cocktail glass. Garnish with a lemon twist.

Dry Rob Roy

Excerpted from The Original Guide to
American Cocktails and Drinks- 6th Edition
Cocktail glass, chilled
Pour ingredients into an iced mixing glass
3 oz. Scotch Whisky
1/2 oz. Dry Vermouth
2-3 dash Angostura Aromatic Bitters
Stir and strain
Garnish with a lemon twist
Pour ingredients into the iced mixing glass. Stir
thoroughly and strain contents into a chilled
cocktail glass. Garnish with a lemon twist.

"The secret to the Manhattan's enduring popularity
can be attributed to the natural affinity
between spirits and fortified wines."

The Balvenie® Single Barrel 15 Year Old Malt Scotch Whisky

Located in the Speyside region of the Scottish Highlands, The Balvenie Distillery began crafting whisky on May 1, 1893 and much of what took place that day continues unchanged. Nowhere else will you find a distillery that still grows its own barley and malts in its own traditional floor maltings. Successive generations of craftsmen have preserved the tradition of producing smooth, accessible malt, honey toned with just a hint of peat. *The Balvenie Single Barrel 15 Year Old Malt Scotch Whisky* typifies their commitment to excellence.

This Speyside classic malt is a 15-year old whisky drawn from a single cask of an individual distillation. The precious contents of each barrel fills a limited edition of hand-numbered bottles — a maximum of 300 bottles from any one cask — so each bottle is unique and unrepeatable. The Balvenie Malt Master selects for bottling only those casks that have the essential characteristics of The Balvenie Single Barrel, most notably honey, vanilla and oaky notes.

The distillery's esteemed range also includes the *Balvenie PortWood Single Malt*, a 21-year old double-barreled whisky. This rare malt is aged first in traditional oak and then transferred to port pipes that previously held fine port wines. The result is an exceptionally complex and robust whisky with a lush body and an array of rich, sweet flavors.

Elegancia

Specialty of Harry Denton's Starlight Room
Created by Jacques Bezuidenhout
Cocktail glass, chilled
Pour ingredients into an iced mixing glass
1 1/4 oz. Herradura Seleccion
    Suprema Tequila
1 oz. Chateau d'Yquem 1994 Vintage
Dash Fee's Orange Bitters
3/4 oz. rooibos tea
Stir and strain
Pour ingredients into the iced mixing glass. Stir thoroughly and strain contents into a chilled cocktail glass.

Heavenly Dram

Specialty of Harry Denton's Starlight Room
Created by Jacques Bezuidenhout
Cocktail glass, chilled
Pour ingredients into an iced mixing glass
1 1/2 oz. The Macallan Sherry Oak 25 Years
    Old Single Malt Scotch
3/4 oz. Garvey Pedro Ximenez Sherry
2 teaspoons honey
1/2 oz. fresh lemon juice
Stir and strain
Garnish with a lemon spiral twist
Pour ingredients into the iced mixing glass. Stir thoroughly and strain contents into a chilled cocktail glass. Garnish with a lemon spiral twist.

Highland Dancer

Specialty of The Carnegie Club
Created by Geoffrey Williams
Cocktail glass, chilled
Pour ingredients into an iced mixing glass
2 1/2 oz. Oban 14-year-old Scotch Whisky
1/2 oz. Williams and Humbert Dry Sack Sherry
Stir and strain
Garnish with an orange twist
Pour ingredients into the iced mixing glass. Stir thoroughly and strain contents into a chilled cocktail glass. Garnish with an orange twist.

Highland Fling

Excerpted from The Original Guide to
American Cocktails and Drinks- 6th Edition
Cocktail glass, chilled
Pour ingredients into an iced mixing glass
3 oz. Scotch Whisky
3/4 oz. Sweet Vermouth
2-3 dashes Angostura Aromatic Bitters
Stir and strain
Garnish with a cherry
Pour ingredients into the iced mixing glass. Stir thoroughly and strain contents into a chilled cocktail glass. Garnish with a cherry.

Irish Manhattan

Excerpted from The Original Guide to
American Cocktails and Drinks- 6th Edition
Cocktail glass, chilled
Pour ingredients into an iced mixing glass
3 oz. Irish Whiskey
1 oz. Sweet Vermouth
3 dashes Angostura Aromatic Bitters
Stir and strain
Garnish with a lemon twist
Pour ingredients into the iced mixing glass. Stir thoroughly and strain contents into a chilled cocktail glass. Garnish with a lemon twist.

Italian Manhattan

Excerpted from The Original Guide to
American Cocktails and Drinks- 6th Edition
Cocktail glass, chilled
Pour ingredients into an iced mixing glass
3 oz. Maker's Mark Bourbon
1 oz. Disaronno Amaretto
1/2 oz. maraschino cherry juice
Stir and strain
Garnish with an orange slice and cherry
Pour ingredients into the iced mixing glass. Stir thoroughly and strain contents into a chilled cocktail glass. Garnish with an orange slice and cherry.

Classic Manhattan

Excerpted from The Original Guide to
American Cocktails and Drinks- 6th Edition
Cocktail glass, chilled
Pour ingredients into iced mixing glass
3 oz. Bourbon
1 oz. Sweet Vermouth
2-3 dash Angostura
    Aromatic Bitters
Stir and strain
Garnish with a cherry
Pour ingredients into the iced mixing glass. Stir thoroughly and strain contents into a chilled cocktail glass. Garnish with a cherry.

Latin Manhattan

Specialty of Nacional 27
Created by Adam Seger
Cocktail glass, chilled
Pour ingredients into an iced mixing glass
2 ¹/2 oz. Cigar Infused Maker's Mark Bourbon*
¹/2 oz. Sweet Vermouth
Splash grenadine
Shake and strain
3 dashes Angostura Aromatic Bitters
Garnish with 2 cherries
Pour ingredients into the iced mixing glass. Shake thoroughly and strain into a chilled cocktail glass. Top with 3 dashes bitters. Garnish with 2 cherries.
*Cigar Infused Maker's Mark Bourbon Recipe
Infuse 1 cigar crushed and wrapped in a cheese cloth in a 1 liter bottle of Makers Mark for 1 week.

Manhattan BH

Specialty of Mosaic Restaurant
Created by Stephanie Kozicki, Matt Rinn
Cocktail glass, chilled
Pour ingredients into an iced mixing glass
2 ¹/2 oz. Basil Hayden's Bourbon
¹/2 oz. Vya Sweet Vermouth
¹/4 oz. Vya Extra Dry Vermouth
2 dashes Angostura Aromatic Bitters
Stir and strain
Garnish with a lemon twist
Pour ingredients into the iced mixing glass. Stir thoroughly and strain contents into a chilled cocktail glass. Garnish with a lemon twist.

"It must have been one heck of a party."

Michael Collins® Irish Single Malt Whiskey

Michael Collins is a historical figure who earned a place along side Gandhi, Martin Luther King and William Wallace. Called the "Big Fellow," Collins was the man at the lead of the political battle for Ireland's independence. To name a whiskey in honor of this beloved and revered man is a courageous move. Well, no worries, *Michael Collins Irish Single Malt* is a most worthy tribute.

The whiskey is made at the only independent Irish-owned distillery in Ireland. It is double-distilled in small batches from barley malt, some of which is peated. The all-important water is drawn from the County Louth Mountains. The whiskey is aged in bourbon seasoned oak barrels stored in 18th century warehouses where the cool, moist Irish air slowly brings the whiskeys to maturity. The single malt is matured between 8 to 12 years and bottled at 80-proof.

Michael Collins Irish Single Malt is an exquisite whisky. The amber hued whiskey has a brilliant bouquet or vanilla, chocolate and ground coffee. Its entry washes the palate with dry cereal grain flavors, an appetizing bounty that gradually gives way to port and succulent fruit notes. The malt finishes long and relaxed. From stem to stern this is a thoroughly engaging whiskey.

The distillery also makes *Michael Collins Blended Irish Whiskey*. It is made from a blend of pot and column-distilled whiskeys barrel aged for a minimum of four years. While less aromatic than the single malt, the blend offers a dry and malty array of delicious flavors. For anyone who's yet to experience the sublime pleasures of Irish whiskey, Michael Collins Irish Single Malt is an ideal entree to the category.

The Manhattan Currant
Specialty of 33 Restaurant & Lounge
Created by Jenn Harvey
Cocktail glass, chilled
Pour ingredients into an iced mixing glass
2 oz. Currant-Infused Knob Creek Bourbon*
1/2 oz. Dubonnet Rouge
2 dashes Angostura Aromatic Bitters
Stir and strain
Garnish with a currant
Pour ingredients into the iced mixing glass. Stir thoroughly and strain contents into a chilled cocktail glass. Garnish with a currant.
*Currant-Infused Knob Creek Bourbon Recipe
Fill container 3/4 full with currants.
Top with bourbon and steep for 3-4 days.*

Manhattan, Rosemary's
Specialty of Rosemary's Restaurant
Created by Michael Shetler, Nick Hetzel
Cocktail glass, chilled
Pour ingredients into an empty mixing glass
1/2 oz. simple syrup
Splash club soda
2 dashes orange bitters
Dash nutmeg
Orange slice
Muddle contents
Add ice
2 oz. Van Winkle Family Reserve Rye Whiskey
1/2 oz. Grand Marnier
1/4 oz. King Eider Vermouth
Stir and strain
Garnish with an orange twist
Pour the club soda, simple syrup, nutmeg, orange bitters and orange slice into the empty mixing glass. Muddle and add ice. Pour in the remaining ingredients. Stir thoroughly and strain contents into a chilled cocktail glass. Garnish with an orange twist.

Mexico City
Specialty of Tommy's Mexican Restaurant
Created by Jacques Bezuidenhout
Cocktail glass, chilled
Pour ingredients into an iced mixing glass
2 oz. 1800 Añejo Tequila
1/2 oz. Cinzano Rosso Vermouth
Dash Angostura Aromatic Bitters
Dash orange bitters
Stir and strain
Garnish with three brandied cherries
Pour ingredients into the iced mixing glass. Stir thoroughly and strain contents into a chilled cocktail glass. Garnish with three brandied cherries.

Midnight Manhattan
Specialty of Stone Rose Lounge
Created by Jeff Isaacson
Cocktail glass, chilled
Pour ingredients into an iced mixing glass
1 1/2 oz. Woodford Reserve Bourbon
1 oz. Grand Marnier
Splash fresh lemon sour mix
Splash simple syrup
1/2 oz. white cranberry juice
Shake and strain
Pour ingredients into the iced mixing glass. Shake thoroughly and strain contents into a chilled cocktail glass.

Nattahnam
Specialty of Indigo Eurasian Cuisine
Created by Jason Castle, Tim Skelton
Cocktail glass, chilled
Pour ingredients into an iced mixing glass
3 oz. Jack Daniels Tennessee Whiskey
1/2 oz. Tuaca Liquore Italiano
1/2 oz. Sweet Vermouth
Stir and strain
Garnish with a cherry
Pour ingredients into the iced mixing glass. Stir thoroughly and strain contents into a chilled cocktail glass. Garnish with a cherry.

New Orleans Manhattan
Excerpted from The Original Guide to American Cocktails and Drinks- 6th Edition
Frangelico coated cocktail glass, chilled
Pour ingredients into an iced mixing glass
3 oz. Brandy
3/4 oz. Sweet Vermouth
Stir and strain
1/2 oz. Frangelico swirled inside
    the chilled cocktail glass, discard excess
Garnish with a cherry
Pour ingredients, except the Frangelico, into the iced mixing glass. Stir thoroughly and strain contents into a chilled cocktail glass that has been coated with 1/2 oz. of Frangelico. Garnish with a cherry.

Perfect Brandy Manhattan

Excerpted from The Original Guide to
American Cocktails and Drinks- 6th Edition
Cocktail glass, chilled
Pour ingredients into an iced mixing glass
3 oz. Brandy
1/2 oz. Dry Vermouth
1/2 oz. Sweet Vermouth
1 dash Angostura Aromatic Bitters
Stir and strain
Garnish with a lemon twist
Pour ingredients into the iced mixing glass. Stir thoroughly and strain contents into a chilled cocktail glass. Garnish with a lemon twist.

Perfect Manhattan

Excerpted from The Original Guide to
American Cocktails and Drinks- 6th Edition
Cocktail glass, chilled
Pour ingredients into an iced mixing glass
3 oz. Bourbon
1/2 oz. Dry Vermouth
1/2 oz. Sweet Vermouth
1 dash Angostura Aromatic Bitters
Stir and strain
Garnish with a lemon twist
Pour ingredients into the iced mixing glass. Stir thoroughly and strain contents into a chilled cocktail glass. Garnish with a lemon twist.

Perfect Rob Roy

Excerpted from The Original Guide to
American Cocktails and Drinks- 6th Edition
Cocktail glass, chilled
Pour ingredients into an iced mixing glass
3 oz. Scotch Whisky
1/2 oz. Dry Vermouth
1/2 oz. Sweet Vermouth
2-3 dashes Angostura Aromatic Bitters
Stir and strain
Garnish with a lemon twist
Pour ingredients into the iced mixing glass. Stir thoroughly and strain contents into a chilled cocktail glass. Garnish with a lemon twist.

Port of Manhattan

Specialty of BarMedia
Created by Robert Plotkin
Cocktail glass, chilled
Pour ingredients into an iced mixing glass
2 oz. Bourbon
3/4 oz. Tawny Port
1/2 oz. Chambord
Stir and strain
Garnish with a lemon spiral twist
Pour ingredients into the iced mixing glass. Stir thoroughly and strain contents into a chilled cocktail glass. Garnish with a lemon spiral twist.

Prohibition Manhattan

Excerpted from The Original Guide to
American Cocktails and Drinks- 6th Edition
Cocktail glass, chilled
Pour ingredients into an iced mixing glass
1 1/2 oz. Rye Whiskey
1 1/2 oz. Sweet Vermouth
3 dashes orange bitters
Stir and strain
Garnish with a lemon twist
Pour ingredients into the iced mixing glass. Stir thoroughly and strain contents into a chilled cocktail glass. Garnish with a lemon twist.

Quebec Manhattan

Excerpted from The Original Guide to
American Cocktails and Drinks- 6th Edition
Cocktail glass, chilled
Pour ingredients into an iced mixing glass
3 oz. Canadian Whisky
1 oz. Dry Vermouth
3 dashes Amer Picon
3 dashes Maraschino Liqueur
Stir and strain
Garnish with a lemon twist
Pour ingredients into the iced mixing glass. Stir thoroughly and strain contents into a chilled cocktail glass. Garnish with a lemon twist.

The Campbell Apartment

📭 **Grand Central Terminal**
   15 Vanderbillt
   New York, NY 10017
☎ **212.953.0409**
▶▌ **www.hospitalityholdings.com**
✉ **info@hospitalityholdings.com**

The **Campbell Apartment** may well be the classiest, most elegant place in New York to sip and marvel. Featuring luxurious cocktails, sultry tunes and a décor once reserved for the upper crust, the cocktail lounge offers guests a virtual excursion back to the grandeur of New York circa the turn of the 20th century. It is one of the "can't miss" nightlife experiences in Manhattan.

The Campbell Apartment was once the private office and salon of tycoon John W. Campbell and for decades considered among the

most remarkable office spaces in Manhattan. The Moroccan inspired interior has been restored to its original splendor and the result is breathtaking. It features a beautiful, 25 foot high ceiling with intricately painted wooden beams, marble walls, tapestry sofas, dark wooden appointments and the original stone fireplace. The wooden bar is situated in front of an expansive leaded glass window. Subtle lighting and jazz and swing music create a pervasive sense of being in a more romantic era.

It's easy to understand why The Campbell Apartment has received such critical acclaim. The ambiance is both sophisticated and convivial. In keeping with the concept, the beverage menu is replete with classic offerings, refined and skillfully prepared cocktails born in simpler times.

Among The Campbell Apartment's repertoire of specialties are the *Flapper's Delight*, a cocktail prepared with Moët & Chandon Champagne, papaya juice and amaretto, served in a flute with a long, spiraled orange twist. For heartier types, there's the ***Prohibition Punch***, a sensational blend of Appleton Estate V/X Jamaica Rum, passion fruit juice and Grand Marnier, topped off tableside with Moët & Chandon Champagne.

The Campbell Apartment offers a rare and unforgettable excursion into a world gone by. —RP

Flapper's Delight
Drink recipe on pg 239

Raincoat
Specialty of Absinthe Brasserie & Bar
Created by Jonny Raglin
Cocktail glass, chilled
Pour ingredients into an iced mixing glass
2 oz. Evan Williams Single Barrel
    1997 Vintage Bourbon
1/2 oz. Monteverdi Nocino della Christina
Splash almond syrup
Dash Angostura Aromatic Bitters
Stir and strain
Garnish with fresh grated cinnamon
Pour ingredients into the iced mixing glass. Stir thoroughly and strain contents into a chilled cocktail glass. Garnish with fresh grated cinnamon.

Classic Rob Roy
Excerpted from The Original Guide to American Cocktails and Drinks- 6th Edition
Cocktail glass, chilled
Pour ingredients into an iced mixing glass
3 oz. Scotch Whisky
1 oz. Sweet Vermouth
2-3 dashes Angostura
    Aromatic Bitters
Stir and strain
Garnish with a
    cherry
Pour ingredients into the iced mixing glass. Stir thoroughly and strain contents into a chilled cocktail glass. Garnish with a cherry.

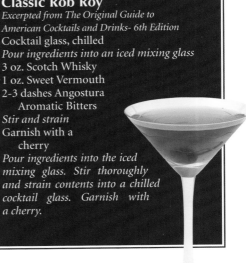

Knob Creek® Kentucky Straight Bourbon

Knob Creek Kentucky Straight Bourbon is exactly what bourbon was intended to be. Its tremendous, semisweet character has timeless appeal, which is why Jim Beam included Knob Creek as a charter member of the Original Small Batch Bourbon Collection, an unparalleled set of four distinctively different styles of handcrafted bourbon.

Knob Creek Bourbon is distilled in small batches and aged for a minimum of 9 years in new white oak barrels. These barrels are first seared over a low flame to bring out the natural sugars in the wood, and then "flash-fired" to create a deep char. It is through the interaction with this rich caramelized layer that Knob Creek gets its deep amber color and savory, semisweet palate.

A few moments alone with Knob Creek are all it takes to fully understand why the 100-proof bourbon has attracted such critical acclaim. The whiskey is enormously aromatic, graced with the aromas of vanilla and baking spices. A few drops of spring water bring out the bourbon's delectable range of flavors. Its finish is warm and spicy.

The collection of small batch bourbons also includes *Booker's*, which is a classically structured whiskey aged 6 to 8 years and bottled unfiltered and uncut at about 126-proof. *Basil Hayden's* is an 8-year old bourbon made with a higher percentage of rye and barley malt for a more flavorful, peppery whiskey. Accessible *Baker's Bourbon* is a 7-year old, 107-proof whiskey distilled with a family strain of jug yeast.

Satin Manhattan

Excerpted from The Original Guide to
American Cocktails and Drinks- 6th Edition
Cocktail glass, chilled
Pour ingredients into an iced mixing glass
2 1/4 oz. Gentleman Jack Rare
   Tennessee Whiskey
3/4 oz. Sweet Vermouth
3/4 oz. Grand Marnier
Stir and strain
Garnish with a lemon twist
Pour ingredients into the iced mixing glass. Stir thoroughly and strain contents into a chilled cocktail glass. Garnish with a lemon twist.

Southern Comfort Manhattan

Excerpted from The Original Guide to
American Cocktails and Drinks- 6th Edition
Cocktail glass, chilled
Pour ingredients into an iced mixing glass
3 oz. Southern Comfort
3/4 oz. Dry Vermouth
Stir and strain
Garnish with a cherry
Pour ingredients into the iced mixing glass. Stir thoroughly and strain contents into a chilled cocktail glass. Garnish with a cherry.

Spanish Manhattan

Specialty of BarMedia
Created by Robert Plotkin
Cocktail glass, chilled
Pour ingredients into an iced mixing glass
2 1/2 oz. Bourbon
3/4 oz. Sherry
Stir and strain
Garnish with a lemon spiral twist
Pour ingredients into the iced mixing glass. Stir thoroughly and strain contents into a chilled cocktail glass. Garnish with a lemon spiral twist.

Tennessee Williams

Specialty of Bookmarks
Created by Jonathan Pogash
Highball glass, ice
Build in glass
1 1/2 oz. Southern Comfort
1/2 oz. Dry Vermouth
2-3 dashes orange bitters
1 oz. pineapple juice
Splash club soda
Garnish with a large mint leaf
Pour ingredients into the iced highball glass in the order listed. Garnish with a large mint leaf.

Texas Trolley

Specialty of Backstreet Café
Created by Sean Beck
Raw sugar rimmed cocktail glass, chilled
Pour ingredients into an iced mixing glass
1 1/2 oz. Booker's Bourbon
1/2 oz. Grand Marnier
1/2 oz. simple syrup
1 oz. fresh lime juice
Shake and strain
Pour ingredients into the iced mixing glass. Shake thoroughly and strain contents into a raw sugar rimmed, chilled cocktail glass.

Uptown Manhattan

Specialty of Harry Denton's Starlight Room
Created by Marco Dionysos
Cocktail glass, chilled
Pour ingredients into an iced mixing glass
1 3/4 oz. Maker's Mark Bourbon
1/2 oz. Amaro Nonino
Dash orange bitters
1/4 oz. brandied cherry juice
Stir and strain
Garnish with 3 brandied cherries
Pour ingredients into the iced mixing glass. Stir thoroughly and strain contents into a chilled cocktail glass. Garnish with three brandied cherries.

Vanilla Manhattan

Specialty of Brûlée the Dessert Experience
Created by Peter Van Thiel
Cocktail glass, chilled
Pour ingredients into an iced mixing glass
2 1/2 oz. Knob Creek Bourbon
1 1/4 oz. Stoli Vanil Vodka
1/4 oz. Sweet Vermouth
Stir and strain
Garnish with a fresh vanilla bean
Pour ingredients into the iced mixing glass. Stir thoroughly and strain contents into a chilled cocktail glass. Garnish with a fresh vanilla bean.

Chapter Four

A Creative Lineage
Cosmos, Kamis, and Gimlets

The popular revival of the *Gimlet* is a clear sign that we're evolving as a species. No drink in all of mixology has spawned as many popular variations of its theme than the classic Gimlet. Yet, as with most things, the original is still unsurpassed.

The Gimlet is the unfettered combination of gin, vodka, light rum or silver tequila mixed with several splashes of Rose's Lime Juice and served chilled in a cocktail glass. Squeeze in the juice from a lime wedge and you've made one of the bona fide classic cocktails.

The origin of the Gimlet can be traced to Colonial India and the expansion of the British Empires. Sailors in Her Majesty's Navy needed the ascorbic acid in fruits such as limes to ward off the debilitating effects of scurvy. The L. Rose & Company of Edinburgh, Scotland answered the call.

In 1867, Lauchlin Rose developed and patented a process for preserving fresh lime juice without the use of alcohol. That same year, the Merchant Shipping Act was passed requiring all Royal Navy and Merchant vessels to dispense a daily ration of lime juice. It was this law that brought about the name "Limeys" for British sailors, as well as generated widespread acclaim for life sustaining Rose's Lime Juice.

Gin and British Navy also enjoy a storied, centuries-old association. In fact, Plymouth Gin has been distilled within walking distance of the Royal Naval base at Plymouth for over 200 years. Officers in Her Royal Majesty's Navy received a daily ration of gin. The large quantities of gin combined with the close proximity of countless bottles of Rose's Lime Juice and the urgent need to ward off scurvy and the doldrums sufficiently explains the origins of the Gimlet.

As for the cocktail's name, the short answer is who knows? A gimlet is a hand tool for drilling small holes, mainly in wood. Certainly seamen working on tall sailing ships would have needed augers like a gimlet. The connection between a hand tool and the drink, however, is a subject for conjecture.

Then there's Surgeon Rear-Admiral Sir Thomas Desmond Gimlette. He was a high-ranking British naval medical officer at the time. How convenient it would have been if he had concocted the Gimlet as an act of civility and in the practice of good medicine.

Unfortunately his obituary in The London Times (October 6, 1943) makes no mention of the cocktail. Rather a pity.

The most public declaration regarding the cocktail may well have been delivered by novelist Raymond Chandler who wrote in his 1953 novel *The Long Goodbye* that "...a real gimlet is half gin and half Rose's Lime Juice and nothing else." Perhaps one could argue about the proportions, but Chandler certainly had the ingredients down.

Until the late '60s, the featured performer in the Gimlet was invariably gin. As Americans turned on to vodka, it became the more popularly requested spirit in the Gimlet. During the same time frame the drink became more frequently requested served on the rocks. While there is no accounting for taste, the dynamics of the Gimlet are unparalleled when made with a crisp, full-bodied gin and presented in a chilled cocktail glass.

Movie buffs and Gimlet enthusiasts will be pleased to learn that famed film director Ed Wood's favorite drink was the Vodka Gimlet. How do we know that? The wacky and utterly fantastic Wood often wrote under the pseudonym "Akdov Telmig," clearly an affectionate salute to his cocktail of choice.

Secrets Revealed of America's Greatest Gimlets

Perfecting the Gimlet is the first step toward a brighter and more prosperous

Zaya™ Gran Reserva 12 Year Old Guatemalan Rum

Where a rum is made is the most significant factor impacting its developing character. The climate, water and soil all contribute to the quality and flavor of the local cane. An excellent example of the affect appellation has on a finished spirit is *Zaya Gran Reserva 12 Year Old Guatemalan Rum*, an ultra premium rum made in the premiere growing region in Guatemala. At the risk of stating the obvious, this magnificent rum couldn't have been made anywhere else.

La Nacional, distiller of renowned Zacapa Centenario, produces Zaya Gran Reserva in exceedingly limited quantities using estate grown sugar cane and artesian water. Long, hot summers and rich, volcanic soil yield premium sugar cane. The rum is double-distilled in copper pot stills and then transferred to oak barriques where it will mature for a minimum of 12 years. The rum is bottled at 80-proof.

If you don't immediately swoon over Zaya Gran Reserva, you likely aren't passionate for world-class añejo rum. It has a deep, captivating mahogany hue and a wafting bouquet loaded with notes of ripe fruit, toasty oak and butterscotch. You'll become a devoted fan after the first whiff. The velvety, medium-weight body delivers a mildly sweet palate imbued with the flavors of vanilla, nutmeg and coconut. The luxurious finish is long and lightly spiced.

Zaya Gran Reserva is a highly sophisticated rum best appreciated neat in a snifter. Then again, it's also delicious featured in a cocktail.

tomorrow. The pursuit will eventually lead you to discovering the tantalizing nuances of the *Kamikaze* and *Cosmopolitan*. It's a good deal. Perfect one cocktail and become master of three.

The first secret lies in achieving a balance between the aromatics in the gin and the sweet, tart flavor of the lime juice such that all are perceptible, yet none predominate. Use too little lime juice and the resulting cocktail will lack vigor and the zesty zeal that is the Gimlet's hallmark. On the other extreme, use too much lime juice and the drink becomes cloying and acerbic.

The traditional portioning is a ratio of three parts gin to one part lime juice. Start there and tweak accordingly. The flavor of the Gimlet will vary slightly depending on the brand of gin you select. Preparing the cocktail with a dry gin will likely require using less lime juice, while a semisweet, more perfumed brand will typically require a larger dose. For that reason, gins with a drier taste profile seem more appropriate for service in Gimlets than their sweeter counterparts.

The venerable Gimlet has earned its niche in the limelight. Few cocktails are as subtle and uncomplicated. To help make the learning curve shorter and less steep, here are the best kept secrets behind America's greatest Gimlets.

• **Spirit Realm** — There is a natural affinity between gin and lime. Maybe they went to camp together, but the zesty, tart flavor of lime seems divinely compatible with gins on both ends of the spectrum. Thus the basis for the Gimlet's celebrity status. One variation on this theme is featuring a flavored gin in a Gimlet. There are numerous citrus and berry infused brands on the market. Bafferts Mint Gin is an intriguing and delicious choice.

It would be an injustice, however, not to consider exploring your creative options when it comes to which base spirit to feature in the cocktail. The enduring popularity of the Vodka Gimlet is testimony that the drink is capable of achieving greatness using a spirit other than gin.

The list of candidates is relatively long, but again the soundest advice is to always choose to promote a premium brand. In this and most other cases, quality trumps all other considerations.

One delicious variation of the Vodka Gimlet is the *Raspberry Gimlet*. It's prepared using raspberry-steeped vodka, or if you'd rather not wait the 2-3 days necessary to make an infusion, select from any of the magnificent raspberry-infused vodkas on the market. Successful premium flavored vodkas are similar to an eaux de vie—light, dry and loaded with character. They taste and smell like sun-drenched, vine-ripened fruit.

The universe is plenty big, however, and there are many more creative spirit options. The first family to look at is rum. While close in looks and personality to a Daiquiri, traditionally concocted *Rum Gimlets* differ from Daiquiris in several key respects. A Rum Gimlet has a more pronounced body and is inherently a sweeter drink than a Daiquiri. The shared attribute between the two cocktails is that pairing the flavor of lime with that of rum is a tried-and-true formula for success.

Once you start to consider the creative possibilities of featuring rum in your next Gimlet the options become almost overwhelming. Even substituting a silver rum for the gin or vodka in the cocktail is a decision loaded with options. For example, a Gimlet made with a Puerto Rican rum like Bacardi or Havana Club will taste markedly different from one based on a silver Jamaican rum, or a super-premium brand of rhum agricole, such as Rhum Clément, 10 Cane, or Haitian Rhum Barbancourt.

And then there are sophisticated and flavorful añejo rums to consider. Their dark rich hues belie that aged rums are light bodied and ideal for use in Gimlets. Rounding out the stellar cast of players is flavored and spiced rums. For instance, raspberry, coconut and citrus-infused rums are superb in a Gimlet. So are rums with lush, fruit flavors like mango and papaya.

Matching the flavor of tequila and lime juice is also a natural. Using a silver tequila in a Gimlet creates a sleek, clean cocktail more along classic lines, while the prominent oaky and vanilla notes in añejo tequilas add another dimension to the drink. If you're

Don Eduardo® Añejo 100% Agave Tequila

One of the patriarchs of the tequila industry was Don Eduardo Orendain Gonzalez. He built his first tequila distillery in 1926. Today, the family owned Orendain Distillery ranks among the major producers of super-premium 100% agave tequilas. Likely their most prestigious achievement to date is *Don Eduardo Añejo 100% Agave Tequila*.

The entire range of Don Eduardo Tequilas is produced at the state of the art Orendain Distillery in Jalisco. The agaves are cultivated on the family's estate outside the town of Tequila. After harvesting, the mature agaves are baked, crushed and slowly fermented using a proprietary strain of yeast. The fermented agave juice is double-distilled in copper pot stills.

The highly acclaimed Don Eduardo Añejo is aged in charred American oak barrels for a minimum of 2 years. During its extended stay in wood, the tequila acquires an amber, golden color and a bouquet rich with flora, vanilla and fruit aromas. It has a complex palate of spice, vanilla and peppery flavors. The finish is long and relaxed.

Delightfully accessible *Don Eduardo Silver Tequila* is a svelte, triple-distilled gem. It has a lightweight body and a fresh, somewhat spicy bouquet. The tequila's satiny body rolls over the palate without undue heat and then slowly dissipates into a crisp and flavorful finish. *Don Eduardo Reposado* is a sensational tequila with some of the exuberance of the silver and the mellow refinement of the añejo. The tequila has a lovely hue and a pepper and vanilla bouquet. It is well textured and generously endowed with flavor.

feeling adventurous, consider basing a Gimlet on mezcal. The light smoke in the finish of most mezcals is an intriguing compliment to the lime flavors.

A burgeoning trend of note is featuring spirits such as shochu, aguardiente, cachaça, grappa, eaux de vie and sake in Gimlets. The pairings are successful because of the simplicity of the drink and each happens to taste great matched with lime juice. The Gimlet is an excellent vehicle to get people to try these lesser known spirits.

- **Scratch Players** — Much of the success of the Gimlet must be credited to the widespread use of Rose's Lime Juice. It is a consistent, high quality product, semisweet without the slightest trace of bitterness. But at the risk of disagreeing with the great Raymond Chandler, the cocktail does not need to be made with Rose's Lime Juice. Indeed, a growing trend within the world of Gimlets is to feature a scratch lime mix, both to freshen things up and to add the flair of craftsmanship to the cocktail.

  The process of making scratch lime juice is not dissimilar to preparing scratch Margarita mix, only the result needs to be slightly denser and decidedly sweeter. This scratch mix can then also be used in Kamikazes, Cosmopolitans and other cocktails traditionally made with a splash or two of Rose's.

  There are two issues to consider when devising a scratch lime juice. The quality of fresh limes varies depending on the season and the source of the fruit. Sometimes limes are sweet and succulent, other times they're small, hard and relatively bitter. This variance will result in needing to use more or less sweetener to achieve a consistent taste profile. Basing the recipe on a different variety of fruit, such as key limes or Mexican limes is another creative avenue to consider.

  The second consideration is selecting a sweetener. In addition to using granulated white sugar or plain simple syrup, sweetener options include cane syrup, agave syrup, or flavored simple syrup. For example, P.F. Chang's China Bistro promotes a sensational cocktail named the *Jasmine Gimlet* that derives its singular flavor in part from the use of jasmine flavored simple syrup as a sweetener.

- **Liqueurs as Modifiers** — Splashing a liqueur into a signature Gimlet is certainly a proven means of creating a bestseller. For example, the *Tuaca Gimlet* is prepared with an additional splash of the liqueur thus rendering the concoction singularly delicious and satiny smooth. Liqueurs such as Chambord, Amaretto, Kahlúa and ZEN Green Tea are all often relied upon to inject Gimlets with some added pizzazz.

  This secret may take you dangerously close to crossing over into the realm of the Kamikaze. After all, adding a measure of Cointreau to a Gimlet transforms the cocktail into a Kamikaze. Some discretion needs to be exercised here lest you market a cocktail as a Gimlet and what the guest actually receives is a specialty Kamikaze.

- **Inspired Machinations** — There's still more creative territory to be traversed. For instance, muddling is an expedient and presentation enhancing method of imbuing a specialty Gimlet with a savory array of fresh fruit. The *Blue Moon* is a signature Gimlet at Bar Masa in Manhattan. It's made with muddled blueberries, sugar, Iichiko Shochu and lime juice. Perhaps splashing in a complementary juice or puree will prove to be the final touch you're looking for. In some quadrants of the universe blending a Gimlet with a base of lime sorbet is just the ticket.

• **End Game** — The lime wedge garnish on the Gimlet accomplishes two objectives. First, and most importantly, it is an additional source of vitamin C. Guests can take the piece of fruit and squeeze the juice into the cocktail if they so choose. It's also interactive and helps people to become more connected to their cocktails.

Secondly the garnish needs to enhance the appearance of the cocktail, the importance of which should not be underestimated. As in all things, first impressions matter. Take care to use only ample sized wedges of impeccably fresh fruit. An old, dried out piece of fruit floating in a cocktail is unappetizing and creates a poor impression.

Secrets Revealed of America's Greatest Kamikazes

In the late '70s the Vodka Gimlet morphed into the *Kamikaze*, an ultra popular cocktail made with vodka, Rose's lime juice and a shot of Cointreau or triple sec. Even now in its third decade, an icy Kamikaze is a "can't miss" proposition.

In addition to an enhanced body, balance and utterly sublime taste, the Kamikaze has one other thing going for it that keeps it popular with both mixologists and their adoring public. That's versatility. The classic cocktail has the great ability to adopt different tastes and clever guises. The blueprint for plumbing its creative depths is revealed in the following best kept secrets behind America's greatest Kamikazes.

• **The Gimlet Foundation** — The place to start when devising a signature Kamikaze is with the recipe for a genuinely magnificent Gimlet and begin tweaking from there. In practical terms, this means the aforementioned secrets of the Gimlet also apply to this cocktail.

While Kamikazes are typically made with vodka, your spirit options are extensive. Flavored vodkas, rums and tequilas are sensational when featured in a specialty Kamikaze. Aged rums and añejo tequilas are viable candidates, as well as the more exotic light spirits, like shochu, aguardiente, cachaça, grappa, eaux de vie and sake. The advice about selecting a premium, moderately dry spirit still applies.

• **Portion Parameters** — There are three dimensions working in a Kamikaze, namely the character of the base spirit, the sweet and tart flavor of the lime juice, and the flavor of the orange liqueur modifier. Each component should be in balance with the others. The traditional portioning of a Kamikaze is three parts vodka and one part each of lime juice and orange liqueur. This ratio provides a good jumping off point.

The Carnegie Club

📫 **CitySpire Center**
156 West 56th Street
New York, NY 10019
☎ **212.957.9676**
⏭ **www.hospitalityholdings.com**
✉ **info@hospitalityholdings.com**

The **Carnegie Club** in Manhattan's CitySpire Center is a swank, upscale cocktail lounge that exudes class. Its romantic appeal is palpable and nearly impossible to resist. More than just another magnificent place, The Carnegie Club is at once three things, an accomplished cocktail joint, a hot jazz club and one of the last bars in the City where smoking fine, hand rolled cigars is permitted, if not encouraged.

The interior of the sprawling Carnegie Club features a 25-foot high ceiling, loft balcony and cathedral-like windows that combine to give the space grandeur. Shelves lined with leather bound books, upholstered sofa chairs, a stone fireplace and bright art deco wallpaper give it an intimate feel, an ideal venue to appreciate great musicians at work. The curling smoke caught in the footlights and waitresses wearing cocktail dresses and pearls complete the grand illusion. Guaranteed, nights fly by all too quickly at The Carnegie Club.

As one would expect, the humidor is well stocked and the staff knowledgeable about cigars. While not everyone in the lively, well-dressed crowd smokes cigars, they all seem to be smiling, tapping their feet and sipping on one of The Carnegie Club's many featured cocktails. The bar offers updated classics like the *Moscow Mule* and *Aviation Cocktail*.

Much of the success of the lounge can be attributed to their sensational signature drinks, one of which is the *Espresso Misu*, an altogether delicious blend of Kahlúa, Stoli Vanil Vodka, freshly brewed espresso and cream. For an effervescent treat order the *Carnegie Confetti* a champagne cocktail made with honey liqueur and pineapple juice.

Regardless of what music's on tap, or who has the mike, The Carnegie Club is always in the groove. —RP

Espresso Misu
Drink recipe on pg 217

The process of tweaking the recipe, as in cooking, is largely where the spark of innovation and brilliance takes place.

• **Orange Keystone** — The most often published recipe for a Kamikaze calls for triple sec as the orange modifier. To assess whether yours is an excellent triple sec, splash some into a glass, give it a healthy swirl and taste. Look for a true to fruit orange flavor, smooth medium-weight body and a clean, crisp finish. Anything less and you should consider making a change.

Blue Curaçao is a popular choice in Kamikazes because of its almost incandescent blue color. The orange liqueur is slightly sweeter than triple sec. A Kamikaze made with Blue Curaçao instead of the triple sec is called a *Divine Wind Kamikaze*.

The preeminent Curaçao liqueur is Cointreau. Created in 1849, super-premium Cointreau is crafted from a blend of oranges from Spain, France, Brazil and South America. The crystal clear liqueur is flawless. In addition to the cache associated with Cointreau, the liqueur will contribute greatly to the cocktail's bouquet and taste, but will leave the color of the cocktail unaffected.

Grand Marnier® Cordon Rouge Liqueur

Grand Marnier Cordon Rouge Liqueur ranks among the finest liqueurs on the planet and is spoken of with justifiable reverence.

This grand dame of liqueurs is the creation of the Lapostolle family, who in 1827, founded a distillery to produce liqueurs in the chateau country of France. By 1870, the firm was experimenting with different blends of cognac-based liqueurs. Louis Alexandre Marnier hit on the notion of combining the peels of bitter Haitian oranges with Fine Champagne cognac. After a decade in development, Grand Marnier was introduced to the world in 1880.

Made in Neauphle-le-Château, Cognac, the liqueur is crafted exactly as it was over a century ago. The orange peels are first slowly macerated in cognac. The infused-spirit is redistilled, blended with the finest cognacs from each of the growing regions, and skillfully sweetened. The liqueur is then barrel aged at the Marnier-Lapostolle cognac cellars at Château de Bourg.

To describe Grand Marnier as exquisite may be underselling it a bit. The liqueur has the captivating color of cognac with radiant yellow and gold highlights. Its light-weight body has the texture of satin and the generous citrus bouquet is laced with the aroma of brandy. The palate is an elegant array of sweet and sour orange flavors followed closely by a lingering cognac finish.

Mixologists around the globe treasure Grand Marnier for its enormous versatility in preparing cocktails.

Kamikazes take on an entirely different dimension when modified with super-premium Grand Marnier. The French classic liqueur is made by macerating the peels of bitter Haitian oranges in Fine Champagne cognac. The result is sublime perfection. Using Grand Marnier as the orange modifier in a specialty Kamikaze will augment the cocktail's color and introduce the complementary flavor of brandy.

There are other exceptional brandy-based orange liqueurs to choose from, each of which will elevate the taste of the finished Kamikaze. It's a select international group comprised of Italian GranGala, Mandarine Napoléon from Brussels and Hardy Extase X.O. from France. As is the case with specialty Margaritas, one available option is to split the orange modifiers and use both Cointreau and one of the brandy-based liqueurs.

• **Liqueur Modifiers** — Take your Kamikazes to the next level by splashing in a liqueur or two. Popular examples include the *Purple Kami*, which is made using raspberry-flavored vodka and Chambord instead of the triple sec and the *Cranberry Kami* featuring Stoli Cranberi Vodka and a liberal dose of all-world PAMA Pomegranate Liqueur. Equally intriguing is the *Radioactive Kamikaze*, the eerie looking combination of Malibu, light rum, 151-proof rum, Blue Curaçao, grenadine and a shot of lime juice.

• **Scratch Base Mix** — Like the Gimlet before it, specialty Kamikazes can also be crafted using scratch lime mix instead of a bottled lime juice. Because of the added dimension of the cocktail, you have more maneuvering room when modifying the base lime mix than with the Gimlet. So feel free to add in complementary flavored juices, purees and syrups, to name but a few. It's a wise course of action. Concocting a devilishly delicious scratch mix goes a long way toward achieving stardom.

• **Kamikaze Postscript** — The standard garnish on the Kamikaze is a generous piece of fresh lime cut into a wedge. The wedge shape facilitates guests squeezing the lime juice into their cocktails. Lime wheels are just for show; lime wedges are the working man's garnish. Kamikazes, however, are also often embellished with long orange peel spirals, slices and orange wheels. Have fun and finish off the cocktail with pizzazz.

Secrets Revealed of America's Greatest Cosmopolitans

"Sex in the City" only confirmed what veteran lounge lizards already knew that when it comes to cocktails the one to be seen with these days is the *Cosmopolitan*. The sleek concoction burst onto the scene in the early 1990s and has been a franchise player ever since. Using the Kamikaze as the creative role model, the Cosmopolitan is constructed with citrus-infused vodka,

Cointreau, lime juice and a splash of cranberry juice. It's then stirred, strained into the coldest, most elegant cocktail glass handy and presented with an ample wedge of fresh lime. Voila, the Kamikaze is transformed into a Cosmopolitan.

One plausible explanation of why the cocktail has enjoyed such success is that it went where its predecessors hadn't — into the fourth dimension. A snapshot of the Cosmopolitan quickly reveals the four dimensions at work, namely the zesty citrus-flavored vodka, the brilliant orange flavor of Cointreau, the sweet/sour taste of the lime base mix and the tart exuberance of cranberries. The added nuance and depth of the Cosmopolitan sparked a creative boom.

A well-crafted Cosmo is universally appealing and a thing of joy. To that end, here are the best kept secrets behind America's greatest Cosmopolitans.

• **The Kamikaze Foundation** — Many of the secrets to making great Cosmopolitans have already been revealed herein. As was the case with the Kamikaze, Cosmopolitans can be made with scores of different premium light spirits. The cocktail reached celebrity

Chambord® Black Raspberry Liqueur

It is hard to imagine sipping a liqueur more luscious and exquisite than *Chambord Black Raspberry Liqueur*. It was inspired by a unique, black raspberry liqueur produced in the Loire Valley of France during the late 17th Century. The liqueur was said to have been introduced to King Louis XIV during one of his visits to the Chateau de Chambord during his reign. It became an overnight success when introduced in the United States in the early 1980s and was a fixture on back bars moments after its arrival. Now twenty years later, Chambord is the featured performer in a large repertoire of cocktails and permanently enrolled in the "must have" class.

Chambord Liqueur is made on the premises of a traditional Loire Valley Chateau south of Paris in Cour-Cheverny France. The liqueur is crafted using only all-natural ingredients. An infusion of fresh raspberries and blackberries is married with a proprietary blend of natural black raspberry fruit extract, cognac, Madagascar vanilla, Moroccan citrus peel, honey, and delicate herbs and spices.

Everything about Chambord is sensational. The intrigue begins with its opaque appearance and extremely deep, ruby/purple hue. The liqueur has a luxuriously textured, medium-weight body and a wafting herbal and fruit bouquet. The semisweet palate is a lavish affair of raspberries, spice, herbs and a taste of honey. The flavors persist on the palate for a remarkably long finish.

In the hands of the inspired, Chambord has no creative limits.

status on the back of Absolut Citron, a preeminent brand of citrus-infused vodka. The vibrant spirit gave the drink added character and flavor dimension.

Preparing a Cosmopolitan with a brand of neutral vodka often results in a flat and disappointing cocktail. With that one possible exception, nearly all other light spirits with discernible taste can be featured in a Cosmopolitan. In addition, there are boatloads of new flavored vodkas and rums to experiment with. The same is also true for aged rums, añejo tequilas and spirits such as shochu, aguardiente, cachaça and sake.

Illustrations abound. A popular derivation of the Cosmo is the *Limón Cosmopolitan*, which is made with the sensational citrus-infused light rum Bacardi Limón. Other creative options are to substitute Mount Gay Eclipse for the Citron to make a *Barbados Cosmo*, or blood orange-infused tequila for the vodka to create the signature *Valhalla*.

The secrets surrounding the use of liqueurs in the Kamikaze apply equally to Cosmopolitans. The cocktail soared to prominence with Cointreau and it remains the most often relied upon modifier. Sample Cointreau neat and you'll better appreciate why it is a timeless classic.

But once again one need not feel limited with respect to selecting flavor enhancing modifiers. Grand Marnier, GranGala and Mandarin Napoléon are right at home in a Cosmopolitan. Blue Curaçao is also frequently selected for service. Not only does it add the right amount of orange flavor to the cocktail, but it also has a special affect on the cocktail's presentation. Case in point is the *Purple Cosmo*, a cocktail made with citrus-vodka, Blue Curaçao and Chambord. Guaranteed that it tastes as sensational as it looks.

The secrets pertaining to the Kamikaze's base lime mix are directly applicable to the Cosmopolitan. While the cocktail attained stardom with Rose's Lime Juice, bottled lime juice is not your only option when it comes to the all-important base mix. Because the Cosmopolitan has such breadth you have more creative latitude when it comes to altering the base. For instance, the *Cosmosaic* is a specialty Cosmopolitan made with a healthy splash of key lime juice.

• **The Fourth Dimension** — How a fruit that grows in bogs can be so delicious is imponderable. Nevertheless, the plucky cranberry has certainly gotten itself a steady gig in the Cosmopolitan. Its light body, tart, crisp flavor and unmistakable reddish hue make a natural ingredient for modifying cocktails.

Even within the fourth dimension there are creative options available to use. Looking to create a Cosmopolitan without its trademark reddish hue? Prepare the cocktail using white cranberry juice. Back up the cranberry's play with a splash of another juice, such as orange, grapefruit, blood orange, grape, pomegranate, or a pomegranate blend. If you're the adventuresome type, replace the cranberry altogether with pomegranate or blood orange juice.

Under the category of adventuresome is a signature cocktail called the *PomIranian*, an innovative variation on the Cosmopolitan concocted with something dubbed "enhanced pomegranate juice." It's made by adding the essential oils of cardamom, nutmeg, red Mandarin and black pepper to pomegranate juice. The resulting cocktail is phenomenal.

So here's to Surgeon Rear-Admiral Sir Thomas Desmond Gimlette (1857-1943), the most likely originator of the Gimlet. His innovation provided the catalyst for the creation of the Kamikaze, which in turn was the inceptive spark that brought us eventually to the Cosmopolitan. *Rule Britannia*!

Courtright's Restaurant

8989 Archer Avenue
Willow Springs, IL 60480
☎ 708.839.8000
▶▶ www.courtrights.com

Located just 25 minutes west of downtown Chicago, **Courtright's Restaurant** is a four-star restaurant situated on two acres of woodland preserve. The destination venue offers innovative American fine dining, an expansive wine cellar and timely, yet unobtrusive service, all in a singularly breathtaking setting. The overall effect is spectacular.

Courtright's is located in a beautiful stone building with an interior that features oak woodwork, high ceilings, muted lighting, a magnificent etched stained-glass window, private upstairs dining rooms, two fireplaces and intimate dining in the restaurant's redwood-lined wine cellar. A wall of windows offers a panoramic view of the surrounding forests and manicured four season garden and gazebo.

The award-winning cuisine at Courtright's is upscale American. Chef Jonathan Harootunian presents guests with seasonally inspired dishes with intriguing flavors and impeccable balance. The restaurant offers several prix-fixe, multi-course degustation menus with wine pairings, as well as a tantalizing selection of a la carte dishes. The chef also features daily foie gras presentations.

The sophisticated and casual lounge in Courtright's is where Marco Recio and his highly skilled bar staff create their delectable line-up of classic cocktails with contemporary twists. An excellent example of their handiwork is the *Bentley Side Car*, a delectable cocktail made with Hennessy X.O. Cognac, Grand Marnier and fresh lime and orange juice. Marco's repertoire also includes the *Chateau Mojito*, a lively blend of Bacardi Limón and Blue Curaçao and a delicious take on the *Espresso Martini* that combines Baileys, Kahlúa, Stoli Vanil, butterscotch schnapps and a chilled shot of espresso coffee. —RP

Bentley Side Car
Drink recipe on pg 163

Barbados Cosmo

Specialty of Stone Rose Lounge
Created by Jeff Isaacson
Cocktail glass, chilled
Pour ingredients into an iced mixing glass
2 oz. Mount Gay Eclipse Rum
1 oz. Cointreau
Splash fresh lime juice
Splash simple syrup
1/2 oz. cranberry juice
Shake and strain
Garnish with a lime wedge
Pour ingredients into the iced mixing glass. Shake thoroughly and strain contents into a chilled cocktail glass. Garnish with a lime wedge.

Blood Orange Cosmopolitan

Specialty of Savoy
Created by Misty Ross, Brandon Craft
Cocktail glass, chilled
Pour ingredients into an iced mixing glass
2 oz. Vox Vodka
Splash fresh lime juice
1/2 oz. cranberry juice
3/4 oz. blood orange juice
Shake and strain
Garnish with a blood orange wheel
Pour ingredients into the iced mixing glass. Shake thoroughly and strain contents into a chilled cocktail glass. Garnish with a blood orange wheel.

"Perfecting the classic Gimlet is the first step toward a brighter and more prosperous tomorrow."

Polar Ice® Vodka

For true enthusiasts, the final measure of a great vodka is how well it performs once it hits the glass. In the final analysis, a product either has what it takes to compete with the big boys, or it doesn't. Well, *Polar Ice Vodka* is a serious contender more than ready to mix it up.

Recently launched in the United States, Polar Ice is made in Canada by the internationally renowned Corby Distilleries. The vodka is made from 100% Canadian wheat and quadruple-distilled in state of the art continuous stills. What makes the production of Polar Ice singular is the use of a patented pressurized extraction process, which rids the spirit of even microscopic impurities. The vodka is then filtered three times for essential purity and bottled at 80-proof.

Polar Ice is a splendid vodka, possibly even an Olympic caliber spirit. It has a firm, featherweight body, satiny texture and a delicate, faintly citrus bouquet. It lilts over the palate like mist leaving behind a most satisfying nothingness, which undoubtedly was exactly what its producers were shooting for. It takes a great deal of effort and knowledge to render a spirit so decidedly neutral.

The brand has a lot going for it, not the least of which is its affordability. Polar Ice is a product of the cocktail generation, and as such, knows its way around a mixed drink. Its a savvy vodka with a bright future ahead of it.

Blue Moon

Specialty of Bar Masa
Created by Mike Vacheresse
Cocktail glass, chilled
Pour ingredients into an empty mixing glass
1 tsp. sugar
10 fresh blueberries
Muddle contents
Add ice
2 oz. Iichiko Shochu
1/2 oz. fresh lime juice
Shake and strain
Place the blueberries and sugar into the empty mixing glass. Muddle and add ice. Pour in the remaining ingredients. Shake thoroughly and strain contents into a chilled cocktail glass.

Color of the Season

Specialty of The Refectory Restaurant & Bistro
Created by Julie Mulisano, Audrey Strange
Cocktail glass, chilled
Pour ingredients into an iced mixing glass
1 1/2 oz. Stoli Strasberi Vodka
1/2 oz. Cointreau
1/2 oz. Monin Pomegranate Syrup
1/2 oz. fresh lime sour mix
Shake and strain
Garnish with a strawberry slice
Pour ingredients into the iced mixing glass. Shake thoroughly and strain contents into a chilled cocktail glass. Garnish with a fresh strawberry slice.

Coriander Gimlet

Specialty of Harry Denton's Starlight Room
Created by Jacque Bezuidenhout
Cocktail glass, chilled
Pour ingredients into an iced mixing glass
1 1/2 oz. Plymouth Gin
3/4 oz. coriander simple syrup*
1 oz. fresh lime juice
Shake and strain
Pour ingredients into the iced mixing glass. Shake thoroughly and strain contents into a chilled cocktail glass.
*Coriander Simple Syrup Recipe - pg 318

Cosblendtini

Specialty of The Spanish Kitchen
Created by Misha Krepon
House specialty glass, chilled
Pour ingredients into an iced blender canister
3/4 oz. Absolut Citron Vodka
3/4 oz. Absolut Vodka
1/2 oz. Cointreau
3/4 oz. cranberry juice
3/4 oz. sweet 'n' sour
Blend ingredients
Garnish with a lemon wheel
Pour ingredients into the iced blender canister. Blend thoroughly and pour contents into a chilled house specialty glass. Garnish with a lemon wheel.

Classic Cosmopolitan

Excerpted from The Original Guide to American Cocktails and Drinks- 6th Edition
Cocktail glass, chilled
Pour ingredients into an iced mixing glass
1 1/2 oz. Absolut Citron Vodka
1/2 oz. Cointreau
1/2 oz. Rose's
  Lime Juice
1/2 oz. cranberry juice
Shake and strain
Garnish with a
  lime wheel
Pour ingredients into the iced mixing glass. Shake thoroughly and strain contents into a chilled cocktail glass. Garnish with a lime wheel.

Cosmopolitan L'Orange

Specialty of Bourbon Street & Voodoo Lounge
Created by Matt Spencer
Cocktail glass, chilled
Pour ingredients into an iced mixing glass
1 3/4 oz. Grey Goose L'Orange Vodka
1 1/4 oz. Grand Marnier
1/2 oz. fresh lime juice
1 1/2 oz. cranberry juice
Stir and strain
Garnish with an orange twist
Pour ingredients into the iced mixing glass. Stir thoroughly and strain contents into a chilled cocktail glass. Garnish with an orange twist.

Cosmosaic

Specialty of Mosaic Restaurant
Created by Stephanie Kozicki
Cocktail glass, chilled
Pour ingredients into an iced mixing glass
1 1/2 oz. Vox Raspberry Vodka
1/2 oz. Cointreau
Splash fresh key lime juice
1 oz. cranberry juice
Shake and strain
Garnish with 2 fresh raspberries
Pour ingredients into the iced mixing glass. Shake thoroughly and strain contents into a chilled cocktail glass. Garnish with 2 fresh raspberries.

Cranberry Kamikaze

Excerpted from The Original Guide to
American Cocktails and Drinks- 6th Edition
Cocktail glass, chilled
Pour ingredients into an iced mixing glass
1 1/2 oz. Stoli Cranberi Vodka
1/2 oz. Triple Sec
1/2 oz. Rose's Lime Juice
1/2 oz. white cranberry juice
Stir and strain
Garnish with a lime wedge
Pour ingredients into the iced mixing glass. Stir thoroughly and strain contents into a chilled cocktail glass. Garnish with a lime wedge.

"Take your Kamikazes to the next level by splashing in a liqueur or two."

Silk Vodka

When you think about Russian vodka, most aficionados will conjure the image of a classically structured spirit with a lean, yet muscular body, a discernible nose and a palate offering waves and waves of flavor. Not only does Russian born *Silk Vodka* match the profile, it does so with great sophistication and finesse. Now here's a vodka worthy of hoarding.

The brand is made in Moscow by Soyuz-Victan, Russia's fastest growing vodka producer. Silk Vodka is Luxe grade, the highest possible quality as determined by the Russian Government. Luxe spirits are made exclusively from the finest selections of wheat, rye and barley grown on the rich and fertile Steppes. A carefully controlled multiple distillation process assures the purest liquid while the grains provide character and soul to the vodka.

Unlike some producers that distill their water, Soyuz-Victan master blenders preserve the character of the source water. Silk is crafted with pristine water sourced from 400-feet deep Artesian wells. The water is filtered through a state of the art, four stage process then passed through a series of mountain crystals and silver ions which removes any remaining impurities.

Silk is spectacular. The vodka is crystal clear with a silky smooth texture and featherweight body. The aroma of sweet grain highlights its generous, pleasant bouquet. The fun really begins though when it fills the mouth with delectable grain and malty flavors that persist long into the flawless finish. Aren't you glad the Cold War is over?

Divine Wind Kamikaze

Excerpted from The Original Guide to
American Cocktails and Drinks- 6th Edition
Cocktail glass, chilled
Pour ingredients into an iced mixing glass
1 ¹/2 oz. Vodka
³/4 oz. Blue Curaçao
¹/2 oz. Rose's Lime Juice
Stir and strain
Garnish with a lime wedge
Pour ingredients into the iced mixing glass. Stir thoroughly and strain contents into a chilled cocktail glass. Garnish with a lime wedge.

Fowl Mouth

Specialty of Savoy
Created by Eric Scheffer
Cocktail glass, chilled
Pour ingredients into an iced mixing glass
3 oz. Grey Goose Vodka
¹/2 oz. Cointreau
Splash fresh lime juice
Shake and strain
Garnish with a lemon twist
Pour ingredients into the iced mixing glass. Shake thoroughly and strain contents into a chilled cocktail glass. Garnish with a lemon twist.

Classic Gimlet

Excerpted from The Original Guide to
American Cocktails and Drinks- 6th Edition
Cocktail glass, chilled
Pour ingredients into an iced mixing glass
3 oz. Gin
1 oz. Rose's Lime Juice
Stir and strain
Garnish with a
    lime wedge
Pour ingredients into
the iced mixing glass.
Stir thoroughly and
strain contents into a
chilled cocktail glass. Garnish
with a lime wedge.

Ibiza White Cosmo

Specialty of Ibiza Dinner Club
Created by Ibiza's staff
Cocktail glass, chilled
Pour ingredients into an empty mixing glass
4 lime wedges
Muddle contents
Add ice
1 oz. Chopin Vodka
¹/2 oz. Cointreau
¹/2 oz. white cranberry juice
Shake and strain
Garnish with 3 fresh cranberries
Place lime wedges into the empty mixing glass. Muddle and add ice. Pour in the remaining ingredients. Shake thoroughly and strain contents into a chilled cocktail glass. Garnish with 3 fresh cranberries.

Italian Stallion Kamikaze

Specialty of BarMedia
Created by Robert Plotkin
Cocktail glass, chilled
Pour ingredients into an iced mixing glass
1 ¹/2 oz. Absolut Citron
³/4 oz. Limoncello
³/4 oz. GranGala
³/4 oz. fresh lime juice
Stir and strain
Garnish with a lime wedge
Pour ingredients into the iced mixing glass. Stir thoroughly and strain contents into a chilled cocktail glass. Garnish with a lime wedge.

Jasmine Gimlet

Specialty of P.F. Chang's China Bistro
Created by P.F. Chang's Staff
Bucket glass, ice
Build in glass
3 oz. Beefeater Wet Gin or Stolichnaya Vodka
¹/2 oz. fresh lime juice
³/4 oz. Monin Jasmine Syrup
Garnish with 2 lime wedges
Pour ingredients into the iced bucket glass in the order listed. Squeeze and drop in 2 lime wedges.

Classic Kamikaze

Excerpted from The Original Guide to
American Cocktails and Drinks- 6th Edition
Cocktail glass, chilled
Pour ingredients into an iced mixing glass
2 1/2 oz. Vodka
3/4 oz. Triple Sec
3/4 oz. Rose's Lime Juice
Stir and strain
Garnish with a
    lime wedge
Pour ingredients into
the iced mixing glass.
Stir thoroughly and strain
contents into a chilled cocktail
glass. Garnish with a lime wedge.

Kurant Affair

Specialty of The Mission Inn Hotel & Spa
Created by Richard Kullack, Frank Romero
Sugar rimmed cocktail glass, chilled
Pour ingredients into an iced mixing glass
1 1/4 oz. Absolut Kurant Vodka
3/4 oz. Chambord
1/4 oz. Triple Sec
1/2 oz. fresh lime juice
1 1/4 oz. cranberry juice
Shake and strain
Garnish with a lime wheel
Pour ingredients into the iced mixing glass. Shake
thoroughly and strain contents into a sugar
rimmed, chilled cocktail glass. Garnish with a
lime wheel.

Lightweight

Specialty of Marcus' Martini Heaven
Created by Marcus' Staff
Cocktail glass, chilled
Pour ingredients into an iced mixing glass
1 1/2 oz. Vodka
1/2 oz. Triple Sec
1 oz. cranberry juice
1 oz. grapefruit juice
Shake and strain
Garnish with a lime wedge
Pour ingredients into the iced mixing glass. Shake
thoroughly and strain contents into a chilled
cocktail glass. Garnish with a lime wedge.

Limón Cosmopolitan

Excerpted from The Original Guide to
American Cocktails and Drinks- 6th Edition
Cocktail glass, chilled
Pour ingredients into an iced mixing glass
1 1/2 oz. Bacardi Limón Rum
1/2 oz. Cointreau
1/2 oz. Rose's Lime Juice
1/2 oz. cranberry juice
Stir and strain
Garnish with an orange twist
Pour ingredients into the iced mixing glass. Stir
thoroughly and strain contents into a chilled
cocktail glass. Garnish with an orange twist.

Love Spell

Specialty of Rio/Voodoo Lounge
Created by Bobby Gleason
Cocktail glass, chilled
Pour ingredients into an iced mixing glass
1 1/4 oz. Finlandia Mango Vodka
1/2 oz. Cointreau
Splash POM Pomegranate Juice
1/2 oz. white cranberry juice
1/2 oz. rock candy syrup
1/2 oz. fresh lime juice
Shake and strain
Garnish with a lemon twist
Pour ingredients into the iced mixing glass. Shake
thoroughly and strain contents into a chilled
cocktail glass. Garnish with a lemon twist.

Mandarin Blossom Cosmopolitan

Specialty of Indigo Eurasian Cuisine
Created by Kimberly Theos, Jason Castle
Cocktail glass, chilled
Pour ingredients into an iced mixing glass
3 oz. Hanger One Mandarin Blossom Vodka
1 oz. Cointreau
Splash fresh lime juice
1 oz. cranberry juice
Shake and strain
Garnish with an orange wheel
Pour ingredients into the iced mixing glass. Shake
thoroughly and strain contents into a chilled
cocktail glass. Garnish with an orange wheel.

Cuba Libre Restaurant & Rum Bar

The Quarter at Tropicana Casino and Resort
Atlantic City, NJ 08401
☎ 609.348.6700
▶▶ www.cubalibrerestaurant.com
✉ info@cubalibrerestaurant.com

Bienvenidos and welcome to **Cuba Libre Restaurant & Rum Bar**. Step across the threshold and treat yourself to a decidedly more romantic time and place. Cuba Libre is a total immersion into the Cuban experience, one evoking the mystique and singular charm of Old Havana and to a time when the city was the "Paris of the Caribbean."

The Atlantic City restaurant and rum bar is located in Tropicana Casino and Resort's *The Quarter*, a bustling, Cuban-themed retail, dining and entertainment center. Cuba Libre's exterior is an authentic, magnificent recreation of the style, feel

and architecture of Havana circa 1950. The building features arched entrances, balconies, a courtyard, stained glass and ornamental wrought iron. The interior is even more magical, if that's possible. Skylights, artful paddle fans, lush and leafy foliage and an open, airy ambience effectively complete the illusion of an al fresco café of a bygone era.

Executive chef Guillermo Pernot's menu is a celebration of *Criollo* home-style cuisine, a joyous blend of native tastes and culinary traditions from Africa, Spain, Asia and Latin America. The fare is flavorful, savory, but only occasionally spicy combinations of beef, chicken, pork and seafood with exotic fruits, root vegetables, herbs and spices. Whatever your definition of delicious is...double it.

As night settles in, Cuba Libre gradually rachets up its pulse and energy level. By the shank of the evening the place has fully transformed into an electrically charged hot spot. The specialties of the house are rum and Latin-inspired drinks with emphasis on signature *Mojitos* and *Caipirinhas*. The bar stocks over 80 brands of premium rum and their cocktail menu is a masterpiece. Hemingway would have loved this place! —RP

Cuba Libre Caipirinha
Drink recipe on pg 125

OP-M

Specialty of Rosemary's Restaurant
Created by Michael Shetler
Cocktail glass, chilled
Pour ingredients into an iced mixing glass
1 oz. Absolut Citron Vodka
1 oz. Absolut Apeach Vodka
3/4 oz. Cointreau
1/4 oz. Chambord
Splash fresh lime juice
1 oz. POM Pomegranate Juice
Shake and strain
Garnish with a fresh raspberry
Pour ingredients into the iced mixing glass. Shake thoroughly and strain contents into a chilled cocktail glass. Garnish with a fresh raspberry.

Orange Crush

Specialty of Rosemary's Restaurant
Created by Michael Shetler
Cocktail glass, chilled
Pour ingredients into an iced mixing glass
2 oz. Hanger One Mandarin Blossom Vodka
3/4 oz. Cointreau
1/2 oz. Grand Marnier
Splash 7UP
1 1/2 oz. fresh orange juice
Shake and strain
Garnish with an orange twist
Pour ingredients into the iced mixing glass. Shake thoroughly and strain contents into a chilled cocktail glass. Garnish with an orange twist.

"The popular revival of the Gimlet
is a clear sign that we're
evolving as a species."

Corazón Tequila® de Agave Blanco

Añejo tequilas are elegant and lip smacking good, but to really appreciate the distiller's craftsmanship, sample the pure and unadulterated style of silver tequila. An excellent example of which is *Corazón Tequila de Agave Blanco*.

Corazón tequilas are distilled in the high altitudes of the Arandas Mountains. These handcrafted, 100% agave tequilas are produced on the sprawling Destiladora San Nicholas Estate using traditional, century old methods abandoned by most as cost prohibitive. The 80-proof tequilas are made from mature, estate grown agaves. After harvesting, the agaves are baked in stainless steel ovens, slowly fermented and double-distilled in the estate's stainless steel pot stills. The results are highly sophisticated spirits worthy of grand cru status.

Corazón Tequila Blanco is drawn directly from the still and rested for 24 hours before bottling. It has a fresh, exuberant personality that can only be found in a spirit unfettered by the effects of barrel aging. The tequila has a lightweight, supple body and a generous floral bouquet. Its initial entry is somewhat demure, but then expands filling the mouth with delectable spicy, peppery flavors. The effect is long lasting and satisfying.

Don't miss out on all that Corazón has to offer. *Corazón Tequila de Agave Reposado* is aged in American oak barrels for a minimum of 6 months. It's aromatic and peppery. After maturing for two years or more *Corazón Tequila de Agave Añejo* is ready for the nearest snifter.

Oyster Cosmo

Specialty of Oyster Restaurant & Nightclub
Created by Larry Failing
Cocktail glass, chilled
Pour ingredients into an iced mixing glass
2 oz. Grey Goose L'Orange Vodka
1/2 oz. Cointreau
Splash fresh orange juice
Splash fresh lime juice
Splash cranberry juice
Shake and strain
Garnish with a lime wedge
Pour ingredients into the iced mixing glass. Shake thoroughly and strain contents into a chilled cocktail glass. Garnish with a lime wedge.

Pomegranate Cosmopolitan

Specialty of 33 Restaurant & Lounge
Created by Ari Bialikamien, Jenn Harvey
Cocktail glass, chilled
Pour ingredients into an iced mixing glass
2 oz. Kettle One Citroen
1 oz. Cointreau
1/2 oz. Rose's Lime Juice
1 oz. POM Pomegranate/Tangerine Juice
Shake and strain
Garnish with a lime wedge
Pour ingredients into the iced mixing glass. Shake thoroughly and strain contents into a chilled cocktail glass. Garnish with a lime wedge.

PomIranian

Specialty of Cyrus
Created by Scott Beattie
Cardamom sugar* rimmed
     cocktail glass, chilled
Pour ingredients into an iced mixing glass
3/4 oz. Hangar One Straight Vodka
3/4 oz. Hangar One Mandarin
     Blossom Vodka
1/2 oz. fresh lime juice
1 oz. enhanced pomegranate juice*
Shake and strain
Pour ingredients into the iced mixing glass. Shake thoroughly and strain contents into a cardamom sugar rimmed, chilled cocktail glass.
*Cardamom sugar is a 50/50 mix of ground cardamom and granulated sugar
*Enhanced Pomegranate Juice - pg 319

Purple Cosmopolitan

Excerpted from The Original Guide to
American Cocktails and Drinks- 6th Edition
Cocktail glass, chilled
Pour ingredients into an iced mixing glass
1 1/2 oz. Citrus Vodka
3/4 oz. Blue Curaçao
1/2 oz. Chambord
1/2 oz. Rose's Lime Juice
1/2 oz. cranberry juice
Shake and strain
Garnish with a lime wheel
Pour ingredients into the iced mixing glass. Shake thoroughly and strain contents into a chilled cocktail glass. Garnish with a lime wheel.

Purple Kami

Excerpted from The Original Guide to
American Cocktails and Drinks- 6th Edition
Cocktail glass, chilled
Pour ingredients into an iced mixing glass
3/4 oz. Raspberry Vodka
3/4 oz. Chambord
1/2 oz. Rose's Lime Juice
3/4 oz. cranberry juice
Shake and strain
Garnish with a lime wheel
Pour ingredients into the iced mixing glass. Shake thoroughly and strain contents into a chilled cocktail glass. Garnish with a lime wheel.

Radioactive Kamikaze

Excerpted from The Original Guide to
American Cocktails and Drinks- 6th Edition
Cocktail glass, chilled
Pour ingredients into an iced mixing glass
1/2 oz. Light Rum
1/2 oz. Coconut Rum
1/2 oz. 151° Rum
1/2 oz. Blue Curaçao
1/2 oz. grenadine
1 oz. Rose's Lime Juice
Shake and strain
Garnish with a lime wedge
Pour ingredients into the iced mixing glass. Shake thoroughly and strain contents into a chilled cocktail glass. Garnish with a lime wedge.

Raspberry Gimlet

Excerpted from The Original Guide to
American Cocktails and Drinks- 6th Edition
Cocktail glass, chilled
Pour ingredients into an iced mixing glass
1 1/2 oz. Vodka
3/4 oz. Chambord
1/2 oz. fresh lime juice
1/2 oz. Rose's Lime Juice
Shake and strain
Garnish with a lime wedge
Pour ingredients into the iced mixing glass. Shake
thoroughly and strain contents into a chilled
cocktail glass. Garnish with a lime wedge.

The Red Zen

Specialty of The Original McCormick & Schmick's
Created by Geoff V. Helzer
Cocktail glass, chilled
Pour ingredients into an empty mixing glass
1 sugar cube
1 oz. fresh lime juice
Muddle contents
Add ice
1 oz. Stolichnaya Vodka
1/2 oz. ZEN Green Tea Liqueur
Splash cranberry juice
2 oz. Red Bull
Shake and strain
Garnish with a lime twist
Place the sugar cube and fresh lime juice into the
empty mixing glass. Muddle and add ice. Pour
in the remaining ingredients. Shake thoroughly
and strain contents into a chilled cocktail glass.
Garnish with a lime twist.

"A well-crafted Cosmo is universally
appealing and a thing of joy."

Cointreau® Liqueur

Cointreau Liqueur is recognized around the world as one of the timeless classic liqueurs. It was created in 1849 by Frenchman Edouard Cointreau in Angers in the Loire Valley. The recipe for Cointreau has since remained a secret and been passed down from generation to generation. Today only five members of the immediate family know the recipe.

Cointreau is crafted from a complex blend of sweet orange peels from Spain, France and Brazil, and bitter, unripe orange peels from South America. A portion of the peels are dried in the sun prior to distillation, the rest are distilled fresh. The peels are macerated in alcohol, and when the infusions have reached their peak flavor, they are double-distilled in copper alembic stills. The distillery has nineteen stills; each designed specifically to produce this incomparable liqueur.

Cointreau must be tasted neat to be fully appreciated. It is perfectly clear with a satiny textured, medium-weight body. The liqueur is impressively aromatic with a highly focused bouquet of freshly cut oranges. It glides over the palate with a tingling wash of sweet orange flavor. The citrus experience continues long into the lingering finish.

Cointreau is particularly versatile in making cocktails. It has a starring role in an impressively long list of cocktails, both classic and contemporary. Cointreau was there at the inception of the Side Car, Margarita and Cosmopolitan. How many other liqueurs have that kind of resumé?

Shanghaipolitan

Specialty of Shanghai 1930
Created by Shanghai's staff
Cocktail glass, chilled
Pour ingredients into an iced mixing glass
1 oz. Mandarin Vodka
1 oz. Citrus Vodka
1/2 oz. Patrón Citrónge Orange Liqueur
Splash mango juice
1/2 oz. sweet 'n' sour
3/4 oz. cranberry juice
Shake and strain
Garnish with a lime wedge
Pour ingredients into the iced mixing glass. Shake thoroughly and strain contents into a chilled cocktail glass. Garnish with a lime wedge.

Shaymus

Specialty of Mosaic Restaurant
Created by Stephanie Kozicki
Cocktail glass, chilled
Pour ingredients into an iced mixing glass
2 oz. Charbay Ruby Red Grapefruit Vodka
1/2 oz. Lorina Sparkling Pink Lemonade
1/2 oz. cranberry juice
Shake and strain
Garnish with a lemon twist
Pour ingredients into the iced mixing glass. Shake thoroughly and strain contents into a chilled cocktail glass. Garnish with a lemon twist.

SocoTini

Specialty of Stone Rose Lounge
Created by Jeff Isaacson
Cocktail glass, chilled
Pour ingredients into an iced mixing glass
2 1/2 oz. Southern Comfort
Splash Rose's Lime Juice
Shake and strain
Garnish with a lime wedge
Pour ingredients into the iced mixing glass. Shake thoroughly and strain contents into a chilled cocktail glass. Garnish with a lime wedge.

Sweetness

Specialty of The Spanish Kitchen
Created by Misha Krepon
Cocktail glass, chilled
Pour ingredients into an iced mixing glass
1 1/2 oz. Stoli Persik Vodka
1/2 oz. Patrón Citrónge Orange Liqueur
1/2 oz. sweet 'n' sour
1/2 oz. Sprite
1/2 oz. cranberry juice
Shake and strain
Garnish with a peach slice
Pour ingredients into the iced mixing glass. Shake thoroughly and strain contents into a chilled cocktail glass. Garnish with a fresh peach slice.

Tuaca Gimlet

Excerpted from The Original Guide to
American Cocktails and Drinks- 6th Edition
Cocktail glass, chilled
Pour ingredients into an iced mixing glass
1 1/2 oz. Vodka
3/4 oz. Tuaca Liquore Italiano
1/2 oz. Rose's Lime Juice
Stir and strain
Garnish with a lime wedge
Pour ingredients into the iced mixing glass. Stir thoroughly and strain contents into a chilled cocktail glass. Garnish with a lime wedge.

Valhalla

Specialty of Absinthe Brasserie & Bar
Created by Jonny Raglin, Jeff Hollinger
Cocktail glass, chilled
Pour ingredients into an iced mixing glass
1 3/4 oz. Blood Orange Infused Tequila*
1/2 oz. Velvet Falernum
Dash Angostura Aromatic Bitters
1/2 oz. fresh lime juice
Shake and strain
Garnish with a clove studded
    flamed orange peel twist*
Pour ingredients into the iced mixing glass. Shake thoroughly and strain contents into a chilled cocktail glass. Garnish with a clove studded flamed orange peel twist.
*Clove Studded Orange Peel - pg 318
*Blood Orange Infused Tequila Recipe
Infuse 1 bottle of tequila with the rinds of 10-12 blood orange rinds. Store in a cool place for 5-7 days. Strain off rinds with cheesecloth.
CAUTION! Extreme care must be used whenever flame is used in or near an alcohol drink.

Watermelon Gimlet

Specialty of 33 Restaurant & Lounge
Created by Ari Bialikamien
Cocktail glass, chilled
Pour ingredients into an iced mixing glass
1 oz. SKYY Citrus Vodka
1/2 oz. Cointreau
1/2 oz. Rose's Lime Juice
2 oz. fresh watermelon puree
Shake and strain
Garnish with a star shaped
    piece of watermelon
Pour ingredients into the iced mixing glass. Shake thoroughly and strain contents into a chilled cocktail glass. Garnish with a star shaped piece of watermelon.

Chapter Five

The Appeal of Rum
Subtropical Classics

R um is among the most dynamic and diverse spirits in the world. It's made in exotic places, graced with brilliant hues, captivating aromas and rich engaging flavors.
Part of rum's immense popularity lies in its diversity. Rums are produced in a broad range of styles, from clear, dry and light-bodied to dark, full-bodied and full-flavored.

Why are rums shooting up the charts? In addition to their "fun in the sun" image, their approachable taste profile means there's no learning curve necessary to enjoy them. But the shared attribute that puts rum on the map is its mixability. It can be used in the preparation of almost any cocktail. When it comes to drink making, premium rums have a taste and aroma that lifts them head and shoulders above any of the other light liquors. A vodka's particular characteristics may go unnoticed in a cocktail, conversely, rum is more often than not a primary flavor ingredient.

Theories abound about the origin of the word "rum." One suggests that it is an abbreviation of the Latin words for sugar, saccharrum officinarum. Another theory suggests that the name "rum" originated on the island of Barbados as a derivation of the words "rumbullion or rumbustion," which were common terms for fighting or causing trouble. On Barbados, rum was also called Kill Devil, likely because as a strong spirit it was used to cure a wide range of afflictions.

Nearly all rums fall into one of two major categories, heavy and light. Heavy rums are typically distilled in pot, or alembic stills. Heavy is an unfortunate label; it gives the impression that they are dense and chewy. The term refers to the fact that heavy rums are loaded with flavoring agents (congeners). They are aromatic, full-bodied and invariably aged in wood.

Light rums are usually distilled in column or continuous stills. As their names imply they have light bodies and crisp, clean palates. They are occasionally aged in oak to round out their character and then filtered to remove the color. Light rums are unsurpassed for their mixability.

An unfortunate misconception about rum is that it's sweet and therefore not in keeping with contemporary tastes. It's true that rum is distilled from sugar cane juice or molasses, but that doesn't mean they are inherently sweet. Quite to the contrary, rums are light-bodied and characteristically dry.

So whether it's their diversity, allure, or enormous mixability, rums are winning flavor with mixologists and their guests. Here then is your road map into the drinks of the subtropics. The journey includes the classic rum and cachaça cocktails from countries where heat and humidity are constants, places like Cuba, Martinique, Puerto Rico and Brazil. It's a memorable excursion and a look into the most famous heat busting drinks of our time.

Secrets Revealed of America's Greatest Daiquiris

The *Daiquiri* is the quintessential rum libation, flavorful and perfectly balanced between sweet and tart. It was born in the Caribbean and eventually its popularity swept across the globe like a blast of good news. Crisp, refreshing and amazingly delicious, the Daiquiri is experiencing a resurgence in the United States that borders on the phenomenal.

This is a trend worth riding. It mirrors the booming popularity of rum, which has quietly become the hottest growth spirits category in the nation. The drink enjoys all of the attributes requisite for longevity. It's easy to make well and loaded with exotic appeal.

The cocktail originated around 1905 in a bar named Venus in Santiago, Cuba, roughly 20

Appleton Estate® V/X Jamaica Rum

Hugely successful **Appleton Estate V/X Jamaica Rum** ranks among the most recognizable Jamaican exports. One sip and you'll appreciate why its reputation is well deserved.

Every step of production takes place on the Appleton Estate in St. Elizabeth Parish, just as it has since 1749. The estate mills its own sugar cane and distills both light-bodied, continuous-distilled spirits and fuller, more complex pot distilled rums. These rums are skillfully blended together and then aged in charred, American oak barrels.

Appleton Estate V/X Jamaica Rum is a spirit masterpiece. The rums used to make up its blend have been aged 5 to 10 years. After blending, the rum is then rested in huge oak vats to allow the constituent elements to become fully integrated. It is bottled at 80-proof.

The V/X on the label stands for "very exceptional," which is definitely an understatement. The rum has a deep golden amber color and a generous bouquet of orange and molasses. The rum's medium-body fills the mouth with the semisweet flavors of caramel, vanilla and spice. Possibly its best feature is the creamy, long lasting and flavor enriched finish.

Appleton Estate V/X is a refined pleasure from start to finish. It is tempting to simply present this rum in a snifter neat, or with a few cubes of ice, and leave it at that. While the rum is certainly elegant enough to warrant the high brow treatment, you'd be missing out on much of its versatility.

miles from the Daiquiri Iron Mine. It was created by a group of American engineers who originally prepared the drink in a tall glass packed with cracked ice. The process started with a teaspoon of sugar and the juice from two fresh limes. The glass was topped off with 2-3 ounces of light rum. The finishing touch was stirring the concoction with a long handled spoon, a technique referred to as "swizzling or frosting."

The Daiquiri's big break came in 1909 when Admiral Lucius W. Johnson, a United States Navy officer, visited the mine and tasted the local favorite. Duly impressed Johnson subsequently introduced it to the bartenders at the Army and Navy Club in Washington, D.C. It was there that the Daiquiri evolved to be mixed in a shaker with the same ingredients and shaved ice. After a thorough shaking, it was poured into a chilled champagne saucer or Martini glass.

The cocktail's fame grew from there. The Daiquiri became a phenomenon in the 1920s and '30s, especially in Cuba when the island was famous for having the swankest clubs, an international clientele and the most capable bartenders in the world. The Daiquiri was one of the drinks made famous in the works of Ernest Hemingway. Its popularity also received a huge boost when in 1961 it was reported that the Daiquiri was President Kennedy's favorite cocktail.

As was the case with the Gimlet, the first secret to mastering the Daiquiri is balance. The three elements that need to be in sync are the tartness of the lime juice, the sweetness of the sugar and the flavor of the featured rum. Err too much in any direction and the cocktail becomes unpalatable. If you make the drink too sweet it will be cloying; too tart and the flavor of the rum will be buried by the acidity and pithy bitterness. While each is unpalatable, perhaps the most objectionable is over portioning the rum in the drink, which will result in an unpleasant and overpowering experience.

A reliable jumping off point for a Daiquiri is the traditional ratio of 1 part rum to 2 parts fresh lime sour mix. The two principal variables will be the flavor of the base lime mix — some are more tart than others — and the character of the featured rum. Your recipe may also be somewhat affected by seasonality issues. Limes vary greatly in flavor and succulence depending on the time of year.

One piece of advice before bounding off on your own. In your enthusiasm to create the best and brightest Daiquiris, don't overlook the original. The classic recipe for a Daiquiri is light rum, sugar and fresh lime juice (a.k.a. fresh lime sour mix), which is then vigorously shaken and strained into a chilled cocktail glass. Few cocktails afford a better opportunity to enjoy a wide array of rums. There's a reason it's the original, after all.

To help get you in a subtropical state of mind, here are the best kept secrets behind America's greatest Daiquiris.

• **Shake or Blend?** — Isn't this the age-old question? The age-old answer is let style dictate form. The decision depends entirely on what type of results you're looking to achieve. If the recipe calls for whole fruit or a puree, then for obvious reasons blending is the preferred method. Blending a Daiquiri will produce a tall and beautiful concoction. Some days there's nothing more welcoming then the sight of an icy cold, frozen fruit Daiquiri.

On the other hand, blending a cocktail with ice might potentially dull the nuances and subtleties that would normally shine through if it had been hand shaken. It's a technique that assures the ingredients are thoroughly integrated and that the cocktail quickly reaches proper serving temperature.

If you are so inclined, try preparing the same recipe by the two different methods and sample the results side by side. One likely finding will be that the blended drink lacks the brilliance and vibrancy of the hand shaken cocktail. A viable response is to bump up the portion of each ingredient. The thinking being that the diminished flavor is a result of being diluted by the ice, so just use more of everything. If a little is good, a little more is better, well, just in this case.

• **Spirit Choices** — The Daiquiri traditionally is prepared with light rum. Flavorful and crystal clear, it's a natural in the leading role. One of the allures of the cocktail is its glorious lime enriched appearance; a clear

Mount Gay® Eclipse Rum

Mount Gay is the oldest rum brand in the world and most recognized brand of Barbadian rum. It is the bestselling rum on Barbados, with nearly 25% of the distillery's output being consumed on the island. The flagship of the company's portfolio, *Mount Gay Eclipse Rum*, was created in 1910 and its name commemorates the total solar eclipse that occurred that year.

Mount Gay Eclipse is produced from estate grown sugar cane and coral filtered spring water. It is comprised of a blend of pot still and continuous still rums aged in charred, American oak barrels for a minimum of 2 years. It is bottled at 80-proof.

The enticement begins with the first glance. Eclipse has a luminous, golden amber hue that is a marvelous entrée for the sensations to follow. The rum has a compact bouquet featuring the aromas of floral, spice, nuts and fresh fruit with a touch of vanilla and oak thrown into the mix.

The rum has a well-textured, light to medium-weight body. Its complex array of flavors settles lightly on the palate and slowly each individual flavor can be discerned. Most prominent among its smooth tastes are tropical fruit, vanilla, a hint of toasty oak, caramel and apricot. Eclipse has a marvelous, semisweet, lightly smoked finish that is both complex and long lasting.

Little wonder Mount Gay Eclipse Rum has gained worldwide renown. It's an accessible, well-balanced rum that can be enjoyed both neat, or featured in a lead role in cocktails and classic mixed drinks.

spirit leaves the color of the lime juice unaffected. Blended Daiquiris made with light rum, however, often have a pale, washed out look to them. One option is to splash in Rose's Lime Juice to bolster the color of the drink, or reach for a bottle of gold rum instead.

The clear advantage of preparing Daiquiris with gold rums is that they look as enticing as they taste. Dark rums contribute a rich amber hue to the cocktail, all without adding excess weight to the drink.

No where is it written that you can't enlist the services of more than one type of rum in your specialty cocktail. For example, the *Charles Daiquiri* is a delectable concoction made with light and dark rum, Cointreau and fresh lime juice. Splitting the spirit base is a proven technique for instilling a Daiquiri with dimension and personality.

Another among the highly marketable features of the Daiquiri is its unsurpassed ability to showcase an unlimited variety of premium rums. Change the base rum and much of the character of the cocktail will change as well. The other absolute about the Daiquiri is the better the rum, the better the resulting drink.

In that vein, consider featuring a premium añejo rum in your next specialty Daiquiri. It adds layers of irresistible flavors, a dark, wood induced color and a set of alluring aromas to the cocktail unobtainable in any other way. Once you start to imagine preparing the cocktail with aged rum, the large window of opportunity will immediately open. No two añejo rums are the same. A rum distilled and aged on the island of Barbados, for example, will taste significantly different than one aged on Trinidad, Jamaica or Cuba for the same length of time. That means a Daiquiri made with Mount Gay Extra Old will be appreciable different than a similarly devised cocktail featuring Appleton Estate V/X, Pyrat X.O., or Guatemalan Zaya Gran Reserva.

There are also many great brands of rum distilled far from the shores of the Caribbean. That list includes stellar brands such as El Dorado Demerara from Guyana, Rum Toucano from Brazil, Gosling's Black Seal from Bermuda and Flor de Caña from Nicaragua. They are all fabulous rums with characters distinctive to their native lands. The Daiquiris they produce are equally distinctive.

Then there are the glorious aged rums from the French speaking islands, those distilled from fresh cane juice rather than molasses. These are the famed Caribbean rhum agricoles, preeminent brands such as Rhum Clemént from Martinique, Rhum Barbancourt from Haiti and French made 10 Cane from Trinidad. There is a fresh herbaceous quality to these world-class rhums that make them highly desirable, especially when crafting Daiquiris.

The Daiquiri is a versatile cocktail and one not to be pigeonholed. The cocktail is an excellent vehicle for featuring a spiced rum or nearly any one of the numerous flavored rums on the market. Imagine the allure of a Daiquiri made with fresh lime juice and Captain Morgan, Cruzan Pineapple, or Appleton Estate Mango Rum. The result is invariably phenomenal. An outstanding example is the specialty Daiquiri named the *Malibu Melvin*, an inspired blend of Malibu, Malibu Pineapple and Malibu Mango rums.

Certainly thought should be given to featuring a premium cachaça in a Daiquiri. These distinctively flavorful Brazilian spirits are typically distilled from fresh cane juice and aged in various types of wood. Among the brands to look for include Ypióca, Pitú, Pirassununga 51 and Água Luca. While considering the spirits from South America don't overlook the service of Peruvian Pisco, a type of clear brandy distilled from premium grape varietals. Piscos are beginning to gain recognition in the American market, largely because of their brilliant fruit flavors and delightful mixability.

• **The Lime Connection** — The chassis of a handcrafted Daiquiri is essentially the same base sour mix found in the undercarriage of a Margarita. The quality and character of the fresh lime sour mix will largely determine the personality of the finished cocktail. Keys to success are using fresh ingredients and balancing the tartness of the lime. When deciding what type of sweetener to use, consider guarapa, a syrup derived from fresh cane juice. It is ideal for use in any rum-based cocktail. Further advice on concocting an excellent lime sour mix can be found in chapter two on Margaritas.

• **The Modifier Spectrum** — Modifiers allow you to take your Daiquiri in any creative direction your imagination and good taste decide to go. It should come as little surprise that the most frequently relied upon Daiquiri modifier is fresh fruit or fruit puree. While Strawberry Daiquiris and Banana Daiquiris will forever remain popular, the options are bounded only by your access to fruit. The cocktail is ideal for showcasing tropical fruit, such as ripe mangos, papaya, kiwis, starfruit or guava. Many exotic fruits are now available year round, both fresh and frozen.

Adding in a measure of similarly flavored rum is an ideal way to enhance the taste of the featured fruit. For example if you're working with fresh mangos, a recommended additional step is to add a measure of Cruzan or Appleton Estate mango-flavored rum. The fresh fruit and the flavored rum harmonize together beautifully.

The next best thing to working with fresh fruit is to use different combinations of juice to modify the drink. For example, the *Florida Daiquiri* is made with grapefruit juice and a splash of grenadine. Passion fruit, pomegranate and pomegranate juice blends, orange juice and prickly pear are all frequently relied upon modifiers.

Liqueurs are also often drafted into service as modifiers. For example, at the legendary La

Cyrus Restaurant

29 North Street
Healdsburg, CA 95448

☎ 707.433.3311

▶▶▶ www.cyrusrestaurant.com

✉ reservation@cyrusrestaurant.com

There are ample reasons to plan a tour of the wine country of Sonoma and near the top of the list is *Cyrus Restaurant*, a magnificent, world-renowned restaurant situated amidst the vineyards and rolling countryside. The upscale Cyrus is a safe haven for spent sophisticates and tired urban warriors looking for a memorable evening and an opportunity to dine, sip and breathe under the star filled sky.

For all of its posh elegance, Cyrus has a relaxed, personable feel about it. The well-lit interior has a timeless appeal marked by arched and vaulted ceilings, fine linen, crystal, china and silver appointed tables. The ambience is welcoming and intimate. Sumptuous warm canapés are served with cocktails and a caviar

cart accompanies each order of Champagne. The contemporary French and American cuisine is offered in a flexible prix fixe format of three to five dishes selected from the extensive menu.

Dining at Cyrus begins with an amuse bouche and finishes with mignardises (chocolates and petits fours) and bon bons. The experience in between is a celebration of the senses, such as delicate foie gras and black sea bass bathed in scallop broth and shitake mushrooms. The dessert selections are divinely inspired and the cheese cart sports over two dozen artisanal varieties. Not surprisingly, the wine menu is extensive and loaded with the best and the brightest Sonoma has to offer.

The bar at Cyrus may well draw as much critical acclaim as its kitchen. The same exacting attention to detail applied to the cuisine is used in the development of their signature cocktails. Among these is the sensational *Clermont Manhattan*, a classic devised with vanilla bean and citrus infused bourbon. Top-notch! —RP

Clermont Manhattan
Drink recipe on pg 70

Floridita Hotel in Havana, the signature of the house is the *La Floridita Daiquiri*, which adds a quarter ounce of Cointreau to the original Daiquiri recipe. The *French Daiquiri* is made with crème de cassis, while Maraschino liqueur is used to make a *Hemingway Daiquiri*. Other liqueur options include Chambord, PAMA, Midori, Crème de Menthe, Limoncello and any of the popular Pucker range of liqueurs. HPNOTIQ and Blue Curaçao are often selected for their seductive coloring.

• **Added Flourish** — Sure, it's understandable that you're eager to present your new specialty Daiquiri to friends, neighbors and guests, but before you do, make sure that it's appropriately dressed for its public debut. Elaborate fruit garnishes and colorful sugar rims are two ways to add pizzazz.

Dark rums are ideal for drizzling, or floating on top of a Daiquiri. They add a great flavor and greatly enhance the drink's presentation. Drizzles and floats are especially effective on light colored, light flavored drinks.

Swirl Daiquiris are another creative way to enjoy different rums. Swirls are frozen drinks prepared simultaneously in two different blenders. The concoctions are then layered or swirled together in a house specialty glass. Each component can feature a different type of rum. For instance, one

ZEN™ Green Tea Liqueur

There are some products with first impressions about as demure as a slap in the face. There's something rather confident about a product that doesn't feel the need to overstate its case. *ZEN Green Tea Liqueur* is delectably understated, yet imbued with nuance and appeal. Rest assured that there isn't another liqueur on the market equal in intrigue as Suntory's ZEN.

For thousands of years, Japanese have enjoyed blending green tea with fine spirits. Suntory has styled ZEN in this tradition. The shining ingredient in the liqueur is ultra-premium Kyoto green tea, leaves cultivated by one of Japan's finest tea brands, Marukyu-Koyama-En. The master distiller uses a blend of whole and ground green tea leaves, herbs, lemongrass and spices to infuse the spirits.

Suntory's ZEN is a class act. It glimmers in a glass with the color of brewed green tea and tantalizes the palate with an array of enticing floral and spice aromas. Its rounded body sports substance without weight, an attribute you'll greatly appreciate when devising cocktails. Its light, delicate mouth feel is a welcome departure from most liqueurs.

The liqueur has a complex of long lasting flavors ranging from the sublime to the exotic. Its initial approach is semisweet and floral, but that's quickly replaced with the flavors of herbs, anise and green tea. At 40-proof ZEN warms the body and revitalizes the mind without drawing attention to itself. From start to lip smacking finish, this is a classy product.

layer could be a raspberry Daiquiri made with Mount Gay Eclipse, while the other a banana Daiquiri made with Cruzan Estate Light Rum. Finish it with a dollop of whipped cream and a drizzle of Appleton V/X Jamaica Rum.

Secrets Revealed of America's Greatest Piña Coladas

In 1954, Bartender Ramon "Monchito" Marrero created the *Piña Colada* at the Caribe Hilton Hotel in San Juan, and ever since it has remained among the most enduring of subtropical classics.

The allure of the Piña Colada is easy to perceive. At its essence is the convergence of three prominent flavors, rum, coconut and pineapple. If you've ever had the drink, you can appreciate the synergy between these three complementary tastes. When working within the Piña Colada framework, don't lose sight of the three flavors that create the drink's famed multifaceted appeal.

In the day, the cocktail was invariably shaken and served in a tall iced glass. It's curious that Piña Coladas are rarely prepared in that manner any more. Perhaps the explanation is that when shaken the drink is more viscous than when blended. It's consistency and texture is similar to a cream drink. Hand shaking also loses a few style points because it does little to enhance the drink's off-white appearance.

On the other hand, blending a Piña Colada has certain advantages. Blending with ice results in a taller drink with a more palatable consistency. Blending also affords the opportunity to work with fresh fruit, something that hand shaking doesn't easily permit. Lastly there's guest expectations to consider, meaning that today most people expect Piña Coladas to be blended concoctions and are thrown when they're not.

Gaining a mastery of the Piña Colada is one merit badge all mixologists should strive to achieve. It is a drink filled with possibilities. With that said, here are the best kept secrets behind America's greatest Piña Coladas.

• **Spirit Choices** — Like the Daiquiri before it, the Piña Colada is traditionally prepared with light rum. One can presume that it is preferred because the rum's transparency will leave the color of the other ingredients unaffected. On the other hand, the Piña Colada's creamy, off-white appearance is not necessarily the drink's strongest attribute. Using a gold or full-bodied, full flavored aged rum may well be an inspired option. In addition to the rich color, the vibrant character of dark rums such as Mount Gay Eclipse, Rhum Barbancourt, Rhum Clemént, or Appleton Estate V/X provides intriguing counterpoints and stand up well to the coconut-pineapple palate of the Piña Colada.

Looking for more Colada options? Certainly start with the largest cache of possibilities, namely flavored rums. Making a Colada with a coconut, or pineapple flavored rum seems like a no-brainer. But banana, mango, citrus and orange flavored rums seem like natural choices as well. So does vanilla, or spiced rum.

Then what happens when you make the drink using more than one in a Colada? It's called magic.

The most famous variation, the *Chi-Chi*, is prepared by substituting vodka for light rum in a Piña Colada. The substitution will create a sleek cocktail, but the vodka will contribute nothing to the drink's personality. On the other hand, using a flavored vodka in the drink could make a huge contribution. Imagine a Chi-Chi made with Stoli Blueberi, Absolut Vanilia, or Van Gogh Dutch Chocolate Vodka? In this day and age of superior flavored vodkas, preparing a Chi-Chi with a neutral vodka seems like a missed opportunity.

If you're getting the idea that the Piña Colada is a highly versatile player, then it won't surprise you that the drink is also marvelous made with tequila, cachaça, pisco and shochu.

XXX Siglo Treinta® Gold Tequila

The short list of brands that give you a lot of tequila for the buck prominently features the name, *XXX Siglo Treinta Gold Tequila*. It is steadily gaining international recognition as a superior quality, great tasting tequila marketed at an inexplicably affordable price, which loosely translates to a perfect bargain.

XXX Siglo Treinta is crafted at the esteemed La Cofradia Distillery, producer of award-winning Casa Noble 100% Agave Tequila. XXX Siglo Treinta Silver and Gold are *mixto* or blended tequilas. They are double-distilled from mature blue agaves and matured for two months in small, American white oak barrels. The new, ultra-premium XXX Siglo Treinta Reposado is a 100% blue agave tequila. All are bottled at 80-proof.

XXX Siglo Treinta Gold is an unexpectedly elegant tequila. It has a lustrous, golden yellow hue and wafting herbaceous bouquet. Its palate quickly expands filling the mouth with a bold set of long lasting, slightly smoky flavors. The tequila is genuinely a pleasure to drink and is splendid featured in a Margarita. *XXX Siglo Treinta Silver Tequila* is a vibrant and joyful spirit with a satiny texture and generous floral bouquet. The tequila is laced with spice and fruit flavors that persist long into the savory finsh.

New to the world stage is ultra-premium *XXX Siglo Treinta Reposado Tequila*, a glorious 100% agave tequila aged nine months in white oak barrels. The spirit is brimming with character, namely a generous, vanilla laced bouquet and a dry palate endowed with spice, oak and white pepper. *Salud!*

• **Coconut and Pineapple Base Mix** — Coconuts are quite the contradiction. How can something so delicious be so incredibly difficult to penetrate? This is one area where science has made life easier for all of us. Coco López Cream of Coconut is just what its name implies. Having originated in Puerto Rico in the early '50s, Coco López is a blend of coconut meat and cane sugar to create a smooth and creamy product. It is a luxuriously rich product with authentic coconut flavor.

Coco López and similar products are viscous and challenging to accurately measure. To accommodate its thick consistency, one tried-and-true technique is to create a scratch Colada mix by blending the Coco Lopez with pineapple juice. Start with an initial ratio of one part coconut cream to 1.5 parts pineapple juice. For example, blend the contents of one, 15-ounce can of the Coco López with 22-23 ounces of pineapple juice. The end result will be a balanced, silky smooth mix where both the pineapple and coconut are equally represented. For added flavor and more consistency, blend the Colada mix with pineapple cubes.

Another technique is to blend ice cream, half & half, or sorbet into the Piña Colada mix. The result is a thicker, more flavorful concoction. This tactic allows a new avenue of creative thought, for in addition to vanilla ice cream, optional flavors to consider are chocolate, French vanilla, banana, strawberry and coffee. Of course, you could argue that there are at least 31 flavors from which to choose.

• **Colada Modifiers** — One of the Piña Colada's more admirable qualities is its versatility. The blended drink's pineapple and coconut base marries well with scores of flavors. For example, a shot of coffee, or chocolate syrup works beautifully in the drink. The Piña Colada also enjoys a special affinity for the sun kissed flavors of fruit, melons, mangos, bananas, oranges, strawberries, raspberries, blueberries and citrus of all kinds.

Liqueurs are ideal modifiers in the drink. Popular examples include the *Kahlúa Colada*, *Green Eyes Colada* with Midori, and the *Stramaretto Colada*, which is a blend of fresh strawberries and Disaronno Amaretto. Two other examples are the *Kokomo Joe Colada*, which is made with crème de banana, orange juice and a banana, and the *Sea Side Liberty*, a Colada made with Mount Gay Eclipse, Cruzan Coconut Rum, Kahlúa, and a float of Appleton Estate V/X Jamaica Rum.

• **Finishing Touches** — Why is it that the better a drink looks, the better it tastes? Who knows, but it's true. A liqueur float is a visually striking way to add flavor and pizzazz to the drink. Lace the top of your Colada with Midori, Kahlúa, or HPNOTIQ and watch what happens. A healthy splash of PAMA will add a bold red color and the fresh flavor of pomegranate. ZEN Green Tea Liqueur is also a contender with its jade green color and subtle tea taste. Better yet, serve the liqueur you're featuring in a sherry or shot glass and let guests have the fun of pouring it into the drink.

Often a dollop of whipped cream is used as an embellishment. Its stark white appearance, however, almost begs for a drizzle of chocolate syrup or a sprinkle of shaved chocolate. Rimming the glass with shredded coconut is another attention grabber.

Secrets Revealed of America's Greatest Mojitos

The *Mojito* has captured the collective American imagination and sparked a boom in restaurants and lounges around the country. While the drink originated in Cuba in the early part of the 20th century, it really became an international hit during the '30s and '40s. The country was flourishing and Havana was a playground for the rich and famous. The place to be seen was the La Bodeguita del Medio bar, the birthplace of the Mojito.

Behind the timeworn wooden bar the La Bodeguita, bartenders would make a seemingly endless procession of Mojitos, 10 to 15 drinks at a time for the likes of Ernest Hemingway and Prince Edward. While the Mojito's fame reached a crescendo in the halcyon days before the Castro regime, it has once again become a popular phenomenon.

The eminently refreshing Mojito is made in a Collins, bucket or specialty glass. Place simple syrup, fresh lime wedges and a generous portion of 5-6 mint leaves in the glass. Muddle the ingredients together, add some ice, 2-3 ounces of light rum and a splash of club soda for effervescence. The final touch is a garnish of fresh mint sprigs.

In addition to being delicious and thirst quenching, the Mojito has a number of rather compelling attributes. The muddled combination of mint leaves, sugar and lime wedges makes for an interesting appearance. And then there's the drink's enhanced production value. Correctly preparing a Mojito takes some time and effort, the theatrics of which is an added benefit. Finally, the drink is amazingly versatile, accommodating a wide range of flavors.

The Mojito bears striking family resemblance to several traditional Brazilian concoctions, the best known of which is the *Caipirinha* (pronounced "kuy-per-REEN-yah"). It is a marvelous drink served in a bucket or tumbler that's made with simple syrup and a quartered lime, both of which are strenuously muddled. The driving force behind this cocktail is cachaça, a clear Brazilian spirit produced from sugar cane. Use between 2-3 ounces of cachaça, add ice and garnish with a fresh lime wedge.

Two other Brazilian borne cocktails are the *Caipirissma* and *Caipiroshka*. The Caipirissma is prepared in the same manner as the Caipirinha, only light rum is substituted for the cachaça, while the Caipiroshka showcases the services of vodka instead of cachaça. All three South American cocktails

Dave & Buster's

📇 **10727 Componsite Dr.**
Dallas, TX 75220
☎ **214.353.0620**
▶▶ **www.daveandbusters.com**

There really were two guys named Dave and Buster. In the '70s, Buster ran a well-frequented bar in Little Rock's Missouri Pacific Train Station, while Dave operated a bustling arcade called "Slick Willy's World of Entertainment." The two became friends and eventually partnered in what we now know and revere as Dave & Buster's.

A great deal regarding their business has changed over the ensuing 30+ years with the exception of its enormous popular appeal and it's decidedly split personality. Dave & Buster's remains two distinct concepts coexisting under the same roof. The first is called the Viewpoint Bar, a place to unwind with friends, watch some sports and put work far out of mind. The interior is as fun as the concept. It's a lively space dominated by the bar and its towering, 20 screen video dome. Left alone to your own devices you can't help but unwind.

The Midway Bar is wall-to-wall entertainment. It sports billiards tables, shuffleboard, video games, a karaoke bar and the latest in virtual reality entertainment. Add in a hard driving back beat, snazzy lighting and you have the makings of a great time.

Dave & Buster's is also a restaurant where the tables are filled with satisfied guests. They're beaming because the food, hearty burgers and mesquite-grilled entrees, is comforting and reasonably priced. The reason for their smiles may also be that Dave & Buster's is unusually adept at making drinks fun and delicious.

A specialty of the house is the *Blarney Stone*, an artful blend of Jameson Irish Whiskey, DeKuyper Pucker Sour Apple and cranberry juice. Also highly recommended is the *Montego Bay*, a Piña Colada made with Malibu, Myers's Rum and banana liqueur. Go have some fun with these guys. —RP

Blarney Stone
Drink recipe on pg 299

are delicious and distinctive. They differ from the Cuban Mojito in the type of spirits used and equally important, none are prepared with muddled mint leaves.

The Mojito is a proven crowd pleaser and an absolute must for every mixologist to perfect. To that end, the following are the best kept secrets behind America's greatest Mojitos.

- **The Muddled Base** — One of the great things about a Mojito is watching its preparation. But beyond its theatrical appeal, the muddling process is essential to achieving the cocktail's depth of flavor. It's arguable that the Mojito's true character can't be reproduced in any other manner. Certainly hand shaking the ingredients won't achieve the desired effect.

The secret lies in the muddling action involving the mint leaves and pieces of lime. The objective is two-fold. First, you're looking to gently crush the mint leaves with the flat of the muddler such that the essential oils are released, but the leaves remain somewhat intact. A mangled heap of leaves in a glass is not appealing. The mint leaves should be removed from the sprig before being placed in the glass. The stems are too bitter for the drink.

Mount Gay® Extra Old Barbados Rum

Barbados is an ideal place to cultivate sugar cane and distill rum. The gently rolling terrain and porous, fertile soil are tailor-made for cultivating sugar cane and the water is drawn from underground aquifers fed with coral filtered spring water. Of the various brands of Barbadian rum, the oldest and most celebrated is Mount Gay. The spacious Mount Gay Rum Estate is located in the northernmost parish of St. Lucy and the crown jewel of their portfolio is *Mount Gay Extra Old Barbados Rum*.

Three years in production, Mount Gay Extra Old is a blend comprised of some of the oldest, most prized barrel-aged rums in the Mount Gay reserves. The mature pot still and continuous still spirits selected for the blend range in age between 12 and 17-years. The rum is bottled at a lip tingling 86-proof.

Mount Gay Extra Old has a rich, amber brown color and brilliant luminescence. The pronounced greenish tint around the edges of the rum confirms its extensive wood aging. It possesses a generous, well-balanced bouquet offering up the sweet aromas of oak, honey, vanilla, and fruit. The more the rum aerates, the more expansive and alluring the bouquet becomes.

Extra Old is remarkably light and delicate, not unlike the body of an aged alembic brandy. The rum immediately fills the mouth and splashes the palate with waves of flavor, tastes of banana, vanilla, caramel and toasted oak. The finish, while not overly protracted, is seamlessly smooth and loaded with flavor. Extra Old is in every sense a luxurious rum.

The object behind muddling the lime wedges is to express the fresh juice while not overly bruising the fruit's bitter white pith. Some of that bitterness is actually a welcomed thing, but too much and the drink will be adversely affected.

Regarding which type of sweetener to use in a Mojito, granulated white sugar is a frequent choice, but to be most effective the sugar must be thoroughly dissolved. Simple syrup is particularly advantageous for that reason. Creative options include sweetening the drink with guarapo (syrup derived from fresh sugar cane juice), brown, raw, or powdered sugar.

Without the muddled fresh mint, the Mojito fails to live up to its advanced billing. The mint is present in nearly every aspect of the cocktail. The predominant variety of mint selected for use in Mojitos is spearmint (Mentha spicata), although some prefer peppermint (Mentha piperita), pineapple mint (Mentha suaveolens) and the yerba buena variety from Latin America.

• **Spirit Options** — The traditional spirit base in a Mojito is light rum and again the better the rum, the better the Mojito. The good news is that there are certainly a great many brands of premium light rum from which to choose. In the pursuit to make a world-class Mojito, strongly consider experimenting with the famed rhum agricoles, such as Rhum Clément from Martinique, Trinidadian 10 Cane Rhum, or Rhum Barbancourt from Haiti. Their vibrant, flavor imbued characters are incomparable when featured in Mojitos. Dark rums are also marvelous in the drink. They add color and waves of dry, often spicy flavors.

Yet, if working with different flavors is high on your list, then showcasing a flavored rum or vodka in the drink is just the ticket. Between the two categories, there's a stellar brand representative of every popular flavor. Imagine the possibilities. You might decide to muddle together Cruzan Raspberry Rum with a handful of fresh raspberries, mint leaves, limes and sugar, or Stoli Blueberi Vodka and a tablespoon of blueberries. Then again you could muddle together a mango flavored rum with muddled papaya, limes, mint and sugar. Using the spirit as either a flavor enhancer or as a counterpoint is part of the artistry.

The Mojito is a superb delivery system for most light spirits. Silver tequila is a great choice. Its exuberant character works well with the muddled mint and sweetened lime juice in a Mojito. Not surprisingly, so does gin. As Bafferts Mint Flavored Gin has proven, mint is a natural complement to the aromatics used in gin. Infusions and exotic products — e.g. aguardiente, cachaça, shochu, sake — are also viable choices.

• **Groovy Modifiers** — As alluded to above, fruit, syrups and juice are often relied upon as modifiers in Mojitos. For example, a specialty at Philadelphia's Cuba Libre Restaurant is the *Sandito Mojito*. It's made with white rum, yerba buena mint leaves, guarapa and freshly squeezed watermelon juice. A partial list of modifier choices includes pomegranates, mango puree or nectar, passion fruit, pineapples, grapefruit or kiwi slices, blood oranges, kumquats, blackberries and prickly pear juice. Whatever you can't find at the local famer's market might be available on your back bar. Liqueurs such as PAMA, Malibu, Chambord, ZEN, Rhum Clément Creole Shrub and Grand Marnier were seemingly created with a flavor starved Mojito in mind.

- **Finishing School** — The final ingredient in the Mojito is a healthy splash of club soda, which adds a welcomed blast of effervescence. But even here you have creative latitude. There's no reason to limit yourself to using plain carbonated water when the world's finest sparkling spring waters are available for service. Then again, why not consider charging a Mojito with champagne or ginger beer? They'll add flavor as well as effervescence.

Cruzan® Estate Light Rum

Rum has been distilled on the Estate Diamond Plantation on the island of St. Croix since 1760. The Cruzan Distillery is famed for crafting light and amazingly flavorful spirits, the brand has become one of the most successful brands of Caribbean rum in the world, lead in no small measure by all world *Cruzan Estate Light Rum*.

It is a blend of triple-distilled rums produced in Cruzan's five-column, continuous still. The blend is aged in charred American oak bourbon barrels between two and three years. After aging, the rum has a golden hue. It is then filtered through activated charcoal to remove impurities and much of the color is obtained during aging.

The Cruzan Estate Light Rum is an unexpected treat; rarely are light spirits so easy to drink neat. The rum is crystal clear, medium-bodied and has a delicate, floral bouquet. It has a dry, light palate, one marked with creamy flavors of vanilla bean and spice. The finish is crisp and of medium duration.

Blindfolded it would be easy to mistake the Cruzan Estate Light for a gold rum. Its body, bouquet and palate reflect its barrel-aging. The rum makes an excellent base for nearly any type of cocktail.

The Cruzan range also includes *Cruzan Estate Dark Rum*, which is a blend of triple-distilled rums aged in oak bourbon barrels for a minimum of 2 years, and *Cruzan Estate Diamond Rum*, a savory, triple-distilled añejo aged in charred American oak barrels for 5 to 10 years.

• **Exit Strategies** — The classic garnishes on the Mojito are mint sprigs and either a lime wheel or wedge. The wedge should be used if you want to provide your guests with an opportunity to squeeze more juice into the drink. If not, the less functional, but more attractive lime wheel might be a better choice.

Many restaurants are adding a segment of sugar cane to their Mojitos. It looks great and performs admirably as a swizzle.

The realm of rum drinks also includes such stalwart libations as the *Zombie*, *Mai Tai*, *Blue Hawaiian*, *Hurricane*, *Scorpion*, *Planter's Punch*, *The Run, Skip and Go Naked* and the *Vicious Virgin*. They're joyful concoctions — tall, colorful and brimming with tropical appeal. A word of caution, be moderate with their rum content. They all share a reputation as being eye rolling strong.

10 Cane Caipirinha

Specialty of Cuba Libre Restaurant and Rum Bar
Created by Cuba Libre's staff
House specialty glass, chilled
Build in glass
Splash fresh lime juice
Splash guarapa
1 lemon wedge
1 lime wedge
Muddle contents
Add ice
2 oz. 10 Cane Rum
Place the lime juice, guarapa, lemon and lime wedge into the empty house specialty glass. Muddle and add ice. Pour in the rum and stir.

Anjou Pear Mojito

Specialty of Backstreet Café
Created by Sean Beck
House specialty glass, ice
Pour ingredients into an iced mixing glass
1 3/4 oz. Bacardi Light Rum
1/4 oz. Calvados
3/4 oz. simple syrup
1 oz. fresh lime juice
1 1/4 oz. Anjou pear puree*
6-8 mint leaves
Shake and strain
2 oz. club soda
Garnish with a lime wheel
Pour ingredients into the iced mixing glass. Shake thoroughly and strain contents into an iced, house specialty glass. Add club soda and stir gently. Garnish with a lime wheel.
*Anjou Pear Puree Recipe - pg 317

Asian Pear Mojito

Specialty of P.F. Chang's China Bistro
Created by P.F. Chang's staff
Pint glass, chilled
Pour ingredients into an empty mixing glass
1 oz. DeKuyper Pucker Sour Apple Schnapps
5 large mint leaves
3 lime wedges
Muddle contents
Add ice
1 1/2 oz. Bacardi Limón Rum
Splash pineapple juice
Shake thoroughly - do not strain
Fill with club soda
Garnish with a fresh mint sprig
Place the Apple Pucker, mint leaves and lime wedges into the empty mixing glass. Muddle and add ice. Pour in the remaining ingredients. Shake thoroughly - do not strain - pour contents into an empty, chilled pint glass. Fill with club soda. Garnish with a fresh mint sprig.

Basil and Pineapple Mojito

Specialty of J BAR
Created by Janos Wilder
Collins glass, chilled
Pour ingredients into an empty mixing glass
1 1/2 oz. Cruzan Light Rum
5 to 6 basil leaves
1/2 oz. basil syrup*
3/4 oz. simple syrup
2 oz. pineapple juice
4 to 5 shakes ground pepper
Muddle contents
Add ice
Shake thoroughly - do not strain
Pour ingredients into the empty mixing glass. Muddle and add ice. Shake thoroughly - do not strain - pour contents into an empty, chilled collins glass.
*Basil Syrup Recipe - pg 317

Batida

Specialty of Nacional 27
Created by Adam Seger
House specialty glass, chilled
Pour ingredients into an iced mixing glass
2 oz. Cachaça
1/3 cup chopped tropical fruit; mango, kiwi, pineapple, etc.
1 1/2 oz. simple syrup
Splash fresh lime juice
Shake thoroughly - do not strain
Pour ingredients into the iced mixing glass. Shake thoroughly - do not strain - pour contents into an empty, chilled house specialty glass.

Berry Basil

Specialty of 33 Restaurant & Lounge
Created by Pej Mortarjem
Cocktail glass, chilled
Pour ingredients into an empty mixing glass
8 blackberries
3 basil leaves
1/2 oz. simple syrup
Muddle contents
Add ice
1 1/2 oz. SKYY Citrus Vodka
Shake and strain
Garnish with a basil leaf
Place the blackberries, basil leaves and simple syrup into the empty mixing glass. Muddle and add ice. Pour in the vodka. Shake thoroughly and strain contents into a chilled cocktail glass. Garnish with a floating basil leaf.

Hard Rock Cafe — Las Vegas

4475 Paradise Rd.
Las Vegas, NV 89109
☎ **702.733.7625**
▶▶ **www.hardrock.com**
✉ **Las_Vegas_Sales@hardrock.com**

The intersection of Harmon and Paradise in Las Vegas is a magical place. It's where you'll find the **Hard Rock Cafe**, and for anyone who has ever tapped his or her foot or listened to the radio, it's a hip slice of heaven.

The place is next to impossible to miss. At the entrance is the famous 85-foot tall Gibson Les Paul guitar neon sign, the strings of which strum riffs from Led Zeppelin's "Stairway to Heaven" in lights. The interior of the Hard Rock is a treasure trove of rock 'n' roll artifacts including Roy Orbison's 1968 Harley Davidson and a $250,000 display of Kiss memorabilia. The walls are covered with signed guitars and platinum records. There is also a life-sized statute of Elvis, along with a number of his guitars and personal effects.

In addition to having an engaging motif, the Hard Rock sports a diverse and eclectic American menu. The Bloody Mary Shrimp are skewered, basted in pesto sauce and served with Bloody Mary salsa and nacho cheese. Specialties include the pulled pork sandwich, Joe Perry's Quesadilla and the Twisted Mac Chicken and Cheese.

The atmosphere in the place is electric, due in no small measure to the lively bar crowd. One of the signatures at the Hard Rock is the *Mixed Berry Tea*, a tall and delicious blend of Stoli Razberi, Stoli Blueberi, Blue Curaçao, sweet 'n' sour and a float of Chambord. Also delectable is the *Black Dog Margarita*, a purple hued specialty made with Cuervo Black Tequila.

Every Hard Rock Cafe around the globe develops its own personality. This famed destination does Vegas and rock 'n' roll proud. —RP

Mixed Berry Tea
Drink recipe on pg 171

Bikini Tini

Specialty of Yard House
Created by Kip Snider
Sugar rimmed cocktail glass, chilled
Pour ingredients into an iced mixing glass
2 oz. Cruzan Banana Rum
1 oz. Malibu Pineapple Rum
1 oz. pineapple juice
Shake and strain
Float with ¹/₂ oz. RémyRed
    Red Berry Infusion
Garnish with an orange slice and lime wedge
*Pour the rums and pineapple juice into the
iced mixing glass. Shake thoroughly and strain
contents into a sugar rimmed, chilled cocktail
glass. Float the RémyRed. Garnish with an
orange slice and lime wedge.*

The Bistro's Singapore Sling

Specialty of P.F. Chang's China Bistro
Created by P.F. Chang's staff
Bucket glass, chilled
Pour ingredients into an iced mixing glass
1 ¹/₂ oz. No.TEN by Tanqueray Gin
¹/₂ oz. Cherry Heering
¹/₄ oz. Cointreau
¹/₄ oz. Strega Liqueur
Splash grenadine
2 dashes Angostura Aromatic Bitters
¹/₂ oz. fresh lime juice
3 oz. pineapple juice
 Shake thoroughyl - do not strain
Garnish with a fresh pineapple wedge
    and cherry
*Pour ingredients into the iced mixing glass.
Shake thoroughly - do not strain - pour contents
into an empty, chilled bucket glass. Garnish with
a fresh pineapple wedge and cherry.*

> "Some days there's nothing more welcoming
> than the sight of an icy cold,
> frozen fruit Daiquiri."

Tarantula® Azul

Considering the hectic lives we all lead, a little help now and again
would be a welcome relief. For example, there are those days when
there's just not enough time to prepare a fabulous tasting Blue
Margarita. In the past, the only option would have been to go
without, or hastily throw something together. Those dark days are
over, thanks to the introduction of *Tarantula Azul*.

    This delicious and innovative product is made in America
from a blend of premium blanco tequilas and all natural citrus
liqueur. Its signature Pacific blue appearance is obtained with added
certified coloring. It's an engaging effect.

Tarantula Azul has a round, medium-weight body and a floral, citrusy bouquet.
Its initial entry is soft and quite mild, but gradually the palate opens revealing a dry,
somewhat tart set of spice and fresh citrus flavors. The tequila doesn't overstay its
welcome, finishing clean and crisp. From start to finish Tarantula Azul drinks fresh and
lively like a well-crafted cocktail.

    Here's a brand that was obviously bred with sheer enjoyment in mind. Poured
over ice, one could easily mistake this sleek tequila for a skillfully crafted cocktail. Its
taste and appearance are so well conceived that they appeal to the senses as a complete
thought. Indeed, add a spot of lime juice and you have a Blue Margarita or a Kamikaze
Azul. It has wonderful applications behind anyone's bar.

Blackberry Mojito

Specialty of J BAR
Created by Patrick Harrington

Collins glass, chilled
Pour ingredients into an empty mixing glass
5 fresh blackberries
4-5 mint leaves
1 oz. simple syrup or 2-3 sugar cubes
1 oz. fresh lime juice
Muddle contents
Add ice
1 ¹/2 oz. Cruzan Estate Light Rum
5 oz. club soda
Shake thoroughly - do not strain
Place the blackberries, mint leaves, simple syrup, and fresh lime juice into the empty mixing glass. Muddle and add ice. Pour in the remaining ingredients. Shake thoroughly - do not strain - pour contents into an empty, chilled collins glass.

Brazilian Margarita

Specialty of Mosaic Restaurant
Created by Stephanie Kozicki

Raw sugar rimmed house specialty glass, ice
Pour ingredients into an iced mixing glass
1 ¹/2 oz. Ypióca Cachaça
¹/2 oz. Kalani Coconut Liqueur
¹/4 oz. DeKuyper Blue Curaçao
1 oz. fresh key lime juice
3 oz. passion fruit juice
Shake and strain
Garnish with a fresh pineapple wedge
Pour ingredients into the iced mixing glass. Shake thoroughly and strain contents into a raw sugar rimmed, iced house specialty glass. Garnish with a fresh pineapple wedge.

Cable Car

Specialty of Harry Denton's Starlight Room
Created by Tony Abou-Ganim

Cinnamon sugar rimmed
    cocktail glass, chilled
Pour ingredients into an iced mixing glass
1 ¹/2 oz. Captain Morgan
    Original Spiced Rum
³/4 oz. Marie Brizard Orange Curaçao
1 ¹/2 oz. fresh lemon sour mix
Garnish with an orange spiral twist
Pour ingredients into the iced mixing glass. Shake thoroughly and strain contents into a cinnamon sugar rimmed, chilled cocktail glass. Garnish with an orange spiral twist.

Classic Caipirinha

Excerpted from The Original Guide to American Cocktails and Drinks- 6th Edition

Old fashioned glass, chilled
Build in glass
4 large lime wedges
³/4 oz. simple syrup
Muddle contents
Add cracked ice
2 ¹/2 oz. Cachaça
Place the lime wedges and simple syrup into the empty, chilled old fashioned glass. Muddle and add cracked ice. Pour in the cachaça.

Caipirinha, Cuba Libre's

Specialty of Cuba Libre Restaurant & Rum Bar
Created by Bob Gallo

Bucket glass, chilled
Pour ingredients into empty mixing glass
2 oz. guarapa
1 lemon wedge
1 lime wedge
Muddle contents
Add ice
2 oz. Pitú Cachaça
Shake thoroughly - do not strain
Pour the guarapa, lemon and lime wedges into the empty mixing glass. Muddle and add ice. Pour in the cachaça. Shake thoroughly - do not strain - pour contents into an empty, chilled bucket glass.

Classic Caipirissma

Excerpted from The Original Guide to American Cocktails and Drinks- 6th Edition

Old fashioned glass, chilled
Build in glass
4 large lime wedges
³/4 oz. simple syrup
Muddle contents
Add crushed ice
2 ¹/2 oz. Light Rum
Garnish with a lime wedge
Place the lime wedges and simple syrup into the empty, chilled old fashioned glass. Muddle and add crushed ice. Pour in the rum. Garnish with a lime wedge.

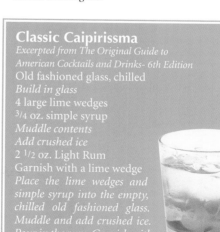

Classic Caipiroshka

Excerpted from The Original Guide to
American Cocktails and Drinks- 6th Edition
Old fashioned glass, chilled
Build in glass
4 large lime wedges
3/4 oz. simple syrup
Muddle contents
Add cracked ice
2 1/2 oz. Vodka
Place the lime wedges
and simple syrup into the
empty, chilled old fashioned
glass. Muddle and add
cracked ice. Pour in the
vodka.

Cali Lemonada

Specialty of The Spanish Kitchen
Created by Kelly Shephard
Sugar rimmed bucket glass, chilled
Pour ingredients into an empty mixing glass
3 lemon wedges
1/2 oz. sugar
Muddle contents
Add ice
1 1/2 oz. Absolut Citron Vodka
1/2 oz. Patrón Citrónge Orange Liqueur
1/2 oz. Sprite
1/2 oz. sweet 'n' sour
1/2 oz. club soda
Shake thoroughly - do not strain
Garnish with fresh mint leaves
Place the lemon wedges and simple syrup into
the empty mixing glass. Muddle and add ice.
Pour in the remaining ingredients. Shake
thoroughly - do not strain - pour contents into a
sugar rimmed, empty, chilled bucket glass.
Garnish with fresh mint leaves.

Rum Toucano™

Any self-respecting cocktail haunt needs **Rum Toucano** on the back bar. It is a classy, romantic spirit imported from the rainforests of Brazil made within a stones throw of the Amazon. In the world of drink making, delectable and exotic is an unbeatable combination.

Rum Toucano is produced by world renowned Ypioca of Fortaleza, the oldest cachaça distillery in Brazil. The Telles family has operated their facility in the tropical state of Ceara since 1846. Toucano is distilled from the pure, first run juice of freshly harvested and unprocessed sugar cane. The 80-proof rum is aged for two years in oak casks and Portuguese bálsamo barrels. The carnauba palm fronds wrapping the bottle are hand-woven by local craftsmen.

Toucano is a South American sensation. The rum has a rich, golden copper hue and an assertive bouquet of herbal, woody aromas. It has a light-weight, oily body and a primarily dry, herbaceous palate similar to an unaged rhum agricole, yet with a more earthy, mineral crisp finish. The effect is sensational.

In its native land this type of spirit is referred to as cachaça rum. Cachaça is the national beverage of Brazil. Toucano is different from most cachaças because it is aged for two years in casks of oak and balsam, which renders it smooth and refined. The rum's crisp, light and unusual taste makes it a natural to feature in a broad range of contemporary cocktails and South American classic drinks.

Carabao Daiquiri

Specialty of Brasserie JO
Created by David Johnston
Cocktail glass, chilled
Pour ingredients into an iced mixing glass
1 1/2 oz. 10 Cane Rum
Seeds from 1 inch of a vanilla bean
1/2 oz. simple syrup
1/2 oz. fresh lime juice
1 1/2 oz. mango nectar
Shake and strain
Garnish with a strip of dried mango
    twisted around straw
Pour ingredients into the iced mixing glass. Shake thoroughly and strain contents into a chilled cocktail glass. Garnish with a strip of dried mango twisted around a straw.

Cazuela

Specialty of Nacional 27
Created by Adam Seger
Pint glass, chilled
Pour ingredients into an empty mixing glass
Equal parts chopped oranges, lemons,
    limes and grapefruit; including
    skins - 2/3 full into mixing glass
Muddle contents
Add pinch sea salt or Kosher salt
Fill with ice
1 1/2 oz. Gran Centenario Plata Tequila
Shake thoroughly - do not strain
Top with Fresca
Place the chopped fruit into the empty mixing glass. Muddle until glass is half fruit, half juice. Add a pinch of sea salt or kosher salt and fill with ice. Add the tequila. Shake thoroughly - do not strain - pour contents into an empty, chilled pint glass. Top with Fresca soda.

Charles Daiquiri

Excerpted from The Original Guide to
American Cocktails and Drinks- 6th Edition
Cocktail glass, chilled
Pour ingredients into an iced mixing glass
1 1/2 oz. Light Rum
3/4 oz. Dark Rum
3/4 oz. Cointreau
1/2 oz. Rose's Lime Juice
1 1/2 oz. fresh lime sour mix
Shake and strain
Garnish with a lime wedge
Pour ingredients into the iced mixing glass. Shake thoroughly and strain contents into a chilled cocktail glass. Garnish with a lime wedge.

Chartreuse Swizzle

Specialty of Harry Denton's Starlight Room
Created by Marco Dionysos
Bucket glass, crushed ice
Pour ingredients into an iced mixing glass
1 1/4 oz. Green Chartreuse
1/2 oz. falernum
1/2 oz. fresh lime juice
1 oz. pineapple juice
Shake and strain
Garnish with a lime wheel
Pour ingredients into the iced mixing glass. Shake thoroughly and strain contents into a crushed ice filled bucket glass. Garnish with a lime wheel.

Chateau Mojito

Specialty of Courtright's Restaurant
Created by Marco Recio
Bucket glass, chilled
Build in glass
6 mint sprigs
1/2 oz. fresh lime juice
1 1/2 tsp. sugar
Muddle contents
Add ice
1 1/2 oz. Bacardi Limón Rum
1 1/2 oz. Blue Curaçao
2 oz. sweet 'n' sour
Swizzle thoroughly
Garnish with a lemon twist and lime wheel
Place the mint sprigs, lime juice and sugar into the empty bucket glass. Muddle and add ice. Pour in the remaining ingredients. Swizzle thoroughly. Garnish with a lemon twist and lime wheel.

Classic Chi-Chi

Excerpted from The Original Guide to
American Cocktails and Drinks- 6th Edition
House specialty glass, chilled
Pour ingredients into
*   an iced blender canister*
1 oz. Vodka
3/4 oz. half & half
2 oz. coconut cream syrup
3 oz. pineapple juice
Blend ingredients
Garnish with a fresh pineapple
      wedge and cherry
Pour ingredients into the
iced blender canister. Blend
thoroughly and pour contents
into a chilled house specialty
glass. Garnish with a fresh pineapple
wedge and cherry.

Coquito

Specialty of Cuba Libre Restaurant & Rum Bar
Created by Bob Gallo
1/2 gallon container
Blend ingredients
2 cups Dark Rum
8 egg yolks, pasteurized
2 tsp. vanilla extract
1 tsp. ground cinnamon
3/4 cup sugar
14 oz. can coconut milk
14 oz. can sweetened condensed milk
12 oz. can evaporated milk
Beat the sugar and egg yolks together until they
form a pale yellow ribbon. Add all the liquid
ingredients. Add cinnamon then adjust to
your own taste. Blend all ingredients well and
refrigerate. Best when served cold. Makes 6-10
servings.

Cucumber Cooler

Specialty of The Original McCormick & Schmick's
Created by Geoff V. Helzer
Bucket glass, chilled
Pour ingredients into an empty mixing glass
3 sugar cubes
2 cucumber slices
3/4 oz. fresh lime juice
Muddle contents
Add ice
1 1/4 oz. Stolichnaya Vodka
1/4 oz. Midori
Shake thoroughly - do not strain
Top with club soda
Garnish with a cucumber slice
Place the sugar cubes, cucumber slices and lime
wedge into the empty mixing glass. Muddle and
add ice. Pour in the remaining ingredients. Shake
thoroughly - do not strain - pour contents into an
empty, chilled bucket glass. Top with club soda.
Garnish with a cucumber slice on the rim.

Classic Daiquiri

Excerpted from The Original Guide to
American Cocktails and Drinks- 6th Edition
House specialty glass, ice
Pour ingredients into an iced mixing glass
1 1/4 oz. Light Rum
1/2 oz. Rose's Lime Juice
2 oz. fresh lime
     sour mix
Shake and strain
Garnish with a lime wedge
Pour ingredients into the iced
mixing glass. Shake thoroughly
and strain contents into an iced
house specialty glass. Garnish with
a lime wedge.

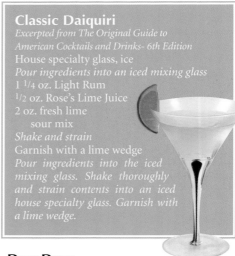

Dew Drop

Specialty of Jade Bar
Created by Wendy Cardiff, Greg Portsche
Sugar rimmed cocktail glass, chilled
Pour ingredients into an iced mixing glass
2 oz. Pyrat XO Reserve Rum
3 dashes Chinese Five Spice
3 dashes lemongrass simple syrup*
1 oz. yuzu juice
1 oz. Margarita mix
Shake and strain
 Garnish with an orange twist
Pour ingredients into the iced mixing glass.
Shake thoroughly and strain into a sugar
rimmed, chilled cocktail glass. Garnish with an
orange twist.
*Lemongrass Simple Syrup Recipe - pg 321

Hard Rock Cafe — New York

🗺 **1501 Broadway**
New York, NY 10036
☎ **212.343.3355**
▸◂ **www.hardrock.com**
✉ **New_York_Reception@**
hardrock.com

With all due respect to the rest of the planet, the center of the civilized world is Manhattan and the hub of the island nation is Times Square. Its energy level is palpable, its vitality infectious. Were extraterrestrials here visiting, you'd find them in Time Square and the odds are that they'd be waiting to get into the Hard Rock Cafe.

The place is one of the "must see" destinations in New York. Located in the heart of Times Square on Broadway and 43rd Street, Hard Rock personifies the excitement

and allure of rock and roll. There are over 500 pieces of rock and roll memorabilia in the place, a priceless collection that includes the original Abbey Road doors, Bo Diddley's handmade "cigar box" guitar and stage costumes worn by Madonna and Gwen Stefani. There is a wall of guitars stacked atop each other and items from Led Zeppelin, Elvis, James Brown, the Ramones and Bruce Springsteen, among others.

When eventually your hunger demands attention, the menu at the Hard Rock Cafe is loaded with solid American performers. Among the featured acts are the Legendary Burger, hickory smoked ribs, grilled salmon, Cajun chicken sandwich and blackened chicken pasta. Don't dare leave without tasting their homestyle cheesecake or hot fudge brownie sundae.

The bar and lounge area create the focal point of the Cafe. The cocktail menu is loaded with creative specialties devised on-site, such as the *Exotic 'Rita*, a classy, upscale cocktail made with Patrón, Cointreau, Monin Pomegranate and Hard Rock's secret Margarita mix. Another specialty worth visiting is the *Red Rocker*, a groovy drink made with Cabo Wabo Reposado, Disaronno Amaretto, cranberry juice and Margarita mix. They're both chartbusters. —RP

Exotic 'Rita
Drink recipe on pg 48

El Pirata

Specialty of Absinthe Brasserie & Bar
Created by Jonny Raglin
Cocktail glass, chilled
Pour ingredients into an iced mixing glass
1 3/4 oz. 10 Cane Rum
1/4 oz. Petit Canne Sugar Cane Syrup
1/4 oz. fresh lemon juice
2 dashes Fee's Mint Bitters
Shake and strain
1/4 oz. Lemon Hart 151° Rum
Garnish with flaming lemon boat
Pour ingredients, except the Lemon Hart 151° Rum, into the iced mixing glass. Shake thoroughly and strain contents into a chilled cocktail glass. Float the lemon boat in the cocktail and carefully pour the 151 into the boat. Light the lemon boat on fire and serve with a skewer to sink the boat once the pith has caramelized a bit.

CAUTION! Extreme care must be used whenever flame is used in or near an alcohol drink.

Farmer's Market Caipirinha

Specialty of Nacional 27
Created by Adam Seger
Old fashioned glass, chilled
Pour ingredients into an empty mixing glass
1 fresh lime cut into 8 wedges
2 oz. seasonal fruit, chopped: sour black cherries, strawberries, raspberries, blackberries, or peaches
Muddle contents
Add crushed ice
1 1/2 oz. simple syrup
2 oz. Ypióca Cachaça
Shake thoroughly - do not strain
Place the lime wedges and chopped fruit into the empty mixing glass. Muddle and add crushed ice. Pour in the remaining ingredients. Shake thoroughly - do not strain - pour contents into an empty, chilled old fashioned glass.

Whaler's® Original Vanille Rum

If someone doesn't enjoy a cocktail made with **Whaler's Original Vanille Rum**, check his pulse and call a medic. This brilliantly flavored rum is an unpretentious, great tasting spirit that's chaffing at the bit to have some fun. Add up its attributes and you've got a back bar winner.

This enticing spirit was originated by Hawaiian Distillers of Honolulu. The rum is distilled using molasses from locally grown sugar cane. Whaler's Original Vanille (pronounced Van-ee) is a dark, highly aromatic rum infused with natural vanilla flavors. The rum has a creamy texture and a delicious palate brimming with vanilla and hints of cocoa. Little wonder why it is the featured act in many contemporary drinks.

The popular Whaler's line of rums also includes **Great White**, a sleek silver rum with a clean, lively palate, and **Original Dark**, an energized spirit endowed with warm, sumptuous flavors. **Whaler's Spiced Rum** has a palate saturated with the flavors of vanilla, caramel and spice.

The dean of the group is **Whaler's Rare Reserve Dark Rum**, an elegant aged rum with a beckoning bouquet and a deliciously complex palate. New to the team are **Killer Coconut**, a vibrant rum loaded with the fresh flavor of coconut, **Pineapple Paradise**, a lavishly flavored pineapple rum and **Big Island Banana**, which is made with natural banana flavorings.

The entire range of Whaler's Hawaiian Rums are bona fide good times waiting to happen.

Florida Daiquiri

Excerpted from The original Guide to
American Cocktails and Drinks- 6th Edition
Cocktail glass, chilled
Pour ingredients into an iced mixing glass
1 1/2 oz. Light Rum
Splash grenadine
1/2 oz. Rose's Lime Juice
1/2 oz. grapefruit juice
1 1/2 oz. fresh lime sour mix
Shake and strain
Garnish with a lime wedge
Pour ingredients into the iced mixing glass. Shake thoroughly and strain contents into a chilled cocktail glass. Garnish with a lime wedge.

French Daiquiri

Excerpted from The Original Guide to
American Cocktails and Drinks- 6th Edition
Cocktail glass, chilled
Pour ingredients into an iced mixing glass
1 3/4 oz. St. James Extra Old Rhum
3/4 oz. Crème de Cassis
1/2 oz. Rose's Lime Juice
2 oz. fresh lime sour mix
Shake and strain
Garnish with an orange twist
Pour ingredients into the iced mixing glass. Shake thoroughly and strain contents into a chilled cocktail glass. Garnish with an orange twist.

Galapagos

Specialty of Absinthe Brasserie & Bar
Created by Xan Devoss
Cocktail glass, chilled
Pour ingredients into an empty mixing glass
1/2 Kaffir lime leaf
1/2 oz. pepper simple syrup*
Muddle contents
Add ice
2 oz. Alto del Carmen Gran Pisco
1/4 oz. fresh lime juice
1/2 oz. fresh grapefruit juice
Shake and strain
Garnish with 3 brandied cherries
Place the lime leaf and pepper syrup into the empty mixing glass. Muddle and add ice. Pour in the remaining ingredients. Shake thoroughly and strain contents into a chilled cocktail glass. Garnish by sinking 3 brandied cherries.
*Pepper Simple Syrup Recipe
1 cup whole black peppercorns per gallon of simple syrup (equal parts sugar and water)

The Garden of Eden

Specialty of The Original McCormick & Schmick's
Created by Geoff V. Helzer, Josh Ryneal
Cocktail glass, chilled
Pour ingredients into an empty mixing glass
1 oz. blood orange juice
2 cucumber slices
2 cilantro sprigs
2 sugar cubes
Muddle
Add ice
1 1/4 oz. Level Vodka
Shake and strain
Garnish with a cucumber slice
Pour the blood orange juice, cucumbers, cilantro, and sugar cubes into the empty mixing glass. Muddle contents and add ice. Pour in the vodka. Shake thoroughly and strain contents into a chilled cocktail glass. Garnish with a cucumber slice on the rim.

Green Eyes Colada

Excerpted from The Original Guide to
American Cocktails and Drinks- 6th Edition
House specialty glass, chilled
Pour ingredients into an iced blender canister
1 1/2 oz. Midori
1 1/2 oz. Citrus Rum
3/4 oz. half & half
2 oz. coconut cream syrup
3 oz. pineapple juice
Blend ingredients
Garnish with a fresh pineapple wedge
    and cherry
Pour ingredients into the iced blender canister. Blend thoroughly and pour contents into a chilled house specialty glass. Garnish with a fresh pineapple wedge and cherry.

Heirloom Tomato Mojito

Specialty of Nacional 27
Created by Adam Seger
Pint glass, chilled
Build in glass
1/2 lime, quartered
1/4 medium-sized green tomato, quartered
1/4 medium-sized Heirloom tomato, quartered
12 basil leaves
Pinch kosher salt
3 pinches fresh black pepper
Muddle contents
Add ice
1 1/2 oz. Gran Centenario Plata Tequila
Top with tonic water
Splash aged balsamic vinegar
Garnish with a basil sprig
Place the limes, tomatoes, basil, salt and pepper
into the empty, chilled pint glass. Muddle and
add ice. Pour in the remaining ingredients.
Garnish with a basil sprig.

Hemingway Daiquiri

Excerpted from The Original Guide to
American Cocktails and Drinks- 6th Edition
Cocktail glass, chilled
Pour ingredients into an iced mixing glass
1 3/4 oz. Light Rum
1/2 oz. Maraschino Liqueur
1 oz. grapefruit juice
1 1/2 oz. fresh lime juice
Shake and strain
Garnish with a lime wheel
Pour ingredients into the iced mixing glass.
Shake thoroughly and strain contents into
a chilled cocktail glass. Garnish with a lime
wheel.

PAMA™ Pomegranate Liqueur

Every once in a while a groundbreaking product comes around and changes the landscape of American back bars. *PAMA Pomegranate Liqueur* is precisely such a product. In the same way Chambord immortalized the essence of black raspberries, PAMA has done the same for the immensely popular pomegranate. This delectable liqueur is a guaranteed franchise player, a back bar classic in the making.

Super-premium PAMA Pomegranate is crafted by Heaven Hill in Bardstown, Kentucky by infusing premium vodka and a small percentage of tequila with the all natural juice of Californian pomegranates. It is bottled at an accessible 34-proof.

PAMA is the world's first authentic pomegranate liqueur and it's a bona fide keeper. The liqueur has a seductive true to fruit reddish hue, a lushly textured, medium-weight body and an alluring bouquet of mixed berry aromas. The sumptuous palate is what really seals the deal. It is imbued with the dry, tart flavors of pomegranate and cranberries. Its finish is flavorful and impressively long.

No mere splash of pomegranate juice could possibly achieve what PAMA is able to accomplish in a cocktail. The liqueur is ideally suited for showcasing in Martinis, Cosmopolitans and Margaritas. In fact, reach for the bottle whenever preparing a cocktail that's in need of a blast of fresh and delectably tart flavor. PAMA is one of the rare "can't miss" ingredients.

Hurricane, Hard Rock Cafe's

Specialty of Hard Rock Cafe- New York
Created by Hard Rock Cafe's staff
House specialty glass, ice
Build in glass
1 oz. Bacardi Light Rum
1 oz. orange juice
1 oz. pineapple juice
1 oz. mango juice
1/4 oz. grenadine
Float with 1/2 oz. Disaronno Amaretto
Float with 1/2 oz. Bacardi Select Rum
Garnish with an orange slice and cherry flag
Pour ingredients into the iced house specialty glass in the order listed. Float the Disaronno and Bacardi Rum. Garnish with an orange slice and cherry flag.

Island Hopper

Specialty of The Refectory Restaurant & Bistro
Created by Kevin McClatchy, Julie Mulisano
Bucket glass, ice
Pour ingredients into an iced mixing glass
1/2 oz. Bacardi Light Rum
1/2 oz. Myers's Original Dark Rum
1/2 oz. Bacardi Cóco Rum
1/2 oz. Cruzan 151° Rum
3 oz. pineapple juice
3 oz. cranberry juice
Shake and strain
Garnish with a paper umbrella
Pour ingredients into the iced mixing glass. Shake thoroughly and strain contents into an iced bucket glass. Garnish with a paper umbrella.

Kahlúa Colada

Excerpted from The Original Guide to
American Cocktails and Drinks- 6th Edition
House specialty glass, chilled
Pour ingredients into an iced blender canister
1 1/2 oz. Light Rum
3/4 oz. Kahlúa
3/4 oz. half & half
2 oz. coconut cream syrup
3 oz. pineapple juice
1 scoop vanilla ice cream
Blend ingredients
Float with 1 oz. Kahlúa
Garnish with a pineapple wedge and cherry
Pour ingredients into the iced blender canister. Blend thoroughly and pour contents into a chilled house specialty glass. Float the Kahlúa. Garnish with a pineapple wedge and cherry.

Kokomo Joe Colada

Excerpted from The Original Guide to
American Cocktails and Drinks- 6th Edition
House specialty glass, chilled
Pour ingredients into an iced blender canister
3/4 oz. Light Rum
3/4 oz. Gold Rum
3/4 oz. Mount Gay Eclipse Rum
3/4 oz. Crème de Banana
1 oz. orange juice
2 oz. coconut cream syrup
3 oz. pineapple juice
Blend ingredients
Garnish with a pineapple wedge
    and banana slice
Pour ingredients into the iced blender canister. Blend thoroughly and pour contents into a chilled house specialty glass. Garnish with a pineapple wedge and banana slice.

La Floridita Daiquiri

Excerpted from The Original Guide to
American Cocktails and Drinks- 6th Edition
Cocktail glass, chilled
Pour ingredients into an iced mixing glass
1 1/2 oz. Light Rum
3/4 oz. Cointreau
3/4 oz. fresh lime juice
2 oz. fresh lime sour mix
Shake and strain
Garnish with a lime wedge
Pour ingredients into the iced mixing glass. Shake thoroughly and strain contents into a chilled cocktail glass. Garnish with a lime wedge.

Mai Tai, P.F. Chang's

Specialty of P.F. Chang's China Bistro
Created by P.F. Chang's staff
House specialty glass, ice
Build in glass
1 1/2 oz. Bacardi Light Rum
1/2 oz. Orange Curaçao
1 oz. orgeat syrup
2 oz. orange juice
2 oz. pineapple juice
Float with 1/2 oz. Myers's Original Dark Rum
Float with 1/4 oz. Bacardi 151° Rum
Garnish with a fresh pineapple slice
Pour the ingredients into the iced house specialty glass in the order listed. Float the Myers's and Bacardi rums. Garnish with a fresh pineapple slice.

Mango Mojito

Specialty of Oyster Restaurant & Nightclub
Created by Thom Greco
House specialty glass, chilled
Build in glass
6-8 mint leaves
2 lime wedges
3/4 oz. mint syrup
3/4 oz. mango juice
Muddle contents
Add ice
1 1/2 oz. Cruzan Mango Rum
Top with club soda
Garnish with a fresh mint sprig
　　and mango wedge
Place the mint leaves, lime wedges, syrup and juice into the empty, chilled house specialty glass. Muddle and add ice. Pour in the rum and top with club soda. Garnish with a fresh mint sprig and mango wedge.

MangoMint Mojito

Specialty of Stone Rose Lounge
Created by Jeff Isaacson
Rocks glass, chilled
Build in glass
2 orange slices
5-6 mint leaves
1/2 oz. simple syrup
Splash club soda
Muddle contents
Add ice
2 oz. Finlandia Mango Fusion Vodka
Garnish with a fresh mint leaf
Place the orange slices, mint leaves, simple syrup and club soda into the empty, chilled rocks glass. Muddle and add ice. Pour in the vodka. Garnish with a fresh mint leaf.

Meet Me In Paradise

Specialty of Joe's Seafood, Prime Steak & Stone Crab
Created by Dan Barringer
Bucket glass, chilled
Build in glass
1 orange wedge
4 drops Fee's Orange Bitters
8 fresh mint leaves
Muddle ingredients
Add ice
1 oz. Bacardi O Rum
2 oz. lemonade
2 oz. ginger beer
Place the orange wedge, bitters and mint into the empty, chilled bucket glass. Muddle and add ice. Pour in the remaining ingredients.

Métro

Specialty of Brasserie JO
Created by David Johnston
Cocktail glass, chilled
Pour ingredients into an iced mixing glass
2 1/2 oz. 10 Cane Rum
1 oz. lemon/mint simple syrup*
Shake and strain
Garnish with a fresh mint sprig
Pour ingredients into the iced mixing glass. Shake thoroughly and strain contents into a chilled cocktail glass. Garnish with a fresh mint sprig.
*Lemon/Mint Simple
　　Syrup Recipe - pg 321

Mexican Mojito

Specialty of Rio/Bamboleo Tequila Bar
Created by Justin Keane, Anthony Alba
House specialty glass, chilled
Pour ingredients into an empty mixing glass
8 mint leaves
2 lime wedges
2 lemon wedges
Muddle contents
Add ice
1 1/2 oz. El Diamante Del Cielo
　　Blanco Tequila
1/2 oz. fresh lime sour mix
Shake thoroughly - do not strain
Garnish with a fresh mint sprig
Place the mint and fruit wedges into the empty mixing glass. Muddle and add ice. Pour in the remaining ingredients. Shake thoroughly - do not strain - pour contents into an empty, chilled house specialty glass. Garnish with a fresh mint sprig.

Mint Morro

Specialty of Jade Bar
Created by Kyle Mason
Sugar rimmed bucket glass, chilled
Pour ingredients into an empty mixing glass
6-8 mint leaves
1 tsp. sugar
1/2 oz. Rose's Lime Juice
1/2 oz. pineapple juice
Muddle contents
Add ice
1 oz. Ketel One Citroen Vodka
1 oz. Myers's Original Dark Rum
Shake thoroughly - do not strain
Garnish with a fresh mint sprig
Place the mint leaves, sugar, lime juice and pineapple juice into the empty mixing glass. Muddle and add ice. Pour in the remaining ingredients. Shake thoroughly - do not strain - pour contents into a sugar rimmed, empty, chilled bucket glass. Garnish with a fresh mint sprig.

Harry Denton's Starlight Room

Sir Francis Drake Hotel
450 Powell Street
San Francisco, CA 94102
☎ **415.395.8519**

▶▶ **www.harrydenton.com**

✉ **michael.pagan@harrydenton.com**

Harry Denton's Starlight Room is as famous a San Francisco landmark as the Bay Bridge and Telegraph Hill, only better. Located on the 21st floor of Union Square's legendary Sir Francis Drake Hotel, the Starlight Room has all of the requisites for a genuinely memorable night on the town, sumptuous food and drinks with live music all presented in an ultra-swank nightclub setting.

The Starlight Room is the creation of restaurateur Harry Denton and reflects his refinement and zeal for life. Its opulent interior is plush and sophisticated with the look and feel of a 1930's jazz club. With fine linen tablecloths, Versace plateware, deep, velvet booths, imported chandeliers and acres of damask drapes and appointments, the place is an extravaganza for the senses. Even the staff is dressed in formal wear or evening gowns.

The menu features impeccably prepared Continental cuisine, including filet mignon Wellington, foie gras au Torchon, antipasti, salmon encrote and caviar by the ounce. With ready access to fresh seafood, half the menu is devoted to dishes such as Oysters Rockefeller, Clams Casino, pan fried crab cakes, scallops and smoked salmon.

The marble topped bar is long, mirrored and exquisite, an incomparably elegant setting to sip one of the Starlight Room's renowned line of *Million Dollar Cocktails*, libations that cost between $100 and $650. Infinitely more affordable is the bar's signature cocktail, the *Cable Car*. Created by famed mixologist Tony Abou-Ganim, the drink is made with spiced rum, Curaçao and fresh lemon sour mix. Equally delectable is the *Cunningham*, a cocktail based on Johnnie Walker Black Label.

The Starlight — dining and dancing high above the city lights, it doesn't get much more romantic than that. —RP

Cunningham
Located on pg 70

Classic Mojito

Excerpted from the Original Guide to
American Cocktails and Drinks- 6th Edition
Bucket glass, chilled
Build in glass
2 lime wedges
5-6 mint leaves
3/4 oz. fresh lime juice
1/2 oz. simple syrup
Muddle contents
Add ice
2 oz. Light Rum
2-3 splashes club soda
Garnish with a lime wedge
    and fresh mint sprig
Place the lime wedges, mint leaves, lime juice
and simple syrup into the empty, chilled bucket
glass. Muddle and add ice. Pour in the rum
and club soda. Garnish with a lime wedge and
fresh mint sprig.

Mojito, Oyster Restaurant's

Specialty of Oyster Restaurant & Nightclub
Created by Thom Greco
Bucket glass, chilled
Build in glass
6-8 mint leaves
2 lime wedges
1 1/2 oz. mint syrup
Muddle contents
Add ice
1 1/2 oz. Bacardi Limón Rum
Splash club soda
Garnish with a fresh mint sprig
    and lime wedge
Place the mint leaves, lime wedges and mint syrup
into the empty, chilled bucket glass. Muddle and
add ice. Pour in the rum and club soda. Garnish
with a fresh mint sprig and lime wedge.

Old Man and the Sea

Specialty of Cuba Libre Restaurant and Rum Bar
Created by Cuba Libre's staff
Bucket glass, ice
Pour ingredients into an iced mixing glass
1 1/4 oz. Cuba Libre White Rum
3/4 oz. fresh lime juice
3/4 oz. guarapa
Splash grenadine
Shake and strain
Fill with grapefruit juice
Garnish with a lime wedge
Pour the ingredietns, except the juice, into the
iced mixing glass. Shake thoroughly and strain
contents into an iced bucket glass. Fill with
grapefruit juice. Garnish with a lime wedge.

Outrigger

Specialty of Joe's Seafood, Prime Steak & Stone Crab
Created by Dan Barringer
House speciality glass, ice
Pour ingredients into an iced mixing glass
1 oz. Malibu Rum
1 oz. Malibu Mango Rum
Splash orgeat syrup
1/2 oz. Torani Watermelon Syrup
1 oz. fresh orange juice
2 oz. pineapple juice
2 oz. mango nectar
Shake and strain
Garnish with a pineapple wedge
Pour ingredients into the iced mixing glass.
Shake thoroughly and strain contents into
an iced house specialty glass. Garnish with a
pineapple wedge.

Peach Batida

Specialty of Nacional 27
Created by Adam Seger
Rocks glass, chilled
Pour ingredients into a crushed iced mixing glass
1/4 cup diced, cachaça marinated peaches*
1 oz. Cachaça
1/2 oz. DeKuyper Peachtree Schnapps
1/2 oz. fresh lime juice
1/2 oz. simple syrup
Shake thoroughly - do not strain
Pour ingredients into the iced mixing glass.
Shake thoroughly - do not strain - pour contents
into an empty, chilled rocks glass.
*Cachaça Marinated Peaches
Peel and dice fresh peaches
    (1 peach will yield 3 drinks).
Place in a glass jar and cover with cachaça, good
for a week.

Pearl Harbor

Specialty of Indigo Eurasian Cuisine
Created by Jason Castle, Tim Skelton
Cocktail glass, chilled
Pour ingredients into an iced mixing glass
2 oz. SKYY Vodka
2 1/2 oz. Midori
Splash pineapple juice
Shake and strain
Garnish with a cherry in bottom of glass
Pour ingredients into the iced mixing glass.
Shake thoroughly and strain contents into a
chilled cocktail glass. Garnish with a cherry in
the bottom of glass.

Classic Piña Colada

Excerpted from The Original Guide to
American Cocktails and Drinks- 6th Edition
House specialty glass, chilled
Pour ingredients into an iced blender canister
1 oz. Light Rum
3/4 oz. half & half
2 oz. coconut cream syrup
3 oz. pineapple juice
Blend ingredients
Garnish with a
      fresh pineapple wedge
*Pour ingredients into the iced
blender canister. Blend thoroughly
and pour contents into a chilled
house specialty glass. Garnish with a
fresh pineapple wedge.*

Pirates Cove

Specialty of The Mission Inn Hotel & Spa
Created by Elizabeth Skrzynecky
Cocktail glass, chilled
Pour ingredients into an iced blender canister
1 1/4 oz. Captain Morgan's
      Parrot Bay Pineapple Rum
3/4 oz. Bacardi O Rum
1 oz. Coco López Coconut Cream
2 oz. pineapple juice
Blend ingredients
Garnish with orange slice,
      cherry and lime wedge
*Pour ingredients into the iced blender canis-
ter. Blend thoroughly and pour contents into
a chilled cocktail glass. Garnish with an orange
slice, cherry and lime wedge.*

Pomegranate Mojito, Cuba Libre's

Specialty of Cuba Libre Restaurant and Rum Bar
Created by Cuba Libre's staff
House specialty glass, chilled
Pour ingredients into an empty mixing glass
6 mint leaves
 2 oz. guarapa
1 1/4 oz. fresh lime juice
Muddle contents
Add ice
1 1/4 oz. Cuba Libre Spiced Rum
Splash pomegranate juice
Shake thoroughly - do not strain
Splash club soda
Garnish with a lime wedge
*Place the mint, guarapa and lime juice into
the empty mixing glass. Muddle and add ice.
Pour in the rum and pomegranate juice. Shake
thoroughly - do not strain - pour contents into
an empty, chilled house specialty glass. Add a
splash of club soda. Garnish with a lime wedge.*

Pomegranate Mojito, Rickshaw's

Specialty of Rickshaw Far East Bistro & Bambú Lounge
Created by Melvin Espinal
Bucket glass, chilled
Build in glass
6-8 mint leaves
 3 pieces fresh mango
 2 oz. fresh lime juice
 2 oz. simple syrup
Muddle contents
Add ice
3/4 oz. PAMA Pomegranate Liqueur
3/4 oz. 10 Cane Rum
Splash club soda
Garnish with a pomegranate wedge
*Place the mint leaves, mango, lime juice and
simple syrup into the empty, chilled bucket glass.
Muddle and add ice. Pour in the PAMA, rum
and add a splash of club soda. Garnish with a
pomegranate wedge.*

Prickly Pear Mexican Mojito

Specialty of Backstreet Café
Created by Sean Beck
Salt rimmed pilsner glass, chilled
Pour ingredients into an empty mixing glass
6 small cilantro leaves
3/4 oz. simple syrup
3/4 oz. fresh lime juice
Muddle contents
Add ice
1 3/4 oz. El Tesoro Platinum Tequila
1/4 oz. Cointreau
1 1/2 oz. fresh prickly pear juice
Shake thoroughly - do not strain
2 oz. club soda
Garnish with a lime wedge
      and cilantro sprig
*Place the cilantro leaves, simple syrup and lime
juice into the empty mixing glass. Muddle and
add ice. Pour in the remaining ingredients and
shake thoroughly - do not strain - pour contents
into a salt rimmed, empty, chilled pilsner glass.
Add the club soda. Garnish with a lime wedge and
cilantro sprig.*

Raspberry Caipirinha

Specialty of Cuba Libre Restaurant and Rum Bar
Created by Cuba Libre's staff
Bucket glass, chilled
Build in glass
1 lemon wedge
1 lime wedge
Splash fresh lime juice
Splash guarapa
Muddle contents
Add ice
1 1/4 oz. Cachaça
3/4 oz. Three Olives Raspberry Vodka
Stir gently
Place the lemon and lime wedge, lime juice and guarapa into the empty, chilled bucket glass. Muddle and add ice. Pour in the remaining ingredients and stir gently.

Robber Baron

Specialty of The Campbell Apartment
Created by Mark Grossich
Pilsner glass, chilled
Build in glass
8-10 fresh mint leaves
1 oz. fresh lime juice
1 oz. simple syrup
Muddle contents
Add ice
2 oz. Grey Goose Vodka
1/2 oz. Midori
Splash club soda
Garnish with a fresh mint sprig
Place the mint leaves, lime juice and simple syrup into the empty, chilled pilsner glass. Muddle and add ice. Pour in the vodka, Midori and club soda. Garnish with a fresh mint sprig.

Rock 'n' Roll Punch

Specialty of Hard Rock Cafe- New York
Created by Hard Rock Cafe's staff
House specialty glass, ice
Pour ingredients into an iced mixing glass
1 1/2 oz. Captain Morgan Original Spiced Rum
Splash fresh lemon juice
Splash fresh lime juice
3/4 oz. Monin Blood Orange Syrup
2 oz. orange juice
Shake and strain
Top with 1 oz. lemon-lime soda
Float with 1/2 oz. Myers's Original Dark Rum
Garnish with a lemon wedge
Pour ingredients into the iced mixing glass. Shake thoroughly and strain contents into an iced house specialty glass. Top with lemon-lime soda. Float the Myers's Rum. Garnish with a lemon wedge.

Royal Mojito

Specialty of Indigo Eurasian Cuisine
Created by Mary Peter, Jason Castle
Hurricane glass, chilled
Pour ingredients into an empty mixing glass
1/8 cup mint leaves
3/4 oz. fresh lime juice
Dash mint simple syrup
Dash sweet 'n' sour
Dash 7UP
Muddle contents
Add ice
1 1/2 oz. Bacardi Light Rum
1/2 oz. Arrow Triple Sec
Shake thoroughly - do not strain
Fill with Champagne
Garnish with lime wedge
Place the mint, lime juice, simple syrup, sweet 'n' sour and 7UP into the empty mixing glass. Muddle and add ice. Pour in the rum and triple sec. Shake thoroughly - do not strain - pour contents into an empty, chilled hurricane glass and fill with Champagne. Garnish with a lime wedge.

Sandito Mojito

Specialty of Cuba Libre Restaurant and Rum Bar
Created by Cuba Libre's staff
House specialty glass, chilled
Pour ingredients into an empty mixing glass
6 mint leaves
1 1/4 oz. guarapa
1 1/4 oz. fresh watermelon juice
1 1/4 oz. fresh lime juice
Muddle contents
Add ice
1 1/4 oz. Cuba Libre White Rum
Shake thoroughly - do not strain
Splash 7UP
Garnish with a lime wedge
Place the mint leaves, guarapa, watermelon juice and lime juice into the empty mixing glass. Muddle and add ice. Pour in the rum and shake thoroughly - do not strain - pour contents into an empty, chilled house specialty glass. Add a splash of 7UP. Garnish with a lime wedge.

Sangre de Fresa

Specialty of Absinthe Brasserie & Bar
Created by Jeff Hollinger

Pilsner glass, chilled
Pour ingredients into an empty mixing glass
2 fresh strawberries
5 basil leaves
1/2 oz. balsamic simple syrup*
Muddle contents
Add ice
1 1/2 oz. Ypióca Cachaça
1/4 oz. fresh lime juice
Shake thoroughly - do not strain
2 oz. club soda
Garnish with a fresh strawberry
    and basil sprig
Place the strawberries, basil leaves and balsamic syrup into the empty mixing glass. Muddle and add ice. Pour in the cachaça and lime juice. Shake thoroughly - do not strain - pour contents into an empty, chilled pilsner glass. Add the club soda. Garnish with a fresh strawberry and basil sprig.
*Balsamic Simple Syrup
Make simple syrup, substituting half the water in simple syrup for balsamic vinegar.

Sea Side Liberty

Excerpted from The Original Guide to
American Cocktails and Drinks- 6th Edition

House specialty glass, chilled
Pour ingredients into an iced blender canister
1 oz. Mount Gay Eclipse Rum
1 oz. Malibu Rum
3/4 oz. Patrón XO Café Coffee Liqueur
3/4 oz. half & half
1 oz. coconut cream syrup
3 oz. pineapple juice
Blend ingredients
Garnish with a pineapple wedge and cherry
Pour ingredients into the iced blender canister. Blend thoroughly and pour contents into a chilled house specialty glass. Garnish with a pineapple wedge and cherry.

Stramaretto Colada

Excerpted from The Original Guide to
American Cocktails and Drinks- 6th Edition

House specialty glass, chilled
Pour ingredients into an iced blender canister
1 oz. Gold Rum
1 oz. Disaronno Amaretto
1/2 cup strawberries
3/4 oz. half & half
2 oz. coconut cream syrup
3 oz. pineapple juice
Blend ingredients
Float with 3/4 oz. Myers's Original Dark Rum
Garnish with a pineapple wedge
    and strawberry
Pour ingredients into the iced blender canister. Blend thoroughly and pour contents into a chilled house specialty glass. Float the rum. Garnish with a pineapple wedge and strawberry.

Strawberry Rum Rita

Specialty of 33 Restaurant & Lounge
Created by Jenn Harvey

Sugar rimmed bucket glass, chilled
Pour ingredients into an iced mixing glass
1 1/2 oz. 10 Cane Rum
1/2 oz. Marie Brizard Grand Orange
Splash Rose's Lime Juice
1/2 oz. sweetened strawberry puree
Shake and strain
Garnish with a fresh strawberry
Pour ingredients into the iced mixing glass. Shake thoroughly and strain contents into a sugar rimmed, chilled bucket glass. Garnish with a fresh strawberry.

Strawberry Shortcake

Specialty of Indigo Eurasian Cuisine
Created by Tiffany Nauman, Jason Castle

House specialty glass, ice
Pour ingredients into an iced mixing glass
3 oz. Arrow Strawberry Liqueur
1 oz. Stoli Strasberi Vodka
Splash Disaronno Amaretto
Splash coconut syrup
2 oz. pineapple juice
Shake and strain
Garnish with a fresh strawberry
Pour ingredients into the iced mixing glass. Shake thoroughly and strain contents into an iced house specialty glass. Garnish with a fresh strawberry on the rim.

Thai Boxer

Specialty of Cyrus
Created by Scott Beattie
Collins glass, chilled
Pour ingredients into an iced mixing glass
1 1/2 oz. Charbay Tahitian Vanilla Bean Rum
1/2 oz. fresh lime juice
1/2 oz. Thai coconut milk
10-15 cilantro leaves
10-15 spearmint leaves
10-15 Thai basil leaves
Splash simple syrup
Shake thoroughly - do not strain
Fill with Cock 'n Bull Ginger Beer
Stir gently
Garnish with Thai basil sprig
Pour ingredients into the iced mixing glass. Shake thoroughly - do not strain - pour contents into a chilled collins glass. Fill with ginger beer. Stir gently. Garnish with a Thai basil sprig.

Trinidad Beachcomber

Specialty of Nacional 27
Created by Adam Seger
Pint glass, ice
Build in glass
1 oz. 10 Cane Rum
1 oz. Sweet Vermouth
1/2 oz. Grand Marnier
1/4 oz. Luxardo Maraschino Liqueur
Dash Angostura Aromatic Bitters
1/2 oz. simple syrup
1 oz. fresh lime juice
Top with club soda
Stir gently
Garnish with a skewer of fresh fruits,
    sprig of mint and straw, with an umbrella
Pour ingredients into the iced pint glass in the order listed. Stir gently. Garnish with a skewer of fresh fruit, mint sprig and long straw, with an umbrella.
NOTE: Skewer of fresh fruit options: pineapple, mango and/or strawberry, orange, lemon, lime and cherry

Tropical

Specialty of 33 Restaurant & Lounge
Created by Ari Bialikamien
Wine glass, chilled
Pour ingredients into an iced mixing glass
2 oz. Bacardi Cóco Rum
1 oz. Marie Brizard Mango Liqueur
1/2 oz. Rose's Lime Juice
1 oz. mango puree
Shake thoroughly - do not strain
Garnish with an orange slice
Pour ingredients into the iced mixing glass. Shake thoroughly - do not strain - pour contents into an empty, chilled wine glass. Garnish with an orange slice.

Tropical Splendor

Specialty of Indigo Eurasian Cuisine
Created by Tim Skelton, Jason Castle
Cocktail glass, chilled
Pour ingredients into an iced mixing glass
2 oz. Malibu Rum
2 oz Banana Liqueur
2 oz. pineapple juice
Shake and strain
Garnish with a skewered pineapple cube
Pour ingredients into the iced mixing glass. Shake thoroughly and strain contents into a chilled cocktail glass. Garnish with a skewered pineapple cube.

The Uptowner

Specialty of Bar Masa
Created by Mike Vacheresse
Cocktail glass, chilled
Pour ingredients into an iced mixing glass
2 oz. 10 Cane Rum
1/2 oz. fresh lime juice
1 oz. Brugal/pineapple simple syrup*
Shake and strain
Pour ingredients into the iced mixing glass. Shake thoroughly and strain contents into a chilled cocktail glass.
*Brugal/Pineapple Simple
    Syrup Recipe - pg 318

Ibiza Dinner Club

528 Second Ave
Seattle, WA 98104
☎ 206.381.9090
▶▶ www.ibizadinnerclub.com
✉ info@ibizadinnerclub.com

Ibiza Dinner Club is a glimpse into the beautiful life, which is a few hefty notches above the good life. The opulent, ultra-swank restaurant is appropriately named after the Spanish Island of Ibiza (Eivissa), an island off the coast of Spain and renowned as Europe's playground. The glamorous Seattle hotspot is in vogue even when closed.

Taking a deep breath before entering Ibiza is advisable. The expansive interior creates a posh and elegant ambience with enormous mirrors, gauzy, high-backed, upholstered banquettes and metal mesh curtain dividers throughout. The high ceilings accommodate a spacious loft and V.I.P. lounge complete with plush

couches and ottomans. The grandeur and scale are palatial. In the center of the action is the bar with its focal point being the towering cylindrical back bar.

The Spanish Mediterranean cuisine is delectable and reasonably priced. The specialty of the house, or one of them, is certainly tapas, such as Tortilla Espinaca and Mushrooms al Ajillo. The menu also features pan seared Chilean Sea Bass, Muscovy duck and foie gras, mango-glazed Ahi, Ceviche Clásico, rack of lamb and Cabrales beef tenderloin skewers. The food is skillfully prepared and exquisitely presented. Leave room for dessert. Popular favorites include the rum flambéed strawberries and crisp pastry fritters called Buñuelos, which are filled with semisweet chocolate and drizzled with vanilla syrup.

The bar offers a long list of well-conceived and executed specialty cocktails, including the *Ibiza White Cosmo*, a luscious combination of Chopin Vodka, Cointreau, white cranberry juice and muddled limes, and *Chocolate Kiss*, a blend of Godiva White and Chocolate Liqueurs, vanilla vodka and Frangelico.

Ibiza Dinner Club is utterly sensational. While the bill of fare is impressively sublime, the added attractions of passion and fashion greatly heighten the experience. —RP

Chocolate Kiss
Located on pg 281

Watermelon Mojito, Carnegie Club's

Specialty of The Carnegie Club
Created by Dawn Durham
Rocks glass, chilled
Pour ingredients into an empty mixing glass
6-8 fresh mint sprigs
1 oz. fresh lime juice
Muddle contents
Add ice
1 1/2 oz. Ketel One Vodka
2 1/2 oz. Marie Brizard Watermelon Liqueur
Shake thoroughly - do not strain
Top with club soda
Garnish with a fresh mint sprig
Place the mint sprigs and lime juice into the empty mixing glass. Muddle and add ice. Pour in the remaining ingredients. Shake thoroughly - do not strain - pour contents into an empty, chilled rocks glass. Top with club soda. Garnish with a fresh mint sprig.

Yerba Buena

Specialty of Tommy's Mexican Restaurant
Created by Jacques Bezuidenhout
Bucket glass, chilled
Build in glass
8-10 mint leaves
1 oz. fresh lime juice
1/2 oz. falernum
Muddle contents
Add ice
2 oz. Corazón Tequila Blanco
Stir gently
Top with Stewart's Ginger Beer
Garnish with a lime wedge and fresh mint sprig
Place the mint leaves, lime juice and falernum into the empty, chilled bucket glass. Muddle and add ice. Pour in the tequila and stir gently. Top with ginger beer. Garnish with a lime wedge and fresh mint sprig.

Watermelon Mojito, Oyster Restaurant's

Specialty of Oyster Restaurant & Nightclub
Created by Thom Greco
House specialty glass, chilled
Build in glass
6 mint leaves
1 lime wedge
3/4 oz. mint simple syrup
Muddle contents
Add ice
1 1/2 oz. Bacardi Grand Melon Rum
3/4 oz. fresh watermelon juice
Top with club soda
Garnish with a fresh mint sprig
    and watermelon wedge
Place the mint leaves, lime wedge and mint syrup into the empty glass. Muddle and add ice. Pour in the rum, watermelon juice and club soda. Garnish with a fresh mint sprig and watermelon wedge.

Chapter Six

20th Century Mixology
Neo–Classic Cocktails

Can you imagine being at a party with Houdini? His death notwithstanding, it would be a blast to be in the same room with the guy. Guaranteed it would be the same watching Professor Jerry Thomas in action behind a bar. Magicians both. Jerry Thomas was our country's most renowned bartender, and although he died in 1870, he is widely recognized as the father of 20th Century mixology.

A tall, strapping young man with engaging looks and cat-like grace, Thomas, it's said, enthralled all those who visited his bars. His roster of establishments included such prestigious venues as the Metropolitan Hotel in New York, Planter's House in St. Louis and the El Dorado Resort in San Francisco. He was the master of his craft, part performer, part tactician, and part entrepreneur. Over the span of his career his standard of excellence inspired many to the upper echelons of the profession and gave rise to the title of principal bartender.

Thomas will best be remembered, however, as the author of the first authoritative guide on making drinks. First published in the 1860s, *The Bon Vivant's Companion* described in detail a rarefied group of 600 cocktails spanning the entire breadth of mixology. More significantly, he used the book to circumscribe the new world of mixology, the substance and intricacies of which had not previously been committed to print.

Thomas was a sensation, a national personage sought out by dignitaries and captains of industry. What's interesting is that while Jerry Thomas was a master showman behind the bar, it was his total and absolute command of the cocktail that attracted a steady stream of distinguished and well-heeled clientele. His repertoire made every bar he tended a destination venue.

Lessons Learned in the 20th Century

There's nothing dated or out of style about the classic cocktails of the 20th century. These drinks have timeless themes and rely on formulations that are every bit as relevant today as they were when first conceived. If you learn to appreciate these basic relationships, then there's no limit on what they can create behind the bar.

Perhaps the best working definition of these cocktails comes from *The Fine Art of Mixing Drinks* (Doubleday 1948), a seminal work written by the professor emeritus of mixology, David Embury. A cocktail, he explained, "must whet the appetite and stimulate the mind. It must always be constructed of the highest quality ingredients, be pleasing to the palate, and yet not so sour, bitter or aromatic as to be unpalatable." Solid advice.

Emburys further specified that "cocktails must delight the eye…have sufficient alcohol to be readily identifiable from papaya juice…and be served thoroughly chilled. The spirit base of a cocktail must consist 50% or more of the volume of the cocktail, never less. The spirit used is the distinguishing ingredient in the drink."

According to Embury, a cocktail must also include two other elements. The first is a modifier, which transforms the base spirit into a homogenized cocktail. These modifiers are typically aperitif wines, bitters, syrups, or a combination of fruit juices. Lastly, a classic cocktail must include a special flavoring agent, which most frequently means the addition of a liqueur or cordial.

All of these cocktail lessons are ably demonstrated by five classic drinks born and raised in the 20th century.

Secrets Revealed of America's Greatest Sidecars

From Main Street to Wall Street, people are rediscovering the unsurpassed character of brandy. Not surprisingly, this renaissance was not born with a snifter in its hand. Instead, the birth of this megatrend came about from people exploring brandy's creative range and limitless mixability.

Bafferts®Mint Gin

In all the gin joints in all the world, how could no one have thought of this before? Infusing a premium gin with the fantastically refreshing character of mint is seemingly as obvious as pairing tequila with lime. There is a natural synergy between the two. This will become evident immediately after opening a bottle of *Bafferts Mint Gin*.

Bafferts Mint is the creation of Hayman Distillers of London. It is crafted using a base of premium, column-distilled grain spirits. During the final distillation, the gin is infused with a mixture of aromatics and botanicals, including all-important essence of fresh mint. It is bottled at 80-proof.

Bafferts Mint is a luscious spirit that effectively seduces the senses. The gin has a generous bouquet that fills the glass with the delicate aromas of mint and citrus zest. Its supple, medium-weight body delivers a layered palate of satisfying, mouth filling flavors. The finish is long, smooth and delectable, one completely without peer.

Aficionados of great tasting light spirits are undoubtedly already familiar with *Bafferts Gin*, a spry, marvelously twisted gin with a unique outlook on life. Instead of looking to wow the senses with a voluminous bouquet and energized palate, the maker's of this delightful gin took an altogether different approach.

The proprietary recipe calls for fewer botanicals than any other premium gin. Therein lies the twist. Bafferts is a light, delicately flavored spirit that makes it a gin even vodka lovers will enjoy.

Brandy is unique within the spirit world. While most types of liquors — vodka, gin and whiskeys — are distilled using cereal grains, brandy is made from grapes. It is essentially wine that is distilled rather than going through the winemaking process. In fact, brandy is a derivative of the German word meaning "burnt wine." As a result, brandy has an incomparably fresh and vibrant flavor. Its personality and character is so universally appealing that it has the rare ability to complement a huge range of other flavors.

When it comes to mixability, brandy is a top performer behind the bar. It creates a foundation with an alluring bouquet and exuberant, fruit-induced flavor. Add a modifier or two and you've got the makings of something truly spectacular. The epitome of all brandy drinks is the venerable *Sidecar*.

This sophisticated cocktail originated in Paris at Harry's New York Bar during the First World War purportedly by an American Army captain. Stories vary regarding the exact circumstances, but all include references to a motorcycle sidecar. In one such account, the captain actually drove his motorcycle into the bar.

The one constant between all of the versions is the principal recipe, which is two parts brandy, one part Cointreau and three parts lemon juice. The drink is shaken with ice and served in a chilled cocktail glass rimmed with sugar.

Smooth and delicious, the Sidecar is a classic cocktail of the 20th century. While an uncomplicated concoction, the drink has many creative possibilities. Here are the best kept secrets behind America's greatest Sidecars.

• **Brandy Selection** — Brandies come in a wide variety of styles. They are made in every wine-producing nation and have as many different looks and personalities as the United Nations. One thing is for certain, the better the brandy, the better the Sidecar.

The upper echelon of the category is reserved for the brandies of Cognac. Their lineage and uncompromised quality have earned them their lofty status among the community of spirits. It is also a highly mixable spirit, and no better cocktail exists for promoting the incomparable characteristics of cognac than the Sidecar.

Cognac houses produce a variety of different grades of cognac, many with the accepted designations — e.g. VS, VSOP, XO Cognac labels bear no age statements. Typically, however, brandies carrying a VS designation have been aged between 4 and 7 years. VSOP cognacs usually have been aged for 5 to 13 years, while XO, Extra, Napoleon, Vielle Reserve or Hors d'Age cognacs range in age from 7 to 40 years. These enormous age spreads account for much of the individuality and distinctions between cognac houses.

For making cocktails, selecting a VS cognac is more than adequate. They typically possess vibrant personalities that are tempered when mixed. As you progress higher up the cognac designations, the more aging the brandy has received the more mellow and refined the cognac. At Courtright's Restaurant, for example, the **Bentley Sidecar** is prepared with the ultra-luxurious Hennessy X.O. As might be expected, the resulting cocktail is sensational.

Many a Sidecar, however, is prepared with a premium brandy other than cognac. Options include Armagnac and Calvados, an alembic distilled apple brandy produced in Normandy. Eaux de vie, such as Poire William and Kirsch, are clear distillates of fruit or grape wine. These brandies are typically rested in glass vessels, which preserve the clarity of the brandy and leave it dry and flavorful.

A popular specialty at upscale 33 Restaurant in Boston is the **Poire Sidecar**, a cocktail made with Marie Brizard Poire William and muddled Bartlett pears. *The Original* McCormick & Schmick's features a delicious version of the cocktail dubbed the **Portland Street Car**. It's made with Oregon pear brandy produced at Clear Creek Distillery in Portland.

American brandies are made in every wine-producing region of the United States, most notably New York, Washington, Oregon and California. Particularly noteworthy are the critically acclaimed brandies of Germain-Robin and Jepson Winery in Ukiah, California. Equipped with copper alembic stills, they are handcrafting brandies from premium grape varietals, such as Pinot Noir, Zinfandel and French Columbard.

Cruzan® Coconut Rum

To be considered a cocktail friendly spirit, a brand needs to have brilliant flavor and an immediately engaging aroma. Just like anything else — some have it and others don't. At the front of the "got it" class is *Cruzan Coconut Rum*.

Made in St. Croix in the U.S. Virgin Islands, Cruzan is world renown for making some of the finest rums that can be served in a glass. Among their newest flavors, Cruzan Coconut is is produced from a blend of triple-distilled rums aged in oak bourbon barrels between 2 and 3 years. After aging, the rum is filtered through activated charcoal to remove impurities and any color. Natural coconut flavorings are added to create the finished product. It is bottled at 55-proof.

Cruzan Coconut Rum is a genuine treat. It has a lightweight, lushly textured body with a prominent coconut bouquet and a touch of natural fruit sweetness in the finish. Everything about this flavored gem screams of fun cocktails, which clearly is why it was created. Because of its relatively low proof, the rum's flavors stay on one's palate for a considerably long time. This persistence makes them ideal for drink making.

If it's true that variety is the spice of life, then the estate's entire portfolio range of cocktail friendly rums will be jazzing things up for years to come. The other flavored rums in the range include *Cruzan Mango*, *Cruzan Banana*, *Cruzan Pineapple*, *Cruzan Orange*, *Cruzan Vanilla* and the dry and tangy *Cruzan Citrus Rum*.

These Californian artisan brandies are ideally suited for use in an ultra-premium Sidecar.

• **Spirit Options** — As great as this cocktail is, the creative urge to tweak and tinker should not be suppressed. A brilliant variation of the Sidecar is obtained substituting brandy with Metaxa 7-Star. It's an elegant Greek spirit made from double-distilled brandy that's infused with aged Muscat wine and a secret botanical mix. The Metaxa melds seamlessly with the Cointreau and fresh lemon sour mix.

Another direction to steer a Sidecar is making the drink with whiskey instead of brandy. Bourbon, Rye, Irish, Scotch and Canadian are completely comfortable paired with Cointreau and mixed with a fresh lemon sour mix. Thus the universal appeal of the Whiskey Stone Sour. No worries if a particular whiskey is finished in port pipes, sherry butts, bourbon barrels, or even Madeira casks, the major components of a Sidecar adapts to them all.

One would be remiss if an aged rum wasn't seriously considered for the leading role in a Sidecar. It's a dynamic way to introduce people to the refined character and lavish flavors of such heavyweights as Mount Gay Extra Old, Rhum Barbancourt Estate Réserve, Rhum Clément VSOP, Pyrat XO, or Zaya Gran Reserva.

• **Creative Modifiers** — Many a Sidecar is made using triple sec instead of premium Cointreau. The obvious explanation is that triple sec is relatively inexpensive. As mentioned in the Margarita chapter, there is a wide range in quality between the various brands of triple sec, so use the best quality available. The difference will be appreciated in the resulting Sidecar. A side by side comparison of the body, bouquet and palate between a quality triple sec and Cointreau is a mismatch. The same holds true for Sidecars made with one versus the other.

Relying on the creative talents of Grand Marnier and Italian GranGala in a specialty Sidecar is a strong creative move however. Both add the robust and complementary flavors of aged brandy and orange citrus to the cocktail.

There are also other liqueurs well suited for use in Sidecars. The *Autumn Sidecar* is prepared with equal parts of Tuaca and Frangelico, while the *Sidecar Royale* is made with VS Cognac, Cointreau and a splash of Benedictine. The soul satisfying *Amber Sidecar* is a signature cocktail at 33 Restaurant. Instead of brandy the drink is concocted with two ounces of Amber, a sublime malt Scotch liqueur made by Macallan and a shot of Cointreau. In lieu of the sweet 'n' sour, the esteemed bar staff muddles limes, lemons and oranges and uses the juice as the base.

• **Fresh Lemon Sour Mix** — As is often done, it is a misnomer to call the Sidecar a "brandy Margarita." While true that both cocktails are made with Cointreau or triple sec, the underlying foundation of the Margarita is lime juice, the Sidecar is lemon. On the other hand, one significant similarity between the two cocktails is that they both taste better when concocted with a fresh sour mix.

The ultimate objective behind creating scratch sweet 'n' sour is to attain a proportion of fresh lemon juice to simple syrup such that it is just slightly tart. Most scratch recipes call for 3 parts lemon juice to 1 part of simple syrup (3:1). If early attempts are too tart, add a higher proportion of simple syrup. If the mix is moderately sweet, like lemonade, increase the proportion of lemon juice.

• **Adding Pizzazz** — The Sidecar is traditionally presented in a sugar-rimmed glass. There are a number of different ways to adhere the sugar, the most frequent of which is to wet the rim of the glass with water and gently dip it into a saucer of granulated sugar. Substitute grenadine for the water and the sugar rim will turn red. Dipping the glass into any variety of juices to produce sugar rims with different flavors and color. A number of purveyors also market sugars (and salts) in a wide array of colors and flavors just for this very purpose.

One final thought regarding adding sugar to the rim of a cocktail glass. Often the wisest course of action is coating only half of the rim instead of its entirety. That offers the recipient the choice of whether to sip the Sidecar with or without an added blast of sugar.

Secrets Revealed of America's Greatest White Russians

The **White Russian** is an unpretentious, straightforward combination of vodka, cream, Kahlúa and ice. Born in the early 1970s, the largely unheralded rocks drink has spawned an amazing number of highly successful progeny, and as such, it now represents a substantial branch of American mixology.

The White Russian's appeal is timeless. Vodka over ice is clean and versatile. Add in the coffee liqueur and cream, it's like drinking an iced coffee with a wee bit more gusto. The caffeinated treat is just as tempting at the start of ones night as it is at the end. There is beauty and grace in simplicity and the most beautiful and graceful of all simple concoctions is the White Russian.

As is the case with most legendary figures, the White Russian comes from noble stock. The drink is the product of the marriage of two equally successful drinks. The **Sombrero** is simply Kahlúa and cream, which is as natural of a combination as adding cream to your morning cup of coffee. It's even a pleasure watching the two ingredients swirl together and slowly transform into one unbeatable taste experience. The other parent is the

Indigo Eurasian Cuisine

📫 1121 Nuuanu Ave.
   Honolulu, HI 96817
☎ 808.521.2900
▶▶ www.indigo-hawaii.com
✉ indigo@cchono.com

One could argue that the most appropriate setting in which to enjoy a sumptuous, expertly prepared dinner is in the heart of paradise. Located in the middle of the Pacific Ocean, the island of Oahu is Eden-esque and the home of **Indigo Eurasian Cuisine**, which consistently ranks among Honolulu's most acclaimed and romantic restaurants.

Indigo is most deserving of its "must see" status. The interior is an aesthetic blend of Moroccan and Asian design. The entry is a narrow brick walkway with large Oriental lanterns lighting the way. The dining room is romantically lit and features linen draped, rattan and bamboo tables and lush, tropical plants. The focal point of the room is a pocket lagoon with a gently cascading waterfall.

Indigo is the brainchild of Chef Glenn Chu, whose vision was to open a restaurant that featured world-class, "East meets West" Eurasian cuisine. The restaurant's popular small dishes allow guests to sample numerous examples of the chef's artistry in one sitting. Included on the expansive menu are such offerings as Miso Marinated Salmon Filet, Black Pepper Encrusted Ahi Steak, Lobster Potstickers and Shanghai Mahogany Duck.

As the evening grows late, the energy level in the restaurant steadily grows as theatergoers and twentysomethings begin pouring into the Indigo's Green Room and the Opium Den & Champagne Bar. The irresistible draws are live jazz, reggae and hip-hop, as well as the bar's amazing collection of tropical-inspired libations. Among the specialties of the house are the *Mandarin Blossom Cosmopolitan*, a sublime cocktail made with Hangar One Mandarin Blossom Vodka, and the *Lychee Martini*, a drink concocted using SKYY Vodka and lychee juice. Paradise never tasted so good.—RP

Mandarin Blossom Cosmopolitan
Located on pg 98

Black Russian, one of the basic building blocks in mixology. While only vodka with an added dose of Kahlúa, the drink is delectable in its simplicity. Combine the two drinks and you've created a legend.

The White Russian is indeed one of the classic drinks to come out of the 20th century. Its ability to creatively inspire is prodigious. Here are the best kept secrets behind America's greatest White Russians.

• **Spirits World** — When it comes to Black and White Russians, almost every type of spirit works. For example, substituting the vodka in a Black Russian with tequila creates a ***Brave Bull***. Add cream to a Brave Bull to make a ***White Bull***. The combination of brandy and Kahlúa is called a ***Dirty Mother*** and splashing in a spot of cream changes it into a ***Dirty White Mother***. Both of the Russians can also be made with light, dark or spiced rum, as well as Irish, Canadian, Bourbon and many types of Scotch whiskeys.

With the finest flavored vodkas at your beck and call, consider making a specialty White Russian using a flavored vodka as the base. Two popular examples are the ***Raspberry White Russian***, which is made with Stoli Razberi, Kahlúa and cream, and the ***Vanilla White Russian***, which is prepared with Absolut Vanilia. In addition, the model works for

Corazón Tequila® de Agave Reposado

One would expect that people in Mexico know a thing or two about tequila. Reposados are the bestselling type of tequila in its country of origin, possibly because they strike a balance between the fresh exuberance of a silver tequila and the mellow refinement of an añejo. Few demonstrate this balancing act as masterfully as ***Corazón Tequila de Agave Reposado***.

Distilled high in the Arandas Mountains, Corazón tequilas are entirely handcrafted at the Destiladora San Nicholas Estate. The 100% agave tequilas are made using traditional, century old methods abandoned by most as cost prohibitive.

Corazón Tequila fully deserves the critical acclaim it is receiving. The 80-proof range of tequilas is made from mature, estate grown agaves. After harvesting, the agaves are baked in stainless steel ovens, slowly fermented and double-distilled in the estate's stainless steel pot stills.

Corazón Tequila Reposado is a supremely enjoyable spirit. It is matured in small, American oak barrels for a minimum of 6 months, which is a sufficient amount of time to soften its character, while leaving the inherent quality of the agave unaffected by the tannins in the wood.

The reposado has a light-weight body and a generous vanilla and floral bouquet. Its mouth filling palate features an array of spicy, slightly peppery flavors that last long into the relaxed finish.

chocolate flavored vodkas, coffee, espresso, pineapple, pomegranate, coconut, mango and orange vodkas to name but a few. Essentially, any flavor that complements the taste of coffee and cream will work in a Russian.

• **Java Liqueurs** — Look under the hood of most White Russians and you'll find they contain Kahlúa, which is by far the bestselling coffee liqueur in the world. The liqueur is produced in Mexico from a base of distilled sugar cane that is steeped with vanilla beans and mountain-grown coffee.

Now in the 21st century, however, there are other coffee liqueur options available with which to construct fabulous Russians. One such welcome addition to the back bar is super-premium Starbucks Coffee Liqueur. It is made with a light, sugar-based spirit that is infused with the company's famed blend of high-grade, Arabica coffee beans. It has the rich, inviting look of espresso and an alluring bouquet of ground coffee. It is drier than the competition and has a delectable "fresh brewed" personality.

Patrón XO Café Coffee Liqueur is another "right product at the right time." Imported by the same folks who make Patrón Tequila, XO Café is made in Mexico from aged añejo tequila and the pure, natural essence of coffee. The liqueur is crafted with a minimal amount of sweetener, which makes it drier and more of a coffee-flavored tequila than a typical liqueur. The marriage of tequila and coffee works beautifully, making Patrón XO Café a superb ingredient for use in White Russians.

Tia Maria is a delicious coffee liqueur from Jamaica. It's made from a blend of premium, aged rums that have been steeped with chocolate and Blue Mountain coffee beans, which are the most expensive and highly sought after coffee beans in the world. The somewhat dry, robust palate of coffee, rum and chocolate flavors make it ideally suited for any Russian-based assignment.

• **Dairy State** — The final act in a White Russian is the splash of cream. Some bartenders use whatever creamer is readily available, such as half & half. In fact, the last ingredient can be milk, chocolate milk, half & half, or heavy cream. The decision which to use is an individual one. For the record, a White Russian finished off with skim milk is referred to as a Skinny Russian. On the other end of the spectrum, you can use melted ice cream in lieu of the milk for a calorie-laden quaff.

Other options do exist, beginning with using a cream liqueur instead of half & half cream. There are numerous brands from which to choose, including Baileys, Carolans, Starbucks, Amarula and Tequila Rose Java. Each will enhance the drink in its own singular way.

• **Modifier Options** — The White Russian is a marvelously versatile drink to experiment with. It adapts especially well to being modified with liqueurs. Imagine splashing in some Chambord atop a White Russian. Chambord's luxurious raspberry flavor is a near perfect complement to the Russian's coffee and cream taste profile.

The same is true for Frangelico, Disaronno Amaretto, Agavero, Irish Mist and Celtic Crossing. For an added dose of vim and vigor consider adding Jägermeister, Goldschläger or Yukon Jack into the mix.

Another option is to change how the drink is formulated. For example, serve the White Russian in a tall glass and add some cola to make the *Colorado Bulldog*. Back off the vodka and you've created a *Smith & Wesson*, or if you'd prefer, substitute club soda for the cola and the drink becomes a *Smith & Kerns*.

It's hard to conceive of a drink with as many creative permutations as the White Russian.

Secrets Revealed of America's Greatest Long Islands

On a space-time continuum, the *Long Island Iced Tea* falls somewhere between the *Harvey Wallbanger* and *Silk Panties*. The tall, sublime concoction originated in the late 1970s at the Oak Beach Inn in Babylon, Long Island. The drink's construction is so unique that its creator, bartender Robert Bott, should be knighted and made to do something with the ozone layer. It takes a peculiarly bent mind to even contemplate

Tequila Espolon® Añejo 100% Agave

In 1996, the first stones were laid in the construction of Destiladora San Nicholas on the rich volcanic soil of Arandas, Mexico. More than a decade later, the relatively young distillery is producing *Tequila Espolon Añejo 100% Agave* , one of a new breed of super-premium brands that derives its lush and seductive character through state of the art production techniques.

The distillery begins the production process with mature agaves grown in the red soil and high altitudes of the Los Altos Mountains. Autoclaves are used to steam bake the harvested agaves before going through a thresher and being milled to express the precious agave juice.

Distillation takes place in technologically advanced column stills. The Espolon range of aged tequilas are matured in Canadian white oak barrels and bottled at 80-proof.

Tequila Espolon Añejo is a top-notch contender, a tequila of substance and style. Its crystal clarity and deep golden color combine for a striking appearance. The tequila is marvelously aromatic with luscious notes of vanilla beans and warm butterscotch. Its soft, round body delivers a spicy, mouth filling palate, followed by a long, warming and semisweet finish. The longer the añejo is left to breathe in the glass, the more of its personality shines through.

The distillery's range of 100% agave tequilas also includes the unaged *Tequila Espolon Silver 100% Agave*, a lively blanco with loads of spicy, peppery, fruit flavor, and *Tequila Espolon Reposado 100% Agave*, which is aged in new oak barrels for six months. It's a refined spirit with a focused bouquet and palate.

combining four light liquors in one glass, no less proceed and make the combination work so well.

In addition to having one of the longest drink names in the business, the Long Island Iced Tea is an inexplicably brilliant creation. Anyone who tells you that they've fathomed why the drink tastes like iced tea is, well, lying. The drink is concocted with half an ounce of gin, vodka, light rum, tequila and triple sec, two ounces of sweet 'n' sour and roughly the same amount of cola. The ingredients are then shaken, which thoroughly mixes the ingredients and dissipates the carbonation from the cola. The drink is served in a tall iced glass with a lemon wedge garnish.

When made properly, the Long Island Iced Tea should taste nearly identical to its brewed, alcohol-free counterpart, with one, not so minor exception; it packs a bona fide wallop. The drink in all of its guises is a tailor-made heat buster, a perfect elixir for the dog days of summer. One note of caution, these drinks are potent. Their effect is markedly increased in the summer heat with the sun pounding down. Long Island Iced Teas and UV rays, they're great when taken in moderation.

Potency notwithstanding, the Long Island Iced Tea is one of the great mixed drinks to emerge from the 20th century. The libation has given flight to a score of creative variations and remains enormously popular, just ask Marge Simpson, one of the drink's legions of devoted followers. Here are the best kept secrets behind America's greatest Long Island Iced Teas.

• **Spirited Formulations** — Because of the large number of ingredients used, many a bar serves their guests Long Islands prepared with inexpensive brands of liquor. While it might make sense from a cost standpoint, it's a mistake from a mixology perspective. As stated, no one really understands why the recipe works, no less works well. Clearly keeping all of the liquor in balance is crucial. The best course of action therefore is to make the drink with quality brands and eliminate the chances of an inferior product disturbing the drink's inner workings.

There are always an adventurous few who don't except boundaries, or the status quo. In their pursuit for the perfect Long Island, an impressive number of creation variations have slipped into the mainstream that call for a different blend of spirits. For example, Hard Rock Cafe popularized a spin-off called the **Manhattan Iced Tea**. It's concocted with gin, vodka, light rum, cola and a float of bourbon. Another is the *Havana Iced Tea*, which features equal parts of light and gold rums, brandy and triple sec.

Then there's the unlimited potential of devising a Long Island with no other types of liquor than flavored rums and flavored vodkas. The possibilities are staggering.

• **Liqueur Essentials** — While its unusual assortment of spirits tends to grab most of the attention, let's not lose sight of the role triple sec has played in the drink's phenomenal success. The liqueur adds body, flavor and sweetness, all things that contribute to the overall effect.

The admonition about only using quality brands in Long Islands also holds true for the triple sec. That having been said, there is no finer Curaçao liqueur than Cointreau. Not surprisingly, the most immediate improvement one can make to their Long Islands is to reach for the top-shelf and make the drink with the good stuff.

A variation on the theme is to craft specialty Long Islands with Grand Marnier, or GranGala as the modifier. They bring a great deal of character to the equation, namely a vibrant palate of orange and brandy flavors. Blue Curaçao makes an excellent substitute for the triple sec as well.

Another lesson learned along the way is that Long Islands taste great modified with liqueurs. Popular examples include the *Green Tea Iced Tea*, which is made with an added float of Midori, the *Italian Iced Tea* is topped off with Disaronno Amaretto and *Raspberry Iced Tea* gets a float of Chambord. Each is thoroughly delicious and satisfying.

• **Modifying the Mix** — Long Islands are made with a base of sweetened lemon juice and cola. Change the composition of that base mix and you'll alter the flavor of the finished drink. For instance, if you use equal parts of cranberry juice and fresh lemon sour mix the drink is converted into the *Long Beach Iced Tea*. The *Florida Iced Tea* is made with the addition of orange juice, the *Hawaiian Iced Tea* is prepared with pineapple juice. The *Bimini Iced Tea* is made with Blue Curaçao, orange juice and pineapple juice, while the *Californian Iced Tea* is made with all premium spirits and added grapefruit juice.

As you might expect, there are several creative variations that call for iced tea in their recipes. Preparing the drink using equal parts of fresh lemon sour mix and iced tea is called the *Plantation Iced Tea*. Substitute citrus flavored vodka to make the *Veranda Iced Tea*.

The cola provides the drink with color and flavor, but several contemporary variations of the Long Island have replaced with the cola with other types of mixers. Two such examples are the *Miami Iced Tea*, made with vodka, rum,

Jade Bar

5700 East McDonald Dr.
Paradise Valley, AZ 85253

☎ 480.948.2100

▶▶ www.sanctuaryoncamelback.com/
content/jadebar.html

✉ info@sanctuaryaz.com

Sanctuary on Camelback Mountain is a luxury resort and spa situated on the northern slope of Camelback Mountain in Paradise Valley, an upscale community wedged between Phoenix and Scottsdale. The resort is frequented by a discerning, well-heeled clientele seeking first class treatment in a spectacular setting. Located on the resort grounds is the impeccably stylish **Jade Bar** and Elements Restaurant.

Award-winning Elements Restaurant is both intimate and elegant and offers guests exquisite American cuisine with Asian accents. Its window-encased interior is tasteful, yet understated with muted colors, sleek lines, private booths and a community table crafted with African woods. The vistas of the nearby mountains and the valley below provide a breathtaking backdrop.

The cuisine is the creation of celebrated Executive Chef Beau MacMillan. The restaurant's menu changes with the seasons and features beautifully presented dishes such as Crab and Spinach Fondue, Maine Lobster "Pot Pie," Clear Gazpacho Gelée and Wasabi Caviar, Spiced Venison Loin, Olive Oil Poached Albacore and Ginger Pork Tenderloin.

Located adjacent to the restaurant is the equally spectacular Jade Bar. A popular haunt with the upwardly mobile set, the Jade Bar has a secluded patio, incomparable views and a long curved bar with a glass and exotic wood top. The bar's cocktail lineup is impressive and cutting edge. Among their renowned cocktails are the *271 Special*, an ultra-premium Margarita made with Herradura Selección Suprema and Grand Marnier Cuvée du Centenaire, the *Asian Pear and Ginger Martini*, a delicate cocktail concocted with Ketel One Citroen, apple and peach schnapps and ginger-flavored simple syrup, and the immensely refreshing *Hibiscus Spiced Tea*, a blend of Hangar One Kaffir Lime Vodka, ginger simple syrup and Hibiscus tea. —RP

Hibiscus Spiced Tea
Located on pg 218

tequila, peach schnapps and equal parts of cranberry juice and lemon-lime soda, and the **Electric Iced Tea**, a specialty at Hard Rock Cafe prepared with Smirnoff Vodka, Beefeater Gin, Bacardi Rum, Blue Curaçao and lemon-lime soda.

The last piece of advice about Long Islands is to use a quality sweet 'n' sour, or better yet, use fresh lemon juice and sweeten it with simple syrup. The natural presumption is that with all of the ingredients in the drink, one won't be able to discern the quality of the base mix. Not so. Rely solely on quality products and you won't be disappointed in the results.

Secrets Revealed of America's Greatest Lemon Drops

The fourth sterling example of cocktail greatness from the 20th century is the **Lemon Drop**. It purportedly originated at a Henry Africa's in San Francisco in the early 1990s. In a time when drinks leaned toward the sweet end of the spectrum, this exceptionally light and refreshingly tart cocktail bucked the trend.

The Lemon Drop is a cocktail made with citrus-infused vodka, simple syrup and fresh lemon juice. The ingredients are shaken vigorously and served in a chilled cocktail glass. The interactive nature of the original garnish likely fueled the Lemon Drop's tremendous popularity. It was a sugarcoated lemon wedge and the ritual was after

Agavero® Tequila Liqueur

Tequila has captured the collective imagination of Americans. For the past 20 years, it has been a headliner in the popular scene. Now the robust and exotic flavor of tequila has been captured in **Agavero Tequila Liqueur**.

It's made with a proprietary blend of a barrel aged reserve tequila, a reposado and a 2-year old añejo. The secret ingredient in Agavero's well-guarded recipe is a unique tea brewed from the Damiana flower, which is an aromatic flower indigenous to the mountains of Jalisco. It is a revered plant in Mexico and is purported to be an aphrodisiac. It is bottled at 64-proof.

You have to taste Agavero Tequila Liqueur to fully appreciate how delicious it is. The liqueur has a supple, medium weight body and a spicy, floral bouquet. Its palate delivers a well-balanced array of herbal enriched, semisweet flavors. The character of the tequila is revealed in the relaxed finish.

Agavero is a romantic hit. It has scores of applications behind the bar, most notably as a modifier in specialty Margaritas. Pouring it over the tequila of your choice with ice seems like a logical way to go as well.

The liqueur's lineage is impressive. For more than a century, the Gallardo family has crafted the much sought after Tequila Gran Centenario at Los Camichines Hacienda in Jalisco, Mexico. In 1857, the head of the family, Don Lazaro Gallardo, created Agavero as a liqueur to savor after dinner.

each sip to take a lick of sugar and suck on the lemon. Slowly that gave way to the drink being presented with a sugared rim.

In its earliest incarnation, the Lemon Drop was little more than a well-presented Vodka Sour. To this day, many reputable drink guides still list the drink's ingredients as citrus-infused vodka, lemon juice and simple syrup. But the cocktail's big break came when mixologists began using Cointreau as the sweetener, instead of simple syrup. The addition catapulted the cocktail into a more elite status. The classic liqueur imbued the drink with better balance, more body and contributed considerably to its depth of character.

The Lemon Drop's appeal is nearly as universal as that of lemonade. There's something especially tantalizing about a cocktail that can deftly deliver so much lip-smacking, mouth-puckering flavor and do it with class. It's a cocktail with great creative potential as well. Here are the best kept secrets behind America's greatest Lemon Drops.

• **Spirit Options** — The Lemon Drop is a clean and uncomplicated cocktail, qualities that make it ideal for presenting top-shelf vodka brands, citrus-infused or otherwise. The better the vodka, the better the Lemon Drop.

For more than a decade, however, the nation's mixologists have refused to leave well enough alone. As it turns out, the cocktail adapts beautifully to a wide array of flavored vodkas. An excellent example is the *Pineapple Drop*, a signature at Seattle's ultra-swank Ibiza Dinner Club. The cocktail is made with Van Gogh Pineapple Vodka, Cointreau and lemon juice. At the Mosaic Restaurant in Scottsdale, the drink to be seen with is *Mia's Drop*, an expertly conceived concoction featuring Charbay Meyer Lemon Vodka, Charbay Red Raspberry Vodka, lemon juice and muddled raspberries.

The Lemon Drop is also marvelous when prepared with light rum, flavored rum and blanco tequila. An illustration of its flexibility is the *Lemon Balm Drop*, a specialty cocktail of the Jade Bar at luxurious Sanctuary on Camelback Mountain. The drink is made with Bombay Sapphire Gin, lemon balm leaves (an herb related to mint with a lemon fragrance), triple sec and fresh lemon sour mix.

• **Liqueur Drops** — Substituting Cointreau for simple syrup in the Lemon Drop elevated it into stardom. Liqueurs are capable of doing that to cocktails. Staying within the orange taste profile, Grand Marnier and GranGala are marvelous in Lemon Drops. An excellent example is the *Herbert Hoover Lemon Drop*, a specialty of The Mission Inn Hotel & Spa in Riverside, California. In addition to Grand Marnier, the drink contains Absolut Citron, a splash of lemon-lime soda and lemonade. The touch of effervescence and the cognac in the Grand Marnier are welcome additions. Another potential leap in evolution is possible modifying with the cocktail with a handful of brands, such as Midori, ZEN, PAMA, limoncello, or Chambord.

- **Base Modifiers** — Making lemon sour mix (a.k.a. sweet 'n' sour, sweetened lemon juice) from scratch is uncomplicated and often yields the finest results. In a classically uncomplicated cocktail like the Lemon Drop, using the freshest ingredients possible makes a perceptible difference.

Another creative course of action is modifying the cocktail's base mix. An example would be the *Prickly Pear Drop*, a specialty cocktail at Scottsdale's Mosaic Restaurant. It's made with Stoli Strasberi Vodka, Cointreau and three teaspoons of prickly pear puree. The drink is shaken and served in a glass rimmed with pink colored sugar.

Finishing a specialty Lemon Drop with a splash of Perrier or San Pellegrino will add effervescence without altering the flavor of the cocktail. In some cases, however especially when the drink is on the tart side, a splash of lemon-lime soda is just the thing to balance it out.

10 Cane™ Rum

Like the Rolls Royce, *10 Cane Rum* is handcrafted and impeccably styled. This Olympic caliber spirit successfully combines French distilling traditions with high-grade sugar cane cultivated on the Caribbean island of Trinidad. The secret behind the rum's amazing flavor and vivacious personality lies in the factors surrounding how it's made.

The process begins with high-grade sugar cane grown in the rich, volcanic soil of the island of Trinidad. After a year, when the cane has reached maturity and the sugar content is at its highest, the select cane is harvested by hand and bundled in tens, hence the name "Ten Cane." To ensure absolute freshness the cane is milled within days of harvesting.

While most rums are produced from black strap molasses, super-premium 10 Cane Rum is distilled from the first pressing of the sugar cane. After fermentation, it is double-distilled in copper alembic stills and aged in small French oak barrels for 6 months. The small batch production yields a full-bodied, character rich spirit. The rum is bottled at 80-proof.

10 Cane is what happens when cognac maker Moët Hennessy sets out to make a world-class rum. They succeed elegantly. The rum has a yellow gold hue and a bouquet of herbal and warm pastry aromas. Its body is supple and beautifully textured. The entry is soft and semisweet, but by mid-palate the rum begins offering up tantalizing flavors of vanilla, spice and cocoa. It has a long, delectable finish.

Make room on the top-shelf because 10 Cane is a guaranteed performer.

Lastly, there are mixologists extraordinaire who advocate adding a dash of Angostura Bitters to Lemon Drops. It may initially give you pause, that is until you actually taste a Lemon Drop concocted with bitters. The additional burst of flavor is much appreciated.

Secrets Revealed of America's Greatest Old Fashioneds

Apologies to our fifth and final neo-classic cocktail, the *Old Fashioned*. The drink may take offense, were that even possible, as it is not a member of the 20th century, rather a product of the previous one. Credit for originating the drink goes to the Pendennis Club, a gentlemen's club in Louisville, Kentucky. In the mid-1880s, the Old Fashioned was popular with the members, one of whom was bourbon distiller Colonel James Pepper. It is said that he introduced it to the bar staff at the Waldorf-Astoria Hotel in Manhattan. That proved to be its gateway to the world.

The Old Fashioned of that era differed from its present incarnation in one significant way. Constructed in a whiskey glass, the recipe called for a small lump of sugar, two dashes of Angostura Bitters and a little amount of water, ostensibly to hasten the sugar dissolving. It further instructed the barman to add a jigger of bourbon, piece of lemon peel and to mix the ingredients with a spoon. The spoon was to be left with the guest. So where's the muddled cherry and orange that so defines today's Old Fashioned?

The now accepted version can trace its lineage back to Prohibition. Times were rough and bootlegged whiskey was even rougher. The muddled cherry and orange slice were no doubt a necessary response to the inferior liquor. With the Repeal, the Old Fashioned sported a new look and loads of fresh fruit character. Along the way, the water in the original recipe was replaced with a splash of seltzer, charged water, and the Old Fashioned was on its way.

The drink's timeless appeal lies in the interplay of the whiskey and murky, muddled base. The cocktail once again proves the adage about the whole being greater than the sum of its parts. Here are the best kept secrets behind America's greatest Old Fashioneds.

• **Spirit Options** — The drink was born and bred to showcase whiskeys and with few exceptions, the Old Fashioned is an ideal vehicle for serving whiskey of all nationalities. Bourbons, ryes, Canadians, Irish and the malts of Scotland are at home in the cocktail. Brandies are also well adapted to the muddled fruit mélange of the Old Fashioned. In Wisconsin, the drink is typically prepared with brandy. Applejack and Calvados are excellent substitutes as well.

And then there's Southern Comfort. For generations the classic American liqueur has been popularly featured in Old Fashioneds. The liqueur's semisweet character and bourbon and peaches flavor melds seamlessly with the muddled fruit and bitters. For example, the *New Orleans Tribute*, a signature cocktail at The Refectory Restaurant & Bistro in Columbus, Ohio, is a muddled Old Fashioned made with Woodford Reserve Bourbon and Southern Comfort. The liqueur takes a leading role in the *Not So Old Fashioned*. The drink is a specialty of Bourbon Street & Voodoo Lounge in Cedar Falls, Iowa and concocted with Southern Comfort, sweet vermouth and the muddled fixings.

The 33 Restaurant & Lounge in Boston has made famous the *33 Old Fashioned*, a delectable drink prepared with fig and almond-infused Jim Beam Black Bourbon. The award for sheer innovative wizardry goes to Scott Beattie of Cyrus Restaurant in Sonoma for his *Burley Old Fashioned*. His muddled masterpiece features 12-year old Weller Bourbon infused with Burley tobacco.

Finally, the *New Age Old Fashioned* is appropriately named. Its recipe features a muddled base comprised of a half ounce of limoncello, a cherry, lemon slice and orange slice. The drink is finished off with a double shot of premium bourbon and a splash of chilled champagne. The drink is exceptionally flavorful and effervescent.

- **Muddling the Works** — For many a bartender the Old Fashioned was a groundbreaking cocktail. It was the drink that needed to be muddled. While now an increasingly frequent tactic for introducing the flavor of fresh ingredients into a cocktail, for decades the Old Fashioned was the only such example in contemporary mixology.

Altering the composition of the muddled base in an Old Fashioned will significantly change how the drink will taste. Two such examples include the *Knob Creek Old Fashioned*, which is prepared with a muddled peach slice instead of the conventional cherry and orange slice, and the *Santa Anita Old Fashioned*, which is made with muddled raspberries and an orange slice.

In parting, the only regrettable thing about the Old Fashioned is its name. The cocktail is far from being a relic, or out of step with contemporary trends. To the contrary, few drinks more perfectly align with what people are looking for from the cocktail experience, namely brilliant fresh flavors in an easy to drink style.

J BAR

3770 East Sunrise Drive
Tucson, AZ 85718

☎ 520.615.6100

▸▸ www.janos.com

✉ janosrest@aol.com

Janos Wilder is among the most celebrated chefs and restaurateurs in the Southwest. His Tucson restaurants are both located in a freestanding building adjacent to the prestigious Westin La Paloma Resort and Spa. Although they are sited under the same roof, fine dining Janos Restaurant and **J BAR** have distinctively different personalities and garner separate, yet equally passionate followings.

Since 1983, Janos Restaurant has featured original, trendsetting cuisine that marries the sensibility and subtlety of French cooking with ingredients indigenous to the Southwest. The upscale interior is every bit as elegant as the food. The decor is a sophisticated blend of French and Spanish colonial aesthetics that provide the backdrop for world-class dining. The award-winning wine menu is expansive and reasonably priced.

The casual J BAR Latin Grill thrives on the other end of the spectrum. There guests can also enjoy expertly prepared cuisine, great service and spectacular views, but in a more casual environment. The 60-seat restaurant has a light and airy feel with a Latino-influenced art, Mexican tile floors, a large patio and stylish bar, while the menu is a brilliant ensemble of the flavors of Mexico, Latin American and the Caribbean.

The bar at J BAR is as much of a draw as the food, tempting guests with such Southwestern and Latin influenced specialty drinks as the *Michelada*, a regional favorite made with Corona, Clamato, lime juice and Worcestershire served on the rocks, and the *Dark Chocolate Jalapeño Raspberry Shake*, a blended masterpiece made with jalapeño-laced ice cream, Absolut Vanilia and Chambord. The *Cranberry Habanero Margarita* is an innovative, delicious cocktail made with gold tequila, Grand Marnier, lime juice and fresh cranberry habanero chutney.

Casual and elegant is an unbeatable attraction. —RP

Dark Chocolate Jalapeño Raspberry Shake

Drink recipe on pg 264

33 Old Fashioned

Specialty of 33 Restaurant & Lounge
Created by Jenn Harvey
Bucket glass, chilled
Build in glass
1 orange slice
1 cherry
$1/2$ oz. simple syrup
2-3 dashes Angostura Aromatic Bitters
Muddle contents
Add ice
1 $1/2$ oz. Fig and Almond Infused
   Jim Beam Black Bourbon*
Splash club soda
Place the orange slice, cherry, simple syrup and bitters into the empty bucket glass. Muddle and add ice. Pour in the bourbon and add a splash of club soda.
*Fig and Almond-Infused Jim Beam
   Black Bourbon Recipe - pg 319

33tini

Specialty of 33 Restaurant & Lounge
Created by Ari Bialikamien
Cocktail glass, chilled
Pour ingredients into an empty mixing glass
3-4 strawberries, stems removed
1 oz. DeKuyper Pucker Sour Apple Schnapps
Muddle contents
Add ice
1 oz. HPNOTIQ
Shake and strain
Garnish with half a strawberry on rim
Place the strawberries and Apple Pucker into the empty mixing glass. Muddle and add ice. Pour in the HPNOTIQ. Shake thoroughly and strain contents into a chilled cocktail glass. Garnish with half a strawberry on the glass rim.

"Jerry Thomas was our country's most renowned bartender."

Pallini™ Limoncello

Few things spread faster than a great idea. Such is the case with limoncello. This European favorite has a refreshing and vibrant character that is unequaled in the American market. No brand illustrates why these light liqueurs have captured the imagination of the world better than *Pallini Limoncello*.

This Italian liqueur is crafted by the Pallini family in Rome according to a recipe dating back more than 100 years ago. It is made from handpicked Sfusato Amalfitano lemons that grow in and around the southern coastal city of Amalfi, which is situated on the sun-drenched Gulf of Salerno. After harvesting, the peels of the tree-ripened fruit are steeped in premium neutral spirits for an extended period of time, typically more than half a year. The lemon peels are then removed and the infused spirit is filtered and sweetened. It is bottled at 52-proof.

Ultra-premium Pallini Limoncello is a class act from start to savory finish. The liqueur features a true to fruit hue with the opacity of homemade lemonade. It has a feather-weight body and a satiny smooth texture more reminiscent of a spirit than a liqueur. The alluring bouquet is generously imbued with the aroma of zesty, freshly squeezed lemons. The limoncello has a soft entry and quickly fills the mouth with crisp, tangy and superbly delicious flavor. The relaxed, lingering finish is balanced and a genuine pleasure.

In the hands of a skilled mixologist, it's a great source for adding exuberance and pizzazz to a wide variety of cocktails and libations.

Amber Sidecar

Specialty of 33 Restaurant & Lounge
Created by Pej Mortarjem
Cocktail glass, chilled
Pour ingredients into an empty mixing glass
2 lime slices
2 lemon slices
2 orange slices
Muddle contents
Add ice
2 oz. Macallan Amber Liqueur
1 oz. Cointreau
Shake and strain
Garnish with an orange slice
Place the fruit slices into the empty mixing glass. Muddle and add ice. Pour in the remaining ingredients. Shake thoroughly and strain contents into a chilled cocktail glass. Garnish with an orange slice.

Autumn Sidecar

Excerpted from The Original Guide to
American Cocktails and Drinks- 6th Edition
Sugar rimmed cocktail glass, chilled
Pour ingredients into an iced mixing glass
1 1/2 oz. VS Cognac
1/2 oz. Tuaca Liquore Italiano
1/2 oz. Frangelico
1 3/4 oz. fresh lemon sour mix
Shake and strain
Garnish with an orange slice
Pour ingredients into the iced mixing glass. Shake contents and strain into a sugar rimmed, chilled cocktail glass. Garnish with an orange slice.

Bentley Sidecar

Specialty of Courtright's Restaurant
Created by Marco Recio
Cinnamon sugar rimmed cocktail glass, chilled
Pour ingredients into an iced mixing glass
1 oz. Hennessy X.O. Cognac
1 oz. Grand Marnier
1 oz. fresh orange juice
1 oz. fresh lime juice
Shake and strain
Garnish with a lime wheel
Pour ingredients into the iced mixing glass. Shake thoroughly and strain contents into a cinnamon sugar rimmed, chilled cocktail glass. Garnish with a lime wheel.

Bimini Iced Tea

Excerpted from The Original Guide to
American Cocktails and Drinks- 6th Edition
House specialty glass, ice
Pour ingredients into an iced mixing glass
1/2 oz. Gin
1/2 oz. Vodka
1/2 oz. Light Rum
1/2 oz. Tequila
1/2 oz. Blue Curaçao
1 1/2 oz. fresh lemon sour mix
1 1/2 oz. orange juice
1 1/2 oz. pineapple juice
1 1/2 oz. cola
Shake and strain
Garnish with a lemon wedge
Pour ingredients into the iced mixing glass. Shake thoroughly and strain contents into an iced house specialty glass. Garnish with a lemon wedge.

Black Cherry Julep

Specialty of 33 Restaurant & Lounge
Created by Jenn Harvey
Bucket glass, chilled
Pour ingredients into an empty mixing glass
Small handful mint leaves
1/2 oz. simple syrup
Muddle contents
Add ice
1 1/2 oz. Black Cherry-Infused
    Jim Beam Black Bourbon*
Stir gently
Garnish with a mint leaf and cherry
Place the mint leaves, lime wedges and simple syrup into the empty bucket glass. Muddle and add ice. Pour in the bourbon and stir gently. Garnish with a mint leaf and cherry.
*Black Cherry-Infused Jim Beam
    Black Bourbon Recipe
Steep 1-2 cups of black cherries in 1 liter of Jim Beam Black Bourbon.
Let sit for 2-3 days.

Black Russian

Excerpted from The Original Guide to
American Cocktails and Drinks- 6th Edition
Rocks glass, ice
Build in glass
1 3/4 oz. Vodka
3/4 oz. Kahlúa
Pour ingredients into the iced rocks glass in the order listed.

Blueberry Amaretto Sour

Specialty of Brûlée the Dessert Experience
Created by Peter Van Thiel
Cocktail glass, chilled
Pour ingredients into an iced mixing glass
2 1/2 oz. Blueberry Amaretto
1 tbsp. sugar
Splash fresh lemon juice
1 1/4 oz. orange juice
1 1/4 oz. fresh lemon sour mix
Shake and strain
Garnish with an orange slice
Pour ingredients into the iced mixing glass. Shake thoroughly and strain contents into a chilled cocktail glass. Garnish with an orange slice.

Burley Old Fashioned

Specialty of Cyrus
Created by Scott Beattie
Bucket glass, chilled
Build in glass
1 orange wheel
1 sugar cube
Splash club soda
Muddle contents
Add ice
1 1/2 oz. Burley Tobacco-Infused
    W.L. Weller 12 Year-Old Bourbon*
3 dashes Angostura Aromatic Bitters
Stir gently
Garnish with 2 Amarena cherries
Place the orange wheel, sugar cube and club soda into the empty bucket glass. Muddle and add ice. Pour in the bourbon and bitters. Stir gently. Garnish with 2 Amarena cherries.
*Burley Tobacco-Infused
    W.L. Weller 12 Year-Old Bourbon
20 cured Burley Tobacco leaves
9 liters W.L. Weller 12 Year-Old Bourbon
Steep for 2-3 days.

Jewel of Russia™ Classic Vodka

As their name clearly suggests, *Jewel of Russia Classic Vodka* drinks like a vodka not from this era. Perhaps even more accurate, it tastes how you imagine a vodka worthy of the Czars should taste. Those looking for a refined and sophisticated experience will most appreciate a slow dance with this luxurious vodka.

One singular feature of The Jewel of Russia Classic is that the vodka is made from a blend of premium rye, hardy winter wheat and deep well artesian water. It's a recipe for greatness. The fermented mash of grains undergoes a multi-column distillation and a 7-step, slow-flow filtration process that removes even microscopic traces of congeners. The finished vodka is bottled at 80-proof.

The Jewel of Russia Classic Vodka is appropriately named. It has a pristine clarity, rounded, satiny texture and an oily, medium-weight body. Even at room temperature the spirit barely generates any heat on the palate. By mid-palate the vodka makes its presence known by completely filling the mouth with crisp, spicy flavors. The vodka has tremendous presence on the palate and a warm, lingering finish.

As magnificent as The Jewel of Russia Classic Vodka is, the distillery has done it one better. Presented in a beautiful, hand painted bottle, The *Jewel of Russia Ultra Vodka* is imbued with a slightly more flavorful palate and subjected to a more strenuous filtration regimen. The family resemblance between these two classy, museum quality spirits is immediately evident, picking a favorite impossible.

California Iced Tea

Excerpted from The Original Guide to
American Cocktails and Drinks- 6th Edition
House specialty glass, ice
Pour ingredients into an iced mixing glass
1/2 oz. Tanqueray Gin
1/2 oz. Vox Vodka
1/2 oz. Bacardi Light Rum
1/2 oz. Sauza Hornitos Reposado Tequila
1/2 oz. Triple Sec
1 oz. cola
2 oz. fresh lemon sour mix
2 oz. grapefruit juice
Shake and strain
Garnish with a lemon wedge
Pour ingredients into the iced mixing glass. Shake thoroughly and strain contents into an iced house specialty glass. Garnish with a lemon wedge.

Charentes Sidecar

Specialty of Cyrus
Created by Scott Beattie
Cocktail glass, chilled
Pour ingredients into an iced mixing glass
1 1/2 oz. Hardy VS Cognac
1/4 oz. Luxardo Maraschino Liqueur
1/4 oz. Marie Brizard Triple Sec
1 oz. fresh lemon juice
Shake and strain
Garnish with a Seville orange zest
Pour ingredients into the iced mixing glass. Shake thoroughly and strain contents into a chilled cocktail glass. Garnish with a Seville orange zest.

Colorado Bulldog

Excerpted from The Original Guide to
American Cocktails and Drinks- 6th Edition
Bucket glass, ice
Build in glass
1 3/4 oz. Vodka
3/4 oz. Kahlúa
1/2 fill cola
1/2 fill half & half
Pour ingredients into the iced bucket glass in the order listed.

Dirty White Mother

Excerpted from The Original Guide to
American Cocktails and Drinks- 6th Edition
Rocks glass, ice
Build in glass
1 3/4 oz. Brandy
3/4 oz. Kahlúa
3/4 oz. half & half
Pour ingredients into the iced rocks glass in the order listed.

Electric Iced Tea

Specialty of Hard Rock Cafe- New York
Created by Hard Rock's staff
Pint glass, ice
Pour ingredients into an iced mixing glass
1/2 oz. Bacardi Light Rum
1/2 oz. Beefeater Gin
1/2 oz. DeKuyper Blue Curaçao
1/2 oz. Smirnoff Vodka
3 oz. sweet 'n' sour
Shake and strain
Fill with 1 oz. lemon-lime soda
Garnish with a lemon wedge
Pour ingredients, except the soda, into the iced mixing glass. Shake thoroughly and strain contents into an iced pint glass. Fill with soda. Garnish with a lemon wedge.

Elit

Specialty of 33 Restaurant & Lounge
Created by Ari Bialikamien
Bucket glass, chilled
Build in glass
3-4 lime slices
1/2 oz. Campari
Muddle contents
Add ice
1 1/2 oz. Bombay Sapphire Gin
Top with club soda
Place the lime slices and Campari into the empty bucket glass. Muddle and add ice. Pour in the gin and top with club soda.

Florida Iced Tea

Excerpted from The Original Guide to
American Cocktails and Drinks- 6th Edition
House specialty glass, ice
Pour ingredients into an iced mixing glass
1/2 oz. Gin
1/2 oz. Vodka
1/2 oz. Light Rum
1/2 oz. Tequila
1/2 oz. Triple Sec
1 oz. cola
2 oz. fresh lemon sour mix
2 oz. orange juice
Garnish with a lemon wedge
Pour ingredients into the iced mixing glass. Shake thoroughly and strain contents into an iced house specialty glass. Garnish with a lemon wedge.

Forbidden City Tea

Specialty of P.F. Chang's China Bistro
Created by P.F. Chang's staff
House specialty glass, ice
Pour ingredients into an iced mixing glass
1/2 oz. Smirnoff Vodka
1/2 oz. Bacardi Light Rum
1/2 oz. Beefeater Gin
1/2 oz. Triple Sec
1/2 oz. Chai tea syrup
4 oz. sweet 'n' sour
Shake and strain
Garnish with a lemon wedge and mint sprig
Pour ingredients into the iced mixing glass. Shake thoroughly and strain contents into an iced house specialty glass. Garnish with a lemon wedge and mint sprig.

Gin Blossom

Specialty of Mosaic Restaurant
Created by Stephanie Kozicki
Cocktail glass, chilled
Pour ingredients into an iced mixing glass
2 oz. Plymouth Gin
1/2 oz. Cointreau
1/2 oz. pomegranate juice
Shake and strain
Garnish with an orange twist
Pour ingredients into the iced mixing glass. Shake thoroughly and strain contents into a chilled cocktail glass. Garnish with an orange twist.

Ginger Sour

Specialty of Rosemary's Restaurant
Created by Michael Shetler, Nick Hetzel
Bucket glass, ice
Pour ingredients into an iced mixing glass
1 1/2 oz. Modern Spirits Candied Ginger Vodka
1/4 oz. Cointreau
Dash orange bitters
1 egg white (pasteurized)
Splash Yuzu concentrate
Splash rock candy syrup
1/2 oz. fresh lemon sour mix
Shake and strain
Fill with Dr. Brown's Dry Ginger Ale
Garnish with a lime wedge
Pour ingredients, except ginger ale, into the iced mixing glass. Shake thoroughly and strain contents into an iced bucket glass. Fill with ginger ale. Garnish with a lime wedge.

Grape Martini

Specialty of Michael's Kitchen
Created by Michael's Kitchen bar staff
Cocktail glass, chilled
Pour ingredients into an iced mixing glass
2 oz. Frïs Vodka
1 oz. Shakka Grape Liqueur
Splash sour mix
Shake and strain
Garnish with multicolored Swedish Fish
Pour ingredients into the iced mixing glass. Shake thoroughly and strain contents into a chilled cocktail glass. Garnish with multicolored Swedish Fish

Green Tea Iced Tea

Excerpted from The Original Guide to
American Cocktails and Drinks- 6th Edition
House specialty glass, ice
Pour ingredients into an iced mixing glass
1/2 oz. Gin
1/2 oz. Vodka
1/2 oz. Rum
1/2 oz. Tequila
1/2 oz. Triple Sec
1 1/2 oz. fresh lemon sour mix
1 1/2 oz. cranberry juice
Shake and strain
Float with 1 oz. Midori
Garnish with a lemon wedge
Pour ingredients, except Midori, into the iced mixing glass. Shake thoroughly and strain contents into an iced house specialty glass. Float the Midori. Garnish with a lemon wedge.

Joe's Seafood, Prime Steak & Stone Crab

✉ **60 East Grand**
Chicago, IL 60611
☎ **312.379.5637**
▶▌ **icon.com/joes/Chicago_home.html**
✉ **joeschicago@icon.com**

Joe's Seafood, Prime Steak & Stone Crab debuted in Chicago in 2000 and Las Vegas in 2004, but its origins can be traced to Miami Beach some 85 years ago. It was then that Joe and Jennie Weiss first began serving cracked stone crabs with mustard sauce at their small seafood restaurant on the beach. The now phenomenally successful Joe's Stone Crab has grown into a local institution with an international reputation.

Its present incarnation is a cooperative effort with famed Lettuce Entertain You Enterprises. The vaulted ceiling, large wraparound dining room and use of mirrors give the restaurant an inviting and spacious feel. Tuxedo clad servers, hardwood

floors, dark wood furniture and clothed tables combine to lend the space a country club ambience.

The cuisine and its execution are as impeccable as the surroundings. Successive generations have spoken of the incomparable stone crabs that they ate at Joe's, the very same that are now available in generous portions at the Chicago Joe's. The twist is that you can also order equally extraordinary seafood and beef dishes, such as swordfish, sauteed scallops and a bone-in filet mignon. The requisite dessert is their legendary key lime pie.

To not sample one of Joe's luxurious signature drinks is to cut short your experience. Special indeed are their **Chocolate Martini**, which is concocted with Stoli Vanil, chocolate liqueur, Godiva White Chocolate and melted Häagen-Dazs ice cream, and the **South Beach Peach**, an effervescent cocktail made with peach schnapps, fresh lime juice and Saracco Moscato d'Asti sparkling wine. Also ideal for the Windy City is **Joe's Hot Buttered Rum**, a soothing mix of Bacardi Vaníla Rum, hot water and rich, homemade batter. The legend continues. —RP

Joe's Hot Buttered Rum
Drink recipe on pg 220

Havana Iced Tea

Excerpted from The Original Guide to
American Cocktails and Drinks- 6th Edition
House specialty glass, ice
Pour ingredients into an iced mixing glass
1/2 oz. Brandy
1/2 oz. Gold Rum
1/2 oz. Light Rum
1/2 oz. Triple Sec
1 1/2 oz. orange juice
1 1/2 oz. fresh lemon sour mix
1 1/2 oz. cola
Shake and strain
Garnish with a lemon wedge
Pour ingredients into the iced mixing glass.
Shake thoroughly and strain contents into
an iced house specialty glass. Garnish with a
lemon wedge.

Hawaiian Iced Tea

Excerpted from The Original Guide to
American Cocktails and Drinks- 6th Edition
House specialty glass, ice
Pour ingredients into an iced mixing glass
1/2 oz. Gin
1/2 oz. Vodka
1/2 oz. Light Rum
1/2 oz. Tequila
1/2 oz. Triple Sec
1 oz. cola
2 oz. fresh lemon sour mix
2 oz. pineapple juice
Shake and strain
Garnish with a lemon wedge
Pour ingredients into the iced mixing glass.
Shake thoroughly and strain contents into
an iced house specialty glass. Garnish with a
lemon wedge.

"Long Island Iced Teas and UV rays,
they're great when taken in moderation."

Glenfiddich® Solera Reserve 15 Year Old Single Malt

The Speyside is situated between the cities of Inverness and Aberdeen. The region has the distinction of being among the most revered of the whisky producing appellations in the world. Speyside malts are famous for their elegance and sophistication. Continuing on in that tradition is the altogether exquisite *Glenfiddich Solera Reserve 15 Year Old Single Malt*.

The one of a kind whisky is aged according to a proprietary system modeled after the Solera process developed by sherry producers in Jerez, Spain. The process is as fascinating as the whisky is delicious.

The master distiller at Glenfiddich selects barrels of whisky that have been aged a minimum of 15 years. Some of the selected malts have been aged in sherry butts, others in bourbon barrels with the rest having matured in new oak casks. The whisky is added to a Solera vat, a large, handcrafted oak vessel that serves as a reservoir.

When whisky is drawn from the Solera vat for bottling, it is replaced with an equal amount of 15-year old malt. In this way, the batch of whisky remaining in the reservoir can "educate" the newly added malts. The process continues in this fashion, assuring consistency in character for each batch.

Solera Reserve is complex and loaded with intriguing nuances. The soft, alluring bouquet is laced with the aromas of sherry and smoky oak. It has a substantial body and a palate underscored with an array of floral, semisweet flavors. It finishes long and satisfying.

Herbert Hoover Lemon Drop

Specialty of The Mission Inn Hotel & Spa
Created by Alan Lee
Sugar rimmed cocktail glass, chilled
Pour ingredients into an iced mixing glass
1 1/4 oz. Absolut Citron Vodka
3/4 oz. Grand Marnier
1/2 oz. lemon-lime soda
2 oz. lemonade
Shake and strain
Garnish with a lemon wedge
Pour ingredients into the iced mixing glass. Shake thoroughly and strain contents into a sugar rimmed, chilled cocktail glass. Garnish with a lemon wedge.

Homemade PIMMS Cup #4

Specialty of Nacional 27
Created by Adam Seger
Bucket glass, ice
Build in glass
1 oz. 10 Cane Rum
1 oz. Sweet Vermouth
1/2 oz. Grand Marnier
1/4 oz. Luxardo Maraschino Liqueur
Dash Angostura Aromatic Bitters
Splash fresh lime juice
Splash simple syrup
2 oz. club soda
Garnish with a skewered lime slice,
    orange slice, cucumber slice, and cherry
Pour the ingredients into the iced bucket glass in the order listed. Garnish with a skewered lime slice, orange slice, cucumber slice, and cherry.

Italian Iced Tea

Excerpted from The Original Guide to American Cocktails and Drinks- 6th Edition
House specialty glass, ice
Pour ingredients into an iced mixing glass
1/2 oz. Gin
1/2 oz. Vodka
1/2 oz. Light Rum
1/2 oz. Triple Sec
2 oz. fresh lemon sour mix
2 oz. cola
Shake and strain
Float 3/4 oz. Disaronno Amaretto
Garnish with a lemon wedge
Pour all ingredients, except the Amaretto, into the iced mixing glass. Shake thoroughly and strain contents into an iced house specialty glass. Float Disaronno Amaretto. Garnish with a lemon wedge.

Jackie Collins

Specialty of Bookmarks
Created by Kenneth McClure
Bucket glass, ice
Build in glass
1 1/2 oz. Stoli Ohranj Vodka
Splash fresh lemon juice
Splash fresh lime juice
Splash simple syrup
Fill with Sprite
Garnish with an orange slice and cherry
Pour the ingredients into the iced bucket glass in the order listed. Garnish with an orange slice and cherry.

Knob Creek Old Fashioned

Excerpted from The Original Guide to American Cocktails and Drinks- 6th Edition
Old fashioned glass, chilled
Build in glass
3 dashes Angostura Aromatic Bitters
1/2 oz. simple syrup
1 peach slice, peeled
Muddle contents
Add ice
2 1/2 oz. Knob Creek Bourbon
Splash club soda
Pour bitters, simple syrup, and peach slice into the empty old fashioned glass. Muddle and add ice. Pour in the bourbon and add a splash of club soda.

La Reinette

Specialty of The Refectory Restaurant & Bistro
Created by Julie Mulisano, Kevin McClatchy
Cocktail glass, chilled
Pour ingredients into an iced mixing glass
1 1/2 oz. Van Gogh Wild Appel Vodka
1/4 oz. Midori
1 1/2 oz. fresh lemon sour mix
Shake and strain
Pour ingredients into the iced mixing glass. Shake thoroughly and strain contents into a chilled cocktail glass.

Lemon Balm Drop

Specialty of Jade Bar
Created by Daniella Gonzalez
Sugar rimmed cocktail glass, chilled
Pour ingredients into an iced mixing glass
5 Lemon Balm leaves
2 oz. Bombay Sapphire Gin
1/2 oz. Triple Sec
1/2 oz. fresh lemon sour mix
Shake and strain
Garnish with a lemon wheel
Pour ingredients into the iced mixing glass.
Shake thoroughly and strain contents into a
sugar rimmed, chilled cocktail glass. Garnish
with a lemon wheel.

Classic Lemon Drop

Excerpted from The Original Guide to
American Cocktails and Drinks- 6th Edition
Sugar rimmed cocktail glass, chilled
Pour ingredients into an iced mixing glass
1 1/2 oz. Absolut Citron Vodka
1/2 oz. Cointreau
1/2 oz. fresh lemon juice
Shake and strain
Garnish with a lemon
       wheel
Pour ingredients
into the iced mixing
glass. Shake thoroughly
and strain contents into
a sugar rimmed, chilled
cocktail glass. Garnish with a
lemon wheel.

Long Beach Iced Tea

Excerpted from The Original Guide to
American Cocktails and Drinks- 6th Edition
House specialty glass, ice
Pour ingredients into an iced mixing glass
1/2 oz. Gin
1/2 oz. Vodka
1/2 oz. Light Rum
1/2 oz. Tequila
1/2 oz. Triple Sec
1 oz. cola
2 oz. cranberry juice
2 oz. fresh lemon sour mix
Shake and strain
Garnish with a lemon wedge
Pour ingredients into the iced mixing
glass. Shake thoroughly and strain contents into
an iced house specialty glass. Garnish with a
lemon wedge.

Classic Long Island Iced Tea

Excerpted from The Original Guide to
American Cocktails and Drinks- 6th Edition
House specialty glass, ice
Pour ingredients into an iced mixing glass
1/2 oz. Gin
1/2 oz. Vodka
1/2 oz. Light Rum
1/2 oz. Tequila
1/2 oz. Triple Sec
2 oz. fresh lemon
       sour mix
2 oz. cola
Shake and strain
Garnish with a
       lemon wedge
Pour ingredients into the
iced mixing glass. Shake
thoroughly and strain
contents into an iced house
specialty glass. Garnish with
a lemon wedge.

Louisiana Lady

Specialty of Marcus' Martini Heaven
Created by Marcus' Staff
Extra fine sugar rimmed
       cocktail glass, chilled
Pour ingredients into an iced mixing glass
1 1/2 oz. Whiskey
1/2 oz. Amaretto
2 oz. fresh lemon sour mix
Shake and strain
Garnish with a lime wedge
Pour ingredients into the iced mixing glass.
Shake thoroughly and strain contents into a
sugar rimmed, chilled cocktail glass.
Garnish with a lime wedge.

Love in a Sidecar

Specialty of Mosaic Restaurant
Created by Stephanie Kozicki
Cocktail glass, chilled
Pour ingredients into an iced mixing glass
1 1/2 oz. A de Fussigny Cognac
1 1/2 oz. Damiana Liqueur
1 1/2 oz. fresh lemon sour mix
Shake and strain
Pour ingredients into the iced mixing glass.
Shake thoroughly and strain contents into a
chilled cocktail glass.

Manhattan Iced Tea

Excerpted from The Original Guide to
American Cocktails and Drinks- 6th Edition
House specialty glass, ice
Pour ingredients into an iced mixing glass
1/2 oz. Gin
1/2 oz. Vodka
1/2 oz. Light Rum
1/2 oz. Tequila
2 oz. cola
2 oz. fresh lemon sour mix
Shake and strain
Float with 3/4 oz. Bourbon
Garnish with a lemon wedge
Pour ingredients, except the bourbon, into the
iced mixing glass. Shake thoroughly and strain
contents into an iced house specialty glass. Float
the bourbon and garnish with a lemon wedge.

Mariposa Sazerac

Specialty of Cyrus
Created by Scott Beattie
Cocktail glass, chilled
Pour ingredients into an empty mixing glass
1 sugar cube
3 dashes Peychaud Bitters
3 dashes Angostura Aromatic Bitters
Muddle contents
Add ice
1 1/2 oz. Old Potrero Single Malt
    Straight Rye Whiskey
Stir and strain
1 dash Herbsaint
Garnish with a lemon zest
Place the sugar cube and bitters into the empty
mixing glass. Muddle and add ice. Pour in the
whiskey and stir gently. Dash the Herbsaint into
the empty, chilled cocktail glass and swirl around
the inside of the glass. Dump the excess. Strain
the shaker contents into the Herbsaint coated
cocktail glass. Garnish with a lemon zest.

Mia's Drop

Specialty of Mosaic Restaurant
Created by Stephanie Kozicki
Pink color sugar rimmed cocktail glass, chilled
Pour ingredients into an empty mixing glass
4 raspberries
Splash simple syrup
Muddle contents
Add ice
1 1/2 oz. Charbay Meyer Lemon Vodka
1/2 oz. Charbay Red Raspberry Vodka
Splash fresh lemon juice
1/2 oz. fresh lemon sour mix
Shake and strain
Garnish with a lemon wedge
Place the raspberries and simple syrup into the
empty mixing glass. Muddle and add ice. Pour in
the remaining ingredients. Shake thoroughly and
strain contents (through a fine strainer to strain out
raspberry seeds) into a pink color sugar rimmed,
chilled cocktail glass. Garnish with a lemon wedge.

Mixed Berry Tea

Specialty of Hard Rock Las Vegas
Created by Naomi Benham
Pint glass, ice
Pour ingredients into an iced mixing glass
1/2 oz. Stoli Razberi Vodka
1/2 oz. Stoli Blueberi Vodka
1/2 oz. Blue Curaçao
2 oz. sweet 'n' sour
Fill with Sprite
Shake and strain
Float with 3/4 oz. Chambord
Garnish with a lemon wheel and a strawberry
Pour ingredients, except the Chambord, into the
iced mixing glass. Shake thoroughly and strain
contents into an iced pint glass. Float the
Chambord. Garnish with a lemon wheel and
strawberry.

New Age Old Fashioned

Excerpted from The Original Guide to
American Cocktails and Drinks- 6th Edition
Old fashioned glass, chilled
Build in glass
3 dashes Angostura Aromatic Bitters
1/2 oz. Limoncello
1 lemon slice
1 orange slice
1 cherry
Muddle contents
Add ice
2 oz. Bourbon
Splash Champagne
Pour bitters, limoncello, lemon, orange, and cherry
into the empty old fashioned glass. Muddle and add
ice. Pour in the bourbon and splash Champagne.

New Orleans Tribute

Specialty of The Refectory Restaurant & Bistro
Created by Julie Mulisano, Kevin McClatchy
Bucket glass, chilled
Build in glass
1 orange slice
1 cherry
Splash club soda
Dash Angostura Aromatic Bitters
1/2 tsp. sugar
Muddle contents
Add ice
1 1/2 oz. Woodford Reserve Bourbon
1/2 oz. Southern Comfort
Place the orange slice, cherry, soda, bitters and sugar into the empty bucket glass. Muddle and add ice. Pour in the remaining ingredients.

The Nickgroni

Specialty of Rosemary's Restaurant
Created by Nick Hetzel
Cocktail glass, chilled
Pour ingredients into an empty mixing glass
1 orange slice
Muddle
Add ice
1 oz. Bombay Sapphire Gin
1 oz. Campari
1 oz. Sweet Vermouth
Splash fresh grapefruit juice
Shake and strain
Garnish with an orange twist
Place the orange slice into the empty mixing glass. Muddle and add ice. Pour in the remaining ingredients. Shake thoroughly and strain contents into a chilled cocktail glass. Garnish with an orange twist.

Not So Old Fashioned

Specialty of Bourbon Street & Voodoo Lounge
Created by Matt Spencer
Old fashioned glass, chilled
Build in glass
1 cherry
1 orange slice
1-2 pinches sugar
Muddle contents
Add ice
1 1/2 oz. Southern Comfort
1/2 oz. Sweet Vermouth
2-4 drops Angostura Aromatic Bitters
1/2 oz. cherry juice
Splash lemon-lime soda
Garnish with an orange wheel and a cherry
Place the cherry, orange slice and sugar into the empty old fashioned glass. Muddle and add ice. Pour in the remaining ingredients. Garnish with an orange wheel and a cherry.

Classic Old Fashioned

Excerpted from The Original Guide to American Cocktails and Drinks- 6th Edition
Old fashioned glass, chilled
Build in glass
3 dashes Angostura Aromatic Bitters
1/2 oz. simple syrup
1 orange slice
1 cherry
Muddle contents
Add ice
1 1/2 oz. Bourbon
Splash club soda
Garnish with an
    orange slice
    and cherry

Pour bitters, simple syrup, orange slice and cherry into the empty old fashioned glass. Muddle and add ice. Pour in the bourbon and club soda. Garnish with an orange slice and cherry.

Pineapple Drop

Specialty of Ibiza Dinner Club
Created by Ibiza's staff
Sugar rimmed cocktail glass, chilled
Pour ingredients into an iced mixing glass
1 oz. Van Gogh Pineapple Vodka
1/2 oz. Cointreau
1/2 oz. fresh lemon juice
Shake and strain
Pour ingredients into the iced mixing glass. Shake thoroughly and strain contents into a sugar rimmed, chilled cocktail glass.

Pineau Sour

Specialty of Brasserie JO
Created by David Johnston
Cocktail glass, chilled
Pour ingredients into an iced mixing glass
1 1/2 oz. Cîroc Vodka
1 oz. Pineau des Charentes
1 oz. fresh lemon sour mix
Shake and strain
Garnish with a peeled grape
Pour ingredients into the iced mixing glass. Shake thoroughly and strain into a chilled cocktail glass. Garnish with a peeled grape.

Lola's

📪 **945 North Fairfax Avenue**
   West Hollywood, CA 90046
☎ **213.736.5652**
▶▶▎ **lolasla.com**
✉ **lolasinfo@aol.com**

Since opening in West Hollywood in 1996, **Lola's** has remained a fashionable, ultra-hip destination venue, all without assuming a veneer of trendiness at times common with happening Angelino restaurants. It's an energized nightspot with an upscale, often star-studded clientele who frequent Lola's for its home style, soul-satisfying American cuisine, repertoire of delectable cocktails and energized, yet relaxed ambience.

The place is airy and remarkably comfortable with outdoor patios and open, well-lit dining rooms. The interior features bright colors, tile floors, maple wood bars, cheetah print upholstery, understated furniture and walls loaded with artwork. One

of its many rooms is dominated by an antique pool table that is in use from open to close.

Lola's is alive and abuzz all the time. The food is unpretentious and delicious. For example, the portabello mushroom topped, ground sirloin burger is huge, perfectly prepared and reasonably priced. The same can be said for their meatloaf with mashed potatoes and the macaroni and cheese.

The fare also includes an array of hot and cold salads, pastas and empanadas. The restaurant is justifiably famous for its Chocolate Bread Pudding

Lola's is also among the bastions of American mixology. Its claim to fame rests largely on the delectable shoulders of about fifty, over-sized, utterly sumptuous Martinis. The bar is the birthplace of the contemporary classic Apple Martini, rightly referred to as *Lola's Apple Martini*. Their menu includes a signature *Pumpkin Martini* as well as a *Kiwitini*, which is made with 42 Below Kiwi Vodka, kiwi juice, pineapple juice and a kiwi slice garnish. The *Thin White Duke* is one of the most requested cocktails. It's a blend of Godiva White Chocolate Liqueur, Stoli Vanil and a splash of cream. Like everything at Lola's, it's unforgettable. —RP

Thin White Duke
Drink recipe on pg 288

Plantation Iced Tea

Excerpted from The Original Guide to
American Cocktails and Drinks- 6th Edition
House specialty glass, ice
Pour ingredient into an iced mixing glass
1/2 oz. Gin
1/2 oz. Vodka
1/2 oz. Light Rum
1/2 oz. Tequila
1/2 oz. Triple Sec
2 oz. fresh lemon sour mix
2 oz. iced tea
Splash cola
Shake and strain
Garnish with a lemon wedge
Pour ingredients into the iced mixing glass. Shake thoroughly and strain contents into an iced house specialty glass. Garnish with a lemon wedge.

Poire Sidecar

Specialty of 33 Restaurant & Lounge
Created by Jenn Harvey
Sugar rimmed cocktail glass, chilled
Pour ingredients into an empty mixing glass
1/2 ripe Bartlett Pear, peeled and cut into cubes
1/2 oz. Cointreau
Muddle contents
Add ice
1/2 oz. fresh lemon juice
2 oz. Marie Brizard Poire William
Shake and strain
Garnish with a pear slice
Place the pear cubes and Cointreau into the empty mixing glass. Muddle and add ice. Pour in the remaining ingredients. Shake thoroughly and strain contents into a sugar rimmed, chilled cocktail glass. Garnish with a pear slice.

The Portland Street Car

Specialty of The Original McCormick & Schmick's
Created by Geoff V. Helzer
Sugar rimmed cocktail glass, chilled
Pour ingredients into an empty mixing glass
1 sugar cube
1 1/2 oz. fresh lemon juice
1 1/2 oz. fresh orange juice
Muddle contents
Add ice
1 3/4 oz. Clear Creek Pear Brandy
1/2 oz. Cointreau
Shake and strain
Garnish with a pear slice
Place the sugar and juices into the empty mixing glass. Muddle and add ice. Pour in the remaining ingredients. Shake thoroughly and strain contents into a sugar rimmed, chilled cocktail glass. Garnish with a pear slice.

Prickly Pear Drop

Specialty of Mosaic Restaurant
Created by Stephanie Kozicki
Pink color sugar rimmed cocktail glass, chilled
Pour ingredients into an iced mixing glass
2 oz. Stoli Strasberi Vodka
1 oz. Cointreau
3 tsp. prickly pear puree
Shake and strain
Garnish with a lemon twist
Pour ingredients into the iced mixing glass. Shake thoroughly and strain contents into a pink color sugar rimmed, chilled cocktail glass. Garnish with a lemon twist.

Purple Haze

Specialty of Hard Rock- New York
Created by Hard Rock's staff
Pint glass, ice
Pour ingredients into an iced mixing glass
1/2 oz. Smirnoff Vodka
1/2 oz. Bacardi Razz Rum
1/2 oz. Beefeater Gin
3 oz. sweet 'n' sour
Shake and strain
Top with lemon-lime soda
Float with 1/2 oz. Chambord
Garnish with a lemon wedge
Pour ingredients into the iced mixing glass. Shake thoroughly and strain contents into an iced pint glass. Top with soda. Float the Chambord. Garnish with a lemon wedge.

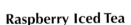

Raspberry Iced Tea

Excerpted from The Original Guide to
American Cocktails and Drinks- 6th Edition
House specialty glass, ice
Pour ingredients into an iced mixing glass
1/2 oz. Gin
1/2 oz. Vodka
1/2 oz. Light Rum
1/2 oz. Tequila
1/2 oz. Triple Sec
2 oz. fresh lemon sour mix
2 oz. cola
Shake and strain
Float with 3/4 oz. Chambord
Garnish with a lemon wedge
Pour ingredients, except the Chambord, into the iced mixing glass. Shake thoroughly and strain contents into an iced house specialty glass. Float the Chambord. Garnish with a lemon wedge.

Raspberry White Russian

Excerpted from The Original Guide to
American Cocktails and Drinks- 6th Edition
Bucket glass, ice
Build in glass
1 ¹/2 oz. Raspberry Vodka
1 ¹/2 oz. Kahlúa
³/4 oz. milk
Pour ingredients into the iced bucket glass in the
order listed.

Santa Anita Old Fashioned

Excerpted from The Original Guide to
American Cocktails and Drinks- 6th Edition
Old fashioned glass, chilled
Build in glass
3 dashes Angostura Aromatic Bitters
¹/2 oz. simple syrup
1 orange slice
5 fresh raspberries
Muddle contents
Add ice
2 ¹/2 oz. Bourbon
Splash club soda
Pour bitters, simple syrup, orange slice, and
raspberries into the empty, chilled old fashioned
glass. Muddle and add ice. Pour in the bourbon.
Add a splash of club soda.

Classic Sidecar

Excerpted from The Original Guide to
American Cocktails and Drinks- 6th Edition
Sugar rimmed cocktail glass, chilled
Pour ingredients into an iced mixing glass
1 oz. V.S. Cognac
¹/2 oz. Cointreau
1 ¹/2 oz. fresh lemon
    sour mix
Shake and strain
Pour ingredients into an iced
mixing glass. Shake thoroughly
and strain contents into a sugar
rimmed, chilled cocktail glass.

Sidecar Royale

Excerpted from The Original Guide to
American Cocktails and Drinks- 6th Edition
Sugar rimmed cocktail glass, chilled
Pour ingredients into an iced mixing glass
1 oz. VS Cognac
¹/2 oz. Cointreau
¹/2 oz. Benedictine
1 ¹/2 oz. fresh lemon sour mix
Shake and strain
Pour ingredients into the iced mixing glass.
Shake thoroughly and strain contents into a
sugar rimmed, chilled cocktail glass.

Skinny Russian

Excerpted from The Original Guide to
American Cocktails and Drinks- 6th Edition
Bucket glass, ice
Build in glass
1 ¹/2 oz. Vodka
1 ¹/2 oz. Kahlúa
³/4 oz. skim milk
Pour ingredients into the iced bucket glass in the
order listed.

Smith & Kerns

Excerpted from The Original Guide to
American Cocktails and Drinks- 6th Edition
Brandy snifter, ice
Build in glass
1 ³/4 oz. Kahlúa
¹/2 fill half & half
¹/2 fill club soda
Pour ingredients into the iced brandy snifter in
the order listed.

Smith & Wesson

Excerpted from The Original Guide to
American Cocktails and Drinks- 6th Edition
Brandy snifter, ice
Build in glass
1 ³/4 oz. Kahlúa
¹/2 fill half & half
¹/2 fill cola
Pour ingredients into the iced brandy snifter in
the order listed.

Top Hat

Specialty of Brasserie JO
Created by David Johnston
Cocktail glass, chilled
Pour ingredients into an iced mixing glass
2 1/2 oz. Château de Montifaud
    VSOP Cognac
1 oz. simple syrup
4-5 drops Fee's Orange Bitters
Shake and strain
1 oz. Green Charteuse
Garnish with an orange twist
Pour ingredients, except the Chartreuse, into the iced mixing glass. Shake thoroughly. Pour the Charteuse into the empty, chilled cocktail glass and swirl around the inside of the glass. Discard the excess and strain shaker contents into the coated cocktail glass. Garnish with an orange twist.

Ultimate Iced Tea

Specialty of Stone Rose Lounge
Created by Jeff Isaacson
House specialty glass, ice
Pour ingredients into an iced mixing glass
1/2 oz. Cîroc Vodka
1/2 oz. No. TEN by Tanqueray
1/2 oz. Bacardi Light Rum
1/2 oz. Jose Cuervo Tradicional
    Reposado Tequila
1/2 oz. Grand Marnier
Splash Coke
2 oz. fresh lemon sour mix
Shake and strain
Garnish with a lemon wedge
Pour ingredients into the iced mixing glass. Shake thoroughly and strain contents into an iced house specialty glass. Garnish with a lemon wedge.

Vanilla White Russian

Excerpted from The Original Guide to
American Cocktails and Drinks- 6th Edition
Bucket glass, ice
Build in glass
1 1/2 oz. Absolut Vanilia Vodka
1 1/2 oz. Kahlúa
3/4 oz. milk
Pour ingredients into the iced bucket glass in the order listed.

Veranda Iced Tea

Excerpted from The Original Guide to
American Cocktails and Drinks- 6th Edition
House specialty glass, ice
Pour ingredients into an iced mixing glass
1 oz. Citrus Vodka
1/2 oz. Gin
1/2 oz. Light Rum
1/2 oz. Triple Sec
1/2 oz. fresh lemon juice
2 oz. fresh lemon sour mix
2 oz. iced tea
Splash cola
Shake and strain
Garnish with a lemon wedge
Pour ingredients into the iced mixing glass. Shake thoroughly and strain contents into an iced house specialty glass. Garnish with a lemon wedge.

Whiskey Stone Sour

Excerpted from The Original Guide to
American Cocktails and Drinks- 6th Edition
Cocktail glass, chilled
Pour ingredients into an iced mixing glass
1 1/4 oz. Whiskey
1 1/4 oz. fresh lemon sour mix
1 1/4 oz. orange juice
Shake and strain
Garnish with an orange slice and cherry
Pour ingredients into the iced mixing glass. Shake thoroughly and strain contents into a chilled cocktail glass. Garnish with an orange slice and cherry.

White Russian

Excerpted from The Original Guide to
American Cocktails and Drinks- 6th Edition
Rocks glass, ice
Build in glass
1 3/4 oz. Vodka
3/4 oz. Kahlúa
3/4 oz. half & half
Pour ingredients into the iced rocks glass in the order listed.

Chapter Seven

America's Foremost Savory Cocktail
Bloody Marys

Paris in the 1920s was a hotbed for American expatriates, writers and artists. Soon word of the **Bloody Mary** made its way back to New York, where it became the drink of choice within high society. Its restorative properties became the rage and made it a fixture at Sunday brunch.

While still popularly served at brunch, the Bloody Mary has now garnered a broader audience and is often seen at Happy Hours as one of the ideal, pre-dinner cocktails. The drink's appeal is timeless. Tall, savory and exuberant, the Bloody Mary is a substantial quaff chock full of garden fresh vegetables, herbs and spices. It's more like a meal with an attitude than a thirst quencher.

The Bloody Mary is perhaps the most singular drink in the lexicon of mixology. It's a drink every bartender makes, and yet no two bartenders make it the same. When made well, the Bloody Mary is an absolute work of art — robust, nutritious and loaded with taste.

Credit for inventing the Bloody Mary goes to Fernand Petiot, a bartender at Harry's New York Bar in Paris in 1924. He dubbed his concoction the "Bucket of Blood." While the drink caught on, the name didn't. It soon became known as the Bloody Mary, likely in honor of Mary Tudor, the unfortunate daughter of King Henry VIII.

Petiot commented on his creation in an interview in *The New Yorker* (July 18, 1964) "I initiated the Bloody Mary of today," he said. "I cover the bottom of the shaker with four large dashes of salt, two dashes of black pepper, two dashes of cayenne pepper, and a layer of Worcestershire Sauce, I then add a dash of lemon juice and some cracked ice, put in two ounces of vodka and two ounces of thick tomato juice, shake, strain, and pour."

The blueprints for constructing nearly all Bloody Marys are seemingly identical. They are comprised of a base spirit, a fill with the mix and a garnish. While a straightforward formula, there is an amazingly large amount of room for creativity.

There are practitioners who make their Bloody Marys from scratch, carefully adding each ingredient directly into the glass in which it is being served. Admittedly there is something satisfying about building a classic Bloody Mary from the ground up, skillfully adding a few dashes of this and a healthy pinch of that. Few drinks are as involved to make and engaging to watch being prepared.

But over the decades the practice of making the drink individually has fallen out of favor, particularly because of the difficulty in attaining consistency. The problem is that some bartenders may use more of one ingredient than another, while others may leave out integral items altogether. Add to this the inordinate amount of time it takes to build the drink from scratch and you have a persuasive case for making scratch Bloody Mary mix in batches.

While naturally there are exceptions, it's advisable to not make more than a gallon of Bloody Mary mix at a time. It is a perishable product. Once a formula has been perfected, take care to write the recipe down. The mix should be kept refrigerated. Most mixes have a refrigerated shelf life of a week or less, after which they should be discarded. Always taste test the mix to ensure freshness and discard if questionable.

If searching for the perfect scratch recipe sounds more involved than the time at hand permits, opting for a bottled Bloody Mary mix offers a viable alternative. Possessing thick, rich bodies, great

Jägermeister® Liqueur

The mere mention of **Jägermeister Liqueur** is enough to raise a knowing smile to the face of any seasoned imbiber. The popular, "must have" elixir has become a classic rite of passage and can be found behind nearly every bar on the planet.

The Mast family founded the Mast-Jägermeister Company in 1878 in Wolfenbüttel, Germany. Jägermeister in German means "master of the hunt." The herbal liqueur was first bottled and widely marketed in 1935, just prior to the beginning of World War II.

Renowned Jägermeister is comprised of a sophisticated blend of 56 roots, herbs and spices from around the world, including gentian roots, valerian, poppy seeds, ginseng and chamomile blossoms. The various botanicals are individually macerated in neutral spirits for up to 6 weeks. They are then filtered and matured in charred oak barrels for a minimum of one year prior to blending. The liqueur is bottled at 70-proof.

Jägermeister is a singular sensation not to be missed. It has a reddish brown hue and a wafting bouquet loaded with spice and peppery aromas. The liqueur immediately fills the mouth with a montage of flavors ranging from bittersweet to spicy hot. The finish is long and herbaceous.

Jägermeister is at its best served chilled, which has prompted countless generations to view the liqueur as something to be consumed as an icy cold shot. While a time-tested method of enjoying the classic brand, it has also become a featured attraction in an increasing number of cocktails.

seasonings and well-balanced flavor, the new generation of fresh and sassy bottled Bloody Mary mixes rival the most delectable house recipes, and the field of entrants run from mild to scalding. Invariably these products originated as specialties of the house and were thought too good to be kept secret. In nearly every case, they were right.

Bottled Bloody Mary mixes are produced in a wide variety of styles to match nearly any needs. Most importantly, they are quality items loaded with great taste. Sure, the process may require sampling several different brands before making a selection, but the result may well be worth it.

Should you select a premixed product for your Mary, consider transferring the mix from its bottle into a reusable quart container. There's no reason on earth why a few modifications can't be made to a bottled mix to make it better suited to your particular tastes. Splash in some olive juice, add crushed roasted garlic, or lace the mix with a heaping tablespoon of fresh salsa. It's your specialty, after all.

This begs the question, is there really a definitive Bloody Mary? Taste is so subjective and dependent on personal preferences, the likely answer is no. Yet all great Bloody Marys share similar attributes. For one thing, they have a thick, almost chewy consistency and appear hearty enough to almost pass as a meal. They also must have at least a slight kick. A world-class Bloody Mary needn't scald the larynx, but it does need to stimulate the senses and impress recipients that they're still alive.

For people looking for a style of drink with flair and substance, this is it. To make the journey more enjoyable, here are the best kept secrets behind America's greatest Bloody Marys.

• **Vodka Marys** — The Bloody Mary is one of the famed vodka drinks. While the particular brand of vodka won't necessarily be readily discernible in the tall, thick drink, it is a mistake to believe that any vodka will do. It requires an extremely keen palate to distinguish between a Bloody Mary prepared with Absolut Vodka and one made with Stolichnaya. On the other hand, it is far easier to perceive the drink made with a lesser brand. When it comes to the vodka in a Bloody Mary, quality is always telling.

While a sublime pleasure, they do not represent the boundary of all that is possible. A few simple alterations to a recipe can transform the flavor of a Bloody Mary into an entirely new taste experience to revel in.

The two most famous of these thematic variations is the **Bloody Caesar**, a classic Mary made with a healthy dose of clam juice, or more likely Clamato Juice. The drink is almost an institution in Canada where its popularity far exceeds that of the conventional Bloody Mary. The other is the **Bloody Bull**, which is made with the addition of beef bouillon to the mix.

With the advent of flavored vodkas, the creative range of the Bloody Mary has greatly expanded. Peppered vodka, such as Absolut Peppar, marries perfectly with the spicy, peppery mix. Citrus-infused vodkas, such as Stoli Citros, Absolut Citron, or Smirnoff Citrus are excellent options. ***Rosemary's Bloody Mary*** at Rosemary's Restaurant in Las Vegas features the talents of Modern Spirits' Celery Peppercorn Vodka. The spirit's vivacious character is perfectly cast in the drink.

Infused vodkas are also ideally showcased in Bloody Marys. For example, the **Mango Bloody Mary** features vodka infused with fresh mango, chili powder, ginger, black pepper, Tabasco, horseradish and V-8 juice. The flavorful spirit marries beautifully with the spices in the drink's mix. At Michael's Kitchen in Hollywood, FL, one of their celebrated infusions is Pepper-Infused Frïs Vodka. It's made with chili peppers, cherry peppers, roasted peppers, olives, caper berries and grilled onions. The mélange is steeped in Frïs Vodka for a minimum of a week and unparalleled in a Bloody Mary.

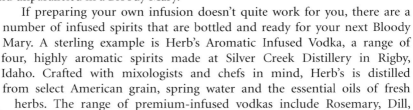

If preparing your own infusion doesn't quite work for you, there are a number of infused spirits that are bottled and ready for your next Bloody Mary. A sterling example is Herb's Aromatic Infused Vodka, a range of four, highly aromatic spirits made at Silver Creek Distillery in Rigby, Idaho. Crafted with mixologists and chefs in mind, Herb's is distilled from select American grain, spring water and the essential oils of fresh herbs. The range of premium-infused vodkas include Rosemary, Dill,

Belvedere® Vodka

Since its American debut in 1996, super-premium **Belvedere Vodka** from Poland has caught on in a seriously big way. It can be found on the back bar of any self-respecting Martini bar and with good reason. Belvedere is a full-bodied, character-laden vodka, one of the first of the modern breed that sparked America's love affair with vodka.

Belvedere Vodka is crafted at the Polmos Zyrardów Distillery from premium rye and underground spring water. It is first distilled in an alembic still, a costly and relatively laborious step, but one that imbues the vodka with a substantial body and robust character. It is then triple-distilled in a continuous still, which lightens it significantly. Lastly, the vodka is filtered three times through a complex of carbon screens rendering it free of any trace congeners or impurities.

Belvedere is deserving of its world-class reputation. The vodka has ideal clarity and a subtle, pleasant bouquet of pine and dried herbs. Its velvety smooth body has heft and substance as it glides over the palate completely filling the mouth with notes of pepper and citrus zest. The lingering, slightly sweet finish is flawless.

This uptown brand gives substance and meaning to any vodka inspired cocktail. Be sure to taste Belvedere neat, or slightly chilled, however, before working with it in earnest behind the bar. It fully deserves to wow you on its own terms before showcasing it in cocktails.

Fennel and Cilantro. The flavor of the namesake-infused herb lingers on the palate for an impressively long time, an attribute that makes them tailor-made for cooking, or use in signature drinks.

The Bloody Mary has also found its way into shooter form. The ***Bloody Nose*** is a fiery combination of Absolut Peppar, horseradish, a raw oyster, and Bloody Mary mix. A slight variation on the theme is the ***Oyster Shooter***, a Louisiana specialty made with Tabasco, horseradish, cocktail sauce, draft beer, and a raw oyster. The famed ***Oyster Shooter*** at 72 Market Street in Venice, CA, is made with tequila, tomato juice, diced avocado, cilantro, jalapeño peppers, green onions, and a raw oyster.

• **Tequila Marias** — It's almost as if tequila was created with the Bloody Mary in mind. The drink mix with its spices and heat is tailor-made to showcase the best qualities of tequila, namely its earthy, spicy and often peppery character.

Substituting tequila for vodka in the drink creates the Bloody Maria. No modifications to the mix are necessary. Silver tequilas are most often selected for the featured role. They are exuberant, flavorful and stand up beautifully in the mix. The aged styles of tequila — reposados and añejos — are often obscured in the Bloody Mary mix. One exception is using an añejo tequila in a hickory flavored mix. The woody character of the aged tequila is a marvelous combination with the hickory notes in the mix.

The World Bar in Manhattan features the ***Mexican Mary***, a specialty made with Patrón Silver Tequila, chipotle hot sauce, chopped cilantro, spices and tomato juice. At Tommy's in San Francisco, the signature ***Bloody Maria*** features Don Julio Blanco Tequila, Cholula Hot Sauce and their homemade Sangrita. This traditional mix is made with tomato juice, hot sauce, orange, grapefruit and lime juices.

• **More Spirit Choices** — Few recipes better illustrate the versatility of the drink than the ***Jäger Salsa Bloody Mary***, which is made with Jägermeister, two teaspoons of medium-hot salsa and Bloody Mary Mix. If the vodka in a Bloody Mary is replaced with gin, the resulting drink is called the ***Red Snapper***. Substitute sake for the vodka to make a ***Bloody Geisha***, aquavit to make the ***Danish Mary***, or bourbon for vodka to make the ***Brown Mary***. When Dry Sack Sherry is paired in equal parts with vodka the drink becomes the ***Bloodhound***.

• **Brewed Marys** — Beer is a marvelous ingredient in these cocktails. For example, the ***Bloody Bastard*** is a savory concoction made with Bass Ale, horseradish and Bloody Mary mix. Add Stoli Citros to convert the recipe into a ***Bloody Russian Bastard***. Another beer laced

Mary is the Mexican classic **Michelata**. It's a tall, iced drink created using tequila and equal parts of Mexican lager and Bloody Mary mix.

One of the more creative Bloody Marys hails from Indigo Eurasian Cuisine in Honolulu. Dubbed simply the **Perfect Mary**, the drink is concocted with SKYY Vodka, horseradish, Worcestershire Sauce and the rest of the usual suspects. That which separates this specialty from the commonplace is the finishing touch — a float of Guinness Irish Stout. The combination of flavors is just about perfect.

• **The Secret Is The Mix** — What makes the Bloody Mary such a classic crowd pleaser lies primarily in the mix. Taste testing is integral to the process of creating a masterpiece. It is important though to always sample the mix over ice, a practice that will best simulate game-like conditions. In addition to cooling the mix, the ice will naturally dilute the drink's consistency and spicy character, factors that must be taken into consideration. Anticipating the diluting effects of ice is crucial.

Where Mary is concerned, thin is not in. A Bloody Mary with a rich, thick consistency immediately conveys quality. It suggests that the drink is substantial, nutritious and that it was prepared with a bevy of vitamin enriched products. It is similar to stew, the thicker and heartier the base, the more life sustaining it is. Most start with a base of tomato juice, however, a great mix can be made using Clamato, or V-8 juice. To thicken things up add a bit of tomato paste to the mix.

Modifiers such as Worcestershire Sauce, prepared horseradish and Tabasco are considered a must. Other often relied upon ingredients include A.1. Sauce, Mexican hot sauce or pureed salsa, pickle juice, barbeque sauce, balsamic vinegar, soy sauce, olive juice, chopped cilantro, fresh lime or lemon juice, Angostura Bitters, and jalapeño pepper juice.

Some people want a Bloody Mary hot and spicy to the point of being nearly combustible. There are others who prefer to survive the experience fully intact. The concept of hot and spicy is a relative one, so caution needs to be exercised when adding heat, regardless of whether it's in the form of spice or sauce. It is far easier to add more heat to a Bloody Mary than to calm one down.

The true creative artistry comes into play when adding the seasonings. Celery salt, salt, and ground black pepper are just the beginning. Cayenne pepper, fresh wasabi, cumin, paprika, crushed red pepper, onion powder, garlic salt or powder, thyme, Chinese mustard, seasoned salt, chili powder, cardamom,

Marcus' Martini Heaven

88 Yesler Way
Seattle, WA 98104

☎ 206.624.3323

▶▶ www.marcusmartiniheaven.com

✉ info@marcusmartiniheaven.com

There's no place else on Earth like **Marcus' Martini Heaven**. A night on the town spent at this completely engaging, subterranean haunt is an experience not to be missed. This destination bar has it all, a romantic setting, tons of class and ambience, an easy to appreciate cuisine and a world-class portfolio of cocktails. In this context, use of the word Heaven is an appropriate description.

Opened in 1997, Marcus' Martini Heaven is located under the historic streets of Pioneer Square in what is known as the Seattle Underground. The bar is situated in what was the lobby of a 19th century hotel at the city's original street level. The place has all of the mystery and allure of a speakeasy. The warm,

inviting interior is an absorbing blend of exposed brick and stone walls, wood beam ceilings, spacious booths, demur lighting and framed works of local artists. As if that wasn't enough to grab your undivided attention, there are large saltwater aquariums to amuse the eyes.

The unassuming cuisine is an ideal accompaniment to the bar's franchise cocktails. The menu includes grilled sandwiches such as Mama Lil's Peppers and Cheese and Sundried Tomato Tapenade and Turkey with Cheese. They also offer a grilled pita and hummus plate that is fabulous.

In addition to the sumptuous fare, what keeps people streaming steadily through Heaven's door is their roster of sumptuous cocktails. High on the list is the popular *La Dolce Vita*, which is made with Campari, gin and fresh orange juice, and the *Louisiana Lady*, a libation crafted using whiskey, amaretto and fresh lemon sour mix. Another specialty of the house is *The Pagan*, a cocktail concocted with Stoli Vanil, Chambord and fresh lemon sour mix.

Heaven underground? In this case it's true. —RP

Louisiana Lady
Drink recipe on pg 170

Italian seasoning, ginger powder, Old Bay Seasoning, whole black peppercorns and basil leaves round out the shopping list. And whether you use a pinch, a teaspoon, or a dash of any of the above is entirely up to you.

Other creative options include the **Bloody Cajun**, which gets its personality from onion powder, thyme, red pepper and paprika, and the **Italian Maria**, a tempting offering made with garlic powder, paprika and prepared Italian seasonings. The **Tex-Mex Mary** is fueled by chili powder and cumin.

• **Coup de Grace** — First impressions matter. The Bloody Mary is a tall, iced drink and must therefore be served in a tall, great looking glass. The drink deserves a glass with a capacity of 12 to 16-ounces, anything less is an insufficient serving size. In addition, present the Mary in a glass with some aesthetic appeal to it.

Another trademark of a well-dressed Bloody Mary is a salted rim. To do so rub a lime wedge against the outside rim of the glass and then dip the glass into a saucer of kosher salt. A sage practice in this day and age is salting half the rim, affording your guests the option of moderating how much salt they consume. If given the time, salt glasses in advance, allowing the lime juice

Chopin® Potato Vodka

It seems most fitting that a classy Polish vodka be named after the country's most renowned and beloved composer—Frederic Chopin. Even more important, **Chopin Potato Vodka** is an opus worthy of bearing the revered composer's name.

Super-premium Chopin is imported from Poland where its ancestry can be traced back five centuries. This small batch vodka is distilled four times in a traditional pot still made exclusively from hand cultivated Stobrawa potatoes grown in the famed agricultural Siedlce region of Poland. The potatoes give Chopin its characteristically light body and distinctively delicious flavor. The water used in its production is drawn from deep, underground wells and is repeatedly filtered for purity. It is bottled at 80-proof.

Chopin Polish Vodka is crystal clear and has an ample bouquet of baked potatoes with notes of pine, caramel and citrus. Upon entry its satiny, light-weight body expands, and fills the mouth with an array of spicy, semisweet flavors that sizzle just slightly on the tongue. The finish is warm, of medium duration and punctuated with the flavors of cocoa and toffee.

The vodka's eye-catching, cork-finished bottle is the same type used to market bestselling **Belvedere Vodka**. These two top-shelf vodkas are typical sisters, related, yet dissimilar. Where Chopin has a bold, zesty character, Belvedere is softer, with a rounder, more sedate personality. Both are exemplary and most deserving of their celebrity status.

and salt combination to harden. Another creative maneuver is adding some black pepper, or crushed red peppers to the salt.

Why has a celery stalk accompanied nearly every Bloody Mary ever served? While opinions differ, one thing is undeniably true; celery is an edible and attractive swizzle. It allows the recipient to both stir the drink and have a nosh. The classic garnish is celery. Use only the tender, interior pieces of the celery and not the fibrous, outer stalks. Also, leave the leafy greens on as it gives the celery a fresh, attractive appearance.

In a democracy there is no law mandating that celery accompany the Bloody Mary. Indeed, there are several other options when it comes to edible swizzles, namely asparagus, beef or turkey jerky, jicima sticks, cucumber spears or something akin to a Slim Jim. Regardless of whether it's edible or not, provide guests with an attractive means of stirring their Bloody Marys.

The final touch to any noteworthy Bloody Mary is the garnish. More than a mere embellishment, the garnish should be considered an ingredient in the drink. The embellishments sitting atop a Bloody Mary contribute to both the flavor of the drink and the enhancement of its overall visual appeal. It's hard to over do it when it comes to garnishes, so don't be stingy, however, do consider how much volume the garnishes will take up in the drink. It's a mistake to add so many finishing touches that the drink overflows its glass.

A fresh lime, or lemon wedge is the other standard garnish on a Bloody Mary. Each adds a delightful citrus tang to the drink. But no need to stop there, optional garnishes include cooked shrimp or prawns, pickled green beans, bleu-cheese stuffed olives, cherry tomatoes, chili pepper rods, sliced bell peppers, speared tomatoes, roasted garlic, cubed cheese, tortilla chips, pepperoncinis or small jalapeños peppers.

• **Hang-Over Free** — The tremendous character of your Bloody Mary mix makes an ideal candidate for promoting it as an alcohol-free specialty drink. Certainly the absence of the base spirit will alter the finished drink, but what's left in the glass is still world-class served over ice. Embellish the alcohol-free version just as you would those Marys that do contain alcohol. The ***Bloody Shame***, as alcohol-free Bloody Marys are sometimes referred to as, is a delicious, exuberant libation.

Bloody Marys are as unique as your signature, and speak volumes about your degree of creativity. Have fun and make a masterpiece.

Bloodhound Bloody Mary

Excerpted from The Original Guide to
American Cocktails and Drinks- 6th Edition
Salt rimmed bucket glass, ice
Build in glass
1 1/2 oz. Vodka
1 oz. Dry Sack Sherry
Fill with Bloody Mary mix*
Garnish with a lime wedge and celery stalk
Pour ingredients into the salt rimmed, iced
bucket glass in the order listed. Garnish with a
lime wedge and celery stalk.
*Bloody Mary Mix Recipe - pg 318

Bloody Bastard Bloody Mary

Excerpted from The Original Guide to
American Cocktails and Drinks- 6th Edition
Salt rimmed bucket glass, ice
Pour ingredients into an iced mixing glass
1/2 fill Bass Ale
1/2 fill Bloody Mary mix*
1/2 tbsp. horseradish
Shake and strain
Garnish with a lime wedge and shrimp
Pour ingredients into the iced mixing glass.
Shake thoroughly and strain contents into the
salt rimmed, iced bucket glass. Garnish with a
lime wedge and shrimp.
*Bloody Mary Mix Recipe - pg 318

"Paris in the 1920s was a hotbed for American
expatriates, writers and artists."

Kutskova® Vodka

Now a commodity nearly synonymous with Russia, vodka originated in the 12th century at an isolated fort named Viakta near the small town of Kutskova, the site of present day Moscow. The spirit was called zhiznennia voda, meaning "water of life," testimony in part to the station it had in early civilization. Today vodka accounts for more than a quarter of all spirits sold in the United States, a megatrend fueled by such top-shelf imports as *Kutskova Vodka*.

This superb spirit is made in Moscow in accordance with a formula first established by the czarist government in 1894. Kutskova is double-distilled in small batches from the highest quality Luxe wheat and soft spring water from the Gzhelka River. The vodka's purity and crystalline clarity can be attributed to its being subjected to rigorous filtration through composites of birch charcoal and diamond quartz sand, which renders the spirit essentially pure. It is bottled at 80-proof.

Kutskova is an exceptional Russian vodka and a genuine treat for the senses. It has a creamy, sweet and grainy bouquet and a full, supple body with a delectable, oily texture. The vodka immediately warms the palate with the semisweet flavors of citrus, toffee and cocoa. The finish is long, warming and flavorful.

Clean, crisp and satisfying, Kutskova is a vodka perfectly suited for serving neat or with a heavy chill. Its modest price tag also makes it an ideal candidate for use in cocktails. *Vashe zdorovie!*

Bloody Bull Bloody Mary

Excerpted from The Original Guide to
American Cocktails and Drinks- 6th Edition
Salt rimmed bucket glass, ice
Build in glass
1 1/2 oz. Vodka
1/2 fill Bloody Mary mix*
1/2 fill beef broth
Garnish with a lime wedge, celery stalk,
    and stick of beef jerky
Pour ingredients into the salt rimmed, iced
bucket glass in the order listed. Garnish with a
lime wedge, celery stalk and stick of beef jerky.
*Bloody Mary Mix Recipe - pg 318

Bloody Caesar Bloody Mary

Excerpted from The Original Guide to
American Cocktails and Drinks- 6th Edition
Salt rimmed house specialty glass, ice
Build in glass
1 1/2 oz. Vodka
Fill with Clamato juice
Garnish with a lime wedge and celery stalk
Pour ingredients into the salt rimmed, iced house
specialty glass in the order listed. Garnish with a
lime wedge and celery stalk.

Bloody Cajun Bloody Mary

Excerpted from The Original Guide to
American Cocktails and Drinks- 6th Edition
Salt rimmed bucket glass, ice
Build in glass
1 1/2 oz. Vodka
1/2 tsp. onion powder
1/4 tsp. crushed thyme leaves
1 pinch crushed red pepper
2 pinches paprika
Fill with Bloody Mary mix*
Garnish with a lime wedge and celery stalk
Pour ingredients into the salt rimmed, iced
bucket glass in the order listed. Garnish with a
lime wedge and celery stalk.
*Bloody Mary Mix Recipe - pg 318

Bloody Geisha

Specialty of BarMedia
Created by Robert Plotkin
Salt rimmed house specialty glass, ice
Build in glass
1 1/2 oz. Sake
Fill with Bloody Mary mix*
Garnish with a lime wedge and celery stalk
Pour ingredients into the salt rimmed, iced house
specialty glass in the order listed. Garnish with a
lime wedge and celery stalk.
*Bloody Mary Mix Recipe - pg 318

Bloody Maria

Excerpted from The Original Guide to
American Cocktails and Drinks- 6th Edition
Salt rimmed bucket glass, ice
Build in glass
1 1/2 oz. Tequila
Fill with Bloody Mary mix*
Garnish with a lime wedge and celery stalk
Pour ingredients into the salt rimmed, iced
bucket glass in the order listed. Garnish with a
lime wedge and celery stalk.
*Bloody Mary Mix Recipe - pg 318

Bloody Maria, Tommy's

Specialty of Tommy's Mexican Restaurant
Created by Jacque Bezuidenhout, Ronaldo Colli
Salt and fresh ground pepper rimmed
    bucket glass, ice
Build in glass
1 3/4 oz. Don Julio Blanco Tequila
Dash Cholula Hot Sauce
Dash Worcestershire Sauce
4 oz. Tommy's Sangrita Bloody Mary Mix*
Stir gently
Garnish with a lime wedge and jicima stick
Pour ingredients into the salt and pepper
rimmed, iced bucket glass in the order listed.
Stir gently. Garnish with a lime wedge and
jicama stick.
*Sangrita Bloody Maria Mix Recipe - pg 322

Bloody Mary, Rosemary's

Specialty of Rosemary's Restaurant
Created by Michael Shetler
Salt rimmed bucket glass, ice
Build in glass
2 oz. Modern Spirits Celery Peppercorn Vodka
8 oz. Rosemary's Bloody Mary Mix*
Stir gently
Garnish with a lime wedge
    and prosciutto-mozzarella stuffed
    cherry pepper
Pour ingredients into the salt rimmed, iced
bucket glass in the order listed. Stir gently. Gar-
nish with a lime wedge and prosciutto-mozza-
rella stuffed cherry pepper.
*Rosemary's Bloody Mary Mix Recipe - pg 322

Bloody Nose
Excerpted from The Original Guide to
American Cocktails and Drinks- 6th Edition
Salt rimmed house specialty glass, ice
Build in glass
1 1/2 oz. Absolut Peppar Vodka
1/2 tbsp. horseradish
Near fill with Bloody Mary mix*
Float a raw oyster
Garnish with a lime wedge and celery stalk
Pour ingredients, except the oyster, into the salt
rimmed, iced house specialty glass in the order
listed. Float a raw oyster and garnish with a lime
wedge and celery stalk.
*Bloody Mary Mix Recipe - pg 318

Bloody Russian Bastard
   ### Bloody Mary
Excerpted from The Original Guide to
American Cocktails and Drinks- 6th Edition
Salt rimmed house specialty glass, ice
Build in glass
2 oz. Bass Ale
1 1/2 oz. Stoli Citros Vodka
1/2 tbsp. horseradish
Fill with Bloody Mary mix*
Garnish with a lime wedge and shrimp
Pour ingredients into the salt rimmed, iced house
specialty glass in the order listed. Garnish with a
lime wedge and shrimp.
*Bloody Mary Mix Recipe - pg 318

Bloody Shame
Excerpted from The Original Guide to
American Cocktails and Drinks- 6th Edition
Salt rimmed house specialty glass, ice
Build in glass
Fill with Bloody Mary mix*
Garnish with a lime wedge and celery stalk
Pour the Bloody Mary mix into the salt rimmed,
iced house specialty glass and garnish with a
lime wedge and celery stalk.
*Bloody Mary Mix Recipe - pg 318

Bloody Tex-Mex Bloody Mary
Excerpted from The Original Guide to
American Cocktails and Drinks- 6th Edition
Salt rimmed house specialty glass, ice
Build in glass
1 1/2 oz. Vodka
1/2 oz. chili powder
2 pinches ground cumin
2 pinches paprika
Fill with Bloody Mary mix*
Garnish with a lime wedge and celery stalk
Pour ingredients into the salt rimmed, iced house
specialty glass in the order listed. Garnish with a
lime wedge and celery stalk.
*Bloody Mary Mix Recipe - pg 318

Brown Mary
Specialty of BarMedia
Created by Robert Plotkin
Salt rimmed house specialty glass, ice
Build in glass
1 1/2 oz. Bourbon
Fill with Bloody Mary mix*
Garnish with a lime wedge and celery stalk
Pour ingredients into the salt rimmed, iced house
specialty glass in the order listed. Garnish with a
lime wedge and celery stalk.
*Bloody Mary Mix Recipe - pg 318

Danish Bloody Mary
Excerpted from The Original Guide to
American Cocktails and Drinks- 6th Edition
Salt rimmed bucket glass, ice
Build in glass
1 1/2 oz. Aquavit
1/2 tsp. horseradish
2 oz. Clamato juice
Fill with Bloody Mary mix*
Garnish with a lime wedge and celery stalk
Pour ingredients into the salt rimmed, iced
bucket glass in the order listed. Garnish with a
lime wedge and celery stalk.
*Bloody Mary Mix Recipe - pg 318

Michael's Kitchen

✉ **2000 Harrison Street**
Hollywood, FL 33020
☎ **954.926.5556**
▶▶ **www.michaels-kitchen.com**
✉ **chef@michaels-kitchen.com**

Open tables at **Michael's Kitchen** are hot commodities in South Florida. The place is more than a mere restaurant; it is a non-stop feast for the senses presented in an expansive dining room wrapped around an open, exhibition kitchen. The action is continuous and enthralling, like watching artists engaged in a choreographed production. It's mastery in motion and at its center is Chef-owner Michael Blum, who clearly loves what he does and does it marvelously well.

Michael's Kitchen is airy, curvy and super hip. The interior features hanging light fixtures, green concrete floors, a large, window-encased wine cellar and richly upholstered booths. The choice seating is definitely the dining bar that hugs the tiled edge of the kitchen. It's like having a front row center view of the action. The rounded bar design is both understated and attention grabbing. The buzz in the place is almost palpable.

The cuisine is delectable and presented with artistry and panache. Seafood is one of the specialties of the house. The Firecracker Yellowfin Tuna Sushi appetizer is delivered in a statuesque cocktail glass on a ceramic tile painted with sauces and embellished with seaweed and fruit. Also among the menu offerings are glazed Asian ribs with a side of devilishly delicious mashed potatoes, Eggplant Caprese and Gnochi with Kobe Beef Bolognaise.

The warm and convivial atmosphere in Michael's Kitchen is only enhanced by their fabulous output of cocktails, many of which are fueled by the bar's large array of infused spirits. One popular specialty is the *Grape Martini*, which is made with Frïs Vodka, Shakka Grape Liqueur and a splash of fresh sour mix.

Michael's Kitchen is deserving of its acclaim. —RP

Grape Martini
Drink recipe on pg 166

Italian Maria
Specialty of BarMedia
Created by Robert Plotkin
Salt rimmed bucket glass, ice
Build in glass
1 1/2 oz. Vodka
1/4 tsp. Italian seasoning
2 pinches garlic powder
2 pinches paprika
Fill with Bloody Mary mix*
Garnish with a lime wedge and beef jerky
Pour ingredients into the salt rimmed, iced bucket glass in the order listed. Garnish with a lime wedge and piece of beef jerky.
*Bloody Mary Mix Recipe - pg 318

Jäger Salsa Bloody Mary
Excerpted from The Original Guide to
American Cocktails and Drinks- 6th Edition
Salt rimmed house specialty glass, ice
Build in glass
1 1/2 oz. Jägermeister
2 tsp. salsa, medium-hot
Fill with Bloody Mary mix*
Garnish with a lime wedge and celery stalk
Pour ingredients into the salt rimmed, iced house specialty glass in the order listed. Garnish with a lime wedge and celery stalk.
*Bloody Mary Mix Recipe - pg 318

"Credit for inventing the Bloody Mary goes to Fernand Petiot."

SKYY® Vodka

SKYY is the Charles Lindbergh of American vodkas, daring to cross what at the time was an empty expanse of super premium vodkas to release what has now become an iconic spirits brand. Marketed in its readily identifiable cobalt blue bottle, the brand was the first to base its claim to fame on essential purity. *SKYY Vodka* is a marvelously neutral spirit deserving of its top-shelf status.

Introduced in San Francisco in 1988, the brand was created by Maurice Kanbar who set out to distill a vodka devoid of impurities called congeners. The result of his pursuit was a column-distilled spirit made from American grain and essentially pure water, which is then subjected to rigorous filtration. It's bottled at 80-proof.

SKYY does a superb job extolling the virtues and portraying the attractive qualities of neutral vodkas. Its light-weight body is pristine and satiny textured. Its initial entry warms the mouth slightly before sliding away into a clean, crisp finish.

Not content to rest on their laurels, the distillery expanded the range with the release of *SKYY90*, an elegant wheat vodka made in a 5-column still and bottled at a lip tingling 90-proof. The spirit has a round, feather-weight body that lilts over the palate with nary a trace of harshness. Its finish is clean and refreshing.

Their medley of flavored vodkas includes *SKYY Melon*, *SKYY Orange*, *SKYY Vanilla*, *SKYY Berry*, and *SKYY Citrus Vodka*, a blend of oranges, lemons, limes, tangerines and grapefruits. All are extremely cocktail friendly.

The Mexican Mary
Specialty of The World Bar
Created by Kenneth McClure
Pilsner glass, ice
Pour ingredients into an iced mixing glass
2 oz. Patrón Silver Tequila
4 dashes Chipotle Hot Sauce
1 pinch finely chopped cilantro
1/2 tsp. celery salt
1 tsp. Worcestershire Sauce
4 oz. tomato juice
Shake and strain
Garnish with a scallion stalk
Pour ingredients into the iced mixing glass. Shake thoroughly and strain contents into an iced pilsner glass. Garnish with a scallion stalk.

Michilata Bloody Mary
Excerpted from The Original Guide to
American Cocktails and Drinks- 6th Edition
Salt rimmed pint glass, ice
Pour ingredients into an iced mixing glass
1 1/2 oz. Reposado Tequila
4 dashes Tabasco Pepper Sauce
2 pinches salt
2 pinches black pepper
2 pinches seasoned salt
1/4 oz. white wine vinegar
1/2 oz. fresh lemon juice
3/4 oz. fresh lime juice
3 oz. tomato juice
Shake and strain
Fill with Tecate Beer
Garnish with a lime wedge
Pour ingredients into the iced mixing glass. Shake thoroughly and strain contents into a salt rimmed, iced pint glass. Fill with Tecate Beer and garnish with a lime wedge.

Oyster Shooter
Excerpted from The Original Guide to
American Cocktails and Drinks- 6th Edition
Rocks glass, chilled
Build in glass
2 dashes Tabasco Pepper Sauce
1/2 tsp. horseradish
3 oz. Draft Beer
Float 1 raw oyster
Pour ingredients into the chilled rocks glass in the order listed. Float the oyster.

Perfect Mary
Specialty of Indigo Eurasian Cuisine
Created by Mary Peter, Jason Castle
Salt rimmed house specialty glass, ice
Pour ingredients into an iced mixing glass
3 oz. SKYY Vodka
Dash ground black pepper
Dash celery salt
1/8 tsp. Tabasco Pepper Sauce
1/4 tsp. horseradish
1/2 tbsp. Worcestershire Sauce
1 oz. fresh lime juice
1 oz. fresh lemon juice
1/2 cup tomato juice
Shake and strain
Float with Guinness Irish Stout
Garnish with an olive, onion, lime wedge
    and cucumber sliver skewered and
    balanced across top of glass
Pour ingredients into the iced mixing glass. Shake thoroughly and strain contents into a salt rimmed iced house specialty glass. Float the Guinness. Garnish with an olive, onion, lime wedge and cucumber sliver skewered and balanced across top of glass.

Ragin' Cajun Bloody Mary
Specialty of Bourbon Street & Voodoo Lounge
Created by Matt Spencer
Salt rimmed house specialty glass, ice
Build in glass
1 1/2 oz. Absolut Peppar Vodka
2 dashes Tabasco Pepper Sauce
2 pinches celery salt
Splash Lea & Perrin's Worcestershire Sauce
Splash fresh lemon juice
Splash fresh lime juice
1/2 oz. A.1. Steak Sauce
3/4 oz. olive juice
1 oz. Cajun pickle juice
Fill with Major Peter's Bloody Mary Mix
Stir gently
Garnish with a pickle, olive and celery stick
Pour ingredients into the salt rimmed, iced house specialty glass in the order listed. Stir gently. Garnish with a pickle, olive and celery stick.

Red Snapper Bloody Mary
Excerpted from The Original Guide to
American Cocktails and Drinks- 6th Edition
Salt rimmed bucket glass, ice
Build in glass
1 1/4 oz. Gin
Fill with Bloody Mary mix*
Garnish with a lime wedge and celery stalk
Pour ingredients into the salt rimmed, iced
bucket glass in the order listed. Garnish with a
lime wedge and celery stalk.
*Bloody Mary Mix Recipe - pg 318

Sichuan Mary
Specialty of P.F. Chang's China Bistro
Created by P.F. Chang's staff
Pint glass, ice
Build in glass
1 1/2 oz. Absolut Peppar Vodka
1/2 oz. Demitri's Bloody Mary Mix
Fill with tomato juice
Garnish with a lime wedge, chili pepper pod,
    and a green onion stalk
Pour ingredients into the pint glass in the
order listed. Garnish with a lime wedge, chili
pepper pod, and a green onion stalk.

"It's almost as if tequila was created
with the Bloody Mary in mind."

Sauza® Hornitos® Reposado 100% Agave Tequila

Tequila Sauza is today the second largest distiller of tequila and the fastest growing spirit brand in the world. Theirs is the bestselling tequila in Mexico. Sauza struck pay dirt with the introduction of *Hornitos Reposado 100% Agave Tequila*.

Hornitos is distilled entirely from mature blue agave at the Sauza La Perseverancia Distillery in Jalisco, Mexico. The harvested agaves are baked, shredded, fermented and double-distilled in both an alembic still and a stainless steel column still. Sauza then ages Hornitos for 4 to 6 months in large vats, which is just enough time in the oak to soften its character without being appreciably affected by the tannins in the wood. As a result, Hornitos has the exuberance and fresh agave character of a blanco tequila with a touch of the mellow refinement of an añejo.

A quick sniff, sip and swallow will quickly reveal why Hornitos has become such a runaway success. The pale golden color belies its complexity and surprisingly full, rounded body. Hornitos has an alluring bouquet concentrated with the rich aromas of pepper, caramel and citrus. Its vibrant palate is an array of semisweet flavors, notably caramel, black pepper, luscious fruit and the herbaceous taste of agave. Hornitos finishes warm and long.

For all of its sophistication and market dominance, Sauza Hornitos is priced well below most top-shelf 100% agave reposados, earning it merit as one of the best tequila values. The brand is game for any tequila-based assignment.

The Upstairs Neighbor

Specialty of Cyrus
Created by Scott Beattie
Collins glass, ice
Build in glass
1 1/2 oz. Hangar One Straight Vodka
Pinch kosher salt
2 grinds fresh black peppercorns
Fresh grated horseradish to taste
1 oz. fresh lemon juice
Fill with Heirloom tomato juice*
Stir gently
Garnish with a skewer of homemade
    pickled vegetables
Pour ingredients into the iced collins glass in the
order listed. Stir gently. Garnish with a skewer of
homemade pickled vegetables.
*Heirloom Tomato Juice Recipe - pg 320

The Vegan Nightmare

Specialty of Savoy
Created by Brandon Craft, James Ducas
Pint glass, ice
Pour ingredients into an iced mixing glass
2 oz. Belvedere Vodka
Dash Worcestershire Sauce
Dash Cholula Hot Sauce
Large pinch salt
Large pinch pepper
Large pinch celery salt
1/4 tsp. wasabi
1 tbsp. tomato paste
1 1/4 oz. veal stock
6 oz tomato juice
Shake and strain
Garnish with a celery stalk, lemon slice
    and bleu cheese stuffed olive
Pour ingredients into the iced mixing glass.
Shake thoroughly and strain contents into the
iced pint glass. Garnish with a celery stalk,
lemon slice and bleu cheese stuffed olive.

Wasabi Mary

Specialty of The Original McCormick & Schmick's
Created by Geoff V. Helzer
Salt rimmed pint glass, ice
Pour ingredients into an iced mixing glass
1 1/2 oz. Absolut Vodka
Pinch celery salt
Pinch pepper
2 dashes Worcestershire Sauce
1/2 tsp. fresh wasabi
6 oz. tomato juice
Shake and strain
Garnish with a pickled green bean,
    celery stalk and lemon twist
Pour ingredients into the iced mixing glass.
Shake thoroughly and strain contents into the
salt rimmed, iced pint glass. Garnish with a
pickled green bean, celery stalk and lemon twist.

Zebra Envy

Specialty of Cyrus
Created by Scott Beattie
Collins glass, ice
Build in glass
1 1/2 oz. Hangar One Straight Vodka
10-15 sweet basil leaves, finely chopped
Pinch gray salt
Pinch black peppercorns, toasted and crushed*
1 tbsp. aged balsamic vinegar
Fill with green tomato juice*
Stir gently
Garnish with fresh mozzarella, green zebra
    tomatoes and basil leaves skewered. Rest
    on top of drink*
Pour ingredients into the iced collins glass in the
order listed. Stir gently. Garnish with fresh moz-
zarella, green zebra tomatoes and basil leaves
skewered. Rest on top of drink.
*Garnish Preparation
Cut the fresh mozzarella and the green zebras
into small matchstick pieces. Alternately skewer
them on a bamboo skewer with sliced basil leaves
intertwined throughout. Dash the skewer with
aged balsamic and sprinkle with gray salt and
toasted pepper. Rest on top of the drink.
*Green Tomato Juice Recipe - pg 320
*Toasted Black Peppercorns Recipe
    1 tbsp. black peppercorns
Stir the peppercorns in a hot pan until they start
popping. Remove from heat. Crush in the bottom
of a glass or with a mortar and pestle.

Chapter Eight

Hot & Steamy Sensations
Hot Drinks

Few countries appreciate a great cup of coffee as much we do. In fact, America is the largest coffee-consuming nation in the world, so it's little wonder that we continue devising so many innovative ways to work with it behind our bars. Where once hot drinks were considered only cold weather fare, the proliferation of cafes and coffee houses has created an environment where specialty coffee drinks have year round appeal.

Most people who rely on coffee for their morning jolt have no idea that coffee is not a bean, but rather the seed of a fruit that grows on large shrub-type plants that reach heights of 15-30 feet. A coffee plant will yield one to two pounds of green berries each growing season. When ripe, the berries turn a deep crimson and closely resemble a plump cranberry.

The secret behind the phenomenal appeal of coffee lies in the roasting process, which burns off certain unwanted acids, while further developing those that provide the finished brew with taste and zestfulness. Roasting also causes beans to become brittle and thus easily ground.

After several minutes in a roaster, the green beans turn a straw, or amber color. Minutes later, the water content in the bean turns to steam and causes it to pop, altering its shape. This internal heat brings about chemical changes within the bean, converting raw components into flavor and aroma enhancing components, such as ketones and aldehydes, the same range of chemicals so important in the making of wine.

Aside from the darkening in color, roasting causes oils to rise to the surface. Up to 15% of a coffee bean is oil. The substance is essential to the appreciation of coffee because it is the oil that delivers the flavor components. The deeper the roast, the more essential oils make it to the bean's surface.

Which degree of roast is best is a matter of debate among coffee aficionados. A roast where the bean has attained a light mahogany color will have trace amounts of oil on the surface. The result is a light-bodied coffee with high acidity and a broad range of flavors. Conversely, dark roasted beans are covered with an oily sheen and deliver a slightly sweet, full-bodied cup of coffee with a bold, robust flavor.

Coffee derives its characteristics from the climatic and soil conditions under which it is grown. There are those who prefer drinking coffee produced by a single variety of bean, such as 100% Colombian, Jamaican, or Kona. While often a bit pricey, it is an interesting way to appreciate the distinctive qualities of a specific growing region.

The majority of commercial coffees are blends, comprised of beans from several different growing regions. While not as exclusive, or expensive, there are appreciable advantages to drinking a blended coffee. The intent of a blend is to marry together complimentary flavors such that the sum of the parts is greater than the whole.

Brewing World Class Coffee

The finest, most exclusive coffee beans will not salvage a poorly prepared cup of coffee. A few carefully heeded words of advice may mean the difference between a luxurious cup of heaven or a bitter, acidic mess. No coffee lover need suffer through a miserable cup of Joe. To that end, the following are the secrets to brewing a world-class cup of coffee.

- **Storing Coffee Beans** — An important aspect of serving a great cup of coffee is to start with fresh beans, or more accurately, to start with freshly roasted beans. The beans will quickly lose their lively aroma and flavor, thus the need for proper storage.

Jim Beam® Bourbon

Now an American institution, Jim Beam is the benchmark by which all other bourbons are measured, if for no other reason than it is the best-selling bourbon in the world. The Beam family has been distilling whiskey at their distillery in Clermont, Kentucky since 1795. It is among the largest and most sophisticated in the world. But for all of their technical sophistication, little has changed in how they produce *Jim Beam Bourbon*.

This most famous of bourbons is distilled from a mash bill comprised of a high proportion of white and yellow corn grown in Indiana and Kentucky, along with lesser percentages of rye and malted barley. The other two crucial ingredients used to make the whiskey are sweet, limestone filtered water from the Long Lick Creek and a strain of spontaneous-type yeast, which was discovered by Jim Beam himself and has been maintained for over 70 years.

Premium Jim Beam Bourbon is aged a minimum of 4 years in oak barrels. During that time it develops a soft, medium-weight body and an enticing bouquet of vanilla, baking spices, cocoa and toasted oak. The whiskey washes over the palate revealing a savory set of flavors including caramel, vanilla, fruit and a hint of smoke. The finish is warm and relaxed.

Quality, price and a classic array of flavors make this Jim Beam Bourbon an absolute "must have" whiskey behind the bar.

Do not store coffee, especially ground coffee, in a refrigerator. The ambient moisture will rob the coffee of its freshness. Even stored in a sealed container, coffee is susceptible to absorbing any food odors present in a refrigerator.

• **Grinding Coffee Beans** — Whole beans maintain their freshness better than ground coffee, so grinding them just before brewing is optimum. Since there are numerous methods to brew coffee, there is no one right gauge of grind. If the grind is too fine, the water will extract an excessive amount of oil and flavors from the coffee. Likewise, the finely ground coffee will clog the filter and cause minute particles of coffee to make their way to the finished cup of coffee. An excessively coarse grind allows hot water to rapidly flow through the filter causing under-extraction and a bitter, flavorless cup of coffee. Most machines require a moderately coarse ground.

• **Water Quality** — The simple truth is that the coffee you brew will be no better than the water you use. Distilled water is by definition flavorless and to some is therefore a detriment. Many tap waters are loaded with alkaline minerals that adversely react with the essential oils in the coffee beans. The phosphates in softened water react even worse with the coffee. Filtered drinking water, or even better, naturally balanced spring water is optimal.

• **Water Temperature** — The water temperature during the brewing cycle is crucially important. It ideally should be between 195° and 205° Fahrenheit. Weak, or older equipment often insufficiently heats all of the water, resulting in under-extraction and weak, bitter coffee. On the other end of the scale, never pour boiling water directly over the coffee. Always wait a few moments before using boiling water taken directly off the burner.

• **Filter Selection: Paper or Gold Plated?** — Most methods of brewing require that ground coffee be placed in either a paper, or gold-plated filter. There are advantages to both. Paper filters are disposable and therefore clean and convenient. They are also inexpensive and an effective method of preventing solids from entering the brewed coffee. Conversely, they filter out more of the desirable oils and colloids, the minute solids that give the brew its body and mouth-feel.

Gold plated filters, on the other hand, allow more of the all-important oils and colloids to pass through to the finished brew. They are durable, moderately priced and quite effective at filtering out solids.

• **Proportioning** — In coffee parlance, a scoop of ground coffee is considered to be two teaspoons. How much coffee you use is obviously a huge factor in determining the quality of the finished product. As a general rule, two scoops of ground coffee and 8-ounces of water will yield a 6-ounce cup of coffee. This basic proportion can be adjusted slightly based on personal preference.

- **Keeping Brewed Coffee Hot** — Prolonged exposure to direct heat will rapidly turn a pot of ideally brewed coffee bitter. Every passing minute that the coffee sits on a burner, a chain of unwanted chemical reactions will continue to destroy and vaporize every desirable quality about the brew. While there appears to be no readily apparent explanation, the best advice is to take the coffee off the burner as quickly as you can.

- **Life Expectancy of Brewed Coffee** — If you've ever worked in an office and drank a cup of old, stale coffee, you'll likely agree that freshness matters. It is therefore highly advisable to serve coffee immediately after the brewing process has stopped. Conventional wisdom suggests that the optimum life expectancy of brewed coffee be between 20-40 minutes, after which it is best discarded.

- **Clean Equipment** — The equipment you use to brew coffee should be cleaned regularly. There are several issues with cleanliness. The first and most compelling is mineral build-up in the machine that can diminish the effectiveness of the equipment, as well as taint the brewing process. The second concern is coffee residue affecting the process. As mentioned, coffee contains essential oils and solids that will remain in the machine. These elements will adversely affect your next pot of coffee.

Amarula® Cream Liqueur

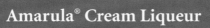

If you're looking for an exotic new taste, this is it. *Amarula Cream Liqueur* is something of an international phenomenon that currently ranks as the second bestselling cream liqueur in the world. To call Amarula a delicious and refreshing change is an understatement. It's a beverage program in a bottle, a guaranteed crowd pleaser.

Amarula is made in South Africa from the fruit of the marula tree, which is better known as the Elephant Tree. The fruit is harvested and fermented in a process similar to winemaking. It is then distilled in copper pot stills and aged for a minimum of two years in small French oak barrels. The liqueur masters then blend the aged liqueur with fresh dairy cream and bottle it at 34-proof.

Your first sip is likely all it will take for you to become an instant fan of Amarula Cream Liqueur. It has a medium-weight body and a subtle, cocoa-enriched bouquet. The liqueur washes the palate with the rich flavors of chocolate, mocha, vanilla, caramel and butterscotch. The finish is clean and quite memorable. The fact that it hails from Africa heightens the whole experience.

Creativity is the benchmark of American mixology. Devising drinks with innovative and singularly different tastes is a straight shot to success. One way to achieve that distinctive taste is to open a bottle of Amarula Cream Liqueur and let your imagination run wild.

Making Sensational Java Drinks

It is estimated that more than 400 billion cups of coffee are consumed each year, easily making it the world's most popular beverage. In fact, coffee is the second-most heavily traded commodity after petroleum.

While there are scores of venerable coffee-based drinks, several standouts have attained rarified status. One such enduring recipe is the *Keoki Coffee*, which is made with equal parts of Kahlúa, brandy and chocolate liqueur, a blend of ingredients that marry beautifully with the robust flavor of coffee. It may be of interest to learn that it's unusual name means "George's Coffee" on Hawaiian, homage to its creator, George Bullington of Bully's Restaurant in southern California.

Another Java classic is the *Irish Coffee*. As the story goes, on a particularly cold evening in 1952, Joe Sheridan, head chef at the Shannon airport restaurant, laced his coffee with a healthy dram of whiskey, a spot of sugar and a layer of whipped cream The utterly delicious drink took on a life of its own after that, becoming a specialty of the airport's bar. That same year, a columnist and travel writer for the San Francisco Chronicle, passed through Shannon on his way home. He sampled several of the coffees and was immediately smitten with the combination.

Word of the Shannon airport's coffee made its way to the Buena Vista Café on Fisherman's Wharf. The drink was replicated and immediately generated a following. Walk into the café now and you'll see a long row of coffee mugs arranged on the bar rail. The bartender will walk back and forth pouring the drink's necessary ingredients into the waiting glasses. The drinks are then finished with whipped cream just moments before being served to the waiting throng.

The appeal of the Irish Coffee is nearly universal despite its simplicity. The drink is made with a splash of simple syrup, a hefty portion of Irish whiskey, a near fill with hot, freshly brewed coffee and a layer of frothed milk or whipped cream.

Naturally, not all Irish Coffees are created equally. The *Irish Coffee Royale* features an additional shot of Kahlúa. Another version includes some Bailey's Irish Cream and a touch of Irish Mist or Celtic Crossing.

Creating delicious coffee-based drinks need not be a complicated process. The warmth and flavor of coffee marries beautifully with a wide range of flavors and products. Indeed, when it comes to creative alchemy, coffee has nearly unlimited possibilities. Here then are the best kept secrets behind America's greatest coffee drinks.

• **Coffee Foundation** — Why fight nature? Scratch the surface of most contemporary coffee drinks and you'll find they contain the classic Kahlúa, by far the bestselling coffee liqueur in the world. The reasons for its frequent use are readily apparent. Kahlúa bolsters the body and flavor of the coffee and sweetens the finished drink. Its easygoing nature accommodates numerous other complementary liqueurs.

Now in the 21st century, however, there are other coffee liqueur options available to mixologists, namely super-premium Starbucks Coffee Liqueur, Patrón XO Café Coffee Liqueur and Tia Maria. Each will contribute a different flavor profile to the drink. As they say, variety behind the bar is a good thing.

• **Esprit de Corps** — Coffee happens to be among the most capable delivery systems for spirits and liqueurs. Cognacs and brandies, Calvados and apple eaux de vie, light and aged rums, aged tequilas, grappas and whiskeys of all types are natural complements to the flavor of coffee.

On the liqueur side, there is an even larger array of complementary flavors from which to work. The range includes chocolate (Godiva and crème de cacao), hazelnut (Frangelico), orange (Grand Marnier, Cointreau and GranGala), mint (crème de menthe), banana (crème de banana), almond (Disaronno Amaretto), anise (Pernod, Absente, anisette, ouzo and sambuca), fruit (Chambord and PAMA), vanilla (Navan), citrus (limoncello) and whiskey-based (Irish Mist, Celtic Crossing and Drambuie).

The artistry comes into play pairing the various spirits and liqueurs with the coffee. Examples of the craft abound. One such concoction is the Courtright Restaurant specialty *Jamaican Coffee*, a luscious combination of Myers's Original Dark Rum, Tia Maria, Dark Crème de Cacao, brandy and hot coffee with a whipped cream garnish. Another is the *Sally Coffee*, which features a blend of Amarula Cream Liqueur, Navan Vanille Cognac Liqueur and coffee.

Other Java specialties of note include the *Mission Inn Coffee*, a classy drink made with a jigger of Courvoisier VSOP Cognac and Frangelico. The *Amadeus Kaffee* is a savory blend of Mozart Black and White Chocolate Creams, Jewel of Russia Wild Bilberry Infusion Vodka and hot coffee.

For something more along the lines of dessert, consider the *Café Brûlée*, a signature of Brûlée the Dessert Experience at the Tropicana Casino and Resort in Atlantic City. The drink is concocted with hot coffee and equal parts of Frangelico, Baileys Irish Cream, Grand Marnier and Kahlúa. It's finished with a generous layer of Baileys-flavored whipped cream. It is a sumptuous experience.

• **Adding a Creamer** — Adding Baileys Irish Cream, Starbucks Cream Liqueur, Amarula, or Carolans Irish Cream to your masterpiece is as natural as pouring cream in your coffee. It's almost as if they were created to be paired with coffee. Other cream liqueurs to use include Cruzan Rum Cream and Tequila Rose Java Cream Liqueur.

• **Java Modifiers** — The roster of potential modifiers with hot coffee is deeper than one might initially expect. First, there's honey, brown sugar and spices such as cinnamon and nutmeg. In addition, companies such as Monin produce extensive lines of flavoring syrups produced with coffee drinks in mind. Flavors cover the gamut

The Mission Inn Hotel & Spa

3649 Mission Inn Avenue
Riverside, CA 92501

☎ **951.341.6767**

▶▶ **www.missioninn.com**

✉ **restaurants@missioninn.com**

Guaranteed that the first glimpse of **The Mission Inn Hotel & Spa** will leave you breathless. Built in 1876, the magnificent property has grown to a full city block in the thick of downtown Riverside, California. It is a sprawling and impressive landmark loaded with intriguing architectural details such as arches, turrets, flying buttresses, towers, covered walkways, an open-air rotunda, interior courtyards, underground catacombs, and a five-story outside spiral staircase. The grounds are lush and equally spectacular.

No two of the Mission Inn's 239 elegant bedrooms and suites are the same. While each has domed ceilings, stained glass windows and carved pillars and niches,

subtle differences abound. Now listed on the National Register of Historic Places, the Inn has played host to heads of state, peace conferences, Hollywood weddings and numerous motion pictures.

The Mission Inn offers a wide range of dining options. The namesake fine dining restaurant indulges it guests amidst a lavish setting of vaulted ceilings, ornate wall sconces and marble accents. Al fresco dining under the stars is one of the allures of the picture perfect Spanish Patio and the much heralded Duane's Prime Steak and Seafood features an award winning wine list. Also not to be missed is the experience of sipping a cocktail in the Presidential Lounge, a former four-room apartment converted into a gentlemen's club-style lounge. All of the outlets are over-the-top classy.

The bars at the Mission Inn are swank, sophisticated and renown for their drink-making abilities. Two sterling examples are the *Billionaire*, a luxury Margarita made with Casa Noble Añejo Tequila and Grand Marnier Cuvée du Cent-Cinquantenaire, and the *Kurant Affair*, a cocktail showcasing Absolut Kurant Vodka and Chambord. —RP

Kurant Affair
Drink recipe on pg 98

such that every creative whim can be fulfilled. For example, Manhattan's World Bar features a signature drink called the *Iced Coffee Valencia* that derives its singular flavor from Valencia orange-flavored syrup.

As coffee and chocolate are classic complementary flavors, hot specialty drinks are often laced with chocolate, be it chocolate syrup, powdered cocoa, or chocolate liqueurs, such as Godiva or crème de cacao. Along the same lines, caramel is a flavor what works well in hot coffee, making caramel syrup a natural player in the creation of these drinks.

- **Capping Your Creation** — Many hot coffee creations are finished with a mound of whipped cream. As the whipped cream melts into the coffee, the sweet cream adds another flavor dimension to the drink. Capping coffee specialties with frothed milk in the fashion of a cappuccino is also a delectable option.

- **Finish with a Flourish** — Every great signature coffee needs a flourish on top to create a grand impression. Drizzle chocolate syrup over the whipped cream, or dust the layer of frothed milk with powdered cocoa. The same can be said for embellishing these drinks with crumbled brownies or cookies. The Mosaic Restaurant serves their popular

Canadian Club® Blended Canadian Whisky

In 1884, Hiram Walker first exported his 6-year old Canadian blended whisky across the Detroit River into the United States. It quickly became the brand of choice by the gentlemen members of exclusive hotels, taverns and men's clubs, earning it the name *Canadian Club Blended Canadian Whisky*. For more than a century it has been the bestselling brand of Canadian whisky in the world.

This famous whisky is comprised of a blend of continuous distilled whiskies. While its exact composition is a closely guarded secret, the blend is made up principally of corn whisky, and lesser proportions of rye, malted rye and malted barley whiskies. These whiskies are blended prior to aging, allowing the elements to thoroughly integrate during their stay in oak.

Canadian Club Whisky has a dry, rounded body and a creamy, pronounced bouquet laced with the aromas of grain, toffee and toasted oak. The whisky lilts over the palate without a trace of bitterness, leaving behind the lip-smacking flavors of caramel, butter, orange zest and notes of cereal. The whisky finishes long and relaxed.

Canadian whisky enthusiasts will also greatly appreciate the 8-year old, "double-matured" *Canadian Club Sherry Cask Whisky* and the super-premium *Canadian Club Classic 12 Year Old Whisky*. It's a blend comprised of corn whisky, and lesser proportions of rye, malted rye and malted barley whiskies. The constituent whiskies are blended together prior to aging, allowing them to become thoroughly integrated. The whisky is then aged for a minimum of 12 years in used bourbon barrels.

Amadeus Kaffee garnished with two chocolate cigarettes sticks. They're small flourishes with big appeal.

After creating a masterpiece, present it in a worthy glass. Insulated glass offers the best of all options. Its thick, yet transparent character allows guests to appreciate how attractive these drinks look.

• **Be Cool** — There is a school of thought that challenges the convention that coffee must be served hot. It explores the creative possibilities of serving freshly brewed and icy cold. There are considerable benefits to creating iced coffee specialties, not the least of which is that they're fabulously delicious, refreshing and quite unexpected.

There are two approaches to preparing iced coffee drinks. One involves transferring freshly brewed coffee into an insulated container and storing it in the cooler. Once the temperature drops it can be used throughout the day or evening. A word of caution: pouring hot coffee directly into an iced glass may cause the glass to crack due to thermal shock.

The other technique, while more involved, adds a classy touch. Pour the hot coffee into an ice filled mixing glass, sloping the hot coffee off the back of a spoon. A swirl or two later, the chilled coffee is poured into an iced service glass. The enhanced service is an appealing benefit. Also, if you're preparing an iced coffee drink, the ingredients can be added to the coffee in the iced mixing glass.

Most iced coffee drinks are presented in 12-16 ounce glasses, ranging in style from wine glasses and specialty snifters to beer glasses and classic shamrock cafés. A heavy pint glass is a popular choice because of its shape and thick, insulating glass.

Exploring the World of Espresso

It was only a matter of time before America's predilection for coffee led us directly to the satisfyingly rich flavor of espresso. Its popularity has never been higher. With increasingly more restaurants and hotels equipping their bars with espresso machines, this is a trend not likely to run out of steam.

Espresso isn't a type of coffee, rather it refers to a brewing process. In Italian, the word espresso translates to *fast*, which is an apt description of the process. Espresso is made by forcing hot water under extreme pressure through finely ground coffee beans. The heat and pressure cause the oils and proteins in the coffee to emulsify to produce a slightly syrupy, more viscous brew.

Making espresso coffee requires the use of a specialized machine that heats, pressurizes and rapidly brews the coffee. It takes roughly 15-25 seconds to brew a cup of espresso with properly ground coffee. Espresso is traditionally served in a demitasse, a small, 2 to 3-ounce china cup, with sugar and a twist of lemon on the side, the lemon peel being a strictly American tradition. Doctoring espresso to one's particular tastes is quite permissible.

Preparing a world-class demitasse of espresso involves both art and science. In an effort to make the learning curve shallow, here are the best kept secrets behind America's greatest espressos.

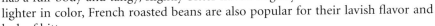

- **Coffee Choice** — Making great espresso is dependent on using good beans. The country of origin, however, is a secondary consideration to the type of roast used. The Italian roast is most commonly selected for espresso beans. The darkest degree of roasting, it turns the beans black and oily. The resulting coffee has a full-body and tangy, slightly bitter flavor. Slightly lighter in color, French roasted beans are also popular for their lavish flavor and lack of bitterness.

- **Daily Grind** — The grinding process dramatically affects the finished espresso. Finely ground espresso produces a bitter and low-acid coffee with a well-developed "crema," a creamy, mustard-colored foam on top of the coffee's surface. This skin, comprised of the coffee's essential oils, is a telling indicator of a well-made cup of espresso. Conversely, with a coarse grind, less of the oils are extracted from the coffee and only a thin skin will develop. Use only freshly ground coffee beans. Stale coffee produces a dull, lifeless cup of espresso.

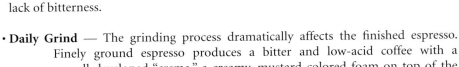

Christian Brothers® VS Brandy

Christian Brothers is one of the oldest and bestselling brands of American spirits. In 1882, the religious order of the Christian Brothers began distilling brandy from California grapes. Their commitment was and remains to create singularly light, flavorful brandies using locally grown grape varietals. Few spirits offer such tremendous character, quality and value of the dollar as *Christian Brothers VS Brandy*.

The Christian Brothers winery and adjacent distillery is a huge, state of the art complex located in the fertile San Joaquin Valley in California. Despite the technological innovations Christian Brothers have built into their facility, little has changed in their artisan approach to making brandy.

The Christian Brothers selected the Thompson Seedless grape as the principal variety, because they possess the highly sought after qualities of high acidity, balanced flavor and low alcohol output. They distill their brandies in huge, copper alembic stills, as well as extremely efficient patent stills. Prior to blending, the brandies are aged in American white oak bourbon barrels a minimum of 4 to 6 years.

The enormously popular Christian Brothers VS Brandy has a tempting and generous fruity bouquet and a soft, supple texture. The full body is imbued with layers of well-balanced fruit flavors. Its finish is warm and lingering.

Christian Brothers XO Rare Reserve Brandy is an elegant blend consisting of a high percentage of well-aged, pot-distilled brandies. It drinks far older than its years.

• **Under Pressure** — Preparing a demitasse of espresso relies on a singular brewing process. Approximately ¼-ounce (7 grams) of finely ground coffee is put into a heavy metal strainer. Before locking the strainer into the machine, the coffee is tapped firmly to ensure uniform extraction. Once the machine is activated, the nearly boiling water (200-205° F) is forced under pressure (1.5 atmospheres) through the packed, ground coffee, directly into a waiting demitasse.

• **Standard Variations** — Years ago, if you ordered a cup of coffee "regular" you'd get it prepared with added cream and sugar. Ask for a cup of regular coffee now and you'll get coffee laced with caffeine. Today, if you walk into a restaurant, bistro or bar and ask for a cup of coffee be prepared for a lengthy interrogation. There are numerous variations of espresso that have long been popular abroad that have caught on here in the U.S. Each combination is just different enough to make it a distinct entity.

For example, a double espresso is prepared using twice the amount of water and ground coffee that's in a single espresso. A short espresso, or a *Ristretto*, is made using less water than in a regular espresso, while an *Americano* is made using more water than is in a single espresso (typically about 4-6 ounces). A *Macchiato* is an espresso served with a dollop of frothed milk on top. A *Doppio* espresso is a double portion of espresso made with only half the amount of water.

The *Caffè con Panna* is an espresso topped with whipped cream, while the *Caffè Correcto* is an espresso "corrected" with a small amount of grappa, cognac, sambuca, or some other spirit.

• **The Creative Spirit** — The robust flavor of espresso marries well with a wide range of spirits and liqueurs. As an example, one of the many noteworthy specialties at Tommy's Mexican Restaurant in San Francisco is the *Café Pacifico*. It's a classy cocktail concocted with Chinaco Blanco Tequila, Kahlúa, cinnamon sugar and a double shot of fresh brewed espresso. Courtright's Restaurant in Willow Springs, Illinois promotes the *Chocolate Raspberry Java*, a superb mix of Chambord and Tia Maria built on an undercarriage of a double shot of espresso.

Stepping Out With Cappuccinos

Cappuccinos are typically prepared with a demitasse of espresso and equal parts of steamed and frothed milk, although this proportion may vary somewhat. The key to making a fabulous cappuccino lies in learning how to properly steam the cold milk such that it produces dense froth.

Whole milk is typically used to make a cappuccino, although 2% reduced fat milk works equally well. Pour the milk into a handled, metal vessel, preferably brass, for frothing. A container or pitcher that is wider at the bottom than the top is considered the most efficient shape. The vessel should be no more than half full at the beginning of the procedure.

Espresso machines are equipped with a steaming nozzle. Place the tip of the nozzle just under the surface of the milk and slowly release the steam. To prevent scalding, the pitcher should be moved in a circular motion. The milk should be frothed to approximately 135-150° F. Since it will continue to heat up after the steaming process is done, the milk will optimally peak at roughly 150-170° F. When done properly, the bubbles of the frothed milk should be compact, tightly knit and long lasting. Milk can be steamed two or three times before being discarded.

Once the milk is frothed, carefully pour some of the steamed milk, about 3 to 4 ounces, into the espresso and then spoon on the frothed milk. An appropriate garnish is a sprinkle of shaved chocolate, a dusting of powdered cocoa, nutmeg, or ground cinnamon on top of the frothed milk.

One of the genuine simple pleasures in life, cappuccinos are delicious and attractive. They also require some hands-on experience to make well. To hasten the process, here are the best kept secrets behind America's greatest cappuccinos.

• **Frothy Latitude** — Among the most popular variations of the cappuccino is the *Caffè Latte*. The drink originated in Italy and is typically prepared using a demitasse of espresso and four parts steamed milk with no froth. In America, the drink is popularly served as one part espresso diluted by four to six parts steamed milk and one part frothed milk.

Another classic variation is the *Café au Lait*, which in French means "coffee with milk." The Café au Lait is served in an oversized cup and made with a demitasse of espresso coffee that is then highly diluted with steamed milk. The proportion of milk to coffee is a matter of personal preference, although it is often made with one part espresso to 4-8 parts steamed milk. A thin layer of frothed milk is often spooned on top.

One obvious twist on the cappuccino is to make it with decaf espresso, which is referred to as a "Harmless," "No fun," or "Sleeper." A dry cappuccino is prepared with a larger percentage of frothed milk and a double cappuccino is made with two demitasses worth of espresso. A *Brevé Cappuccino* is made using half & half instead of milk, while a *Skinny Cappuccino* is prepared with nonfat milk.

The *Mochaccino*, also known as the *Café Mocha,* is a cappuccino made with either frothed chocolate milk, or a healthy portion of chocolate syrup or powdered cocoa. A *Vienna Cappuccino* is made with equal parts of espresso, hot cocoa and whipped cream and the *Caramella* is a cappuccino with added caramel sauce.

• **Spirit Options** — Cappuccinos make ideal delivery vehicles for most spirits and liqueurs. If the product tastes great mixed with coffee, it'll be that much better served in a cappuccino.

A specialty at Houston's Backstreet Café is *Patricia's Bittersweet Goodnight*, a locally renowned latte made with Maker's Mark Bourbon, Amaretto Disaronno, Frangelico and Tuaca Liquore Italiano. Its wafting set of aromas alone makes it worth the price. Another is the *Island Hopping Java*, which features Malibu and Mount Gay Eclipse Rum, Frangelico and a demitasse of freshly brewed espresso and steamed milk.

The *Goodnight Kiss*, a signature at upscale Rosemary's Restaurant in Las Vegas, is made with Godiva Chocolate Liqueur and Nocello Nut Liqueur, chocolate syrup,

Mosaic Restaurant

📠 **10600 East Jomax Rd.**
   Scottsdale, AZ 85255
☎ **480.563.9600**
▶▶I **www.mosaic-restaurant.com**
✉ **eat@mosaic-restaurant.com**

Mosaic Restaurant is a posh Arizona venue that combines all of the elements to create an evening of exceptional dining. The natural beauty of the Sonoran Desert at sunset and moonrise complements the upscale restaurant's innovative, globally inspired cuisine.

The interior design of Mosaic is exquisite. There are three intimate dining rooms, each with their own feel and ambiance and two expansive patios offering the best in al fresco dining with glorious views of the Pinnacle Peak Mountains. The impeccable attention to detail creates a visually pleasing and harmonious atmosphere. It's a mosaic with every tile perfectly placed.

Chef Deborah Knight has created a menu brimming with innovation and creativity, an eclectic selection of vegetarian, seafood and wild game dishes. For starters there's Bacon-Wrapped Kangaroo Tenderloins, or Snapping Turtle Soup. The chef offers three, 5-course tasting menus nightly, in addition to the restaurant's celebrated ala carte menu. Popular entrees include Crisp Roasted Pheasant with Pumpkin Risotto, or the chef's signature dish consisting of wild boar chop, loin of venison and Muscovy duck.

The restaurant's comfortable yet elegant cocktail lounge offers guests a sensational repertoire of skillfully crafted libations. An outstanding example is a cocktail dubbed *Paradise Found*, a luxurious Margarita made with ultra-premium El Tesoro Paradiso Tequila, Grand Marnier Cuvée du Centenaire, mandarin orange puree and fresh lime sour mix. Others include the *Nazdarovie*, a classy concoction created with Jewel of Russia Wild Bilberry Infusion Vodka, Grand Marnier and English Breakfast Tea, and *Love in a Side Car*, a glorious drink comprised of A. de Fussigny Cognac, Damiana Liqueur and fresh lemon sour mix.

Mosaic also prides itself on its award-winning wine menu that includes boutique bottlings from every region in the world. No oasis in the desert could offer more. —RP

Paradise Found
Drink recipe on pg 53

espresso and steamed milk. A favorite at Refectory Restaurant in Columbus, Ohio is *Captain Chai*, a latte crafted with Captain Morgan Private Stock Rum, Oregon chai and frothed milk. The drink is spicy, warm and brilliantly flavored.

- **Iced Cappuccinos** — Iced cappuccinos have made it possible to sip and savor these drinks even in the heat of summer. It's made by pouring 8-ounces of cold milk and two, freshly brewed demitasses of espresso into an iced mixing glass. Shake the concoction vigorously and then serve in an iced, 16-ounce specialty glass. Garnish with whipped cream and a sprinkle of shaved chocolate.

An iced caramella is made in the same manner, the only addition being a tablespoon each of chocolate and caramel syrup. It, too, is garnished with whipped cream, but it deserves a drizzle of chocolate and caramel syrup. Substitute hazelnut syrup for the caramel and add a shot of Hennessey V.S.O.P and Starbucks Coffee Liqueur and you've made a *Chocolate Biscotti*.

So go ahead, add a scoop of French vanilla ice cream to your cappuccino. Splash in some chocolate syrup or caramel sauce. Drop in a dollop of whipped cream and crumble a fudge brownie on top. The creative possibilities are only bounded by your imagination.

Courvoisier® VS Cognac

Located in the heart of Jarnac, France, Courvoisier makes its cognacs from the finest brandies distilled in the premiere crus, or growing regions. The brandies are double-distilled in small copper alembic stills and cellared in handmade Limousin and Tronçais oak barrels. At any one point, the chateau has over 45,000 casks of brandy aging and adds about 3000 new barrels each year.

The chateau's line of cognacs is a work of art in itself. The series begins with *Courvoisier VS Cognac* (very special). While some producers consider the VS mark to be merely an entry-level product, Courvoisier VS is indeed something special. It is a crafted blend of brandies from the premiere crus — Grande Champagne, Petite Champagne and the Fins Bois. The blend contains brandies aged for 4 years, as well as those aged a minimum of 7 years. The marriage of young and old brandies creates a cognac with a lush, floral bouquet and a delectable fruity palate with some oak undertones.

Famed *Courvoisier VSOP* is a Fine Champagne cognac, meaning it is a blend of brandies from the prized Grande Champagne and Petite Champagne districts of Cognac. The brandies used in its blend are matured a minimum of 6 years, with most aged in excess of 10 years.

Courvoisier VSOP is a classically structured cognac. It has a soft, round body and an assertive bouquet loaded with fruit and floral notes. The brandy has a layered palate of chocolate, citrus and nuts.

A Look At The World of Tea

Some 4700 years ago, the Chinese Emperor Shen Nung was boiling water when some leaves from a nearby Camellia sinensis plant, now known as the black tea shrub, landed in the open pot. Intrigued by the brew's aroma, the emperor drank the mixture and declared that it "gave vigor to the body, lent contentment to the mind and instilled determination of purpose." Also known as the Divine Healer, Shen Nung set out to learn more about the attributes of the plant and is largely responsible for the cultivation of tea.

The tea plant is an evergreen shrub and a member of the Camellia family. It grows in the tropics and subtropical areas of the world's temperate zones, specifically in Indonesia, India, Sri Lanka and in many parts of Asia, including China. The tea plant flourishes in high altitudes and   requires abundant rainfall, especially during the hot season. In the wild, the plant can grow in excess of 45 feet in height, but in cultivation it is normally kept under 6 feet, this for the practical reason of making it easier to harvest the tender shoots and top leaves.

Catering to tea consuming guests begins with a balanced offering of tea styles with which to satisfy even the most discriminating of palates.

Black tea is the most widely distributed type of tea in the United States. Each variety has a distinctive flavor. For example, Assam is a black tea from India with a full-body and pronounced, malty palate, while Darjeeling, also from India has a delicate taste. Darjeeling tea is prized for its quality, which is reflected in its price. Orange Spice is black tea with small pieces of orange peel, cinnamon and cloves.

Several varieties of black teas are used to create now famous blends. English Breakfast tea is a blend of Sri Lanka and Assam (Indian) teas. Irish Breakfast tea is a combination of various Indian teas and Earl Grey is a popular blend comprised of three varieties of black tea flavored with the oil of bergamot.

Green tea, also known as China tea, is not allowed to ferment before drying, which allows it to retain much of the natural taste, color and aroma. It is often served as a single variety and not blended with other teas. Gunpowder is widely considered the highest quality of Chinese green tea. It has small, tightly rolled leaves and a subtle aroma and flavor.

White tea is picked and harvested before the leaves open, leaving the buds still covered by fine white hair. They contain less caffeine and more anti-oxidants than other varieties. White teas are not allowed to ferment. They are often floral, somewhat sweet and not at all "grassy," a characteristic of green teas. There are many varieties of white tea, but they are all scarcer and therefore more expensive than the other types of tea.

Oolong tea, which is also referred to as red tea, is allowed to partially ferment prior to drying. Most oolong teas have delicate, fruity flavors and floral bouquets. Jasmine tea is made from a blend of green and oolong with fresh jasmine blossoms, the tea has a flowery aroma and a fresh, mild flavor.

Herbal tea consists of the dried flowers and leaves of plants other than Camellia sinensis. Herbal teas can also be made using fresh flowers, herbs, seeds, fruit, or various spices. They are typically caffeine-free.

Brewing World Class Tea

You don't need to be hosting a high tea to need to know how to properly brew tea. It is a relatively straightforward process. Here are a few pointers that if heeded, the end result will be a marvelous cup of tea.

- **Water Quality** — A cup of tea can only be as good as the water used to make it, and therefore spring water or bottled drinking water will yield the best results. Start with cold water and bring to a rolling boil. When making green tea, the water should be just off the boil.

- **Tea to Water Ratio** — Typically one teaspoon of loose tea, or one tea bag, is used per 6-ounces of water, although some people prefer increasing the ratio to two teaspoons (or bags) for every 6-ounces of water. When using loose tea, fill the infuser or metal ball no more than half full. The tea leaves

Jacques Cardin® Cognac VSOP

Jacques Cardin is a classy range of spirits making their debut in the United States. Enthusiasts will greatly appreciate what this brand brings to the table, beginning with the sophisticated and unexpectedly affordable *Jacques Cardin Cognac VSOP*.

This superior cognac is a mélange of eaux de vie aged in small French oak casks for a minimum of four years. The JC VSOP has an enticing amber hue with gold highlights. The bouquet is a lavish array of herbs, butterscotch, spice and vanilla bean aromas. Its silky, medium-weight body delivers a lively, layered palate featuring the prominent flavors of honey, ginger, cocoa and cinnamon. A long, flavorful finish seals the deal.

Ah, but the brand has more to offer. The *Jacques Cardin Apple Flavored VSOP* is a mélange of cognacs selected for their distinctive pear, apricot and apple bouquets. The result is something genuinely special. Within minutes of pouring, the satisfying aroma of tree-ripened apples comes wafting forth. The cognac has a velvety, medium-weight body, a delightful, slightly spicy palate and an incomparable, baked apple finish.

The *Jacques Cardin Jasmine Flavored VSOP Cognac* is an assemblage of well-aged eaux de vie. A distillate from India is added to the blend producing the cognac's signature personality. The enticing aroma and flavor of jasmine is pervasive and long lasting. The combined effect is sensational.

will quickly expand when wet and swell to the point of impeding the free flow of water through the infuser.

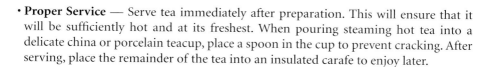

• **Preparation Techniques** — Always preheat the teapot. Fill with hot water and let stand for a few minutes and drain before use. Allow loose tea to steep for 3 to 5 minutes. Since tea bags contain more finely chopped tea, it requires a shorter brewing time to attain the same degree of extraction. To prevent tea from becoming bitter, always remove the tea bags or loose tea immediately after brewing. Never allow prepared tea to boil.

• **Proper Service** — Serve tea immediately after preparation. This will ensure that it will be sufficiently hot and at its freshest. When pouring steaming hot tea into a delicate china or porcelain teacup, place a spoon in the cup to prevent cracking. After serving, place the remainder of the tea into an insulated carafe to enjoy later.

Making Sensational Tea Drinks

Consumption of tea in the United States is skyrocketing. One explanation for its popularity is the medical studies showing that regular consumption of tea has been

associated with lowering the risk of heart disease and some types of cancer. Black and green teas contain flavonoids that are highly effective antioxidants. Tea is also lower in caffeine than coffee, something a growing number of Americans consider important. An 8-ounce cup of tea contains approximately 60% less caffeine than a typical cup of coffee. Most herbal teas don't contain any caffeine.

Regardless of what sparked the current boom in the U.S., tea and all that surrounds it are piping hot. To stoke the fires somewhat, here are the best kept secrets behind America's greatest tea drinks.

• **Some Like it Hot** — The traditional path for tea-based drinks is serving them warm. That end of the spectrum is represented by drinks like the *Blueberry Tea* — Disaronno Amaretto, Grand Marnier and hot herbal tea — and the *Earl of Grey*, which is made with Scotch whisky and Earl Grey tea. Fanciers of something a wee bit stronger might want to sample the *Irish Tea*, a hearty brew made with Irish Mist, a dram of Jameson and Irish breakfast tea. The drink has a marvelous bouquet eclipsed only by its bracing constitution. Also from the UK is *Winnie's Hot Honey Pot*, a fanciful combination of Drambuie, honey, lemon juice and English breakfast tea. The drink has all of the makings of a happy ending.

• **Or Something Cooler Perhaps?** — Making drinks that feature iced tea is a natural. P.F. Chang's promotes the *Green Tea-Ni*, a cocktail made with organic green tea and Charbay Green Tea Vodka.

The *My Kentucky Mojito* is an amazingly refreshing concoction devised from a base of Maker's Mark Bourbon. Prepared similarly to the famed Latin, mint-laced classic, the drink also contains a splash of Cointreau and iced tea. The mint and tea lends the drink an herbal quality that plays beautifully with the classically sweet notes in the bourbon.

Another highly creative use of iced tea is the *N'Orleans Chiller*. Constructed with Bacardi Limón and Cruzan Orange rums, the drink also features a healthy dose of iced herbal tea. It is a crisp and delectably flavorful specialty. The same can be said for the *Acapulco Afternoon*, a tall, iced signature drink made with Sauza Hornitos Reposado Tequila and equal parts of lemonade and iced tea. Add in a splash of Squirt and a few sliced lemons and limes and you're set for the afternoon. Float some Chambord on top and you've got the *Acapulco Sunset*.

• **Soothing Chai** — People are increasingly discovering the tranquility of chai tea, a soothing drink made from spiced, sweetened tea mixed with milk. While there are any number of variations of chai, it's typically made from Darjeeling or Assam black tea, a sweetener, milk and a mixture of spices referred to as the chai masala.

Some recipes of chai accentuate the flavor of the spices; others the character of the milk. The masala usually features spices such as anise, cinnamon, ginger, nutmeg, cloves and cardamom. Some chai tea recipes also call for the use of black peppercorns, bay leaves, fennel seeds, grated ginger, vanilla and star anise. The array of spices are added to the tea and steeped. A mixture of milk (whole, non-fat or soy) and water are then added to taste It can be sweetened with sugar, brown sugar, or honey.

• **Tea Ice-Capades** — The first World's Fair in the United States was held in St. Louis in 1904. One of the exhibitors was a tea plantation owner named Richard Blechynden. He had intended to serve fair goers samples of his hot tea, but an unexpected heat wave spoiled his plans. In an effort to salvage his investment, he offered the parched throngs glasses of brewed tea served with ice. It became an immediate hit and sparked a new American tradition.

There are three methods of preparing great iced tea. The first entails brewing tea as usual, with the exception that it is prepared using twice as much loose tea or twice as many tea bags. After the brewed tea has cooled, it can be served in a tall glass filled with ice. Depending on the type of tea used, the brew may turn cloudy when poured over ice. Although this will not affect its taste, some people do not care for the appearance. To clarify the tea, add a small amount of boiling water and stir.

The second is the cold-water method. It involves using 1 1/2 times to twice the number of tea bags as would usually be used for the volume of water. The tea is allowed to slowly steep in the cold water for 6 to 8 hours. Once it has attained the desired strength, the tea bags are removed and the tea is ready to drink.

Nacional 27

⌂ **325 West Huron**
   Chicago, IL 60610
☎ **312.664.2727**
▶▎ **www.nacional27.net**
✉ **info@nacional27.net**

Passion for the flavors and textures of Latino culture led Executive Chef Randy Zweiban to create one of Chicago's most acclaimed restaurants, **Nacional 27**. The number in its name refers to how many Latin and South American cuisines are inclusive in the venue's concept. The downtown eatery has become a fixture in the Chicago restaurant scene, renowned for the vibrancy of its food and the electrically charged atmosphere.

The interior of Nacional 27 is dramatic, swank yet thoroughly comfortable. The place has a tropical feel, thanks in part to high ceilings, billowy gauze curtains, tubular light fixtures, exotic woods, wooden tables and subdued lighting. Late on weekend nights, Nacional 27 shifts gears and dons the look and sound of a dance club as the center tables in the dining room are peeled away and the DJ beckons couples to the bamboo dance floor with a mix of modern salsa, merengue and techno-Latino tunes.

The draw remains the bold and divinely inspired, modern Latin cuisine. A common sight in the lounge is people enjoying starters such as Ahi Tuna & Watermelon, Smoked Chicken Empanadas and Barbecued Lamb Tiny Tacos. The entrees are magnificent and include Florida Black Grouper "Huachinango," Slow Roasted Gunthorp Farms Pork "Cubano," and Prime Chimichurri Crusted Sirloin.

In addition to serving outstanding food, Nacional 27 has garnered a following based on their award-winning cocktails. *El Corazón* is a signature cocktail made with Corzo Silver tequila, passion fruit puree, pomegranate juice and fresh lemon sour mix. The house specialties *Batida*, *Caipirinha* and *Mojito* are each sensational, as is the *Cazuela*, a cocktail made with Gran Centenario Plata Tequila and muddled slices of grapefruit, orange, lime, and lemon.

Nacional 27 is zesty and an imminently pleasurable slice of life. —RP

El Corazón
Drink recipe on pg 47

The sun tea method uses the same tea-to-water ratio as the cold-water method. The water and tea are placed in a loosely sealed glass jar and set out in the direct sunlight for 2 to 4 hours. The sunlight slowly brews the tea. Once brewed, the tea bags are removed and it is served over ice.

One creative option is to freeze brewed tea in ice cube trays and use the resulting cubes in glasses of iced tea. This will prevent the iced tea from becoming overly diluted. Along the same lines, freeze fruit juice in ice cube trays and drop a few cubes in a glass of iced tea for a blast of flavor.

Creating Hot Cocoa Classics

Hot cocoa's origins go far beyond Bosco or Ovaltine. In fact, cocoa beans were so revered by the Aztecs they were used as money. While Cortez lusted after the Aztec's gold and riches, he and his men had little fondness for the bitter mixture, that is until they added cane sugar.

Upon returning to Spain, Cortez introduced King Charles V and his Royal Court to sweetened hot cocoa, and not surprisingly, it became the rage of the aristocracy. For more than a century, cocoa remained the domain of the wealthy and privileged. By the early 19th century however, steam-operated grinding machines caused prices to drop dramatically. The innovation greatly improved the flavor of cocoa and led to large-scale manufacturing.

Cocoa trees grow only in tropical climates in a band 20 degrees north and south of the Equator. They produce kernels, or nibs, which contain up

Starbucks™ Cream Liqueur

Cream liqueurs are something special. Perhaps they appeal directly to a special part of our brains, because they seem to have nearly universal appeal. Who wouldn't crave flavor-laced cream infused with a dram of alcohol? Those cravings are bound to thump off the charts once you taste *Starbucks Cream Liqueur*. Strap yourself in because this is great stuff.

Super-premium Starbucks Cream Liqueur is made with dairy fresh cream, sugar-based spirits and is flavored with the company's famed blend of high grade, Arabica coffee beans. It's bottled at 30-proof and packaged in a replica art deco cocktail shaker.

Sure, most cream liqueurs will taste good when chilled, but a truly world-class brand will taste delicious even when sipped neat. Such is the case with delectable Starbucks Cream Liqueur. The recent arrival has the look of café au lait and a discernible brewed coffee aroma. The liqueur has a supple, medium-weight body that coats the palate with chocolate and toffee flavors. The finish is where it really shines. As the liqueur slowly ebbs away the slightly dry, coffee flavors become prominent.

Change is a good thing, especially when it involves an ingredient so popular in mixology as cream liqueurs. This has all the attributes of a franchise player in the making. Not only will Starbucks Cream Liqueur contribute a singularly marvelous coffee dimension to your cocktails, it will do so without adding cloying sweetness. What more can one ask?

to 54% cocoa butter. After the beans are crushed, heat is used to liquefy the cocoa butter to form chocolate paste. When dried, it is crushed and pulverized into a fine powder. Most premium producers of cocoa powder add a small amount of alkaline salts to the paste prior to drying. The salts render the powder darker, give it a more intense chocolate flavor and allow it to stay in solution longer in liquid.

One of the great things about making a cup of cocoa is that it doesn't require specialized equipment or training. Although there are many ways to make hot cocoa, the following is a typical scratch recipe.

In a saucepan over a low flame, whisk together 1/2 cup of cocoa powder, 1/3 cup sugar and 1/2 cup of water. After the powder and sugar go into solution, stir in another 1/2 cup of water and a cup of milk. Keep stirring over low to moderate heat for approximately 10 minutes, stirring from the bottom of the saucepan to prevent scalding. Once the mixture is hot, remove the pan from the burner and allow it to cool. Serve with whipped cream, marshmallows or both for a finishing touch.

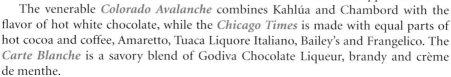

Creating great tasting drinks with hot cocoa is almost foolproof. It's about as straightforward as mixology gets. Here then, are the best kept secrets behind America's greatest hot cocoa drinks.

• **Cocoa Cocktails** — Nowhere is it written that you can't lace hot cocoa with something a wee bit stronger than syrup. As a collective they're outrageously delicious. It's hard to make a mistake when working with hot cocoa.

At Scottsdale's Mosaic Restaurant, the hot drink to ask for is the *Peppermint Bark*, a lip-smacking good libation featuring DeKuyper Peppermint Schnapps, Mozart White Chocolate Cream, homemade Mexican vanilla hot chocolate and whipped cream.

The venerable *Colorado Avalanche* combines Kahlúa and Chambord with the flavor of hot white chocolate, while the *Chicago Times* is made with equal parts of hot cocoa and coffee, Amaretto, Tuaca Liquore Italiano, Bailey's and Frangelico. The *Carte Blanche* is a savory blend of Godiva Chocolate Liqueur, brandy and crème de menthe.

• **Cocoa Modifiers** — A 3/4 full cup of hot cocoa is almost begging for an added blast of flavor. It could be a splash of hot fudge or chocolate sauce; after all, chocolate and caramel complement the flavor of hot cocoa. If adding a sauce is more concentrated than what you're looking for, perhaps a splash of black raspberry or vanilla syrup is called for.

Some recipes call for the addition of vanilla extract, cloves, cinnamon, lemon juice, instant espresso powder or mint chocolate chips for flavor. Cornstarch or arrowroot can be added for thickening. Substituting brown sugar for regular granulated sugar is another creative option.

Then there's the *Mayan Hot Cocoa*, made famous in the movie *Chocolat*. It's made with milk, pure cocoa, unbleached flour, dark brown sugar, powdered sugar, vanilla, grated nutmeg, cloves, crumbled cinnamon and chili pepper. The drink is spicy and highly aromatic.

- **Ice Cream** — After modifying the cocoa base, it may well be time to drop in a scoop or two of ice cream. Shortly after splash down, the melting ice cream forms a frothy layer on the cocoa. It creates a fabulous presentation. The coup de grace is there's a wide variety of ice cream flavors that work with the satisfying taste of hot cocoa, a list that includes banana, chocolate, French vanilla, raspberry, strawberry and Almond Roca, to name but a few.

An example is the *Café Glace*, a specialty at Brûlée the Dessert Experience in Atlantic City. It's a hot, decadent blend of Pyrat XO Reserve Rum, a demitasse of espresso and a generous fill of hot chocolate. The finishing touch is a scoop of vanilla ice cream. The combined effect is spectacular.

Warmth coupled with soul satisfying flavor make an irresistible combination. Whether crafted with coffee, espresso, tea or cocoa, a well-conceived hot drink is a timeless thing of beauty. More importantly, they're capable of soothing frayed nerves and thawing frostbitten extremities. Have fun, experiment and concoct the next international phenomenon.

Starbucks™ Coffee Liqueur

It's hard to imagine a better conceived and more welcomed product than *Starbucks Coffee Liqueur*. Considering that there will soon be a Starbucks on every street corner in the U. S., it's safe to presume that Americans have an insatiable hankering for Starbucks' coffee. Now that signature flavor is available in a delectable coffee liqueur. The question remains though, what took so long?

Super-premium Starbucks Coffee Liqueur is an impressive product that ranks with the best in its class. It is made with a light, sugar-based spirit that is infused with the company's famed blend of high grade, Arabica coffee. The 40-proof liqueur has the rich, inviting look of brewed espresso, a satiny, light-weight body and an alluring bouquet of fresh ground coffee. It rolls over the palate without a trace of sweetness, another attribute that distinguishes it from the competition. The coffee-steeped finish is delicious, slightly bitter and remarkably long lasting. The overall result is a sensational recreation of the Starbucks experience.

In a nation fueled by coffee, exploring your drink making options when it comes to coffee-infused products makes good sense. Starbucks' light body and dry, authentic flavor is perfectly suited for mixology. For example, Starbucks exquisite balance makes it the definitive choice for making a coffee Martini. It yields cocktails that are noticeably less sweet, which is perfectly in step with contemporary trends. Kudos Starbucks!

Amadeus Kaffee

Specialty of Mosaic Restaurant
Created by Stephanie Kozicki
Coffee mug, preheated
Build in glass
1 1/2 oz. Jewel of Russia Wild Bilberry
    Infusion Vodka
1/4 oz. Mozart Black Chocolate Pure 87
1/4 oz. Mozart White Chocolate Cream
5 oz. Mosaic house special blend coffee
Garnish with 2 chocolate cigarette sticks
Pour ingredients into the preheated coffee mug in the order listed. Garnish with 2 chocolate cigarette sticks.

Apple Rum Tea

Specialty of Backstreet
Created by Sean Beck
Zombie glass, ice
Pour ingredients into an iced mixing glass
1 3/4 oz. Mount Gay Eclipse Rum
Splash fresh lime juice
1/2 oz. simple syrup
1 oz. cold Hibiscus tea
3 oz. fresh apple juice
Stir and strain
Garnish with a green apple slice
    and edible flower
Pour ingredients into the iced mixing glass. Stir thoroughly and strain contents into an iced Zombie glass. Garnish with a green apple slice and edible flower.

Café Brûlée

Specialty of Brûlée the Dessert Experience
Created by Peter Van Theil
Snifter glass, preheated
Build in glass
3/4 oz. Frangelico
3/4 oz. Baileys Irish Cream
3/4 oz. Grand Marnier
3/4 oz. Kahlúa
Fill with coffee
Garnish with Baileys whipped cream*
Pour ingredients into the warmed snifter in the order listed. Garnish with Baileys whipped cream.
*Baileys Whipped Cream
1 oz. Baileys blended into 3 oz. whipped cream.

Café Glace

Specialty of Brûlée the Dessert Experience
Created by Peter Van Thiel
Coffee mug, preheated
Build in glass
2 oz. Pyrat XO Reserve Rum
2 oz. espresso
Fill with hot chocolate
Top with a scoop of vanilla ice cream
Pour ingredients into the preheated coffee mug in the order listed, leaving room for the scoop of vanilla ice cream. Top with a scoop of vanilla ice cream.

Captain Chai

Specialty of The Refectory Restaurant & Bistro
Created by Julie Mulisano, Kevin McClatchy
Coffee mug, preheated
Build in glass
1 1/2 oz. Captain Morgan Private Stock Rum
Steam equal parts Oregon Chai and milk
Garnish with frothed chai milk
Steam equal parts of Oregon Chai and whole milk. Pour the rum and steamed chai milk into the preheated coffee mug. Garnish with steamed chai milk foam.

Chocolate Raspberry Java

Specialty of Courtright's Restaurant
Created by Marco Recio
Coffee mug, preheated
Build in glass
1 1/2 oz. Chambord
1 1/2 oz. Tia Maria
4 oz. espresso
Garnish with whipped cream and a
    dusting of cocoa powder
Pour ingredients into the preheated coffee mug in the order listed. Garnish with whipped cream and a dusting of cocoa powder.

Espresso Misu

Specialty of The Carnegie Club
Created by Mark Grossich
Cocktail glass, chilled
Pour ingredients into an iced mixing glass
1 oz. Stoli Vanil Vodka
1 oz. Kahlúa
1 oz. cold espresso
1 oz. half & half
Shake and strain
Garnish with 3 espresso beans
Pour ingredients into the iced mixing glass. Shake thoroughly and strain contents into a chilled cocktail glass. Garnish with 3 espresso beans.

Godiva Chocolate Cherry

Specialty of The Mission Inn Hotel & Spa
Created by Brooke Crothers
Coffee mug, preheated
Build in glass
1 oz. Godiva Chocolate Liqueur
1 oz. Cherry Brandy
Fill with hot chocolate
Garnish with whipped cream and a cherry
Pour ingredients into the preheated coffee mug in the order listed. Garnish with whipped cream and a cherry.

Goodnight Kiss

Specialty of Rosemary's Restaurant
Created by Michael Shetler
Coffee mug, preheated
Build in glass
1 oz. Godiva Chocolate Liqueur
1 oz. Nocello Nut Liqueur
1 oz. chocolate syrup
2 oz. hot espresso
Fill 3/4 full with steamed milk
Place 2 drink stirs over rim of glass in an X pattern
Garnish with prepared whipped cream and a chocolate kiss
Pour ingredients into the preheated coffee mug in the order listed. Place 2 drink stirs over rim of glass in an X pattern. Garnish with prepared whipped cream and a chocolate kiss.

Green Tea-ni

Specialty of P.F. Chang's China Bistro
Created by P.F. Chang's staff
Cocktail glass, chilled
Pour ingredients into an iced mixing glass
2 oz. Charbay Green Tea Vodka
1/4 oz. Simple Syrup
1 oz. Revolution Organic Green Tea
     (room temperature)
Shake and strain
Garnish with a lemon wheel
Pour ingredients into the iced mixing glass. Shake thoroughly and strain contents into a chilled cocktail glass. Garnish with a lemon wheel on edge of glass.

Heated Affair

Specialty of Tommy's Mexican Resturant
Created by Jacques Bezuidenhout
Coffee mug, preheated
Build in glass
2 oz. Gran Centenario Reposado Tequila
4 oz. hot organic spiced apple cider*
Float heavy whipping cream
Sprinkle grated nutmeg
Pour ingredients into the preheated coffee mug in the order listed. Garnish with a float of heavy whipping cream and a sprinkle of grated nutmeg.
*Organic Spiced Apple Cider Recipe
Heat organic apple cider with a small tea steeper filled with cloves, orange peel, allspice and a cinnamon stick. Simmer to taste.

Hibiscus Spiced Tea

Specialty of Jade Bar
Created by Greg Portsche
Bucket glass, heated or with ice
Build in glass
2 oz. Hanger Kaffir Lime Vodka
1/4 oz. Ginger Simple Syrup
4 oz. Hibiscus tea
Garnish with a lemon twist
Pour ingredients into the bucket glass in the order listed. Garnish with a lemon twist.

Hot Buttered Rum, Cyrus

Specialty of Cyrus
Created by Scott Beattie
Coffee mug, preheated
Build in glass
1 1/2 oz. Charbay Tahitian Vanilla Bean Rum
2 1/2 oz. hot buttered rum batter*
2 1/2 oz. hot water
Stir thoroughly
Garnish with a sprinkle of ground nutmeg
Pour the rum into the preheated coffee mug. Add the batter and hot water. Stir until ingredients are combined. Garnish with a sprinkle of nutmeg.
*Hot Buttered Rum Batter Recipe - pg 320

The Original McCormick & Schmick's Seafood Restaurant

235 SW First Ave.
Portland, OR 97204

☎ 503.224.7522

▶▶ www.mccormickandschmicks.com

Appropriately located in a building constructed in 1886, *The Original McCormick & Schmick's Seafood Restaurant* is an ultra-popular eatery that takes enormous pride in its dedication to tradition. That respect can be seen in every facet of this highly successful family of restaurants, from its classic approach to making cocktails to its hale and hearty bill of fare featuring fresh seafood and premium beef.

The spacious interior of McCormick & Schmick's mirrors the look and feel of its historic facade. There are high ceilings, exposed brickwork, brass, art deco light

fixtures, beveled glass and dark wood paneling. The focal point of the space is the massive wooden bar with ornate accents and a towering, bottle-lined back bar. The ambience is lively, engaging and enjoyable.

McCormick & Schmick's adherence to traditional values is also evident in their liberal portions, reasonable prices and attentive servers who take guest's orders from memory. The restaurant's menu is printed daily, reflecting the availability of fresh seafood. It offers a selection of more than 30 varieties of seafood from Alaskan halibut and New Zealand grouper to Atlantic salmon and Florida Yellowfin tuna. All of the seasonal dishes feature regionally inspired preparations. The food is sumptuous.

The same approach carries over to the bar, where the staff impeccably prepares their cocktails using only fresh ingredients. The bar's impressive roster of classic concoctions includes the *Northwest Raspberry Martini*, which is paired with fresh raspberry puree, muddled lemons, Stolichnaya Vodka and a splash of triple sec and cranberry juice, and the *Cucumber Cooler*, a tall iced libation made with muddled slices of cucumber and lime, Stolichnaya Vodka and a splash of Midori.

Tradition never tasted so marvelous. —RP

Cucumber Cooler
Drink recipe on pg 128

Hot Buttered Rum, Joe's

Specialty of Joe's Seafood, Prime Steak & Stone Crab
Created by Dan Barringer
Nutmeg, cassia bud and cardamom
    sugar rimmed* coffee mug, preheated
Build in glass
2 oz. Bacardi Vanilía Rum
4 oz. hot buttered rum batter*
1 oz. hot water
Steam with a cappuccino steamer until
   contents are heated throughout
Pour ingredients into a preheated, nutmeg,
cassia bud and cardamom sugar rimmed cof-
fee mug. Heat with a cappuccino steamer until
thoroughly heated.
*Hot Buttered Rum
   Batter Recipe (Joe's) - pg 320
*Nutmeg, Cassia Bud and Cardamom
   Sugar Rim Recipe - pg 321

Hot Buttered Rum, Rosemary's

Specialty of Rosemary's Restaurant
Created by Michael Shetler, Dorothy Lopreore
Cinnamon sugar rimmed
    coffee mug, preheated
Build in glass
1 tbsp. butter
1 tbsp. brown sugar
Pinch nutmeg
Pinch cinnamon
2 dashes Rosemary's house made
    vanilla extract*
Muddle contents
2 oz. Captain Morgan Private Stock Rum
Fill ¾ full with hot water
Stir gently
Garnish with ¼ oz. heavy whipping
    cream, well-shaken
Place the butter, brown sugar, nutmeg, cinnamon
and vanilla into the cinnamon sugar rimmed,
empty, preheated coffee mug. Muddle thoroughly.
Add the rum and hot water to ¾ full. Stir gently
until all ingredients are combined. Garnish with
heavy whipping cream shaken well.
*Rosemary's House Made Vanilla Extract
Infuse 1 liter brandy with whole vanilla beans
and macerate for a minimum of 90 days.

Patrón® XO Café Coffee Liqueur

It is estimated that more than 450 billion cups of coffee are consumed worldwide each year, easily making it the planet's most popular beverage. A large percentage of those cups of Joe are consumed right here in the United States. In fact, America is the largest coffee-consuming nation in the world, making super-premium *Patrón XO Café Coffee Liqueur* the right product at the right time.

Imported by the same folks who make Patrón 100% Blue Agave Tequila, XO Café is made in Mexico from 100% agave tequila and pure, natural essence of coffee. The 70-proof liqueur is crafted with a minimal amount of sweetener, which makes it drier and more of a coffee-flavored tequila than a typical liqueur.

Patrón XO Café is a thoroughly satisfying product that has developed a considerable following. It has a luxuriously smooth, medium-weight body and an engaging bouquet of cocoa, vanilla and freshly roasted coffee. It has a surprisingly dry palate that at once fills the mouth with the balanced flavors of coffee and mellow aged tequila. The liqueur's finish is long and memorable.

Patrón XO Café is an excellent twist on the conventional. The marriage of tequila and coffee is luscious, making the liqueur a superb ingredient in a wide array of contemporary cocktails. It is outstanding with everything from vodka and tequila to ice cream and hot chocolate. Top-shelf all the way.

Iced Coffee Valencia

Specialty of The World Bar
Created by Kenneth McClure
Pilsner glass, ice
Pour ingredients into an iced mixing glass
1 oz. Grand Marnier
1/2 oz. Orange Curaçao
3/4 oz. half and half
1 oz. Valencia orange syrup
4 oz. cold coffee
Shake and strain
Garnish with whipped cream and
    a candied orange peel
Pour ingredients into the iced mixing glass. Shake thoroughly and strain contents into an iced pilsner glass. Garnish with whipped cream and a candied orange peel.

Iced Mint Mocha Chip

Specialty of Bookmark
Created by Kenneth McClure
Pint glass, ice
Pour ingredients into an iced mixing glass
1 oz. Godiva Chocolate Liqueur
1 oz. Van Gogh Dutch Chocolate Vodka
1/2 oz. chocolate syrup
1/2 oz. mint syrup
1 oz. heavy cream
5 oz. cold coffee
Shake and strain
Garnish with whipped cream, chocolate
    shavings, mint leaf and drizzle of
    Green Creme de Menthe
Pour ingredients into the iced mixing glass. Shake thoroughly and strain contents into an iced pint glass. Garnish with whipped cream, chocolate shavings, mint leaf and a drizzle of Green Creme de Menthe.

Irish Coffee

Excerpted from The Original Guide to
American Cocktails and Drinks- 6th Edition
Irish coffee glass, preheated
Build in glass
1 1/4 oz. Irish Whiskey
1/2 oz. simple syrup
Near fill with hot coffee
Garnish with frothed milk or whipped cream
Pour ingredients into the preheated Irish coffee glass in the order listed. Garnish with frothed milk or whipped cream.

Irish Coffee Royale

Excerpted from The Original Guide to
American Cocktails and Drinks- 6th Edition
Irish coffee glass, preheated
Build in glass
1 1/4 oz. Irish Whiskey
1 oz. Kahlúa
1/2 oz. simple syrup
Near fill with hot coffee
Garnish with frothed milk or whipped cream
Pour ingredients into the preheated Irish coffee glass in the order listed. Garnish with frothed milk or whipped cream.

Island Hopping Java

Specialty of Backstreet Café
Created by Sean Beck
Irish coffee glass, preheated
Build in glass
3/4 oz. Malibu Rum
3/4 oz. Mount Gay Eclipse Rum
1/2 oz. Frangelico
Splash simple syrup
2 oz. hot espresso
2/3 fill with steamed coconut milk mixture*
Stir gently
Garnish with shredded, toasted coconut
    and toasted almond slices
Pour ingredients into the preheated Irish coffee glass in the order listed. Stir gently. Garnish with shredded, toasted coconut and toasted almond slices.
*Steamed Coconut Milk
    Mixture Recipe -pg 322

Latin Panda

Specialty of Rickshaw Far East Bistro & Bambú Lounge
Created by Rickshaw's staff
Coffee mug, preheated
Build in glass
1/4 oz. Absolut Vanilia Vodka
1/4 oz. Baileys Irish Cream
2 oz. hot espresso
3/4 fill with steamed milk
Garnish with a layer of frothed milk
Splash Coke
Pour ingredients into the preheated coffee mug in the order listed. Garnish with frothed milk and a splash of Coke.

The Mission Inn Coffee

Specialty of The Mission Inn Hotel & Spa
Created by Brooke Crothers, Gerard Carvajal
Coffee mug, preheated
Build in glass
1 1/2 oz. Courvoisier VSOP
1 oz. Frangelico
Fill with hot coffee
Garnish with whipped cream
    and chopped nuts
Pour ingredients into the preheated coffee mug
in the order listed. Garnish with whipped cream
and chopped nuts.

Montego Bay

Excerpted from The Original Guide to
American Cocktails and Drinks- 6th Edition
Coffee mug, preheated
Build in glass
3/4 oz. Tia Maria
3/4 oz. Appleton Estate V/X Jamaica Rum
3/4 oz. Cruzan Banana Rum
Near fill with hot coffee
Garnish with whipped cream
    and shaved chocolate
Pour ingredients into the preheated coffee mug
in the order listed. Garnish with whipped cream
and a sprinkle of shaved chocolate.

"The appeal of Irish coffee is nearly universal
despite its simplicity."

Celtic Crossing® Liqueur

Celtic Crossing Liqueur is a post-prandial performer of the highest caliber. It has done for Irish whiskeys what Drambuie did for Scotch malts; namely deliver soul-satisfying character of whiskey in a honey-tempered and heather soft liqueur.

Made in Bailieboro, Ireland, Celtic Crossing is made from a recipe first devised over 150 years ago. It is skillfully crafted from a blend of barrel-aged Irish whiskies and cognac, and then sweetened with a touch of heather honey. The real question surrounding Celtic Crossing is how did it become so flavorful without sporting a hefty body and syrupy consistency?

Clearly someone knows the answer, but they're not talking. What is known about this liqueur is that it has an exceptionally light body and a velvety smooth texture. Its wafting bouquet is laced with the comforting aromas of honey, vanilla and toasted oak. Perhaps Celtic Crossing's most laudable quality is its palate, which features the sumptuous flavors of honey, spice and a dram-sized taste of Irish whiskey. The finish is delectably long and soothing.

Like most top-notch liqueurs, Celtic Crossing is delicious and ideally balanced. It is best appreciated when sipped neat, or with a single cube of ice. It does, however, also enjoy numerous applications behind the bar. It blends marvelously with coffee, cappuccino and hot cocoa, as well as adding a complementary flavor to a wide range of whiskies and many other liqueurs.

N'Orleans Chiller

Excerpted from The Original Guide to
American Cocktails and Drinks- 6th Edition
House specialty glass, ice
Pour ingredients into an iced mixing glass
1 1/2 oz. Citrus Rum
1 1/2 oz. Orange Rum
1 oz. orange juice
1 oz. fresh lemon sour mix
2 oz. cold herbal tea
Shake and strain
Garnish with an orange slice
Pour ingredients into the iced mixing glass. Shake
thoroughly and strain contents into an iced house
specialty glass. Garnish with an orange slice.

Nutty Mocha

Specialty of Jade Bar
Created by Greg Portche
Coffee mug, preheated
Build in glass
1 oz. Godiva White Chocolate Liqueur
1 oz. Frangelico
1 oz. Fonte's Espresso
2 oz. steamed milk
Top with foam
Garnish with chocolate syrup
    swirled on foam
Pour the into the preheated coffee mug in the or-
der listed. Garnish with chocolate syrup swirled
on the foam.

Our Man In Jamaica

Specialty of Dave & Buster's
Created by Barry Carter
Clear glass footed coffee mug, preheated
Build in glass
1 1/4 oz. Myers's Original Dark Rum
3/4 oz. Baileys Irish Cream
4 oz. hot coffee
Garnish with whipped cream, a cherry
    and grated nutmeg
Pour ingredients into the preheated glass mug in
the order listed. Garnish with whipped cream, a
cherry and grated nutmeg.

Patricia's Bittersweet Goodnight

Specialty of Backstreet Café
Created by Sean Beck
Irish coffee glass, preheated
Build in glass
1/2 oz. Maker's Mark Bourbon
1/2 oz. Disaronno Amaretto
1/2 oz. Frangelico
1/2 oz. Tuaca Liquore Italiano
2 oz. hot espresso
4-6 oz. bittersweet steamed chocolate milk*
Garnish with cocoa powder and
    two stir straws
Pour ingredients into the preheated Irish coffee glass
in the order listed. Garnish with cocoa powder and
2 stir straws.
*Bittersweet Chocolate Milk Recipe - pg 318

Peppermint Bark

Specialty of Mosaic Restaurant
Created by Stephanie Kozicki, Ulyssio Williams
Coffee mug, preheated
Build in glass
2 oz. DeKuyper Peppermint Schnapps
1/2 oz. Mozart White Chocolate Cream
3 oz. Mexican vanilla hot chocolate
Garnish with whipped cream and
    a peppermint stick
Pour ingredients into the preheated coffee mug
in the order listed. Garnish with whipped cream
and a peppermint stick.

Peter Prescription

Excerpted from The Original Guide to
American Cocktails and Drinks- 6th Edition
Coffee mug, preheated
Build in glass
1 1/4 oz. Appleton Estate V/X Jamaica Rum
1/2 oz. Tia Maria
1/2 oz. Grand Marnier
1/2 oz. Chambord
Near fill with hot coffee
Garnish with whipped cream and
    shaved chocolate
Pour ingredients into the preheated coffee mug
in the order listed. Garnish with whipped cream
and sprinkle of shaved chocolate.

Royal Street Coffee

Excerpted from The Original Guide to
American Cocktails and Drinks- 6th Edition
Coffee mug, preheated
Build in glass
3/4 oz. Disaronno Amaretto
3/4 oz. Kahlúa
1/2 tsp. nutmeg
Near fill with hot coffee
Garnish with whipped cream
Pour ingredients into the preheated coffee mug in
the order listed. Garnish with whipped cream.

Sally Coffee

Specialty of Courtright's Restaurant
Created by Marco Recio
Coffee mug, preheated
Build in glass
1 1/2 oz. Amarula Cream Liqueur
1 1/2 oz. Navan Vanille Cognac Liqueur
Near fill with hot coffee
Garnish with whipped cream and
        powdered cocoa
Pour ingredients into the preheated coffee mug
in the order listed. Garnish with whipped cream
and powdered cocoa.

Shanghai Millionaire

Specialty of Rickshaw Far East Bistro & Bambú Lounge
Created by Rickshaw's staff
Coffee mug, preheated
Build in glass
1/4 oz. Baileys Irish Cream
1/4 oz. Kahlúa
1/4 oz. Chambord
2 oz. espresso
3/4 fill steamed milk
Layer of froth
Pour ingredients into the preheated coffee mug in
the order listed.

Steamed Carmel-Apple Cider

Specialty of Jade Bar
Created by Greg Portsche
Coffee mug, preheated
Build in glass
1 1/2 oz. Hardy V.S. Cognac
1/2 oz. Hiram Walker Butternip Schnapps
1/2 oz. Granny Smith Sour Apple Schnapps
4 oz. steamed apple juice
Garnish with a cinnamon stick
Pour ingredients into the preheated coffee
mug in the order listed. Garnish with a
cinnamon stick.

Suntan

Specialty of The Mission Inn Hotel & Spa
Created by Brooke Crothers
Bucket glass, ice
Build in glass
1 1/4 oz. Crème de Pêche de Vigne
5 oz. cold sun-brewed tea
Garnish with a lemon slice and mint sprig
Pour ingredients into the iced bucket glass in
the order listed. Garnish with a lemon slice and
mint sprig.

Tight Sweater

Excerpted from The Original Guide to
American Cocktails and Drinks- 6th Edition
Coffee mug, preheated
Build in glass
1/2 oz. Frangelico
1/2 oz. Kahlúa
1/2 oz. Disaronno Amaretto
1/2 oz. Baileys Irish Cream
Near fill with hot coffee
Garnish with whipped cream
        and powdered cocoa
Pour ingredients into the preheated coffee mug
in the order listed. Garnish with whipped cream
and powdered cocoa.

Tropical Tea

Specialty of The Refectory Restaurant & Bistro
Created by Julie Mulisano, Paul Meyers
Wine glass, ice
Build in glass
1 oz. Grand Marnier
1 oz. Caravella Limoncello
Near fill with hibiscus elder tea
        (room temperature)
Garnish with a lemon wedge
Pour ingredients into the iced wine glass in the
order listed. Garnish with a lemon wedge.

Winnie's Hot Honey Pot

Excerpted from The Original Guide to
American Cocktails and Drinks- 6th Edition
Coffee mug, preheated
Build in glass
1 oz. Drambuie
1/2 oz. honey
1/2 oz. fresh lemon juice
Near fill with English breakfast tea
Serve with a lemon slice
Pour ingredients into the preheated coffee mug
in the order listed. Serve with a lemon slice.

Chapter Nine

Class by the Glass
Champagne & Wine Cocktails

Champagne has a nearly universal appeal. Perhaps no other product enjoys such a sterling reputation for outstanding quality. It is also the one wine that may be appropriately served any time of day, with any meal and with just about any type of food.

It's unlikely that when Dom Pierre Pérignon discovered the process of making champagne he had any idea his sparkling wine would spawn a fabulous array of sensational cocktails. Champagne-based drinks are synonymous with celebrations and special occasions. So exceptional are these cocktails that they have the capacity of turning any night into something genuinely memorable.

The new breed of champagne libations is among the latest trends sweeping the country. These cocktails are light, effervescent and exceptionally delicious. With the advent of the reusable bottle-stopper that keeps champagne carbonated overnight, you can pour champagne by the glass without being concerned that the unused portion will go flat and be wasted.

Champagne is deserving of its fame. The wine is skillfully produced, has impeccable quality and is able to wow the senses and satisfy the soul. Why has it attained such celebrity status? A number of singular and most significant factors are at the heart of the explanation and none of them involve luck.

The wine is made northeast of Paris in the region of France within the Department of Marne. Champagne is made from various grape varietals, including Chardonnay and two black grapes — Pinot Noir and Pinot Meunier. The region's climate and chalky soil are ideal for cultivating grapes. They are harvested by hand, pressed carefully so as not to crush the delicate skins and allowed to ferment naturally. Afterwards the vintner marries the wines together to create its individual blend, called a cuvée.

Champagne attains its famous spritz through a process called méthode champenoise. Before bottling, sugar and yeast are added, which initiates a secondary fermentation in the bottle. The process raises the wine's alcohol content and imbues the champagne with effervescence. Secondary fermentation takes about a month, after which the champagne is matured in cellars up to three years. The final stage involves the removal of sediment and the bottle being recorked.

Champagnes are principally produced in three versions. Blanc de Blanc Champagnes are made entirely from Chardonnay grapes. A Blanc de Noir Champagne is made from Pinot Noir and Pinot Meunier, and a Rosé Champagne is produced from any of these varietals with its alluring tint obtained from the juice being in contact with the grape skins.

Like all wines, the qualities, characteristics and personalities of Champagnes and sparkling wines differ greatly. It only stands to reason that choosing the most appropriate Champagne or sparkling wine for use in a particular cocktail is a significant success factor. The better the sparkler, the better the cocktail.

The Essentials

The original recipe for the Champagne Cocktail can be found in Professor Jerry Thomas' seminal work, *The Bon Vivant's Companion or How to Mix Drinks*. Published in 1862, the guide cites the formula to be one-half teaspoon of sugar, one or two dashes of bitters and one piece of lemon peel. It further instructs that the ingredients were to be poured into a tumbler one-third full of broken ice, and fill balance with wine. Shake well and serve. Use one bottle of Champagne to every six large glasses.

For nearly a century and a half the cocktail has remained relatively unchanged. The contemporary version of the drink is made directly into a Champagne flute, tulip glass, or saucer. Typically a sugar cube is placed into

Absente™ Absinthe Refined

Once there was no more celebrated and notorious a spirit than Absinthe. The so-called "Green Muse" was at the height of fashion with the café society of Paris during the early 20th century. Famous artists, writers and poets like Picasso, Baudelaire, Hemingway, Degas, Manet, Toulouse-Lautrec and Oscar Wilde all famously indulged in Absinthe, that is until its production was banned in 1915. With the introduction of *Absente Absinthe Refined*, a new era of enlightenment beckons.

The liqueur is distilled in France by Destilleries et Domaines de Provence from a masceration of botanicals. Absente derives its brilliant color and seductive flavor from a botanical mix including star anise, angelica, peppermint and wormwood; not the grande variety that caused the initial ban, but with the less bitter and decidedly safer Southern wormwood, also known as "petite Absinthe." The liqueur is bottled at 110-proof.

Absente Absinthe Refined is breathtaking. It has a captivating green color and broad bouquet of spicy herbal treats. The dazzling array of aromas is worth the trip alone. The liqueur's initial entry is strong, sizzling and predominantly spicy, but gradually the dry anise and mint flavors begin to move forward and remain on the palate long after the other, more delicate nuances have faded. Absente is complex and elegant, a classic in the making.

A standard method of preparation is to create a cocktail by slowly pouring water over sugar cubes placed on a slotted spoon and balancing the spoon on a glass containing equal parts of Absente and water.

the glass and saturated with one or two dashes of Angostura Bitters, after which cold Champagne is slowly added. Anticipate that the Champagne will create an immediate froth when it comes into contact with the sugar, thus the need to pour the wine slowly. The finishing touch is twisting a lemon rind such that its essential oils are expressed in the direction of the glass. The spiraled lemon twist is then dropped into the cocktail and served.

The venerable *Champagne Cocktail* was named one of the ten best drinks by Esquire Magazine in 1934. One famous variation on the drink originated at London Savoy Hotel in the 1920s. The *Savoy Champagne Cocktail* was made with an Angostura Bitters saturated sugar cube, equal parts of Grand Marnier and V.S. Cognac, filled with chilled Champagne and garnished with an orange twist.

In addition to the category's namesake and founder, there are other classic and absolutely essential Champagne cocktails that must be sipped and savored to be fully appreciated.

• *Bellini* — Created at Harry's Bar in Venice, Italy, the Bellini is a classic cocktail made with cold white peach puree and chilled Prosecco, although the drink is now more frequently made with Champagne. The proportions range from equal parts of puree to Champagne (or Prosecco) to three parts puree to one part wine.

• *Black Velvet* — One of the classic Champagne cocktails, the Black Velvet is said to have originated at the Brook's Club in London in 1861. It's an innovative blend with equal parts of Guinness Irish Stout and Champagne.

• *Death in the Afternoon* — Ernest Hemingway is credited with creating this drink at Harry's New York Bar in Paris in the 1920s. It's prepared by mixing a jigger of Pernod and a generous fill of chilled Champagne.

• *French 75* — Said to have originated in Paris during World War I, the classic cocktail is made with gin, fresh lemon sour mix and Champagne. Substitute bourbon for the gin to make the *French 95*. There is also a cognac-based version of the cocktail, the *French 125*.

• *Kir Royale* — The libation is a combination of Champagne, crème de cassis and a lemon twist. The balance of the three flavors is sublime. Considering it's prominent role, selecting a premium brand of cassis for use in this particular cocktail is highly advisable. A contemporary version is the *Champagne Framboise*, which pairs Champagne with raspberry liqueur, such as Chambord. Combine equal parts of raspberry liqueur and cognac and fill with chilled Champagne to create the classic *Rue de la Paix*.

• *Mimosa* — Originated sometime in France in the 1920s, the Mimosa is made by combining equal parts of fresh orange juice and Champagne. The drink has launched numerous variations, including the *Puccini* (tangerine juice), *Pizzetti* (orange and grapefruit juice) and *Ruddy Mimosa* (orange and cranberry juice).

- **Nelson's Blood** — Despite its slightly daunting name, the Nelson's Blood is a sensationally delicious and refreshing cocktail. It's prepared with a jigger of tawny Port and Champagne. As for the name? England's greatest naval hero, Admiral Horatio Viscount Nelson, was mortally wounded in 1805 at the Battle of Trafalgar. His brilliant tactics led to the defeat of the combined French and Spanish fleets. Nelson's body was returned to England in a cask of rum, the alcohol to serve as a preservative until he could be buried with full honors at St. Paul's Cathedral. As the story goes, during the voyage the sailors onboard secretly emptied the cask of rum so as to drink "Nelson's Blood," which became the name of another classic drink.

- **Ritz Fizz** — Created at the Ritz-Carlton Hotel in Boston, the now famous Ritz Fizz is concocted using Disaronno Amaretto, Blue Curaçao, fresh lemon sour mix and Champagne.

Secrets Revealed of America's Greatest Champagne Cocktails

Champagne is a bona fide treasure with no creative limits. With that firmly in mind, here are the best kept secrets behind America's greatest Champagne cocktails.

- **Exotic Sparklers** — Although celebrated, Champagne is not the only variety of sparkling wine that can be used in the construction of this style of cocktail. It is, however, the only sparkling wine that can be labeled as Champagne. What's important to note is that when you change the flavor and character of the sparkling wine in a cocktail, the resulting cocktail is creatively altered as well.

Dubonnet® Rouge

Dubonnet Rouge is a sweetened, fortified aperitif that has for decades been the bestselling wine of its type in America. As an aperitif wine it is typically consumed before dinner to awaken and stimulate the appetite. While still popularly served as an aperitif, Dubonnet Rouge is under going a resurgence as an integral ingredient in many classic contemporary cocktails.

Considered the grand dame of aperitifs, the fortified wine was created by Frenchman Joseph Dubonnet in 1846 who intended it to be a restorative elixir for the French Foreign Legion on their missions to Africa and Asia. The wine is produced in two versions, both of which are still made according to the same secret recipe devised 150 years ago.

Dubonnet Rouge is produced on a base of premium red wine that is infused with a proprietary blend of herbs, spices, peels and quinine. The wine is fortified with grape spirits to an elevated strength of 19% alcohol by volume. The famed aperitif is light and refreshing, characteristically aromatic with a delicate body and a palate of tangy fruit. The finish is long and subtly effervescent.

Dubonnet Blanc is crafted on a base of white wine, fortified with grape spirits and infused with botanicals. It is drier than its red wine counterpart.

While both versions are a genuine pleasure to sip neat or over ice, they are enormously delicious when featured in specialty cocktails, most notably signature Martinis and Manhattans.

American sparkling wines have steadily increased in renown and popularity. These wines are made from premium varietal grapes in a similar manner to Champagne. Also popular is Prosecco, a delicious sparkling wine made north of Venice in the Veneto region of Italy.

Creative examples of other sparkling wines to consider abound. Brasserie JO in Chicago serves a cocktail dubbed the **Apple Sour**, which is made with Daron Calvados and Bel Normande Sparkling Apple Juice Cider, while their cocktail **April in Paris** is finished with Klipfel Crémant d'Alsace Brut. One of the signature drinks at the World Bar in Manhattan is the **Sake Blossom**, which is finished with Gekkeikan Sparkling Sake. Lastly, the Mosaic Restaurant in Scottsdale, Arizona promotes a specialty **The Bull**, a cocktail made with Absolut Kurant, Chambord and sparkling Shiraz.

Like most commodities, sparkling wines come in many different grades of quality. It is especially important in this respect to hold inviolate the adage about always buying quality and you won't be disappointed. These cocktails will only be as great as the character of the Champagne or sparkling wine used in its creation.

• **Spirited Options** — This is a style of drinks in which brandies, light liquors — gin, vodka, rum and tequila — are the star players.

For example, the World Bar in Manhattan promotes a classy signature cocktail fueled by cognac dubbed the **World Cocktail**. It's concocted with Rémy Martin XO Cognac, white grape juice, bitters and Pineau des Charentes, a French aperitif made from a blend of cognac and fresh grape juice from the autumn pressing. The drink is hand shaken, strained into a chilled glass and filled with Veuve Clicquot Champagne.

At Harry Denton's Starlight Room in San Francisco one of the headline attractions is a sensational specialty called **Drinking the Stars**, a luxurious combination of Dom Pérignon Champagne and 1979 Chateau Ravignan Bas Armagnac that has been infused with Madagascar vanilla, black raisins and oranges.

Not surprisingly, many of the famous Champagne-based drinks showcase cognac in their recipes, including the **Champagne Imperial**, a blend of cognac, Grand Marnier, a bitters-saturated sugar cube and Champagne, the **Champs Elysees Cocktail**, which features V.S. Cognac, B & B Liqueur, fresh lemon sour mix and Champagne and the **De Gaulle Cocktail**, a cocktail made with cognac, Chambord, fresh lemon juice and Champagne.

Many a champagne drink is prepared with a light spirit. For instance, Boston's 33 Restaurant promotes the **Ambrosia**, a champagne cocktail made with apricot-infused Bombay Gin and elderberry juice, while The Carnegie Club's **Havana Fizz** is prepared with muddled fresh mint, lime juice, simple syrup, Bacardi 8 Rum and Champagne. Appleton Estate V/X Jamaica Rum is the driving force behind the World Bar's interpretation of the classic **Prohibition Punch**.

The **Flirtini** at Manhattan's Stone Rose Lounge pairs Grey Goose L'Orange Vodka, pineapple juice and Champagne, while the **French 59** at Brasserie JO in Chicago is made with Tanqueray Gin, G.E. Massenez Créme de Gingembre Liqueur, fresh lemon sour mix and a fill of Cremant d'Alsace Brut. The

Platinum Apricot Bellini is a specialty at Rosemary's Restaurant in Las Vegas. It's a sensational cocktail concocted using Gran Patrón Platinum Tequila, apricot puree and J Vintage Brut from J Vineyards & Winery.

Modifying Champagne cocktails with liqueurs is another advisable creative tact. Stellar examples include the *Best Seller*, a specialty at Manhattan's Bookmarks made with Grand Marnier, Pimm's No. 1, Belvedere Vodka and Champagne, and the *Sweeny 75*, a specialty of Harry Denton's Starlight Room in San Francisco concocted with Mathilde Framboise Liqueur, Beefeater Gin, fresh lemon sour mix and Champagne. The drink is flavorful and exceedingly delicious. Another noteworthy signature cocktail from Harry Denton's is the *Starry Night*, which features Edmond Briottet Crème du Mûre and Brut Champagne. The combination is stirred, poured into a chilled Champagne glass and finished with a fill of Cremant d'Alsace.

For a light change of pace, the *Caribbean Champagne* is made with crème de banana, light rum and a fill of Champagne, or the *Down Under*, a cocktail featuring Disaronno Amaretto, fresh lemon sour mix, orange juice and Champagne. Another flavorful concoction is the *What's Your Honey Dew*. It's made with Midori, lemonade and a fill of Champagne. Some may want to consider getting a *Lobotomy*, a delicious cocktail made with Disaronno Amaretto, Chambord, pineapple juice and Champagne.

• **Muddled Affairs** — Muddling fresh products into these elegant cocktails is a winning strategy for introducing fresh flavors into these cocktails. An example is the *Blueberry Fizz*, one of the delightful sparkling specialties at Bookmarks. The cocktail is prepared with about a dozen muddled blueberries, lime juice and simple syrup, Grand Marnier and a generous fill of Moët & Chandon Champagne. Other creative examples of muddling include the *Gin-Berry Fizz*, which is prepared with muddled strawberry liqueur steeped raspberries, No. TEN by Tanqueray, fresh lemon sour and Champagne, and the *Yuzu Champagne Cocktail* from Bar Masa. It's prepared with muddled sugar, rose water and yuzu peels and a long pour of Champagne.

• **Modified Elegance** — There is a wide array of flavors and products that can be used in these cocktails, with bitters, fruit juice and purees being the often relied upon modifiers. The Refectory Restaurant in Columbus, Ohio has made famous the *Grande Dame*, a Champagne cocktail prepared with Monin Pomegranate Syrup, pineapple juice, Grand Marnier and a fill of Champagne. At 33 Restaurant in Boston, the Prosecco laced *Rhubarb Razz* derives much of its delectable nature from a dose of rhubarb puree.

Oyster Restaurant & Nightclub

⌂ 77 E. Market Street
  Wilkes-Barre, PA 18701
☎ 570.820.0990
▶▶l www.oysterrestaurant.com
✉ thom@oysterrestaurant.com

Oyster Restaurant & Nightclub is like a South Beach experience in Pennsylvania. The place has an airy, elegant feel, a menu loaded with steamy seafood and a serious penchant for attracting the nightlife. When the weather cooperates there's a patio replete with a swimming pool, opium den bed seating and discreet lighting where guests mingle, dance and enjoy the night skies.

Oyster is an upscale venue that's ideal for couples seeking an evening of affordable elegance. The space is divided into somewhat private dining rooms using white gauzy curtains and curved brass fixtures, which creates an intimate and relaxed atmosphere. The interior design features hardwood floors, red brick walls with brass light fixtures, clothed tables and dark fabric, high-back chairs.

True to its name, the cuisine at Oyster is all about seafood with a deliciously spicy Pan-Pacific flair. For starters there are Asian Crab Cakes Wasabi, Seared Kobe Beef Carpaccio and Duck & Shitake Potstickers. The entrees are beautifully prepared and include Shanghai Lobster, Seared Diver Scallops and the marvelously opulent Thai Fish Hot Pot with Lobster, Scallops, Shrimp, Squid and Oysters. The generous portions cap off a first rate dining experience.

Following the chef's lead, the bar has crafted a repertoire of classy and stylish drinks. Signatures of the house are the *Marilyn Monroe Martini*, a sophisticated cocktail made with Stoli Strasberi Vodka and champagne and the *Colossal Shrimptini*, a blend of Absolut Peppar Vodka, dry vermouth, Tabasco and an exquisitely large shrimp garnish. The *Mango Oyster* is concocted with a muddled base of limes, mint leaves, mango juice and simple syrup and savory Cruzan Mango Rum.

The only things the Oyster Restaurant experience lacks are sand, palm trees and insufferable humidity. —RP

Marilyn Monroe Martini
Drink recipe on pg 21

- **Avoiding the Big Bang** — Care needs to be taken when uncorking a bottle of Champagne. The wine inside is under extreme pressure (90 pounds per square inch) and it can turn a cork into a dangerous projectile in an instant. The following are some pointers on opening a bottle of Champagne or sparkling wine:

1. Before opening a bottle of Champagne make sure that it is directed safely away from guests and yourself. Place a cloth napkin or towel over the bottle while loosening the wire enclosure on the cork. It is not necessary to completely remove the wire cage prior to opening the bottle.

2. Keep a firm grip on the cork throughout the procedure. Wrap your thumb and index finger tightly around the cork, digging the wire muzzle into the cork. To loosen, hold the cork tightly and turn the bottle. Do not let the cork cause a popping sound. This is considered bad form and may precipitate Champagne to gush out of the bottle.

3. Champagne and sparkling wines are meant to be served chilled, about 44°F. Serve Champagne after it has been thoroughly chilled in a bucket of icy water or immediately after it has been taken out of the refrigerator. Opening a warm or slightly chilled bottle of Champagne or sparkling wine is a messy proposition.

4. Champagne should be served in chilled glassware. Chilling Champagne glasses can easily be accomplished by storing them in a cooler, placing in crushed ice for five to ten minutes, or filling each glass with ice water for a minute or two.

Grand Marnier ® Cuvée du Cent Cinquantenaire

Grand Marnier Cuvée du Cent Cinquantenaire may very well be the pinnacle of elegance and sophistication. Introduced in 1977 to commemorate the 150th anniversary of Marnier-Lapostolle. Grand Marnier Cuvee du Cent Cinquantenaire is skillfully crafted at the Marnier-Lapostolle distillery in Neauphle le-Château. After the infusion of Haitian orange peels and barrel-aged cognacs have been redistilled, they are blended with exceptionally old, Grande Champagne cognacs ranging in age up to 50 years. The liqueur is then aged at least two more years in Limousin oak barrels

The Cuvee du Cent Cinquantenaire is a luxurious liqueur. It has a burnished amber hue and a delicate, silky smooth body. The wafting bouquet is lavishly endowed with the aromas of well-aged cognac and citrus. It has a sensationally full and rich palate prominently featuring the flavor of cognac with vibrant orange notes. The finish is delectably long and warming.

The liqueur is sophistication personified. To fully appreciate its grandeur, allow it to fully breathe in a snifter. The longer you wait, the better it becomes.

In 1927, the company celebrated its centenary with the release of *Grand Marnier Cuvée du Centenaire*. It is made on a base of cognacs ranging in age up to 25 years. The liqueur has a luxuriously textured body, a generous, citrus-laced bouquet and a delectable palate of well-aged cognac with vibrant orange notes. The finish is delectably long and warming.

• **Final Act** — These are beautiful, stylish drinks and they deserve to be sent out in public with an appropriate garnish. A traditional embellishment is adding sugar to the rim of the glass. Today there are numerous flavors and colors of cocktail sugars on the market. For instance, the **South Beach Peach** is a specialty cocktail at Chicago's Joe's Seafood, Prime Steak & Stone Crab. The cocktail is presented with a rim of lavender-vanilla sugar, which enhances both its appearance and flavor.

Fresh fruit is the most frequently relied upon embellishment for these effervescent cocktails. Lemon and orange twist spirals are both attractive and practical, as they add flavor of the fruits' essential oils to the drink. The **Ambrosia Cocktail** is garnished with skewered dried apricots, while the **Carnegie Club's Watermelon Fizz** is appropriately finished with three speared watermelon balls. Creative options abound.

Wine Drinks Pressed For Success

The popularity of wine borders on phenomenal. It remains the most frequently requested drink for women in this country and second only behind beer for men. For some, the world of wine-based drinks is circumscribed by the Spritzer, Cooler and the Kir, the classic blend of white wine and crème de cassis. The realm of possibilities, however, is far greater than that and well worth exploring, so here then are the best kept secrets of America's greatest wine drinks.

Both red and white wines are versatile bases for drink making. They each have a range of flavors that meld easily with scores of other ingredients and there are numerous, highly creative libations that rely on wine as a base. For instance, a specialty of Bookmarks in Manhattan, the **Plum Drop** is a sensational cocktail created from a mix of Syrah, California plum wine and Disaronno Amaretto. Created at 33 Restaurant in Boston, the **White Passion** is a drink made with dry white wine, DeKuyper Pucker Sour Apple, Cointreau and a splash of ginger ale.

The **Zintini** is a delectably refreshing cocktail served at The Carnegie Club. It's crafted using Ivan Tamas Estates Zinfandel, Absolut Kurant and a few liberal dashes of Cointreau, crème de cassis and peach schnapps. One of the marquee specialties at Rosemary's Restaurant in Las Vegas is the **Ambrosia Cocktail**, an appropriately named drink featuring Neige Apple Cider Ice Wine, Grey Goose L'Orange Vodka, Lillet, fresh lemon sour and pomegranate juice. The drink is hand shaken, strained into a chilled sherry glass and finished with a float of ice wine and an apple slice.

The Restoration is a flavorful mix of dry red wine, brandy, Chambord and fresh lemon sour mix served in a tall, iced glass. Others may want to seek the shelter of a **Port In A Storm**, which is the combination of red wine, brandy and port. Two other classic wine recipes are the **Hot Mulled Wine**, a red wine drink with an irresistible aroma and equally captivating taste, and the **Wine Cobbler**, a savory blend of white wine, triple sec, orange juice, fresh lemon sour mix and a splash of soda.

The Ultimate Summer Libation

When you turn up the thermostat and crank up the thirst, few libations are more satisfying than *Sangria*. It is essentially a punch, an extraordinary blend of wine, fresh fruit and an assortment of spirits and liqueurs. There isn't one definitive version of the Sangria. It is a drink perfectly suited for individuality and an artisan's touch. Often served in a pitcher, Sangria can also be made in single servings.

    This light, thirst-quenching classic is typically made with a moderately priced red wine. The famed wines from the Rioja or Penedes regions of Spain are quite appropriate, as are California Zinfandel or Cabernet Sauvignon. In fact, wine choices are limited only by availability and personal preference. *Nacional 27's White Sangria* in Chicago promotes a savory version of the drink, which is concocted with South American Sauvignon Blanc or Chardonnay, while *Rio's White Sangria* in Las Vegas is built on a base of Pinot Grigio.

    Champagne, sparkling wine or club soda is occasionally added to Sangria for a refreshing splash of effervescence. An example is *Rosemary's Restaurant's Red Sangria*. It's made with, among other things, light to medium-bodied red wine, a bevy of juices and dry sparkling wine. The popular *Rosemary's Restaurant's White Sangria* is made with light-bodied dry white wine and sparkling wine.

HPNOTIQ® Liqueur

HPNOTIQ (pronounced "hypnotic") is a classy, irresistible liqueur from France. The aquamarine hued gem is made from a blend of premium triple-distilled vodka, aged cognac and a proprietary mix of natural tropical fruit juices. Try as you might you won't be able to detect their individual identities.

    Calling HPNOTIQ a liqueur is almost a misnomer. While as versatile as a liqueur, the product is more like a skillfully crafted cocktail in a cork-finished bottle. The cognac used in its production is a blend of brandies from the Petite Champagne, Fins Bois and Borderies regions.

    The moment HPNOTIQ hits the glass you know you're in for a singular treat. The liqueur has an alluring turquoise blue color and a light, spirit-like body. Its prominent bouquet is laced with the aromas of ripe fruit and citrus. The mouth-filling palate is tart and loaded with nuance, an intriguing mix with a taste reminiscent of grapefruit, mandarin and a hint of brandy on the finish. No learning curve necessary here.

    HPNOTIQ is a bona fide pleasure to work with behind the bar. It was obviously created for a cocktail glass and is outstanding served chilled straight up, or on the rocks. It also plays well with others mixing beautifully with most styles of rum, tequila, a slew of flavored vodkas and champagne. Mentioning that the liqueur tastes great with nearly all types of juice comes close to stating the obvious.

The Sangria is a forgiving concoction, so you can't go too far astray. A few pointers usually prove helpful, however. To that end, here are the best kept secrets to America's greatest Sangrias.

• **Spirited Designs** — The Sangria's wine and fruit base makes a wonderfully hospitable environment for many different spirits, liqueurs and fortified wines. All-stars such as Cointreau, crème de cassis, peach schnapps, apricot liqueur, Chambord, fraise and numerous of their ilk are used in Sangrias. Along with the Sauvignon Blanc and Chardonnay, the **White Sangria** at Nacional 27 derives some of its marvelous flavor from a bracer of Pisco, a Peruvian brandy.

The Spanish Kitchen in Beverly Hills celebrates summer with two very different versions of the drink. **The Spanish Kitchen White Sangria** gets its kicks with Cruzan Orange and Pineapple Rums, DeKuyper Tropical Pineapple Schnapps and white wine, and their **Red Sangria** is fueled by Cruzan Citrus Rum, Brandy Presidente and red wine. Both are heavenly.

• **Fresh, Fresh, Fresh** — Most seasonal fruits make excellent additions in Sangria. Especially suitable are the citrus fruits, such as oranges, lemons, and limes. Their high acidity offsets the drink's natural sweetness and keeps the other fruit in the drink from discoloring. Also popular are fragrant fruit and berries, such as peaches, nectarines, blackberries, strawberries and pitted cherries, as well as apples, pears, or grapes.

A luscious example of creative "fruiting" is the Backstreet Café's **Pomegranate & Peach Sangria**, a blend of pomegranate juice, fresh pureed peaches, guava nectar, orange juice, Cointreau and New Zealand Sauvignon Blanc. It's worth the trip.

Muddle the fruit along with sugar or simple syrup before adding in the other ingredients. It is also highly advisable to let the Sangria steep so the flavor of the wine, fruit and spirits has time to become fully integrated. If you make Sangria in advance, add soft fruit, such as pears and strawberries, just before serving to prevent them from getting mushy.

Ambrosia

Specialty of 33 Restaurant & Lounge
Created by Jenn Harvey
Cocktail glass, chilled
Pour ingredients into an iced mixing glass
2 oz. Apricot-Infused Bombay Gin*
1 oz. Elderberry flower juice
Shake and strain
Top with 1 oz. Veuve Clicquot
    Yellow Label Champagne
Garnish with a dried apricot on a skewer
Pour ingredients, except the Champagne, into the iced mixing glass. Shake thoroughly and strain contents into a chilled cocktail glass. Top with 1 oz. Champagne. Garnish with a dried apricot on a skewer
*Apricot-Infused Bombay Gin Recipe - pg 317

Ambrosia Cocktail

Specialty of Rosemary's Restaurant
Created by Michael Shetler
Cocktail glass, chilled
Pour ingredients into an iced mixing glass
2 oz. Grey Goose L'Orange Vodka
1/2 oz. Marie Brizard Apry
1/4 oz. Lillet Blanc
1/4 oz. Neige Apple Ice Wine
1/4 oz. fresh lemon sour mix
1 1/2 oz. POM Pomegranate Juice
Shake and strain
Float 1 bar spoon of Neige Apple Ice Wine
Garnish with an apple twist
Pour ingredients into the iced mixing glass. Shake thoroughly and strain contents into a chilled cocktail glass. Float 1 bar spoon of Neige Wine. Garnish with an apple twist.

April in Paris

Specialty of Brasserie JO
Created by Adam Seger
Cocktail glass, chilled
Pour ingredients into an iced mixing glass
1 oz. Homemade Parfait d'Amour
1 1/2 oz. passion fruit nectar
Shake and strain
1 1/2 oz. Klipfel Crémant d'Alsace
    Brut Sparkling Wine
Garnish with a strip of orange zest cut
    over the glass
Pour the Parfait d'Amour and nectar into the iced mixing glass. Shake thoroughly and strain contents into a chilled cocktail glass. Top with 1 1/2 oz. sparkling wine. Garnish with a strip of orange zest cut over the glass.

The Best Seller

Specialty of Bookmarks
Created by Dawn Durham
Cocktail glass, chilled
Pour ingredients into an iced mixing glass
1 oz. Belvedere Vodka
1/2 oz. Grand Marnier
1/2 oz. Pimm's No. 1
Shake and strain
Top with Veuve Clicquot Yellow
    Label Champagne
Garnish with an orange twist
Pour ingredients, except for the Champagne, into the iced mixing glass. Shake thoroughly and strain contents into a chilled cocktail glass. Top with Champagne. Garnish with an orange twist.

Blueberry Fizz

Specialty of Bookmarks
Created by Jonathan Pogash
Champagne flute, chilled
Pour ingredients into an empty mixing glass
10-12 fresh blueberries
1 tsp. sugar
1/4 oz. fresh lime juice
1/4 oz. simple syrup
Muddle contents
Add ice
Splash Grand Marnier
3 oz. Moët & Chandon White
    Star Champagne
Stir and strain
 Garnish with 3 blueberries on a pick
Place the blueberries, sugar, lime juice and simple syrup into the empty mixing glass. Muddle and add ice. Pour in the remaining ingredients. Stir gently and strain into a chilled Champagne flute. Garnish with 3 blueberries on a pick.

The Bull

Specialty of Mosaic Restaurant
Created by Stephanie Kozicki, Matt Rinn
Cocktail glass, chilled
Pour ingredients into an iced mixing glass
2 oz. Absolut Kurant Vodka
1/4 oz. Chambord
Shake and strain
Float 1 oz. Sparkling Shiraz
Garnish with a lemon twist
Pour the vodka and Chambord into the iced mixing glass. Shake thoroughly and strain contents into a chilled cocktail glass. Float the sparkling Shiraz. Garnish with a lemon twist.

P.F. Chang's China Bistro

Mary Brickell Village
901 S. Miami Ave.
Miami, FL 33131
☎ 305.358.0732
▶▶ www.pfchangs.com

Arguably the best seats in the house at P.F. Chang's China Bistro are at the bar facing the expansive exhibition kitchen. No need to glance at the wall-mounted television because what's going on in front of you is imminently more entertaining. With more than 150 restaurant's nationwide, the chefs and cooks at P.F. Chang's are virtuosos with the wok, the most challenging of culinary arts and the definitive method for producing authentic Chinese cuisine.

The stylish, high energy bistro is decked out in the dramatic colors, fabrics and images of China. The interior is sophisticated and richly appointed with deep booths, carved wooden screens, Asian art and oversized urns and vases. As traditional as the setting might be, the feel in the restaurant is upbeat, fast-paced and contemporary.

P.F. Chang's menu is a lavish offering of innovative modern Chinese dishes with Southeast Asian influences. Many are presented with light sauces prepared tableside to allow the natural flavors to fully emerge. Signature dishes include Oolong Marinated Sea Bass, Orange Peel Beef, Cantonese Shrimp and the immensely popular Chang's Chicken in Soothing Lettuce Wraps.

The restaurant's popularity can also be attributed to a creative roster of outstanding cocktails, such as the **Asian Pear Mojito**, which features Bacardi Limón Rum, DeKuyper Pucker Sour Apple and a splash of fresh pineapple juice, and **Cantaloupe Chang's**, a cocktail made with muddled cantaloupe, SKYY Melon Vodka, Marie Brizard Watermelon Liqueur, Thai basil and fresh lemon sour mix.

Watching the uniformed crew at work is mesmerizing, as is the constant towering flame shooting up from the woks as they stir and toss ingredients. Great show, great follow through. —RP

Asian Pear Mojito
Drink recipe on pg 122

Classic Champagne Cocktail

Excerpted from The Original Guide to
American Cocktails and Drinks- 6th Edition
Champagne glass, chilled
Build in glass
1 sugar cube, soaked with Angostura
   Aromatic Bitters
Fill with Champagne
Garnish with a
   lemon twist
Place the sugar cube
in the bottom of the
chilled Champagne glass.
Soak with bitters. Fill with
Champagne. Garnish with
a lemon twist.

Champagne Imperial

Excerpted from The Original Guide to
American Cocktails and Drinks- 6th Edition
Champagne glass, chilled
Build in glass
1 sugar cube soaked with
   Angostura Aromatic Bitters
1/2 oz. Courvoisier VSOP Cognac
1/2 oz. Grand Marnier Cuvée du Centenaire
Fill with Champagne
Garnish with a lemon twist
Place the sugar cube in the bottom of the
chilled Champagne glass. Soak with bitters.
Add the Cognac and Grand Marnier. Fill with
Champagne. Garnish with a lemon twist.

Limoncé® Liqueur

Italy is well known for crafting some of the finest products on Earth. While sports cars, leather goods, cheese and wine certainly top the list, the nation is also internationally famous for making limoncello, a remarkably light and refreshing lemon flavored liqueur. It is standard fare on back bars throughout Europe. Over the past several years, Americans have been discovering how marvelously wonderful these liqueurs can be. Leading this popular phenomenon is *Limoncé Liqueur*.

Made in Trieste, Italy at the renowned Stock Distillery, Limoncè gets its fabulous flavor from sun-drenched lemons grown on the Mediterranean coast. The peels of the fruit are steeped for an extended period of time in pure grain spirits, after which the infused-alcohol is filtered and sweetened. The liqueur is bottled at 60-proof.

Limoncè is deserving of the critical acclaim it is receiving. The liqueur looks like freshly squeezed lemonade and has a wafting, lively bouquet with notes of citrus and flora. It has a feather-weight body that rolls over the palate and immediately fills the mouth with the zesty, tangy flavor of lemons. It's a vibrant sensation brimming with life and kinetic vitality. The lingering finish is warming and bittersweet.

Limoncé is the bestselling limoncello in Italy. The liqueur is tailor-made for American mixology and can be used to invigorate a wide variety of contemporary cocktails. It's often added to Mojitos, Manhattans, Lemon Drops and Martinis for an added burst of flavor.

Champs Elysees Cocktail

Excerpted from The Original Guide to
American Cocktails and Drinks- 6th Edition
Champagne glass, chilled
Pour ingredients into an iced mixing glass
1 oz. VSOP Cognac
1 oz. B&B Liqueur
2 dashes Angostura Aromatic Bitters
1 1/2 oz. fresh lemon sour mix
Shake and strain
Fill with Champagne
Pour ingredients, except Champagne, into the
iced mixing glass. Shake thoroughly and strain
contents into a chilled Champagne glass. Fill
with Champagne.

The Corsage for Mother's Day

Specialty of Joe's Seafood, Prime Steak & Stone Crab
Created by Dan Barringer
Cocktail glass, chilled
Pour ingredients into an iced mixing glass
1 1/2 oz. California Riesling Wine
1/2 oz. Sweet Sparkling Wine
1/2 oz. Alizé Red Passion
1/2 oz. Ceres Pear Juice
1 oz. Rose flower simple syrup*
Shake and strain
Garnish with a floating mini rose
Pour ingredients into the iced mixing glass. Shake
thoroughly and strain contents into a chilled
cocktail glass. Garnish with a floating mini rose.
*Rose Flower Simple Syrup Recipe - pg 322

Down Under

Excerpted from The Original Guide to
American Cocktails and Drinks- 6th Edition
House specialty glass, ice
Pour ingredients into an iced mixing glass
1 1/2 oz. Disaronno Amaretto
1 1/2 oz. fresh orange juice
1 1/2 oz. fresh lemon sour mix
Shake and strain
Fill with Champagne
Pour ingredients, except the Champagne, into
the iced mixing glass. Shake thoroughly and
strain contents into an iced house specialty glass.
Fill with Champagne.

Drinking the Stars

Specialty of Harry Denton's Starlight Room
Created by Jacques Bezuidenhout
Champagne glass, chilled
Build in glass
4 oz. Dom Pérignon Champagne
1 1/2 oz. Armagnac Infusion*
Garnish with a lemon spiral twist
Pour ingredients into the chilled Champagne
glass in the order listed. Garnish with a lemon
spiral twist.
NOTE: Keep drink ingredients on ice.
*Armagnac Infusion Recipe - pg 317

Flapper's Delight

Specialty of The Campbell Apartment
Created by Mark Grossich
Champagne glass, chilled
Build in glass
1/2 oz. Disaronno Amaretto
1/2 oz. papaya juice
Fill with Moët & Chandon
     White Star Champagne
Garnish with an orange twist
Pour the ingredients into the chilled Champagne
glass in the order listed. Garnish with an
orange twist.

Flirtini

Specialty of Stone Rose Lounge
Created by Jeff Isaacson
Cocktail glass, chilled
Pour ingredients into an iced mixing glass
1 1/2 oz. Grey Goose L'Orange Vodka
1 oz. pineapple juice
Shake and strain
Fill with Champagne
Pour the vodka and pineapple juice into the
iced mixing glass. Shake thoroughly and strain
contents into a chilled cocktail glass. Fill with
Champagne.

French 125

Excerpted from The Original Guide to
American Cocktails and Drinks- 6th Edition
Champagne glass, chilled
Pour ingredients into an iced mixing glass
1 oz. VS Cognac
2 oz. fresh lemon sour mix
Shake and strain
Fill with Champagne
Garnish with a lemon twist
Pour Cognac and sour mix into the iced mixing
glass. Shake thoroughly and strain contents
into a chilled Champagne glass. Fill with
Champagne. Garnish with a lemon twist.

French 33

Specialty of 33 Restaurant & Lounge
Created by Ari Bialikamien
Champagne glass, chilled
Pour ingredients into an iced mixing glass
1 oz. WET by Beefeater
1/2 oz. peach nectar
Splash fresh lemon juice
Shake and strain
Fill with Prosecco
Garnish with a lemon twist
Pour ingredients, except the Prosecco, into the iced mixing glass. Shake thoroughly and strain contents into the chilled Champagne glass. Fill with Prosecco. Garnish with a lemon twist.

French 59

Specialty of Brasserie JO
Created by David Johnston
Ginger sugar rimmed cocktail glass, chilled
Pour ingredients into an iced mixing glass
1 1/2 oz. Tanqueray Gin
1 oz. G.E. Massenez Crème de Gingembre
Splash simple syrup
Splash fresh lemon juice
Shake and strain
Fill with 2 oz. Cremant d'Alsace
   Brut Sparkling Wine
Garnish with a lemon twist
Pour ingredients, except the sparkling wine, into the iced mixing glass. Shake thoroughly and strain contents into a ginger sugar rimmed, chilled cocktail glass. Fill with sparkling wine. Garnish with a lemon twist.

> "The new breed of Champagne libations is among the latest trends sweeping the country."

Metaxa® Five Star Greek Specialty Liqueur

The Greek culture is one of the oldest on Earth and the bedrock of modern civilization. It also prides itself as the country of origin of *Metaxa Five Star Greek Specialty Liqueur*, an absolutely delicious spirit often thought of as a brandy, but in reality it is something much more. If you haven't been fortunate enough to taste Metaxa, be prepared with your first sip to become a fan for life.

This famous Greek import has been made according to the same recipe since 1888. Three different grape varietals — Savatiano, Sultanina and Black Corinth — are crushed to produce a special wine, which is the base for all of the Metaxa vintages. This wine is then double-distilled and placed in handmade, French Limousin oak casks for aging, which for Metaxa Five Star is five years. After aging, the distillate is blended with Muscat wine from the Samos and Lemnos and infused with a secret mix of botanicals, one of which is rose petals. It is further aged and bottled at 76-proof.

This expression of Metaxa is worthy of its world-class reputation. It has a burnished amber appearance and a voluminous bouquet of raisins, ripe plums and toasted oak. Its body is soft, lush and supple and on the palate the Five Star is fresh, fruity and imminently satisfying. The spirit finishes long and flavorful. It's a first class experience.

The famous Metaxa range also includes the *Seven Star* (3 years old), *Grand Olympian Reserve* (12 years old), *Grande Fine* (15 years old) and the *Private Reserve* (20 years old). Only age distinguishes one from the other.

French 75

Excerpted from The Original Guide to
American Cocktails and Drinks- 6th Edition
Champagne glass, chilled
Pour ingredients into an iced mixing glass
1 oz. Gin
2 oz. fresh lemon sour mix
Shake and strain
Fill with Champagne
Garnish with a lemon twist
Pour the gin and fresh lemon sour mix into the
iced mixing glass. Shake thoroughly and strain
contents into a chilled Champagne glass. Fill
with Champagne. Garnish with a lemon twist.

Fuzz Up

Specialty of Cyrus
Created by Scott Beattie
Cocktail glass, chilled
Pour ingredients into an iced mixing glass
3/4 oz. Hangar One Citron
    "Buddha's Hand" Vodka
3/4 oz. Hangar One Straight Vodka
1/2 oz. fresh lemon juice
1 1/2 oz. Red Indian peach puree*
Shake and strain
Splash sparkling wine
Garnish with a thin slice of Red Indian Peach
Pour ingredients, except the sparkling wine, into
the iced mixing glass. Shake thoroughly and
strain contents into a chilled cocktail glass. Add
a splash of sparkling wine. Garnish with a thin
slice of Red Indian Peach.
*Red Indian Peach Puree Recipe - pg 322

Gin-Berry Fizz

Specialty of The Campbell Apartment
Created by Mark Grossich
Pilsner glass, chilled
Build in glass
1 tbsp. fresh raspberries
Splash Hiram Walker Strawberry Liqueur
Muddle contents
Add ice
1 1/2 oz. No. 10 by Tanqueray Gin
Splash fresh lemon juice
Splash simple syrup
Top with Moët & Chandon White
    Star Champagne
Garnish with a fresh strawberry
    and 3 fresh skewered raspberries
Place the raspberries and liqueur into the chilled
pilsner glass. Muddle and add ice. Add the
remaining ingredients. Garnish with a fresh
strawberry and 3 fresh raspberries skewered.

Grande Champagne Cocktail

Specialty of Brasserie JO
Created by David Johnston
House specialty glass, ice
Build in glass
1 oz. Chateau de Montifaud VSOP Cognac
1 oz. Cointreau
1/2 oz. G.E. Massenez Crème de Cassis
3-4 drops Fee's Orange Bitters
Stir gently
Fill with 2 oz. Cremant d'Alsace
    Brut Sparkling Wine
Garnish with strip of orange peel
Pour ingredients, except the sparkling wine,
into the iced house specialty glass. Stir gently.
Fill with sparkling wine. Garnish with a strip of
orange peel.

Grande Dame

Specialty of The Refectory Restaurant & Bistro
Created by Julie Mulisano, David McMahon
Champagne glass, chilled
Build in glass
1/2 oz. Grand Marnier
1/4 oz. Monin Pomegranate Syrup
1 oz. pineapple juice
Fill with Champagne
Pour ingredients into the chilled Champagne
glass in the order listed.

Havana Fizz

Specialty of The Carnegie Club
Created by Kenneth McClure
Cocktail glass, chilled
Pour ingredients into an empty mixing glass
6-8 sprigs fresh mint
1/2 oz. fresh lime juice
1/2 oz. simple syrup
Muddle contents
Add ice
2 oz. Bacardi 8 Rum
Shake and strain
Fill with Champagne
Garnish with a mint sprig
Place the mint, lime juice and simple syrup into
the empty mixing glass. Muddle and add ice.
Pour in the rum. Shake thoroughly and strain
contents into a chilled cocktail glass. Fill with
Champagne. Garnish with a mint sprig.

Hot Mulled Wine

Excerpted from The Original Guide to
American Cocktails and Drinks- 6th Edition
Punch bowl or decanter
Pour ingredients into a saucepan
36 oz. Dry Red Wine
1/4 cup mulling spices
1/2 cup sugar
12 oz. cranberry juice
Simmer for 30 minutes or to taste
Garnish with thinly sliced lemon
  and orange wheels
Pour ingredients into a saucepan. Simmer for 30
minutes or to taste and serve in a punch bowl
or decanter with clear glass mugs. Garnish with
thinly sliced lemon and orange wheels. Makes
8-10 servings.

Huck Yu

Specialty of Cyrus
Created by Scott Beattie
Cocktail glass, frozen
Pour ingredients into an iced mixing glass
1 oz. Hangar One Straight Vodka
1/2 oz. Limoncello
1 oz. Verjus
1/4 oz. Yuzu Orange Juice
1/4 oz. huckleberry simple syrup*
Shake and strain
Fill with sparkling wine
Pour ingredients, except the sparkling wine, into
the iced mixing glass. Shake thoroughly and
strain contents into a frozen cocktail glass. Fill
with sparkling wine.
*Huckleberry Simple Syrup Recipe - pg 320

Jonny's Appleseed

Specialty of Absinthe Brasserie & Bar
Created by Jonny Raglin
Cocktail glass, chilled
Pour ingredients into an iced mixing glass
1 1/2 oz. Domaine Dupont
  Calvados Hor d'age
1/2 oz. apple simple syrup*
1/2 oz. fresh lemon juice
Shake and strain
Garnish with a thin slice of Granny Smith apple
Float 3/4 oz. Rose Champagne on the garnish
Pour ingredients, except the sparkling wine,
into the iced mixing glass. Shake thoroughly
and strain contents into a chilled cocktail glass.
Garnish with a thin slice of Granny Smith apple.
Float the Champagne on top of the apple slice.
*Apple Simple Syrup Recipe - pg 317

Limonsecco

Specialty of Bookmarks
Created by Kenneth McClure
Rocks glass, chilled
Pour ingredients into an empty mixing glass
3 lemon slices
1 1/2 oz. Pallini Limoncello
1/2 oz. fresh lemon juice
Muddle contents
Add ice
1 oz. SKYY Citrus Vodka
Fill with Prosecco
Garnish with a lemon slice
Place the lemons, Limoncello and lemon juice
into the empty mixing glass. Muddle and add
ice. Pour in the vodka. Shake thoroughly and
strain contents into a chilled rocks glass. Fill with
Prosecco. Garnish with a lemon slice.

Lobotomy

Excerpted from The Original Guide to
American Cocktails and Drinks- 6th Edition
Champagne glass, chilled
Pour ingredients into an iced mixing glass
3/4 oz. Disaronno Amaretto
3/4 oz. Chambord
3/4 oz. pineapple juice
Shake and strain
Fill with Champagne
Pour ingredients, except the Champagne, into
the iced mixing glass. Shake thoroughly and
strain contents into a chilled Champagne glass.
Fill with Champagne.

Mission Belle

Specialty of The Mission Inn Hotel & Spa
Created by Brooke Crothers
Champagne glass, chilled
Build in glass
1/4 oz. Disaronno Amaretto
1/4 oz. Apricot Brandy
Fill with Brut Champagne
Pour ingredients into the chilled Champagne
glass in the order listed.

Nelson's Blood

Excerpted from The Original Guide to
American Cocktails and Drinks- 6th Edition
Champagne glass, chilled
Build in glass
1 1/2 oz. Tawny Port
Fill with Champagne
Garnish with an orange twist
Pour ingredients into the chilled Champagne
glass in the order listed. Garnish with an
orange twist.

The Refectory Restaurant & Bistro

🏠 **1092 Bethel Road**
   Columbus, OH 43220
☎ **614.451.9774**
▶▶ **www.therefectory.citysearch.com**
✉ **refectory@rrohio.com**

The Refectory Restaurant & Bistro offers quiet sanctuary and a soul satisfying dining experience. The continental cuisine restaurant is located in two historic buildings. The first was built as a church in 1853 and some 60 years later it was moved 200 yards south and joined with an older, one-room schoolhouse. In this century the combined buildings house the acclaimed Refectory Restaurant, which caters to its congregation one exceptional dinner at a time.

The unique architecture and construction creates a peaceful ambience and a discernible air of gracious elegance. The east wing, or the original schoolhouse, now houses the lounge, full bar and main dining room, while the west wing is reserved for the non-smoking dining room. The dramatic interior features the original hand-hewn beams, exposed wooden roof, red brick walls, stained glass windows, subdued lighting, deep, secluded booths and large stone hearth. The tables are clothed and candles abound. The effect is intimate and exceedingly romantic.

The classic and contemporary northwestern French cuisine is the specialty of Chef de Cuisine Richard Blondin. The seasonal menu includes the likes of Smoked Salmon Rillette, Pan Seared Baby Lamb Loin, homemade pâté and Pan Seared Crispy Mild Spiced Duck Magret. An ever-changing, biweekly bistro menu is available weekdays in the schoolhouse or on the patio surrounded by the chef's herb garden. A wine menu with over 700 selections complements the world-class cuisine.

The philosophy of exceeding guest expectations carries over to the bar, where cocktails are the specialty of the house. A sterling example is the **Blueberry Ballad**, a delectable combination of cherry vodka, limoncello, POM Blueberry-Pomegranate Juice and club soda.

All in all, the landmark eatery guarantees a memorable evening. —RP

Blueberry Ballad
Drink recipe on pg 299

Paradise Fizz

Specialty of Jade Bar
Created by Greg Portsche
Champagne glass, chilled
Build in glass
1 tbsp. sugar
1/2 oz. Midori
1/2 oz. Fruja Mango Liqueur
1/2 oz. pineapple juice
Fill with Veuve Clicquot Yellow
    Label Champagne
Garnish with a lemon twist
Pour ingredients into the chilled Champagne glass
in the order listed. Garnish with a lemon twist.

Passion Fruit Bellini

Specialty of 33 Restaurant & Lounge
Created by Jenn Harvey
Champagne glass, chilled
Build in glass
1/2 oz. Cointreau
1/2 oz. passion fruit puree
Splash simple syrup
Fill with Prosecco
Garnish with an orange twist
Pour ingredients into the chilled Champagne glass
in the order listed. Garnish with an orange twist.

Pernod Pom Royale

Specialty of Nacional 27
Created by Adam Seger
Champagne flute, chilled
Pour ingredients into an iced mixing glass
1 oz. Pernod
2 dashes Angostura Aromatic Bitters
1 oz. pomegranate juice
Stir and strain
Fill with Brut Champagne
Garnish with a orange twist
Pour ingredients, except the Champagne, into
the iced mixing glass. Stir gently and strain
contents into a chilled Champagne flute. Fill with
Champagne. Garnish with an orange twist.

Hennessy® Privilège V.S.O.P. Cognac

Founded in 1765, Hennessy is the most successful cognac house in the world. It is the owner of the largest reserve of old cognacs with some 230,000 barrels aging at any one time. Among their chief assets is an unbroken lineage of seven generations of master blenders from the Fillioux family. This assures a familial knowledge of the Hennessy cellars and a heritage of individuals proven unsurpassed at art of blending eaux de vie. Among its famous repertoire is the acclaimed *Hennessy V.S.O.P. Privilège Cognac*.

Created in 1817 for the future King George IV of Great Britain, Privilège V.S.O.P., is assembled from more than 60 eaux de vie obtained primarily from the Grande and Petite Champagne growing regions. The constituent cognacs are aged 15 years in seasoned Limousin casks, thereby limiting the influence of the tannins in the wood.

Privilège is a most appropriate name for this delectable cognac. It has a rich amber hue, a lush, velvety textured body and a bouquet punctuated with the aromas of cinnamon, flora, honey and ripe peaches. Its initial entry is smooth and engaging, followed by a long lasting finish laced with a flavorful and somewhat spicy finish.

Hennessy has made a worldwide franchise of the V.S. cognac market. *Hennessy V.S. Cognac* is assembled from more than 40 different Grande and Petite Champagne brandies, along with some from the Borderies and Fins and Bons Bois. The constituent cognacs are aged a minimum of three years.

Platinum Apricot Bellini

Specialty of Rosemary's Restaurant
Created by Michael Shetler, Francesco LaFranconi
Champagne glass, chilled
Build in glass
1 oz. Gran Patrón Platinum Tequila
1/4 oz. Marie Brizard Apry
2 1/2 oz. apricot nectar puree*
Top with Jordan Vineyards J Vintage Brut
Garnish with a fresh mint sprig
Pour ingredients into the chilled Champagne glass in the order listed. Garnish with a fresh mint sprig.
*Apricot Nectar Puree Recipe - pg 317

Plum Drop

Specialty of Bookmarks
Created by Geoffrey Williams
Cocktail glass, chilled
Pour ingredients into an iced mixing glass
1 oz. California Plum Wine
1 1/2 oz. Syrah
1/2 oz. Disaronno Amaretto
Stir and strain
Pour ingredients into the iced mixing glass. Stir gently and strain contents into a chilled cocktail glass.

Pomegranate & Peach Sangria

Specialty of Backstreet Café
Created by Sean Beck
Glass pitcher, 64 oz., ice
Build in pitcher
Bottle New Zealand Sauvignon Blanc (26.2 oz.)
1 1/2 oz. Cointreau
8 oz. pomegranate juice
7 oz. fresh pureed peaches
6 oz. guava nectar
4 oz. orange juice
2 oz. simple syrup
Stir
1 peach cut into slices
1 orange cut into slices
1 lime cut into slices
Garnish with freshly cut fruit
Combine all ingredients, except the sliced fruit, and stir well. Add freshly sliced fruit. Serve in glass of choice over ice.
Makes 6-10 servings

Port in a Storm

Excerpted from The Original Guide to
American Cocktails and Drinks- 6th Edition
House specialty glass, ice
Pour ingredients into an iced mixing glass
4 oz. Dry Red Wine
2 oz. Tawny Port
3/4 oz. Brandy
Stir and strain
Garnish with a mint sprig
Pour ingredients into the iced mixing glass. Stir thoroughly and strain contents into an iced house specialty glass. Garnish with a mint sprig.

Prohibition Punch

Specialty of The Campbell Apartment
Created by Mark Grossich
Snifter glass, ice
Pour ingredients into an iced mixing glass
1 1/2 oz. Appleton Estate V/X Jamaica Rum
3/4 oz. Grand Marnier
Splash fresh lemon juice
1 oz. passion fruit juice
1 oz. cranberry juice
Shake and strain
Fill with Moët & Chandon White
    Star Champagne
Pour ingredients, except the Champagne, into the iced mixing glass. Shake thoroughly and strain contents into an iced snifter glass. Fill with Champagne.

Raspberry Champagne Cocktail

Specialty of Bar Masa
Created by Mike Vacheresse
Champagne glass, chilled
Pour ingredients into an empty mixing glass
1 oz. Raspberry/Shiso Puree*
5 oz. Champagne
Stir
Garnish with a fresh raspberry
Pour the puree and Champagne into the empty mixing glass. Stir gently to mix and pour into an empty, chilled Champagne glass. Garnish with a fresh raspberry.
*Raspberry/Shiso Puree Recipe - pg 322

Raspberry Sangria

Specialty of 33 Restaurant & Lounge
Created by Ari Bialikamian
Wine glass, ice
Build in glass
2 oz. Alba Vineyard Red Raspberry Wine
1 oz. Carmen Merlot
1 oz. Brandy
1/2 oz. Cointreau
Dash simple syrup
1/2 oz. orange juice
Garnish with floating mixed berries
Pour ingredients into the iced wine glass in the order listed. Garnish with floating mixed berries.

Red Sangria, Rosemary's

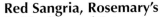

Specialty of Rosemary's Restaurant
Created by Michael Shetler
Pint glass, ice
Pour ingredients into an iced mixing glass
Pour Rosemary's Sangria* into an iced mixing glass. Shake thoroughly and strain into an iced pint glass. Garnish with fresh orange slices, grapes and a lime wedge floated in the glass.
　　*Rosemary's Red Sangria
　　1 gallon+ container
　　Mix all ingredients and refrigerate overnight
　　50.8 oz. (2 x 750ml bottle) Light to Medium
　　　Bodied Red Wine
　　12.7 oz. (1/2 x 750ml bottle) Dry
　　　Sparkling Wine
　　10 oz. Rosemary's House Brandy Extract**
　　16 oz. fresh orange juice
　　4 oz. fresh lime juice
　　4 oz. fresh ruby red grapefruit juice
　　4 oz. POM Pomegranate Juice
　　6 oz. simple syrup
　　Makes about 1 gallon
**Rosemary's House Brandy Extract
1 liter Brandy
1 whole vanilla bean
Macerate stock brandy with whole vanilla bean for minimum of 90 days

Rhum Clément VSOP

Estate produced Rhum Clément is one of Martinique's preeminent agricole rhums, a traditional style of rum in which fresh cane juice is distilled, rather than molasses. After many years absence, the super-premium brand is once again available in the United States, a venerable range led by critically acclaimed *Rhum Clément VSOP.*

Founded in 1887 by Homère Clément, the distillery is located on the site of an old sugar refinery. The prestigious VSOP is made in accordance with the Appellation d'Origine Contrôlée Martinique from a blend of column-distilled agricole rhums and aged for a minimum of three years in re-charred bourbon barrels. The rhum is then transferred to seasoned cognac barrels for further aging, typically for a year.

A snifter of Rhum Clément VSOP is a museum-grade exhibition. The mahogany hued rhum has a soft, medium-weight body and voluminous bouquet of spicy, semisweet, bakery-fresh aromas. Its breadth of flavors is magnificent, a savory array of chocolate, fig, ripe plums, amaretto and red wine that slowly fade into a memorable finish.

The range includes *Clément Premiére Canne*, a classy silver agricole rhum distilled from the free running juice from seven varieties of Martinique cane. *Clément Créole Shrubb* is a heralded 80-proof liqueur made from a blend of silver and aged rhums and infused with bitter oranges and Creole spices

The entire line of spirits crafted by Clément is exceptional and showcase the fresh, vibrant qualities of agricole rhum from Martinique.

Red Sangria, The Spanish Kitchen's

Specialty of The Spanish Kitchen
Created by Danny Rodriguez
House specialty glass, ice
Build in glass
Fill the iced house specialty glass with The Spanish Kitchen Red Sangria*, leaving room for 1 scoop sangria soaked fruit. Mix fruit in carefully.

    *The Spanish Kitchen's Red Sangria
    Build in container
    5 gallon container
    Combine all ingredients
    8 red apples (cut into 12 pieces)
    8 oranges (cut into 12 pieces)
    1 liter Brandy Presidente
    1 liter Cruzan Citrus Rum
    8 liters San Antonio Velvet Burgundy
    4 liters Sprite
    16-24 oz. canned mandarin oranges
      with juice
    1 oz. whole cloves wrapped in coffee filter
      (remove after 24 hours)
    Makes 14 liters

Restoration

Excerpted from The Original Guide to
American Cocktails and Drinks- 6th Edition
Bucket glass, ice
Pour ingredients into an iced mixing glass
4 oz. Dry Red Wine
3/4 oz. Brandy
3/4 oz. Chambord
1 1/2 oz. fresh lemon sour mix
Shake and strain
Garnish with a lemon twist
Pour ingredients into the iced mixing glass. Shake thoroughly and strain contents into an iced bucket glass. Garnish with a lemon twist.

Rhubarb Razz

Specialty of 33 Restaurant & Lounge
Created by Jenn Harvey
Champagne glass, chilled
Build in glass
1/4 oz. Framboise
1/2 oz. Rhubarb puree
Splash simple syrup
Fill with Prosecco
Garnish with 2 floating raspberries
Pour ingredients into the chilled Champagne glass in the order listed. Garnish with 2 floating raspberries.

Ritz Fizz

Excerpted from The Original Guide to
American Cocktails and Drinks- 6th Edition
House specialty glass, ice
Pour ingredients into an iced mixing glass
1 oz. Disaronno Amaretto
1/2 oz. Blue Curaçao
1 1/2 oz. fresh lemon sour mix
Shake and strain
Fill with Champagne
Garnish with a lemon twist
Pour ingredients, except the Champagne, into the iced mixing glass. Shake thoroughly and strain contents into an iced house specialty glass. Fill with Champagne. Garnish with a lemon twist.

Rue de la Paix

Excerpted from The Original Guide to
American Cocktails and Drinks- 6th Edition
Champagne glass, chilled
Pour ingredients into an iced mixing glass
1 oz. Chambord
1 oz. VSOP Cognac
Stir and strain
Fill with Champagne
Garnish with a lemon twist
Pour the Chambord and cognac into the iced mixing glass. Stir thoroughly and strain contents into a chilled Champagne glass. Fill with Champagne. Garnish with a lemon twist.

Sake Blossom

Specialty of The World Bar
Created by Kenneth McClure
Champagne glass, chilled
Build in glass
1 1/2 oz. lychee puree
4 1/2 oz. Gekkeikan Sparkling Sake
Garnish with a cherry
Pour ingredients into the chilled Champagne glass in the order listed. Garnish with a cherry.

Savoy Champagne Cocktail

Excerpted from The Original Guide to
American Cocktails and Drinks- 6th Edition
Champagne glass, chilled
Build in glass
1 sugar cube, soaked with Angostura
    Aromatic Bitters
1/2 oz. Grand Marnier
1/2 oz. VS Cognac
Fill with Champagne
Garnish with a lemon twist
Place the sugar cube in the bottom of the chilled
Champagne glass. Soak with bitters. Pour in the re-
maining ingredients. Garnish with a lemon twist.

Savoy Sangria

Specialty of Savoy
Created by Brandon Craft
House specialty glass, ice
Pour ingredients into an iced mixing glass
1/2 oz. Christian Brothers Brandy
8 oz. Savoy's Sangria*
Shake and strain
Garnish with an orange slice and cherry
Pour ingredients into the iced mixing glass.
Shake thoroughly and strain contents into an
iced house specialty glass. Garnish with an
orange slice and cherry.
    *Savoy Sangria Base Recipe
    1 gallon container
    Combine all ingredients
    1.5 liters Spanish Red Wine
    3/4 cup sugar
    2 anise stars
    2 cloves
    1 lemon peeled, in wedges
    2 limes peeled, in wedges
    3 oranges peeled, in wedges
    6 halved cherries
    Mix and refrigerate for 12 to 18 hours
    Makes about 1.5 liters

South Beach Peach

Specialty of Joe's Seafood, Prime Steak & Stone Crab
Created by Dan Barringer
Lavender vanilla sugar rimmed
    cocktail glass, chilled
Pour ingredients into an iced mixing glass
2 oz. Saracco Moscato D'Asti Italian
    Sparkling Dessert Wine
2 oz. DeKuyper Peachtree Schnapps
1/2 oz. fresh lime juice
1 oz. fresh orange juice
Shake and strain
Pour ingredients into the iced mixing glass. Shake
thoroughly and strain contents into a lavender
vanilla sugar rimmed, chilled cocktail glass.

Splendor Cocktail

Specialty of 33 Restaurant & Lounge
Created by Ari Bialikamien, Jenn Harvery
Cocktail glass, chilled
Pour ingredients into an iced mixing glass
2 oz. Pineapple-Infused Vodka*
1/2 oz. Cointreau
1/2 oz. Welch's White Grape Juice
Shake and strain
1/2 oz. Alba Vineyard Red
    Raspberry Wine, sink to bottom
Pour ingredients, except the raspberry wine,
into the iced mixing glass. Shake thoroughly
and strain contents into a chilled cocktail glass.
Carefully sink the raspberry wine to the bottom
of the cocktail glass.
* Pineapple-Infused Vodka Recipe
Steep pineapple in vodka for 3-4 days

Starry Night

Specialty of Harry Denton's Starlight Room
Created by Marco Dionysos
Champagne flute, chilled
Build in glass
Near fill with Brut Champagne
    or sparkling wine
1/4 oz. Briottet Crème du Mûre
Garnish with a lemon spiral twist
Pour ingredients into the chilled Champagne
flute in the order listed. Garnish with a lemon
spiral twist.

Sweeney 75

Specialty of Harry Denton's Starlight Room
Created by Jacques Bezuidenhout
Bucket glass, ice
Pour ingredients into an iced mixing glass
1 1/2 oz. Beefeater London Dry Gin
1/2 oz. Mathilde Framboise Liqueur
1 oz. fresh lemon sour mix
Shake and strain
Fill with Brut Champagne or sparkling wine
Garnish with a lemon spiral twist
Pour ingredients, except the Champagne,
into the iced mixing glass. Shake thoroughly
and strain contents into an iced bucket glass.
Fill with Champagne. Garnish with a lemon
spiral twist.

Rickshaw Far East Bistro and Bambú Lounge

⌂ **2810 Westheimer**
Houston, TX 77098
☎ **713.942.7272**
▶▶ **www.rickshaw-bambu.com**
✉ **info@rickshawbambu.com**

O ne of the country's great restaurant towns, Houston is a magnificent melting pot of diverse cuisines from every region and land. **Rickshaw Far East Bistro and Bambú Lounge** mirrors that pattern within its Pan-Asian menu, which presents guests with a lavish array of dishes from Hong Kong, Japan and Thailand with flavor influences from India, the Philippines and Korea. It's fusion cuisine at its finest.

The interior of Rickshaw is open, stylish and contemporary chic. The decor features exposed ceilings, lush fabrics, silk curtains, sepia-toned photomurals of turn of the century Hong Kong on the walls and handcrafted Mondrian glass panels separate the dining room from the lounge. The open kitchen is flanked by

a curving sushi bar typically lined with diners. On Thursday, Friday and Saturday nights, when dinner is over and the kitchen closes, the energy level in the place shifts gears as the Bambú Lounge comes to life. The lighting changes and the place pulses to the beat of the talented and popular house DJ's.

Favorite dishes at Rickshaw include Teriyaki Chicken Wraps, Crab Cakes, Portabella Ahi, Miso Marinated Sea Bass and Hong Kong Duck. The sushi menu is equally extensive and the dishes magnificently prepared.

The roster of signature cocktails at the Bambú Lounge is as diverse and well-conceived as the cuisine. Specialties include the *Ultimate Lemon Drop*, a cocktail made with Ketel One Citroen and Pallini Limoncello, *Chocolate Cake Martini*, SKYY Citrus and Frangelico and the *Comfortable Italian Fortress*, a sensational blend of PAMA Liqueur, Citadelle Gin, Amaretto, Southern Comfort and a mix of juices.

Rickshaw Far East Bistro and Bambú Lounge are hot and spicy destinations not to be missed. —RP

Comfortable Italian Fortress
Drink recipe on pg 301

Vanilla Kiss

Specialty of The Mission Inn Hotel & Spa
Created by Brooke Crothers
Champagne glass, chilled
Build in glass
1/4 oz. Absolut Vanilia Vodka
1/4 oz. DeKuyper Pucker Island Blue Schnapps
Fill with Brut Champagne
Garnish with a lemon twist
Pour ingredients into the chilled Champagne glass in the order listed. Garnish with a lemon twist.

Watermelon Fizz

Specialty of The Carnegie Club
Created by Jonathan Pogash
Champagne glass, chilled
Pour ingredients into an empty mixing glass
1 tsp. sugar
1 lemon slice
Muddle contents
Add ice
1/2 oz. Marie Brizard Watermelon Liqueur
Shake and strain
Fill with Moët & Chandon White
    Star Champagne
Garnish with 3 watermelon balls on a skewer
Place the sugar and lemon slice into the empty mixing glass. Muddle and add ice. Pour in the watermelon liqueur. Shake thoroughly and strain contents into a chilled Champagne glass. Fill with Champagne. Garnish with 3 watermelon balls on a skewer.

Jewel of Russia™ Berry Infusion

It is safe to say that the **Jewel of Russia Berry Infusion** is unlike any other product you've ever encountered. This traditional Russian spirit is a contemporary classic in the making and something that must be sampled to fully appreciate.

The Jewel of Russia Berry Infusion is made according to a distillation technique devised 300 years ago. The fresh cranberries used in the infusion are hand picked and crushed in a vat. The mash of fresh fruit is then steeped with super-premium Jewel of Russia Vodka for an extended period of time. The infusion is then filtered and bottled at 40-proof.

The result is outrageously delicious. The spirit has a lustrous red color, a satiny feather-weight body and a lavish set of fresh fruit aromas. On the palate it's all about delivering the luscious flavors of berries and a hint of chocolate. The infusion is relatively low in alcohol so it generates no heat and has no biting edge. The flavors persist well into the soft lingering finish. It's so soft and delicate that one would be hard pressed to identify it as alcohol.

Its sibling is the **Jewel of Russia Wild Bilberry Infusion**, which is made by the same process exclusively from wild bilberries, which are similar to Scandinavian Lingonberries. Both of these Russian state treasures are worthy of sampling neat or with a slight chill. But make no mistake, these infusions are ideally featured in specialty cocktails. Slam dunk.

They both are essential drink making equipment and the opportunity to use espresso coffee in blended drinks is an opportunity too rich to pass up.

Frozen cappuccinos are an excellent vehicle around which to build a noteworthy signature drink. The **Kasbah Caffe** is a good example of an espresso shake. It's a delicious after dinner drink concocted using espresso coffee and two types of ice cream. Its attention grabbing appearance only seals the deal.

The drink starts with four ounces of cold espresso coffee, an amount equal to two demitasses. Pour the coffee into the blender canister and add in ¾ ounces each of Starbucks Coffee Liqueur, Godiva Chocolate Liqueur and brandy, a splash of milk and two scoops (approximately 8 ounces) of chocolate ice cream. Blend the ingredients and pour the drink into a house specialty glass. Next, spoon on a layer of frothed milk and garnish with a crumbled fudge brownie. The best word to use to describe the drink is luxurious.

The same could be said about the **Liquid Postres**. A signature at The Spanish Kitchen in Beverly Hills, the lavish concoction is prepared with Godiva Chocolate Liqueur, Kahlúa, Cointreau, Baileys Irish Cream, vanilla ice cream and freshly brewed espresso.

Another amazingly delicious drink made with espresso coffee is called the **California Dreamin'**. This tall specialty is created using ½ ounce portions of Kahlúa, Stoli Vanil, Baileys Irish Cream and Chambord. Add in two scoops (approximately 8 ounces) of French vanilla ice cream and a double shot of cold espresso coffee. The drink is finished with a thick layer of frothy steamed milk and a sprinkle of shaved chocolate.

Made with added caramel sauce, the **Caramella** is a popular twist on the cappuccino. It was obviously the inspiration for the **Caramella Soprano**. This blended sensation is made with chilled espresso and two scoops of vanilla ice cream. The fuel element in the drink is equal parts of Jack Daniels, Starbucks Coffee Liqueur and Starbucks Cream Liqueur. Before pouring the blended ingredients into the specialty glass, ribbon the inside of the glass with caramel and chocolate sauce. It, too, is finished with frothed milk, a drizzle of chocolate and caramel syrup and a chocolate biscotti.

So go ahead, add a few shots of espresso to your next vanilla milkshake, or blended Brandy Alexander. The world will be better off for it.

• **Ice Cream Drinks** — Even in this day and age of health awareness, chefs still prepare trays of tempting desserts. Few people go out to dinner with the intent to calorie-bulk on a dessert. Yet, when faced with devilishly irresistible treats, their heads nod yes as they make their selections.

This time-tested concept also works beautifully behind your own bar. Tempting guests with delectable, dessert-like libations are a "can't miss" proposition. They appeal to the child in all of us, and whether they admit it or not, people are attracted to the instant gratification of taste.

Ice cream is an ideal vehicle for liqueurs and distilled spirits. Its sweet, creamy consistency accepts a wide variety of flavors, so being extremely creative is easy. Here's an experiment proving that an ice cream drink can be every bit as satisfying as dessert on a plate.

Start by placing two heaping scoops of French vanilla ice cream into a blender. Add 2 ounces of Kahlúa, a ripe banana, 1/2 cup of fresh raspberries, an ounce of chocolate syrup, and a healthy measure of milk and blend thoroughly. Pour the contents into a chilled specialty glass and garnish with a dollop of whipped cream and a drizzle of chocolate syrup. While there is no such thing as a universal crowd pleaser, this concoction comes awfully close.

The Mosaic Restaurant promotes two sterling ice cream libations. The **Chocolate Covered Grasshopper** is a delicious blend of green crème de menthe, crème de cacao, Godiva Chocolate liqueur and vanilla ice cream, while the **Peach Sickle** is made with vanilla ice cream, Absolut Apeach, Absolut Vanilia and fresh peach slices.

DeKuyper® Pucker® Sour Apple

If you're still capable of cranking out a smile, then you still have enough life in you to enjoy *DeKuyper Pucker Sour Apple*. Everything about this product screams of fun, from the lighthearted packaging to its spry, low proof character. DeKuyper did their homework and created a winner

Pucker Sour Apple is one of a line of similarly constructed sweet 'n' sour schnapps that are balanced with surgical precision to be just this side of tart. What differentiates this snazzy line of schnapps from the rest of the field is that they have just enough zing to make them something special; any more tartness and the effect would be dashed. The tartness works especially well when it is used as the principal flavoring agent in cocktails.

The liqueur has a light, delicate body and a cheerful apple green hue, two qualities ideal for drink making. Sipped neat, the liqueur will bring about a pucker, but when mixed, the tangy tartness acts as a counterbalance. The sour apple flavor seems true enough and persists for a remarkably long time.

Versatility must be DeKuyper Sour Apple Pucker's middle name. While the schnapps initially earned its reputation for greatness as the primary ingredient in the Appletini, it is now featured in everything from Martinis and Margaritas to Daiquiris and Cosmos. You can now find it in uptown cocktails and downtown shooters. Sour Apple Pucker is a contemporary gem.

Vanilla ice cream is most frequently used in specialty drinks because it provides a somewhat neutral base upon which a wide array of flavors can be added. There is, however, no reason to work exclusively with vanilla ice cream. There are at least 31 flavors from which to choose, so experiment. In addition to ice cream, there's also frozen yogurt, sherbet and sorbet to consider. Each will lend a different taste and texture to the concoction.

There are few creative limitations when choosing flavorings for ice cream drinks. In addition to using fresh fruit, options include chocolate, caramel, and butterscotch syrup, peanut butter, iced coffee or espresso, crushed cookies and candy bars.

The back bar is also rich with possibilities. Nothing could be more ideally suited to creating world-class ice cream libations than coffee liqueurs such as Kahlúa, Starbucks and Tia Maria. Yet, why stop there? Midori is marvelous when paired with fresh kiwis and lime sherbet, or papayas with lemon sorbet. Consider pairing coconut rum with chocolate ice cream and Mandarin oranges, or making a specialty float using Malibu, cola and ice cream.

On the extreme end of the creativity curve is the *Dark Chocolate Jalapeño Raspberry Shake Martini.* A signature at Tucson's J BAR, it's an absolutely lovely and delicious drink made with Chambord, Absolut Vanilia, milk and two scoops of homemade dark chocolate jalapeño ice cream. The cocktail looks as intriguing as it tastes.

Another highly creative concoction is *Mel's Chocolate/PB/Nana Shake*, a delicious creation made with Kahlúa, Appleton Estate Jamaica Rum, chocolate syrup, peanut butter, milk, vanilla ice cream, and a fresh banana. It's so big and satisfying that it could be served as an entrée.

In many respects, ice cream drinks are about exceeding expectations and indulging your guests' desires. Thoroughly decadent and loaded with pleasure, ice cream libations are guaranteed to do just that.

• **Adult Smoothies** — These aren't the smoothies that your momma used to make for you. If smoothies can be customized with one or more nutritious additives, why can't you doctor them with a little Kahlúa, Midori or a bracer of Maker's Mark?

The results are in. Smoothies do taste considerably better with an additional shot or two from the bar. As an example, the *Blue Aloha Smoothie* is a tall, frosty concoction made with frozen vanilla yogurt, pineapple juice and blueberries. Many might stop there. While the smoothie is delightful and undoubtedly healthful, the addition of Charbay Blood Orange Vodka and

Midori propel the drink into a whole other level of greatness. Rev up your blender and try it for yourself.

Wait, before you do that, first consider these two sinfully delicious libations. The first is the **Caribbean Dream Smoothie**. It's an adult smoothie concocted with Cruzan Estate Light Rum, Cruzan Mango Rum, mangoes, peaches, orange sorbet and lemon sorbet. You can throw in some wheat germ and B vitamins if you're a stickler for nutrition, but for those of us who prefer taste to wholesomeness, this recipe is a bona fide winner.

The same can be said for the **Chocolate Banana Smoothie**, the delectable combination of Mount Gay Extra Old Rum, Kahlúa, a ripe banana, chocolate syrup, milk and frozen vanilla yogurt.

Since your blender is already handy, go ahead and make the **Cranberry Crazed Smoothie**. It's a blended gem prepared with Stoli Cranberi Vodka, Chambord, cranberry juice, fresh strawberries and blueberries, plain yogurt and several healthy scoops of raspberry sorbet. If scrumptious is still a word, then this smoothie is scrumptious. The **Melon Marvel Smoothie** might be a bit more vitamin-enriched. It's made with Malibu and Mount Gay Eclipse rums, cubed watermelon and honeydew melons, fresh lime juice, honey, orange juice and vanilla yogurt. Despite being nutritious, the drink is sensational.

One jazzed up smoothie is called **In The Moo'ed**. The drink is a luscious blend of vanilla yogurt, peanut butter, chocolate syrup, milk and a whole banana. It's converted into an adult smoothie with the addition of Absolut Vanilia Vodka and Starbucks Coffee Liqueur.

Now some people might feel somewhat guilty drinking a smoothie that just plain tastes great with no overriding health claims. There's no reason that you can't add antioxidants, such as vitamins A, E and beta-carotene, or fiber, such as wheat germ and oat bran, or sources of protein, such as bee pollen, brewers yeast and soy. Also falling into the beneficial range are flaxseed oil, ginkgo biloba, ginseng, lecithin, protein powder, wheat grass, echinacea, calcium, folic acid and vitamins B, C, D and K.

Then there are smoothie modifiers that just plain taste great. They may be intended to add flavor or provide a welcome touch of sweetness. Either way, these are ingredients that are bound to satisfy the kid in all of us. This tasty category includes, but is not limited to chocolate or caramel sauce, coffee, agave nectar, espresso coffee, Reese's peanut butter cups, candy bars, walnuts, vanilla extract, cinnamon, nutmeg,

Rio All-Suite Hotel & Casino

✉ **3700 West Flamingo Rd.**
    Las Vegas, NV 89103
☎ **866.746.7671**
▶▶ **www.harrahs.com/casinos/**
         rio/hotel-casino

In a city renown for its sensational late night attractions, the **Rio All-Suite Hotel & Casino** stands out as one of Las Vegas' stellar destinations. The magnificent hotel and casino sports 13 restaurants, 2 nightclubs, 2 swank lounges and 3 wedding chapels, just in case your night goes exceedingly well.

Among its many popular draws is the VooDoo Steak & Lounge, which sits atop the Rio on the 50th and 51st floors. The menu features sumptuous American cuisine with a French Creole flair. It's an intimate dining experience with candlelight and breathtaking rooftop vistas of the city at night. The decor throughout is lively, bright and festive, evocative of Brazil and the Carnivale.

Food and pleasure go hand in hand at the Rio. There is a seemingly endless selection of cuisines from which to choose, beginning with the Carnival World Buffet, an extraordinary, acre-sized feast offering guests with insatiable appetites a run for their money. Those looking for gourmet Italian food should head to Antonio's Ristorante, while barbeque fare can be found at Rub. That's just the beginning. There's Gaylord Indian Restaurant, Hamada's Asiana, Buzio's Seafood, and the All-American Bar & Grille. The Rio is like a self-contained epicurean holiday.

Enthusiasts of great cocktails are also well catered to. A popular specialty at the VooDoo Lounge is *Love Spell*, a savory blend of Finlandia Mango Fusion Vodka, Cointreau, lime juice, simple syrup, pomegranate and white cranberry juice. The **Mexican Mojito** is a signature at the iBaR. Its muddled construction includes El Diamante del Cielo Blanco Tequila and fresh lemon sour.

You can easily enjoy a spectacular vacation and never leave the Rio. —RP

Love Spell
Drink recipe on pg 98

grenadine, chai tea, coconut cream, coconut milk, peanut butter, raspberry or strawberry preserves, honey, malted milk powder, maple syrup, cookies, unsweetened coconut and brown sugar.

While drinking adult smoothies might not make you healthier, they will certainly make you feel better.

- **Classics Revisited** — While blended *Margaritas*, *Daiquiris* and *Piña Coladas* get most of the attention, innovators are also promoting blended variations of other well-established specialties. A frozen *Long Island Iced Tea* is fast becoming a popular favorite. The *Rum Runner* is also excellent served frozen, so too are tropical classics such as the *Mai Tai*, *Zombie*, and *Scorpion*. Blending with ice lowers their potency, while their broad range of flavors completely fills the glass. In the summer, take your favorite Sangria recipe and try serving it blended. For an effervescent twist, add a splash of Champagne to these classics.

- **Swirls** — Swirling does to a frozen drink what layering Kahlúa, Baileys and Grand Mariner does for the B-52. It adds pizzazz and enhances the drink's eye appeal. Swirling involves preparing two different drinks

Shakka™ Kiwi Liqueur

Shakka Kiwi Liqueur is part of a line of innovative and marvelously flavorful eaux de vie produced by famed Cruzan Rum. Created with bartenders in mind and inspired by Hawaii's laidback way of life, this highly mixable liqueur is an unexpected blast of good taste. Uncork the fun and expect great things to happen to your drinks.

The Shakka Liqueurs are American born and made from pure grain distillates and all natural flavorings. All of the products are modestly priced and bottled at a responsible 30-proof. The kiwi version has a translucent, true to fruit green hue, a smooth, refreshingly light body and a focused bouquet of lush fruit and floral aromas. The palate is a balanced affair with the tart, crisp flavor of ripe kiwis most prominent. The finish is clean and quick, a great quality for such a mixable product.

The creative range also includes *Shakka Grape*, a rather fanciful liqueur with the delightful look and taste of a Grape Nehi. It's a genuinely singular, attention-grabbing product. The other member of the trio is the fire engine red *Shakka Apple Liqueur*.

The Hawaiian word "shakka" is a local greeting loosely meaning, "How's it going?" Behind the bar, though, Shakka means expanded creative capabilities. The liqueurs enjoy nearly unlimited drink making applications. Their light bodies make them naturals for showcasing in specialty cocktails and are flavorful enough for use in blended drinks. *Okole ma luna!*

simultaneously in two different blenders, and then pouring them together in the same specialty glass. The effect is dramatic and greatly enhances the resulting drink's presentation. Among the original swirled recipes is the **Pain in the Butt**, a sensational blend of a Rum Runner and a Strawberry Daiquiri. The key to a great swirl is marrying together two different colored drinks with complementary tastes.

- **Frozen Lemonade** — One of America's favorite potables, lemonade is an exceptionally versatile mixer and perfectly suited for blending. Blending lemonade with ice and a spirit or two is ideal for the summer months. Bourbon and frozen lemonade makes an interesting variation on a whiskey sour. Consider blending lemonade with Midori or Amaretto. Lemonade also marries well with tequila, light rum, and dark rums, such as Myers's and Appleton Estate.

Banana Split

Specialty of Courtright's Restaurant
Created by Marco Recio
House specialty glass, chilled
Pour ingredients into an empty blender canister
1/2 oz. Crème de Banana
1/2 oz. Kahlúa
1/2 oz. Tequila Rose
3 oz. milk
Blend thoroughly with 1 scoop of ice
Garnish with whipped cream and a cherry
Pour ingredients into the empty blender canister. Blend thoroughly and pour contents into a chilled house specialty glass. Garnish with whipped cream and a cherry.

Bananas Barbados

Excerpted from The Original Guide to
American Cocktails and Drinks- 6th Edition
House specialty glass, chilled
Pour ingredients into an empty blender canister
1 1/4 oz. Mount Gay Eclipse Rum
3/4 oz. Crème de Banana
1 dash vanilla extract
1 ripe banana
2 oz. fresh lemon sour mix
Blend thoroughly with 1 scoop of ice
Float 1 oz. Mount Gay Extra Old Rum
Pour ingredients, except the Mount Gay, into the empty blender canister. Blend thoroughly and pour contents into a chilled house specialty glass. Float 1 oz. Mount Gay Extra Old Rum.

> "The electric blender has single-handedly added another dimension to drink making."

Jose Cuervo® Especial® Tequila

If you walk into a bar and don't see a bottle of *Jose Cuervo Especial Tequila* on the back bar, turn around and leave. The brand has grown to be the world's bestselling brand of tequila and known affectionately around the planet simply as "Cuervo Gold." More than just a familiar name, it is the brand that helped launch a cultural revolution

Jose Cuervo Especial is made in the town of Tequila at the 200-year old family distillery, La Rojeña. It is a premium gold style Joven tequila produced from a trademark blend of double-distilled reposado tequilas and other high-grade agave spirits. The blend is further rested allowing the constituent spirits to become fully integrated, after which it is bottled at 80-proof.

The explanation of why Jose Cuervo Especial has become an international phenomenon doesn't have as much to do with how it's made, but rather its accessible personality once it hits the glass. The tequila has an enticing golden hue, a smooth medium-weight body and an expansive herbal and floral bouquet. Its palate immediately fills the mouth with spicy, herbal flavors that persist well into the long and warming finish.

There is only one Jose Cuervo Especial and without it all tequila-related commerce at the bar grinds to a halt. When it comes to drink making, the brand has unlimited creative range. From the shot glass to Margarita glass, it is a standard bearer.

Banilla

Specialty of Mosaic Restaurant
Created by Stephanie Kozicki
House specialty glass, chilled
Pour ingredients into an empty blender canister
1 1/2 oz. Stoli Vanil Vodka
1/2 oz. 99 Bananas Liqueur
1 oz. pineapple juice
1 oz. orange juice
2 scoops vanilla ice cream (4-6 oz. each)
Blend thoroughly with 1 small scoop of ice
Garnish with a fresh pineapple
Pour ingredients into the empty blender canister. Blend thoroughly and pour contents into a chilled house specialty glass. Garnish with a fresh pineapple.

Bukhara Coffee

Excerpted from The Original Guide to
American Cocktails and Drinks- 6th Edition
House specialty glass, chilled
Pour ingredients into an empty blender canister
1 1/4 oz. Stoli Vanil Vodka
3/4 oz. Baileys Irish Cream
1/2 oz. Godiva Chocolate Liqueur
2 oz. cold coffee
2 scoops vanilla ice cream (4-6 oz. each)
Blend thoroughly with 1 small scoop ice (optional)
Garnish with whipped cream
    and shaved chocolate
Pour ingredients into the empty blender canister. Blend thoroughly and pour contents into a chilled house specialty glass. Garnish with whipped cream and shaved chocolate.

California Dreamin'

Specialty of BarMedia
Created by Robert Plotkin
House specialty glass, chilled
Pour ingredients into an empty blender canister
1/2 oz. Kahlúa
1/2 oz. Stoli Vanil Vodka
1/2 oz. Baileys Irish Cream
1/2 oz. Chambord
2 oz. cold espresso
2 large scoops French vanilla ice cream
    (8 oz. each)
Blend thoroughly
Spoon on a layer of frothed milk
Garnish with a sprinkle of shaved chocolate
Pour ingredients into the empty blender canister. Blend thoroughly and pour contents into a chilled house specialty glass. Spoon on a layer of frothed milk. Garnish with a sprinkle of shaved chocolate.

Caramella Soprano

Specialty of BarMedia
Created by Robert Plotkin
Caramel and chocolate syrup ribboned house
    specialty glass, chilled
Pour ingredients into an empty blender canister
3/4 oz. Jack Daniels Tennessee Whiskey
3/4 oz. Starbucks Coffee Liqueur
3/4 oz. Starbucks Cream Liqueur
2 oz. cold espresso
2 large scoops vanilla ice cream (8 oz. each)
Blend thoroughly
Spoon on a layer of frothed milk
Garnish with a chocolate biscotti
Pour ingredients into the empty blender canister. Blend thoroughly and pour contents into a ribboned, chilled house specialty glass. Spoon on a layer of frothed milk. Garnish with a biscotti.

Caribbean Dream Smoothie

Specialty of BarMedia
Created by Robert Plotkin
House specialty glass, chilled
Pour ingredients into an empty blender canister
1 1/4 oz. Cruzan Estate Light Rum
1 oz. Cruzan Mango Rum
1/2 cup mangos, peeled and cubed,
    fresh or frozen
1/2 cup peaches, peeled and sliced,
    fresh or frozen
1-2 scoops orange sorbet (4 oz. each)
1-2 scoops lemon sorbet (4 oz. each)
Blend thoroughly with 1 small scoop ice (optional)
Garnish with an orange wheel
Pour ingredients into the empty blender canister. Blend thoroughly and pour contents into a chilled house specialty glass. Garnish with an orange wheel.

Caribbean Gridlock

Excerpted from The Original Guide to
American Cocktails and Drinks- 6th Edition
House specialty glass, chilled
Pour ingredients into an empty blender canister
3/4 oz. Appleton Estate V/X Jamaica Rum
3/4 oz. Bacardi Light Rum
3/4 oz. Mount Gay Eclipse Rum
3/4 oz. Rose's Lime Juice
2 oz. fresh lime sour mix
2 oz. orange juice
Blend thoroughly with 1 scoop of ice
Float 3/4 oz. Gosling's Black Seal Rum
Garnish with a lime, lemon and orange wedge
Pour ingredients, except the Rum, into the empty blender canister. Blend thoroughly and pour contents into a chilled house specialty glass. Garnish with a lime, lemon and orange wedge.

Chocolate Covered Banana

Excerpted from The Original Guide to
American Cocktails and Drinks- 6th Edition
House specialty glass, chilled
Pour ingredients into an empty blender canister
1 ³/4 oz. Appleton Estate V/X Jamaica Rum
1 ¹/2 oz. Godiva Chocolate Liqueur
1 ripe banana
Splash half & half
2 scoops vanilla ice cream (4-6 oz. each)
Blend thoroughly with 1 small scoop ice (optional)
Garnish with whipped cream, a drizzle of
    Gosling's Black Seal Rum and a
    sprinkle of shaved chocolate
Pour ingredients into the empty blender canister.
Blend thoroughly and pour contents into a
chilled house specialty glass. Garnish with
whipped cream, a drizzle of Gosling's Black Seal
Rum and shaved chocolate sprinkles.

Chocolate Covered Grasshopper

Specialty of Mosaic Restaurant
Created by Stephanie Kozicki
House specialty glass, chilled
Pour ingredients into an empty blender canister
1 oz. Mozart Black Chocolate Pure 87
¹/2 oz. Green Crème de Menthe
¹/2 oz. DeKuyper White Crème de Cacao
2 scoops vanilla ice cream (3-4 oz. each)
Blend thoroughly with 1 small scoop of ice
Garnish with a cherry
Pour ingredients into the empty blender canister.
Blend thoroughly and pour contents into a chilled
house specialty glass. Garnish with a cherry.

Cranberry Crazed Smoothie

Specialty of BarMedia
Created by Robert Plotkin
House specialty glass, chilled
Pour ingredients into an empty blender canister
1 ³/4 oz. Stoli Cranberi Vodka
³/4 oz. Chambord
3 oz. cranberry juice
¹/4 cup strawberries, fresh or frozen
¹/4 cup blueberries, fresh or frozen
4 oz. plain yogurt
2-3 scoops raspberry sorbet (3-4 oz. each)
Blend thoroughly with 1 small scoop ice (optional)
Garnish with a fresh strawberry
Pour ingredients into the empty blender canister.
Blend thoroughly and pour contents into a
chilled house specialty glass. Garnish with a
fresh strawberry.

The Cure

Specialty of 33 Restaurant & Lounge
Created by Jenn Harvey
Cocktail glass, chilled
Pour ingredients into an empty blender canister
1 oz. 42 Below Manuka Honey Vodka
1 ripe banana
1 tbsp. honey
1 oz. milk
Blend thoroughly with 1 small scoop of ice
Garnish with a swirl of honey into glass
Pour ingredients into the empty blender canister.
Blend thoroughly and pour contents into a chilled
cocktail glass. Garnish with a swirl of honey into
the glass.

Dark Chocolate Jalapeño
Raspberry Shake Martini

Specialty of J BAR
Created by Patrick Harrington, Janos Wilder
Cocktail glass, chilled
Pour ingredients into an empty blender canister
1 ¹/2 oz. Chambord
1 oz. Absolut Vanilia Vodka
2 scoops Dark Chocolate Jalapeño Ice Cream*
    (4-6 oz. each)
1 oz. milk
Blend thoroughly
Garnish with a fresh raspberry
Pour ingredients into the empty blender canister.
Blend thoroughly and pour contents into a chilled
cocktail glass. Garnish with a fresh raspberry.
*Dark Chocolate Jalapeño
    Ice Cream Recipe - pg 319

Rosemary's Restaurant

🕮 **8125 West Sahara**
    Las Vegas, NV 89117
☎ **702.869.2251**
▶▶ **www.rosemarysrestaurant.com**
✉ **info@rosemarysrestaurant.com**

Chef-owned **Rosemary's Restaurant** exudes a classy, contemporary elegance and is a marvelous escape from the hustle, bustle, noise and glare that has become part of Las Vegas' public persona. Its impeccably prepared cuisine, relaxed yet attentive service and boatloads of ambience afford guests a most enjoyable sanctuary for the senses.

The interior of Rosemary's is casual, intimate and inviting. The warmly lit dining room features clothed tables, plush carpet, extensive artwork on the walls and low ceilings. The marble-topped bar is spacious and ideally designed for dining. Perhaps

the best seats in the house are at the food bar adjacent to the open kitchen where you can watch the chefs in action and engage the staff throughout the night.

For all of its acclaim and acknowledgements, Rosemary's is relaxed, unpretentious and inexplicably reasonably priced. The cuisine is French inspired, beautifully presented Nouveau American. Specialties include Hugo's Texas BBQ Shrimp served over bleu cheese slaw, Pan Roasted Sea Scallops, Seared Foie Gras and Honey Creole Mustard Glazed Salmon. All of the entrees are paired with wine and craft beer recommendations. Make a point to leave room for dessert, as the Chocolate Flourless Cake is outrageously delicious.

Life at the bar is equally marvelous. Not to be outdone by the restaurant's award-winning cuisine, Rosemary's specialty cocktails are exquisite. An outstanding example is their signature house *Manhattan*, a muddled drink made with fresh orange slices, orange bitters, Grand Marnier, King Eider Vermouth and Knob Creek Bourbon. Equally engaging is the *Silver Yuzu Margarita*, a blend of Patrón Silver Tequila, Cointreau, yuzu concentrate, agave nectar and fresh lime and lemon juice.

Rosemary's Restaurant is one of life's more delectable experiences. —RP

Rosemary's Manhattan
Drink recipe on pg 75

E Pluribus Unum

Excerpted from The Original Guide to
American Cocktails and Drinks- 6th Edition

Cocktail glass, chilled
Pour ingredients into an empty blender canister
3/4 oz. Frangelico
3/4 oz. Chambord
3/4 oz. Kahlúa
2 scoops chocolate ice cream (4 oz. each)
Blend thoroughly with 1 small scoop ice (optional)
Garnish with a sprinkle of shaved
  white chocolate
Pour ingredients into the empty blender canister.
Blend thoroughly and pour contents into a
chilled cocktail glass. Garnish with a sprinkle of
shaved white chocolate.

Ed Sullivan

Excerpted from The Original Guide to
American Cocktails and Drinks- 6th Edition

House specialty glass, chilled
Pour ingredients into an empty blender canister
1 1/4 oz. Bacardi Light Rum
3/4 oz. Disaronno Amaretto
1/2 cup strawberries, fresh or frozen
1/2 oz. half & half
2 oz. fresh lime sour mix
Blend thoroughly with 1 scoop of ice
Fill with Champagne
Garnish with a fresh strawberry
Pour ingredients, except the Champagne, into
the empty blender canister. Blend thoroughly
and pour contents into a chilled house specialty
glass. Fill with Champagne. Garnish with a fresh
strawberry.

> "A well–prepared blended drink
> is a thing of beauty."

Jose Cuervo® Black Medallion™ Tequila

This tequila was not crafted with a shot glass in mind. To the contrary, *Jose Cuervo Black Medallion Tequila* is imbued with boatloads of flavor, which makes it ideally suited for today's cocktail culture. It's intended to be sipped on the rocks, or mixed with any number of items. While many tequilas shrink under such conditions, Cuervo Black shines.

Like all of the Jose Cuervo tequilas, the Black Medallion is double-distilled at the 200-year old family distillery, *La Rojeña*, from blue agaves grown in the foothills near the town of Tequila. It is comprised of a signature blend of añejo tequilas aged in charred oak barrels for 12 months. The blend is further rested allowing the constituent spirits to become fully integrated, after which it is bottled at 80-proof.

True to their word, Jose Cuervo Black Medallion is sufficiently bold and distinctive to perform beautifully when mixed. The tequila has a lustrous mahogany amber hue, and a generously spicy and herbaceous bouquet. The velvety body generates exceptionally little heat, but does fill the mouth with a host of tantalizing flavors, including cocoa, cinnamon, apple and toffee. The finish is splendid, long, soft and flavorful. Black Medallion is a spirit with grace and exuberance, a rare combination for a modestly priced spirit.

Its outgoing personality makes it an ideal choice for featuring in your next specialty Margarita, or mixed with cola, which has become an phenomenally popular way to enjoy the brand.

Gorilla Milk

Excerpted from The Original Guide to
American Cocktails and Drinks- 6th Edition
House specialty glass, chilled
Pour ingredients into an empty blender canister
1 oz. Bacardi Light Rum
3/4 oz. Kahlúa
3/4 oz. Baileys Irish Cream
1/2 oz. Crème de Banana
1 oz. half & half
2 scoops vanilla ice cream (4-6 oz. each)
Blend thoroughly
Garnish with a pineapple wedge
    and banana slice
Pour ingredients into the empty blender canister.
Blend thoroughly and pour contents into a
chilled house specialty glass. Garnish with a
pineapple wedge and banana slice.

In The Moo'ed

Specialty of BarMedia
Created by Robert Plotkin
House specialty glass, chilled
Pour ingredients into an empty blender canister
1 1/4 oz. Absolut Vanilia Vodka
1 oz. Starbucks Coffee Liqueur
1/2 ripe banana
4 oz. milk
2 oz. chocolate syrup
2 oz. peanut butter
3-4 scoops vanilla frozen yogurt (3-4 oz. each)
Blend ingredients with 1 small scoop ice (optional)
Garnish with a banana slice
Pour ingredients into the empty blender canister.
Blend thoroughly and pour contents into
a chilled house specialty glass. Garnish with a
banana slice.

Irish Daiquiri

Specialty of Courtright's Restaurant
Created by Marco Recio
House specialty glass, chilled
Pour ingredients into an empty blender canister
1 1/2 oz. Malibu Rum
1 1/2 oz. Baileys Irish Cream
4 oz. strawberry puree
Blend thoroughly with 1 scoop of ice
Garnish with a fresh strawberry
Pour ingredients into the empty blender canister.
Blend thoroughly and pour contents into a
chilled house specialty glass. Garnish with a
fresh strawberry.

Jardinera

Excerpted from The Original Guide to
American Cocktails and Drinks- 6th Edition
House specialty glass, chilled
Pour ingredients into an iced blender canister
2 oz. Sauza Tres Generaciones Plata Tequila
3/4 oz. Cruzan Vanilla Rum
1/2 cup pineapple cubes
2 oz. coconut cream syrup
2 oz. fresh lime sour mix
Blend thoroughly with 1 scoop of ice
Garnish with shredded coconut
    and shaved chocolate
Pour ingredients into the iced blender canister.
Blend thoroughly and pour contents into a chilled
house specialty glass. Garnish with shredded
coconut and shaved chocolate.

Kasbah Cafe

Specialty of BarMedia
Created by Robert Plotkin
House specialty glass, chilled
Pour ingredients into an empty blender canister
3/4 oz. Starbucks Coffee Liqueur
3/4 oz. Godiva Chocolate Liqueur
3/4 oz. Brandy
2 oz. cold espresso
2 large scoops chocolate ice cream (8 oz. each)
Blend thoroughly
Spoon on a layer of frothed milk
Garnish with crumbled fudge brownie
Pour ingredients into the empty blender canister.
Blend thoroughly and pour contents into a chilled
house specialty glass. Spoon on a layer of frothed
milk. Garnish with crumbled fudge brownie.

Kiwi Cooler

Specialty of Mosaic Restaurant
Created by Stephanie Kozicki
House specialty glass, chilled
Pour ingredients into an empty blender canister
1 1/2 oz. Stoli Strasberi Vodka
1/2 oz. Cointreau
1/4 oz. Kiwi Liqueur
1/4 oz. fresh lemon sour mix
1/4 oz. Lorina Sparkling Pink Lemonade
4 oz. strawberry puree
Blend thoroughly with 1 small scoop of ice
Garnish with a fresh strawberry
Pour ingredients into the empty blender canister.
Blend thoroughly and pour contents into a
chilled house specialty glass. Garnish with a
fresh strawberry.

Liquid Postres

Specialty of The Spanish Kitchen
Created by Misha Krepon
Beer mug, chilled
Pour ingredients into an empty blender canister
3/4 oz. Godiva Chocolate Liqueur
3/4 oz. Baileys Irish Cream
3/4 oz. Kahlúa
1/2 oz. Patrón Citrónge Orange Liqueur
1 1/2 oz. cold espresso
1 scoop vanilla bean ice cream (6-8 oz.)
Blend thoroughly with 1 scoop of ice
Garnish with whipped cream
Pour ingredients into the empty blender canister.
Blend thoroughly and pour contents into a
chilled beer mug. Garnish with whipped cream.

Melon Marvel Smoothie

Specialty of BarMedia
Created by Robert Plotkin
House specialty glass, chilled
Pour ingredients into an empty blender canister
1 1/4 oz. Malibu Rum
3/4 oz. Mount Gay Eclipse Rum
1/2 cup watermelon, cubed
1/2 cup honeydew melon, cubed
1 tbsp. honey
1 oz. fresh lime juice
4 oz. fresh orange juice
1 scoop vanilla frozen yogurt (4 oz.)
Blend thoroughly with 1 small scoop ice (optional)
Garnish with a skewered watermelon cube
Pour ingredients into the empty blender canister.
Blend thoroughly and pour contents into a chilled
house specialty glass. Garnish with a skewered
watermelon cube.

"There are few creative limitations when choosing flavorings for ice cream drinks."

Tequila Rose® Strawberry Cream Liqueur

The Tequila Rose story is a simple one to tell. It came, it saw, it conquered. Seriously, how else would you describe the liqueur's meteoric rise to stardom? When Tequila Rose debuted in 1997, there was nothing on the market remotely like it, and since it has hit the popular scene, the brand hasn't looked back.

Tequila Rose Strawberry Cream Liqueur is a blend of cream, tequila and natural strawberry flavorings. To call marrying these flavors together innovative would be an understatement. But as throngs of devotees will attest, the combination works exceptionally well.

Tequila Rose has a true to Crayola pink hue. While not necessarily the most rugged color they could have chosen, it may well be the only pink product behind the bar. The lavish bouquet is that of strawberries and cream, which also best describes the palate. To fully appreciate how its flavors fully integrate, Tequila Rose should be sampled chilled, either straight up or on the rocks.

The liqueur may be at its best when playing a featured role in a cocktail or mixed libation. Tequila Rose is great when mixed over ice with a fruit-flavored liqueur, or blended with strawberry ice cream and presented as a creamy liquid dessert. It also works beautifully with coffee and chocolate. If you can't have fun with Tequila Rose, maybe you're no longer breathing.

The successful franchise now also includes coffee-flavored *Tequila Rose Java Cream Liqueur* and milk chocolate *Tequila Rose Cocoa Cream*.

Montego Bay

Specialty of Dave & Buster's
Created by D&B Mixologists in Dallas, TX
House specialty glass, chilled
Pour ingredients into an empty blender canister
1 oz. Malibu Rum
1/2 oz. Crème de Banana
1/2 oz. pomegranate syrup
1 1/2 oz. orange juice
1 1/2 oz. pineapple juice
Blend thoroughly with 1 scoop of ice
Float 1/2 oz. Myers's Original Dark Rum
Garnish with a lime wedge, orange slice
    and cherry flag
Pour ingredients into the empty blender canister.
Blend thoroughly and pour contents into a
chilled house specialty glass. Float 1/2 oz. Myers's
Rum. Garnish with a lime wedge, orange slice
and cherry flag.

Pain In The Butt

Excerpted from The Original Guide to
American Cocktails and Drinks- 6th Edition
House specialty glass, chilled
Blend separately and combine
Step 1
Pour the following ingredients into an empty
    blender canister
3/4 oz. Bacardi Select Rum
3/4 oz. Bacardi Light Rum
3/4 oz. Crème de Banana
3/4 oz. Blackberry Brandy
1/2 oz. grenadine
1/2 oz. Rose's Lime Juice
2 oz. fresh lime sour mix
Blend thoroughly with 1 scoop of ice
Pour into the chilled house specialty glass
    to 1/2 full
Step 2
Pour the following ingredients into an empty
    blender canister
1 1/4 oz. Mount Gay Eclipse Rum
3/4 oz. Chambord
1/2 cup strawberries, fresh or frozen
1/2 oz. Rose's Lime Juice
2 1/2 oz. fresh lime sour mix
Blend thoroughly with 1 scoop of ice
Pour on top of first drink to fill
Garnish with a pineapple wedge and cherry
Blend each drink separately. Pour "Step 1"
blender canister contents into the chilled house
specialty glass to half full. Fill with "Step 2"
blender canister contents. Garnish with a
pineapple wedge and cherry.

Peach Perfecta

Specialty of 33 Restaurant & Lounge
Created by Jenn Harvey
Cocktail glass, chilled
Pour ingredients into an empty blender canister
1 oz. Stoli Persik Vodka
1 oz. Prosecco
1/2 oz. simple syrup
1 oz. white peach puree
Blend thoroughly with 1 small scoop ice (optional)
Float 1/2 oz. Aqua Perfecta Framboise
    Eau de Vie
Garnish with a fresh peach slice
Pour ingredients into the empty blender canister.
Blend thoroughly and pour contents into a
chilled cocktail glass. Float 1/2 oz. Aqua Perfecta
Framboise. Garnish with a fresh peach slice.

Peach Sickle

Specialty of Mosaic Restaurant
Created by Stephanie Kozicki
House specialty glass, chilled
Pour ingredients into an empty blender canister
1 oz. Absolut Apeach Vodka
1 oz. Absolut Vanilia Vodka
1/2 fresh peach, peeled and cut
    into smaller pieces
2 scoops vanilla ice cream (4-6 oz. each)
Blend thoroughly with 1 small scoop ice (optional)
Garnish with a fresh peach slice
Pour ingredients into the empty blender canister.
Blend thoroughly and pour contents into a
chilled house specialty glass. Garnish with a
fresh peach slice.

Snow Cone

Specialty of Dave & Buster's
Created by D & B Mixologists in Houston, TX
House specialty glass, chilled
Build in glass
Step 1
3/4 oz. DeKuyper Pucker
    Watermelon Schnapps
Splash pomegranate syrup
Pour the schnapps and pomegranate syrup into
the empty, chilled house specialty glass
Fill with crushed ice
Step 2
Pour the following ingredients into an empty
blender canister
3/4 oz. Malibu Rum
3/4 oz. Blue Curaçao
1/2 oz. Three Olives Cherry Vodka
Splash sweet 'n' sour
2 oz. Sprite
Flash blend and pour over the crushed ice filled,
house specialty glass
Garnish with a marachino cherry
Step 1. Pour the watermelon schnapps and
pomegranate syrup into the empty, chilled house
specialty glass, then fill with crushed ice. Step
2. Flash blend the remaining ingredients in an
empty blender canister. Pour over the crushed
ice. Garnish with a marachino cherry.

Tropical Rock

Specialty of Hard Rock Café- New York
Created by Hard Rock Café's staff
House specialty glass, chilled
Pour ingredients into an empty blender canister
1 oz. Bacardi Razz Rum
1 oz. DeKuyper Crème de Banana
6 oz. Piña Colada Mix
Blend thoroughly with 1 scoop of ice
Sink 1/2 oz. Midori
Float 1/2 oz. Midori
Garnish with a cherry
Pour ingredients, except the Midori, into the
empty blender canister. Blend thoroughly. Pour
1/2 oz. Midori into an empty, chilled house
specialty glass, then fill with blender contents.
Float remaining 1/2 oz. Midori. Garnish with
a cherry.

Chapter Eleven

Desserts by the Glassful
After-Dinner Classics

There is a sense of complete satisfaction that settles in after a great dinner. That moment when you set your fork down and triumphantly proclaim membership in the "clean plate club" is close to paradise on Earth. Close, but not quite there...not while there's still strength in the arms for dessert.

A marvelous way to cap off a sensational dinner experience is with a sumptuous cocktail. Sipping something marvelous after dinner is like putting an exclamation mark on the evening. Dessert drinks come in many different styles and are drop-dead delicious. What sets them apart from their plate-bound brethren is that these desserts also contain a dram or two of alcohol, which easily makes them the best of both worlds.

Like kitchen-originated desserts, the brotherhood of after dinner libations is a highly creative lot. There are primarily two ways to go with these drinks. Some prefer to quaff something neat, warm and soothing. Other tastes run toward the creamy and delicious, something akin to dessert, only better. Fortunately, there are libations ready to satisfy any taste or after-dinner request.

Secrets Revealed of America's Greatest After-Dinner Drinks

Any discussion of dessert drinks should begin with those celebrated libations that have achieved late night celebrity status. Perhaps the king of all after-dinner cocktails is the ***Brandy Alexander***. This classic libation was originally made with cream and a shot of brandy and crème de cacao. Now blending the ingredients with ice cream, or hand shaking them with melted ice cream is the prevailing technique as it yields a richer, thicker drink. Served with a dusting of nutmeg, the Brandy Alexander is the reason why many of us eat dinner, simply to get to the last course.

But few things exist that cannot be improved upon. Consider substituting the ubiquitous crème de cacao in your specialty Alexander with Godiva Chocolate Liqueur, or Van Gogh Dutch Chocolate Vodka. Your selection will bring about a creatively different drink. As an example, the ***Brûlée Alexander*** at fashionable Brûlée the Dessert Experience, is concocted with Godiva White Chocolate Liqueur.

Chicago's Nacional 27 devised a magnificent variation on the theme dubbed the ***Century Alexander***. Priced at $55, the signature is a museum-grade cocktail made with

Blandy's 1935 Verdelho Madeira, Camus XO Cognac, Liqueur Créole Clément and homemade tres leches ice cream.

Joining the Alexander in stature is the **Stinger Cocktail**, the postprandial darling of the first half of the 20th century. The drink is little more than a combination of brandy and crème de menthe. When vigorously shaken with ice the aerated cocktail becomes lighter than the sum of its parts, literally tingling with light foam. It's a marvelous drink, especially when made with an elegant brandy. A V.S.O.P. Cognac performs the role handily. Likewise, the better the crème de menthe, the better the Stinger.

Personal preference will dictate the cocktail's proportioning. Most recipes call for five parts brandy to one part crème de menthe. A drier version of the drink would be 7 or 8 parts brandy to one part menthe, while a 3:1 Stinger is slightly sweeter. Either formula, however, will be result in spontaneous applause.

Also famous from the last century is the **Frappé**, which is not a specific drink, rather a style of service. Frappés are libations served over mounded shaved or crushed ice and served in Champagne saucers with short straws. In some cases, it's just a liqueur or cordial served over ice, such as green crème de menthe, other times it's a cocktail devised specifically as a frappé. Classic examples include **Mulatta Frappé**, the combination of Bacardi Gold Rum, dark crème de cacao and

Jim Beam® Black Bourbon

Made in Clermont, Kentucky since 1795, Jim Beam is an American institution and the most famous name in bourbon. It is the benchmark by which all other American whiskeys are measured, if for no other reason than it is the bestselling bourbon in the world. While the 80-proof bourbon and their stellar collection of small batch whiskeys get most of the attention, **Jim Beam Black Bourbon** has quietly become one of the top whiskey values here and abroad.

Jim Beam Black is distilled from a high proportion of white and yellow corn grown in Indiana and Kentucky, and lesser percentages of rye and malted barley. In 2001, the distillery reintroduced the brand with an additional year of aging under its belt. The whiskey is now matured in oak a minimum of 8 years and bottled at 86-proof.

What they didn't change is the bourbon's tremendous personality and character. The bouquet is still irresistible, sweet and brimming with the aromas of corn, vanilla, caramel and toasted oak. While the whiskey remains enormously flavorful, the additional time in the barrel has tempered some of its natural exuberance. Its palate is sweet and grainy and the finish warm and long. The entire experience is top-notch, extraordinary considering its modest price.

Jim Beam Black Bourbon has genuinely come of age, proving once again that leaving well enough alone isn't always the best policy. Use it in any bourbon-based cocktail you'd like to ascend into the great range.

lime juice, **Coffee Marnier Frappé**, which features equal parts of Kahlúa and Grand Marnier, and the **Mocha Frappé**, a drink made with Kahlúa, white crème de menthe, white crème de cacao and Cointreau.

After-dinner drinks have enjoyed enduring popularity and remain a major focus of mixology. From a hospitality perspective these cocktails form the evening's final impression, the last chance to wow. Who said you can't have dessert and drink it too? Well, perhaps no one, but nevertheless here are the best kept secrets behind America's greatest after-dinner drinks.

- **Neat and Tidy** — One famous category of after-dinner drinks is comprised of those served neat in brandy snifters. Many of their predecessors were devised to act as a digestive, calming ones system after a hearty repast. Not surprising, a majority of these drinks are made with a base of brandy, such as the **French Connection**, a velvety blend of VSOP Cognac and Grand Marnier. Consider also the **Framboise Kiss**, which combines VSOP Cognac and a splash of framboise or Chambord. The combination of the cognac and a hint of raspberries is irresistible.

  The key to a great after-dinner drink is to deliver a lot of flavor. A case in point is the **Moulin Rouge**, a neat drink made with VSOP Cognac, crème de cassis, dry sherry and a few dashes of bitters. Another drink served in a snifter that's brimming with rich flavors is the **Raspberry Café**, a simple yet delicious mix of Kahlúa, Chambord and a splash of Baileys Irish Cream. Convert the drink into the **Raspberry Russian** by adding in a shot of Stoli Razberi Vodka. It's an outstanding after-dinner treat.

- **The Dessert Cart** — If you're looking for something more along the lines of a drinkable dessert, the **Chocolate Safari Martini** is irresistible. A signature at Courtright's Restaurant, the cocktail is a silky slice of heaven made with a double shot of Amarula Cream Liqueur modified with Stoli Vanil, Kahlúa and a splash of Chambord. Along the same lines is Dave & Buster's **Venti Mocha Martini**, a specialty featuring Starbucks Coffee Liqueur, Stoli Vanil and Baileys Irish Cream topped with whipped cream and a drizzle of chocolate sauce.

  Few better understand the allure of drinkable desserts than the beverage gurus at Brûlée. High on their list of favorites is the **White Chocolate Raspberry Muse Martini**. It's made with equal parts of Dooley's Original Toffee Cream Liqueur, Godiva White Chocolate Liqueur, Stoli Vanil and Chambord, to which white chocolate sauce and fresh raspberries are added. Also topping the charts is their diet buster named the **Java Tini**, a lavish blend of chilled, freshly brewed espresso, Stoli Vanil, Kahlúa, Frangelico, Baileys and both Godiva chocolate and white chocolate liqueurs.

A specialty at Joe's Seafood, Prime Steak & Stone Crab, the potable dessert of choice is the **Drumstick**. The drink is prepared with Stoli Vanil, vanilla simple syrup and a healthy portion of melted Häagen-Dazs Vanilla Ice Cream. The ingredients are shaken vigorously and presented in a cocktail glass rimmed with chocolate syrup, crushed graham crackers and chopped peanuts and coated on the inside with a ribbon of chocolate syrup. Topped with a drizzle of chocolate syrup and sprinkled graham crackers and nuts, this signature drink is as visually engaging as it is delicious.

Taking a different tact altogether is the **American Apple Pie**, a specialty of the All-American Bar and Grille at the Rio Al-Suite Hotel and Casino in Las Vegas. The drink tastes remarkably like baked apple pie

Metaxa® Seven Star Greek Specialty Liqueur

Greece is one of the oldest civilizations on Earth and the birthplace of the Olympics. Nestled between the Aegean and Ionian Seas, the ancient land is also an ideal place for the cultivation of premium grape varietals, the juice of which is at the essence of national treasure **Metaxa Seven Star Greek Specialty Liqueur**, a sensational botanical-infused spirit.

This acclaimed Greek import has been made according to the same recipe since 1888. Three different grape varietals — Savatiano, Sultanina and Black Corinth — are crushed to produce a special wine, which is the base for all of the Metaxa vintages. This wine is then double-distilled and placed in handmade, French Limousin oak casks for aging, which for Metaxa Seven Star is seven years. After aging, the distillate is blended with Muscat wine from the Samos and Lemnos and infused with a secret mix of botanicals, one of which is rose petals. It is further aged and bottled at 80-proof.

Metaxa Seven Star is a remarkably elegant product. It has a mahogany hue, darker and richer than Metaxa Five Star, and an engaging bouquet of plump raisins, vanilla and honey. The liqueur's light-weight body has the texture of velvet. The Metaxa Seven delivers a magnificent array of flavors, all of which are fresh, ripe and delicious. The finish is refined and delectable.

The famous Metaxa range also includes the **Five Star** (5 years old), **Grand Olympian Reserve** (12 years old), **Grande Fine** (15 years old) and the **Private Reserve** (20 years old). Only age distinguishes one from the others.

and is made with a shot of Bacardi Big Apple Flavored Rum, Baileys Irish Cream, Starbucks Coffee Liqueur and cream. All it's missing is the crust.

Another innovative dessert drink is Mosaic Restaurant's **Float Up the Creek**, a fanciful combination of Knob Creek Bourbon, Kahlúa and a near fill with Mug Root Beer. The ingredients are shaken and strained into a chilled cocktail glass containing a large scoop of vanilla ice cream. The cocktail ingredients and ice cream swirl together creating a memorable effect. Also noteworthy is a drink called the **Toasted Coconut**. The cocktail hails from Joe's Seafood, Prime Steak & Stone Crab and is made with Bacardi Cóco Rum, butterscotch schnapps, macadamia syrup, coconut cream and cream soda. The drink is a multifaceted, hand shaken gem taken straight off the dessert cart.

• **Updated Classics** — Another significant branch of postprandial mixology is comprised of those drinks crafted more along classic lines, spirited cocktails featuring more panache than calories. An excellent example is Mosaic Restaurant's **Charleston Chew**, a luxurious blend of Barbeito "Charleston" Sercial Madeira, Disaronno Amaretto and a splash of Grand Marnier. The cocktail is shaken, served straight up and garnished with sliced almonds.

Another Mosaic specialty in this category is the **Canadian Maple**. The drink features a jigger of Crown Royal, splashes of Kahlúa, Mozart Black Chocolate Pure 87, half & half and a bit of Canadian maple syrup. Surprisingly well-balanced, it's a delectable nightcap.

At Houston's Rickshaw Far East Bistro, a popular after-dinner selection is the **Pineapple Upside-Down Cake**. The drink is concocted using a base of vanilla bean ice cream and pineapple infused Rain Vodka, Absolut Vanilia and pineapple juice. Garnished with a pineapple wedge, the cocktail is a fresh and delightful finale to a marvelous meal.

Other updated classics include the **Charleston Truffle**, a swank, sophisticated specialty of The Campbell Apartment, in Manhattan. The cocktail is made principally with Van Gogh Dutch Chocolate Vodka and mere splashes of Godiva Chocolate and crème de cacao. Another inspired concoction is the **Babylon Sister**, a delicious and well-conceived signature cocktail of Absinthe Brasserie & Bar in San Francisco. The drink pairs Aqua Perfecta Kirsch and Luxardo Maraschino with a touch of cream. It's hand shaken and served in a chocolate sauce painted cocktail glass and garnished with three brandied cherries.

• **Lactose Tolerance** — Cream drinks are silky smooth, outrageously delicious and one of the classic categories of after dinner cocktails. Joining the Brandy Alexander as one of the established stars of the group is the **Grasshopper**, the combination of cream, green crème de menthe and white crème de cacao. Its creamy, chocolate-mint personality is timelessly appealing.

Concocting after-dinner drinks with cream as the base has been popular for the better part of a century. Not only does the cream serve as an effective vehicle for delivering a huge array of flavors, it's also a marvelous digestive. While a well-established style of drink, it still has a great deal of contemporary appeal. Case in point, a specialty at P.F. Chang's is the **Chang's Key Lime Pie Martini**, a delightful blend of Licor 43 Cuarenta y Tres Liqueur, key lime juice, half & half and whipped cream. The ingredients are hand shaken and strained into a cocktail glass rimmed with crushed graham crackers and garnished with a floating lime wheel.

The **Lemon Meringue Martini** is a sought after specialty at Courtright's Restaurant for good reason. Bearing close resemblance to the classic dessert, the cocktail is the delectable pairing of Ketel One Citroen, limoncello and cream served in a cocktail glass rimmed with sugared graham cracker crumbs. Following the same theme is the **Turtle Sundae**, a creation of The Refectory Restaurant made with Godiva Chocolate Liqueur, Tuaca, Butterscotch, Frangelico and cream. Another sumptuous dessert drink at Refectory is the **Mocha Mudslide Merger**, made with Starbucks Cream Liqueur with Van Gogh Espresso Vodka and Kahlúa.

The **XO Café** well illustrates the creative range of these cocktails. It marries the flavors of Patrón XO Café, Pyrat XO Reserve Rum, Amoretti Pistachio Dessert Sauce and heavy cream. The realm of possibilities also includes the **Tiramisu**, a marvelous recreation of the Italian classic made with a healthy dose of Kahlúa, Disaronno Amaretto, crème de cacao and melted vanilla ice cream.

• **Layered Elegance** — Pousse Cafés are layered cordial drinks comprised of three or more stripes. In French, the name translates to "push coffee," a reference to its popularity as an after-dinner drink. Among the classic layered drinks is the B & B. The drink, layered Benedictine Liqueur and brandy, originated in the 1930s at the famous 21 Club in Manhattan. A more recent example is the **B-52**, a layered concoction featuring Kahlúa, Baileys Irish Cream and topped with Grand Marnier. It's unrivaled both in beauty and enduring popularity.

Carrying on this proud tradition is the altogether engaging **Black Twilight**, a signature drink at 33 Restaurant and Lounge in Boston. Presented in a sherry glass, it's made with Burmeister 10-Year-Old Tawny Porto, Godiva Chocolate Liqueur and capped off with Effen Black Cherry Vodka.

When prepared properly, the ingredients in these drinks will form distinct layers. This occurs as a result of

Savoy

📬 **641 Merrimon Ave.**
   Asheville, NC 28804
☎ **828.253.1077**
▶▌ **www.savoyasheville.com**
✉ **info@savoyasheville.com**

I f you appreciate flawlessly prepared cuisine, creative cocktails and an inviting, convivial ambiance, then your travels must include a trip to beautiful Ashville, North Carolina and **Savoy**. Having once housed a gasoline station, its exterior may be understated, but in all other regards, Savoy is an A-list, over-the-top, delight for the senses.

The interior of the restaurant has the look and feel of Tuscany, rustic, yet chic. The color washed walls in shades of yellow and red are adorned with black and white photographs of Italian cityscapes. The bar is constructed out of concrete, the furniture antique and the decor complemented by hand forged wrought iron appointments. The dining area seats about 84. The combination creates a warm and inviting atmosphere.

The main underpinning of the cuisine is seafood, most of which is flown in fresh from Honolulu. Recent entrée offerings include Hawaiian Escolar, Pacific Rainbow Runner, Sautéed Black Tiger Shrimp, Pacific Opah and Branzino Arrosto, pan roasted sea bass served atop a saffron and asparagus risotto with Prince Island mussels, sea scallops and roasted tomatoes. Equally impressive is the restaurant's award-winning wine menu.

Part of Savoy's fame is based on their featured selection of creative drinks. Case in point is **The Bee's Knees**, a clever spin on a classic cocktail. The drink is made with a hefty portion of small batch Knob Creek Bourbon, limoncello and a modicum of honey. Equally tempting is Savoy's **Blood Orange Cosmopolitan**, which features Grey Goose Vodka, fresh lime, blood orange and cranberry juices.

Classy and unpretentious, the Savoy is an elegant establishment deserving of its success. —RP

The Bee's Knees
Drink recipe on pg 68

using liqueurs with different densities, or specific gravities. The effect achieved is similar to the way oil will float on water or vinegar, thereby creating two layers in the glass.

To accomplish the layering effect, pour the first liqueur directly into the glass and the second off the back of a spoon to slow the force of the pour. The spoon should be positioned just above the level of the first product. Each successive layer is poured using this same technique. The ingredients should be poured in the order specified in the recipe as ingredients are listed from heaviest to lightest.

A layered drink like the B-52 should be served in a chilled glass. This will help keep the ingredients at their proper serving temperature and improve the drink's presentation.

> "A marvelous way to cap off a sensational dinner experience is with a sumptuous cocktail."

Ardbeg® Islay Single Malt Scotch Whisky

There are few spirits on Earth that capture unbridled passion and the sense of discovery as the peaty and iodine-laced flavors in *Ardbeg Islay Single Malt Scotch Whisky*. If you're looking for an exotic adventure but still have to show up for work in the morning, we recommend saving the airfare and having a dram or two of this magnificent, award-winning whisky.

Ardbeg is made on Islay (pronounced eye-luh), a wind-swept island located off the rugged west coast of Scotland. Its blustery climate is dominated by the sea of Hebrides and the unpredictable North Atlantic. Built in 1815, the famed Ardbeg distillery sits by the waters edge and is one of the oldest and smallest distilleries in Scotland. The local peat used in production is floor malted and the pure, soft water comes from two lochs several miles uphill. For decades used as the core of popular blended Scotches, the Ardbeg single malt is aged for 10 years in seasoned American oak casks and bottled at 92-proof.

Ardbeg is a bold and robust whisky with the distinction of being the most heavily peated single malt. It is generously graced with the aromas of iodine, peaty smoke and sea air. On the palate, the medium-weight body delivers a huge array of briny and salty flavors. The finish is long with a muscular heft to it.

Ardbeg is one of the classic malts for the ages.

American Apple Pie

Specialty of Rio/All American Bar and Grille
Created by Anthony Alba
Cocktail glass, chilled
Pour ingredients into an iced mixing glass
1 oz. Bacardi Big Apple Rum
³/4 oz. Baileys Irish Cream
³/4 oz. Starbucks Coffee Liqueur
1 oz. heavy whipping cream
Shake and strain
Garnish with an apple slice and
    2 cinnamon sticks tied with a cherry stem.
Pour ingredients into the iced mixing glass. Shake thoroughly and strain contents into a chilled cocktail glass. Garnish with an apple slice and 2 cinnamon sticks tied with a cherry stem.

B-52

Excerpted from The Original Guide to
American Cocktails and Drinks- 6th Edition
Sherry glass, chilled
Layer ingredients
¹/3 fill with Kahlúa
¹/3 fill with Baileys Irish Cream
¹/3 fill with Grand Marnier
Layer ingredients in the chilled Sherry glass in the order listed.

B & B

Excerpted from The Original Guide to
American Cocktails and Drinks- 6th Edition
Sherry glass, chilled
Layer ingredients
¹/2 fill with Benedictine
¹/2 fill with Brandy
Layer ingredients in the chilled Sherry glass in the order listed.

Babylon Sister

Specialty of Absinthe Brasserie & Bar
Created by Jonny Raglin
Chocolate sauce ribboned cocktail glass, chilled
Pour ingredients into an iced mixing glass
³/4 oz. Aqua Perfecta Kirsch Eau de Vie
¹/2 oz. Luxardo Maraschino Liqueur
Splash simple syrup
¹/2 oz. half & half
Shake and strain
Garnish with 3 brandied cherries
Pour ingredients into the iced mixing glass. Shake thoroughly and strain contents into a chocolate sauce ribboned, chilled cocktail glass. Garnish with 3 brandied cherries.

Black Twilight

Specialty of 33 Restaurant & Lounge
Created by Jenn Harvey
Sherry glass, chilled
Layer ingredients
¹/2 oz. Burmester 10-Year-Old Tawny Porto
¹/2 oz. Godiva Chocolate Liqueur
¹/2 oz. Effen Black Cherry Vodka
Layer ingredients in the chilled Sherry glass in the order listed.

Brûlée Alexander

Specialty of Brûlée the Dessert Experience
Created by Peter Van Thiel
Cocktail glass, chilled
Pour ingredients into an iced mixing glass
2 oz. Brandy
³/4 oz. Godiva White Chocolate Liqueur
³/4 oz. créme
Shake and strain
Garnish with chocolate shavings
Pour ingredients into the iced mixing glass. Shake thoroughly and strain contents into a chilled cocktail glass. Garnish with chocolate shavings

Butterscotch Delight

Specialty of Bourbon Street & Voodoo Lounge
Created by Patrick Snyder
Cocktail glass, chilled
Pour ingredients into an iced mixing glass
1 oz. Absolut Vodka
¹/2 oz. Baileys Irish Cream
¹/2 oz. DeKuyper ButterShots Schnapps
¹/2 oz. Chambord
Shake and strain
Pour ingredients into the iced mixing glass. Shake thoroughly and strain contents into a chilled cocktail glass.

Canadian Maple

Specialty of Mosaic Restaurant
Created by Stephanie Kozicki, Deborah Knight
Raw sugar rimmed cocktail glass, chilled
Pour ingredients into an iced mixing glass
1 ¹/2 oz. Crown Royal Canadian Whiskey
¹/4 oz. Kahlúa
¹/4 oz. Mozart Black Chocolate Pure 87
2 tbsp. Maple Gold Pure Maple Syrup
Splash half & half
Shake and strain
Pour ingredients into the iced mixing glass.
Shake thoroughly and strain contents into a raw
sugar rimmed, chilled cocktail glass.

Century Alexander

Specialty of Nacional 27
Created by Adam Seager
Cocktail glass, chilled
Pour ingredients into an iced mixing glass
1 ¹/2 oz. Camus Borderies XO Cognac
¹/2 oz. 1908 Malmsey or Bual Madeira
¹/2 oz. Liqueur Créole Clément
3 oz. tres leches ice cream
Shake and strain
Garnish with a homemade maraschino cherry*
    and dust with freshly grated nutmeg
Pour ingredients into the iced mixing glass.
Shake thoroughly and strain contents into a
chilled cocktail glass. Garnish with a homemade
maraschino cherry and dust with freshly grated
nutmeg.
*Homemade Maraschino
    Cherry Recipe - pg 320

"Dessert drinks come in many different styles
and are drop dead delicious."

Hennessy® X.O. Cognac

In 1870, more than a century after it was founded, the house of Hennessy released the first X.O. cognac, a delicate and masterful spirit that earned as much critical success as an export as it did on the Continent. Now over 130 years later, **Hennessy X.O. Cognac** remains one of the world's most acclaimed and prestigious spirits.

This magnificent cognac is an assemblage comprised of more than 100 eaux de vie principally from Grande and Petite Champagne regions, with lesser percentages obtained from the other primary appellations. The constituent elements are aged up to fifty years in seasoned Limousin oak barrels and receive further aging after blending to allow the cognacs in the assemblage to fully integrate.

The Hennessy X.O. is a full and supremely elegant cognac. It has a deep mahogany hue and a creamy, velvety textured body. The bouquet is lively and grows with each passing minute, offering aromas of ripe plums, figs, chocolate and a bevy of spices. The cognac washes over the palate with the robust flavors of cinnamon, vanilla, pears and black pepper. The finish is first class — long and flavorful.

The renowned portfolio also includes **Hennessy Paradis Extra Cognac**. Created in 1979, it is an assemblage comprised of predominantly Grande and Petite Champagne eaux de vie with a minimum age of 25 years and many that exceed 100 years old.

Chang's Key Lime Pie Martini

Specialty of P.F. Chang's China Bistro
Created by P.F. Chang's staff
Crushed graham cracker rimmed
    cocktail glass, chilled
Pour ingredients into an iced mixing glass
2 oz. Licor 43 Cuarenta y Tres
1/2 oz. simple syrup
1/2 oz. key lime juice
1 oz. half & half
3 circles of whipped cream
Shake and strain
Garnish with a floating lime wheel
Pour ingredients into the iced mixing glass. Shake thoroughly and strain contents into a crushed graham cracker rimmed, chilled cocktail glass. Garnish with a floating lime wheel.

Charleston Chew

Specialty of Mosaic Restaurant
Created by Stephanie Kozicki
Cocktail glass, chilled
Pour ingredients into an iced mixing glass
2 1/4 oz. Barbeito Charleston Sercial Madeira
1/2 oz. Disaronno Amaretto
1/4 oz. Grand Marnier
Shake and strain
Garnish with a Marcona almond
Pour ingredients into the iced mixing glass. Shake thoroughly and strain contents into a chilled cocktail glass. Garnish with a Marcona almond.

Charleston Truffle

Specialty of The Campbell Apartment
Created by Mark Grossich
Shaved chocolate rimmed cocktail glass, chilled
Pour ingredients into an iced mixing glass
2 1/2 oz. Van Gogh Dutch Chocolate Vodka
1/2 oz. White Crème de Cacao
Shake and strain
Float with Godiva Chocolate Liqueur
Pour ingredients into the iced mixing glass. Shake thoroughly and strain contents into a shaved chocolate rimmed, chilled cocktail glass. Float with Godiva Chocolate Liqueur.

Chocolate Kiss

Specialty of Ibiza Dinner Club
Created by Ibiza's staff
Cocktail glass, chilled
Pour ingredients into an iced mixing glass
1/2 oz. Godiva White Chocolate Liqueur
1/2 oz. Godiva Chocolate Liqueur
1/4 oz. Vanilla Vodka
1/4 oz. Frangelico
Shake and strain
Pour ingredients into the iced mixing glass. Shake thoroughly and strain contents into a chilled cocktail glass.

Chocolate Martini

Specialty of Joe's Seafood, Prime Steak and Stone Crab
Created by Dan Barringer
Chocolate syrup ribboned cocktail glass, chilled
Pour ingredients into an iced mixing glass
1 oz. Stoli Vanil Vodka
1 oz. DeKuyper Dark Crème de Cacao
1 oz. Godiva White Chocolate Liqueur
3 oz. melted Häagen-Dazs Vanilla Ice Cream
Shake and strain
Garnish with Praline pecans
Pour ingredients into the iced mixing glass. Shake thoroughly and strain contents into a chocolate syrup ribboned, chilled cocktail glass. Garnish with Praline pecans.

Chocolate Safari Martini

Specialty of Courtright's Restaurant
Created by Marco Recio
Cocktail glass, chilled
Pour ingredients into an iced mixing glass
2 oz. Amarula Cream Liqueur
3/4 oz. Stoli Vanil Vodka
3/4 oz. Kahlúa
Splash Chambord
Shake and strain
Garnish with a Hershey's Kiss
    in the bottom of the glass
Pour ingredients into the iced mixing glass. Shake thoroughly and strain contents into a chilled cocktail glass. Garnish with a Hershey's Kiss in the bottom of the glass.

Coffee Marnier Frappé

Excerpted from The Original Guide to
American Cocktails and Drinks- 6th Edition
Cocktail glass, chilled
Build in glass
Fill to a mound with crushed ice
1 oz. Kahlúa
1 oz. Grand Marnier
Splash fresh orange juice
Short straw
Fill the chilled cocktail glass to a mound with
crushed ice. Pour ingredients in the order listed
and add a short straw.

Concerto

Specialty of Mosaic Restaurant
Created by Stephanie Kozicki
Chocolate rimmed cocktail glass, chilled
Pour ingredients into an iced mixing glass
1 1/2 oz. Chopin Vodka
1/2 oz. Mozart Black Chocolate 87 Pure
1/2 oz. Mozart White Chocolate Cream
1/4 oz. Chambord
Shake and strain
Pour ingredients into the iced mixing glass. Shake
thoroughly and strain contents into a chocolate
rimmed, chilled cocktail glass.

Crème Bruleé Martini

Specialty of Jade Bar
Created by Alex John
Cocktail glass, chilled
Pour ingredients into an iced mixing glass
2 oz. Stoli Vanil Vodka
1 oz. Frangelico
1/2 oz. Cointreau
1/2 oz. cream
Shake and strain
Garnish with ground nutmeg
Pour ingredients into the iced mixing glass. Shake
thoroughly and strain contents into a chilled
cocktail glass. Garnish with ground nutmeg.

Drumstick

Specialty of Joe's Seafood, Prime Steak & Stone Crab
Created by Dan Barringer
Chocolate crushed graham cracker and
   peanut rimmed cocktail glass, chilled
Pour ingredients into an iced mixing glass
1 oz. Stoli Vanil Vodka
1 oz. vanilla simple syrup*
4 oz. melted Häagen-Dazs Vanilla Ice Cream
Shake and strain
1 oz. chocolate syrup
Garnish with ribboned chocolate
   syrup, chopped peanuts, and crushed
   graham crackers
Pour ingredients into the iced mixing glass and
shake thoroughly. Ribbon half of the chocolate
syrup inside the prepared, chilled cocktail
glass. Strain contents. Garnish with remaining
chocolate syrup, chopped peanuts, and crushed
graham cracker.
*Vanilla Simple Syrup Recipe - pg 322

Espresso Martini

Specialty of Courtright's Restaurant
Created by Marco Recio
Cocktail glass, chilled
Pour ingredients into an iced mixing glass
1 1/2 oz. Baileys Irish Cream
3/4 oz. Kahlúa
3/4 oz. Stoli Vanil Vodka
3/4 oz. Butterscotch Schnapps
2 oz. cold espresso
Shake and strain
Garnish with 3 espresso beans and
   a lemon twist
Pour ingredients into the iced mixing glass.
Shake thoroughly and strain contents into a
chilled cocktail glass. Garnish with 3 espresso
beans and a lemon twist.

Shanghai 1930

📠 **133 Steuart St.**
San Francisco, CA 94105
☎ **415.896.5600**
▶▶ **www.shanghai1930.com**
✉ **info@shanghai1930.com**

Scan the 20th century and you'll likely not find a more uncertain, romantically charged place and time than Shanghai during the 1930s. Dubbed the "Paris of the Orient," Shanghai was a city teeming with spies and an atmosphere of international intrigue and fatalism. In a time when an evening might be your last, memories were especially meaningful. Such is the palpable mystique of **Shanghai 1930**, a San Francisco restaurant renowned for its multi-regional Chinese cuisine.

The interior is right out of 1930s China with the feel of a speakeasy or opium den. The art deco and nouveau décor is a blend of nuances from East and West. The lounge is dominated by a 40-foot aquamarine bar with an expansive back bar. The rich wood accents and subdued lighting creates a romantic, yet convivial

atmosphere, a perfect setting to enjoy one of the expertly prepared classic cocktails that are the specialty of the house.

The menu takes an approach to fusion cuisine best described as authentic Asian "street food." Preparing fresh seafood is a particular specialty and entrees include dry-wok fired Kung Pao Prawns, "Zhao Liew" Fish Pillows, Fish on a "Vine" and "Three Coins in the Fountain", a signature dish made with medallions of sea scallops in a Sa-te sauce.

The bar menu at Shanghai 1930 is a dance of seduction. The lounge has made famous the **Shanghaipolitan**, an involved drink made with mandarin and citrus vodkas, Patrón Citrónge Orange Liqueur and a bevy of juices, and **Sexual Healing**, a cocktail comprised of vodka, Lillet, Grand Marnier and lychee syrup.

To be whisked away to another time and place is the romantic journey awaiting you at Shanghai 1930. —RP

Sexual Healing
Drink recipe on pg 27

Float up the Creek

Specialty of Mosaic Restaurant
Created by Stephanie Kozicki, Matt Rinn
Cocktail glass, chilled
Pour ingredients into an iced mixing glass
1 ¹/2 oz. Knob Creek Bourbon
¹/4 oz. Kahlúa
Shake and strain
1 scoop vanilla ice cream
Top with Mug Root Beer
Place 1 scoop vanilla ice cream in the bottom
of the chilled cocktail glass. Pour bourbon
and Kahlúa into the iced mixing glass. Shake
thoroughly and pour contents over the ice cream.
Top with Mug Root Beer.

Framboise Kiss

Excerpted from The Original Guide to
American Cocktails and Drinks- 6th Edition
Brandy snifter, heated
Build in glass
1 ¹/2 oz. XO Cognac
¹/2 oz. Chambord
Pour ingredients into the heated brandy snifter
in the order listed.

French Connection

Excerpted from The Original Guide to
American Cocktails and Drinks- 6th Edition
Brandy snifter, heated
Build in glass
1 ¹/2 oz. V.S. Cognac
1 ¹/2 oz. Grand Marnier
Pour ingredients into the heated brandy snifter
in the order listed.

"Sipping something marvelous after dinner is like putting an exclamation mark on the evening."

Rémy Martin® XO Excellence Cognac

Established in 1724, Rémy Martin Cognac is one of the preeminent cognac houses. The firm features Fine Champagne cognacs, assemblages comprised of brandies from the Grande and Petite Champagne regions. Rémy Martin is the only major cognac house to distill all of its brandies on the lees, which it is argued yields spirits with a greater range of complexity. No expression better illustrates the firm's signature style than the impeccable ***Rémy Martin XO Excellence Cognac.***

This most famous designation is an assemblage comprised of more than 100 eaux de vie derived from Grande (85%) and Petite Champagne (15%). The constituent elements are aged between 10 and 37 years in seasoned Limousin oak barrels and receive further aging after blending to allow the cognacs in the assemblage to fully integrate.

Rémy XO Excellence is a rare and sublime pleasure. The cognac has an alluring mahogany hue with gold highlights and a wafting bouquet of cinnamon, oranges, plums and subtle floral notes. The light, velvety body delivers waves of delectable spicy, ripe fruit flavors that persist remarkably long on the palate.

The distinguished top end of the Rémy Martin portfolio features the likes of ***Rémy Martin Extra***, whose blend has a minimum age of 35 years, and the world's most recognized ultra-premium spirit, ***Louis XIII de Rémy Martin***. With its youngest brandy registering 40 years in age, the famous cognac is appropriately packaged in Baccarat crystal.

Goodnight Kiss

Specialty of Savoy
Created by Eric Scheffer
Chocolate syrup ribboned cocktail glass, chilled
Pour ingredients into an iced mixing glass
1 1/2 oz. Stoli Vanil Vodka
1 oz. Godiva Chocolate Liqueur
1 oz. Godiva White Chocolate Liqueur
Shake and strain
Garnish with chocolate shavings
Pour ingredients into the iced mixing glass. Shake thoroughly and strain contents into a chocolate syrup ribboned, chilled cocktail glass. Garnish with chocolate shavings.

Grasshopper

Excerpted from The Original Guide to American Cocktails and Drinks- 6th Edition
Cocktail glass, chilled
Pour ingredients into an iced mixing glass
3/4 oz. White Crème de Cacao
3/4 oz. Green Crème de Menthe
2 oz. half & half
Shake and strain
Pour ingredients into the iced mixing glass. Shake thoroughly and strain contents into a chilled cocktail glass.

Hazelnut Torte

Specialty of Bookmarks
Created by Mark Grossich
Cocktail glass, chilled
Pour ingredients into an iced mixing glass
1 oz. Frangelico
1 oz. Baileys Irish Cream
1 oz. Stoli Vanil Vodka
1/2 oz. White Crème de Cacao
Shake and strain
Garnish with sliced almonds
Pour ingredients into the iced mixing glass. Shake thoroughly and strain contents into a chilled cocktail glass. Garnish with sliced almonds.

Java Tini

Specialty of Brûlée the Dessert Experience
Created by Randi Montague, Peter Van Thiel
Cocktail glass, chilled
Pour ingredients into an iced mixing glass
3/4 oz. Stoli Vanil Vodka
3/4 oz. Kahlúa
3/4 oz. Godiva White Chocolate Liqueur
3/4 oz. Godiva Chocolate Liqueur
3/4 oz. Baileys Irish Cream
3/4 oz. Frangelico
1 oz. cold espresso
Shake and strain
Pour ingredients into the iced mixing glass. Shake thoroughly and strain contents into a chilled cocktail glass.

Lemon Meringue Martini

Specialty of Courtright's Restaurant
Created by Marco Recio
Sugar and crushed graham cracker rimmed cocktail glass, chilled
Pour ingredients into an iced mixing glass
1 1/2 oz. Ketel One Citroen Vodka
1 oz. Limoncello
1 1/2 oz. half & half
Shake and strain
Garnish with a lemon twist
Pour ingredients into the iced mixing glass. Shake thoroughly and strain contents into a sugar and crushed graham cracker rimmed, chilled cocktail glass. Garnish with a lemon twist.

Mocha Frappé

Excerpted from The Original Guide to American Cocktails and Drinks- 6th Edition
Cocktail glass, chilled
Build in glass
Fill to a mound with crushed ice
1 oz. Kahlúa
1/2 oz. White Crème de Menthe
1/2 oz. White Crème de Cacao
1/2 oz. Cointreau
Short straw
Fill the chilled cocktail glass to a mound with crushed ice. Pour ingredients in the order listed and add a short straw.

Mocha Mudslide Merger

Specialty of The Refectory Restaurant & Bistro
Created by Julie Mulisano, Audrey Strange
Cocktail glass, chilled
Pour ingredients into an iced mixing glass
1 oz. Starbucks Cream Liqueur
1/2 oz. Van Gogh Double Espresso Vodka
1/2 oz. Kahlúa
Shake and strain
Pour ingredients into the iced mixing glass.
Shake thoroughly and strain contents into a
chilled cocktail glass.

Moulin Rouge

Excerpted from The Original Guide to
American Cocktails and Drinks- 6th Edition
Brandy snifter, heated
Build in glass
1 1/2 oz. Briottet Crème de Cassis
1/2 oz. V.S.O.P. Cognac
1/2 oz. Dry Sherry
1-2 dashes Angostura Aromatic Bitters
Garnish with a lemon twist
Pour ingredients into the heated brandy snifter
in the order listed. Garnish with a lemon twist.

"There are libations ready to satisfy any taste or after dinner request."

Patrón® 100% Agave Añejo Tequila

The famed artisan tequilas of Patrón are skillfully distilled and blended in the high altitudes of the mountains surrounding Jalisco. These 100% agave tequilas have remained preeminent since they were introduced in America in the mid-1980s, due largely to the enormous following of the brand's flagship, *Patrón 100% Agave Añejo Tequila*.

The entire range of Patrón tequilas are made relying on time-proven techniques. The mature agaves are baked, crushed and slowly fermented. They are then double-distilled in copper pot stills, balanced to 80-proof and repeatedly filtered for purity. Aging takes place in small, 180-liter American oak barrels.

Patrón Añejo is an incomparable masterpiece with a luxurious, satiny smooth gold body. The tequila is generously aromatic with light fruity notes. Its palate is a rich complex of caramel, citrus and spice. The finish is long and semisweet.

Patrón 100% Agave Silver Tequila is a rare and exuberant gem, loaded with the fresh aromas of lemon and white pepper. The supple body delivers on the promise of buttery sweet and peppery flavors. It is a supremely elegant blanco tequila.

The latest addition to the family is *Patrón 100% Agave Reposado Tequila*. It is aged a minimum of 6 months, during which it picks up a trace of golden color and a splash of toasted oak flavor. The tequila is mellow and inviting with a relaxed finish.

Mulatta Frappé

Excerpted from The Original Guide to
American Cocktails and Drinks- 6th Edition
Cocktail glass, chilled
Build in glass
Fill to a mound with crushed ice
1 1/4 oz. Bacardi Gold Rum
3/4 oz. Dark Crème de Cacao
1/4 oz. Rose's Lime Juice
1/4 oz. fresh lime juice
Garnish with a lime wedge
Fill the chilled cocktail glass to a mound
with crushed ice. Pour ingredients in the order
listed and add a short straw. Garnish with a
lime wedge.

Nutty Nail

Specialty of Mosaic Restaurant
Created by Stephanie Kozicki, Matt Rinn
Bucket glass, ice
Build in glass
1 1/2 oz. Highland Park 12 years old Scotch
1/2 oz. Drambuie
1/4 oz. Frangelico
Stir ingredients
Pour ingredients into the iced bucket glass in the
order listed. Stir thoroughly.

Orient Express Martini

Specialty of P.F. Chang's China Bistro
Created by P.F. Chang's staff
Cinnamon sugar rimmed cocktail glass, chilled
Pour ingredients into an iced mixing glass
1 oz. Smirnoff Vanilla Vodka
1/2 oz. Frangelico
1/2 oz. Baileys Irish Cream
1/2 oz. half & half
1 oz. espresso
Shake and strain
Garnish with a lemon twist
Pour ingredients into the iced mixing glass.
Shake thoroughly and strain contents into a
cinnamon sugar rimmed, chilled cocktail glass.
Garnish with a lemon twist.

Pineapple Upside-Down Cake

Specialty of Rickshaw Far East Bistro & Bambú Lounge
Created by Rickshaw's staff
Cocktail glass, chilled
Pour ingredients into an iced mixing glass
1 3/4 oz. Vanilla Bean and Pineapple-
     Infused Rain Vodka
1/2 oz. Absolut Vanilia Vodka
Splash grenadine
Splash simple syrup
1 oz. pineapple juice
Shake and strain
Garnish with a pineapple and cherry flag
Pour ingredients into the iced mixing glass.
Shake thoroughly and strain contents into a
chilled cocktail glass. Garnish with a pineapple
and cherry flag.

Raspberry Café

Excerpted from The Original Guide to
American Cocktails and Drinks- 6th Edition
Brandy snifter, heated
Build in glass
1 oz. Kahlúa
1 oz. Chambord
3/4 oz. Baileys Irish Cream
Garnish with a lemon twist
Pour ingredients into the heated brandy snifter
in the order listed. Garnish with a lemon twist.

Raspberry Russian

Excerpted from The Original Guide to
American Cocktails and Drinks- 6th Edition
Brandy snifter, heated
Build in glass
3/4 oz. Kahlúa
3/4 oz. Stoli Razberi Vodka
3/4 oz. Chambord
3/4 oz. Baileys Irish Cream
Garnish with a lemon twist
Pour ingredients into the heated brandy snifter
in the order listed. Garnish with a lemon twist.

Raspberry Truffle

Specialty of The Refectory Restaurant & Bistro
Created by Julie Mulisano, Alex Reger
Cocktail glass, chilled
Pour ingredients into an iced mixing glass
1 oz. Godiva Chocolate Liqueur
1/2 oz. Vox Raspberry Vodka
1/2 oz. Amarula Cream Liqueur
Shake and strain
Pour ingredients into the iced mixing glass.
Shake thoroughly and strain contents into a
chilled cocktail glass.

The Thin White Duke

Specialty of Lola's
Created by Loren Dunsworth
Grated Hershey's Kiss rimmed
    cocktail glass, chilled
Pour ingredients into an iced mixing glass
1 1/2 oz. Godiva White Chocolate Liqueur
1 1/2 oz. Stoli Vanil Vodka
Splash half & half
Shake and strain
Pour ingredients into the iced mixing glass. Shake thoroughly and strain contents into a grated Hershey's Kiss rimmed, chilled cocktail glass.

Tiramisu

Excerpted from The Original Guide to
American Cocktails and Drinks- 6th Edition
Cocktail glass, chilled
Pour ingredients into an iced mixing glass
3/4 oz. Godiva Chocolate Liqueur
3/4 oz. Disaronno Amaretto
3/4 oz. Kahlúa
3 oz. melted vanilla ice cream
Shake and strain
Garnish with whipped cream
    and shaved chocolate
Pour ingredients into the iced mixing glass. Shake thoroughly and strain contents into a chilled cocktail glass. Garnish with whipped cream and shaved chocolate.

Toasted Coconut

Specialty of Joe's Seafood, Prime Steak & Stone Crab
Created by Dan Barringer
Simple syrup and toasted coconut
    rimmed cocktail glass, chilled
Pour ingredients into an iced mixing glass
2 oz. Bacardi Cóco Rum
1/2 oz. Monin Macadamia Nut Syrup
1/4 oz. DeKuyper ButterShots Schnapps
2 oz. coconut cream syrup
2 oz. vanilla cream soda
Shake and strain
Pour ingredients into the iced mixing glass. Shake thoroughly and strain contents into a simple syrup and toasted coconut rimmed, chilled cocktail glass.

Turtle Sundae

Specialty of The Refectory Restaurant & Bistro
Created by Julie Mulisano
Chocolate sauce ribboned
    cocktail glass, chilled
Pour ingredients into an iced mixing glass
1/2 oz. Godiva Chocolate Liqueur
1/2 oz. Tuaca Liquore Italiano
1/2 oz. Butterscotch Schnapps
1/2 oz. Frangelico
Shake and strain
1 oz. heavy cream, chilled
Pour the heavy cream into the prepared, chilled cocktail glass. Pour remaining ingredients into the iced mixing glass and shake thoroughly. Swirl the shaker contents into the cocktail glass.

Venti Mocha Martini

Specialty of Dave & Buster's
Created by Maria Kerschner, Will Jacobus
Cocoa powder rimmed cocktail glass, chilled
Pour ingredients into an iced mixing glass
1 1/2 oz. Starbucks Coffee Liqueur
1/2 oz. Stoli Vanil Vodka
1/2 oz. Baileys Irish Cream
Shake and strain
Garnish with whipped cream drizzled
    with Hershey's Chocolate Syrup
Pour ingredients into the iced mixing glass. Shake thoroughly and strain contents into a cocoa powder rimmed, chilled cocktail glass. Garnish with whipped cream drizzled with Hershey's Chocolate Syrup.

The Spanish Kitchen

826 North LaCienega Blvd.
Los Angeles, CA 90069

☎ 310.659.4794

▶▶I www.thespanishkitchen.com

✉ information@spanishkitchen.com

Evocative of Hollywood's Golden Era, **The Spanish Kitchen** is styled after a famous Mexican Restaurant of the same name whose heyday was in the 1940s. The restaurant is a popular haunt that attracts a lively and beautiful crowd, a stream of folks looking for an authentic Mexican experience steeped in bona fide Hollywood glamour.

The restaurant is reminiscent of a colonial Spanish hacienda constructed with materials from south of the border. The interior is bright, airy and brilliantly colored. The decor is authentically Mexican with tiled walls, chandeliers, wrought iron, crescent shaped booths, antique doors and candlelit tables. It is a traditional and cultural immersion that beautifully sets the stage for an evening of fun.

The cuisine at The Spanish Kitchen is a celebration of the exuberant flavors of southern Mexico. Much of the seafood and poultry portion of the menu is rubbed with recados, which are dry marinades that enhance flavors as they are grilled over an open mesquite flame. Entrees include Enchiladas de Cangrejo, a seasoned and sautéed Blue crabmeat topped with a Salsa Poblano-Tequila Lobster Sauce, and Paella, a mélange of fresh mussels, clams, scallops, shrimp, chicken and spicy sausage cooked with saffron rice.

The bar at The Spanish Kitchen also operates at a world-class level. The back bar is loaded with a broad collection of premium tequilas and mezcals. The drink menu is a work of art, as are their the Margaritas and Sangrias. Special kudos to the specialty *Liquid Postres*, a luxurious blend of espresso, Cointreau, Godiva, Baileys, Kahlúa and vanilla bean ice cream. It is an ideal drink to cap off an evening.

An ultra-hip location, marvelous cuisine and irresistible cocktails qualify The Spanish Kitchen as a Hollywood landmark. —RP

Liquid Postres
Drink recipe on pg 268

White Chocolate Raspberry Muse Martini

Specialty of Brûlée the Dessert Experience
Created by Peter Van Thiel
Cocktail glass, chilled
Pour ingredients into an iced mixing glass
3/4 oz. Dooley's Original Toffee
　　Cream Liqueur
3/4 oz. Stoli Vanil Vodka
3/4 oz. Chambord
3/4 oz. White Godiva Chocolate Liqueur
3/4 oz. white chocolate sauce
3-4 fresh raspberries
Shake and strain
Pour ingredients into the iced mixing glass. Shake thoroughly and strain contents into a chilled cocktail glass.

XO Café

Specialty of Rosemary's Restaurant
Created by Michael Shetler, Francesco LaFranconi
Chocolate syrup ribboned, crushed
　　espresso beans and pistachio rimmed
　　cocktail glass, chilled
Pour ingredients into an iced mixing glass
1 oz. Patrón XO Café Coffee Liqueur
1/2 oz. Pyrat XO Reserve Rum
1/2 oz. Amoretti Pistachio Dessert Sauce
1 oz. heavy cream
Shake and strain
Pour ingredients into the iced mixing glass. Shake thoroughly and strain contents into a chocolate syrup ribboned, crushed espresso beans and pistachio rimmed, chilled cocktail glass.

Chapter Twelve

Drinks with Timeless Appeal
Modern Classics

In 1888, the population of the United States was a mere 60.4 million, Benjamin Harrison defeated incumbent Grover Cleveland for the presidency and the cocktail was experiencing its first golden era. In the cultural centers of the country, the gentry made popular a drink called the *Golden Slipper*. This layered concoction featured Yellow Chartreuse, Danziger Goldwasser and an egg yolk suspended between the two layers. Since you dare not risk having the egg yolk drip down from the corners of your mouth, it was accepted etiquette to consume the Golden Slipper in one swallow.

Cocktails have enjoyed several golden ages, most having directly followed an American war. Its current renaissance, however, may well go down in the books as the most impressive. The degree of innovation demonstrated behind bars today rivals the creative output of any previous generation. The creative abilities and skills of great contemporary mixologists, the likes of Jacques Bezuidenhout, Adam Seger, Scott Beattie, Jonathan Pogash and Francesco LaFranconi are as divinely inspired as their predecessors.

As in ages past, the mantra today when it comes to concocting drinks is "balance, taste and quality." While arguing the relative balance and taste of contemporary cocktails compared to those of the past ultimately renders down to personal preference, quality is the factor that decidedly favors today's drinks.

Since the mid-1980s, the spirits industry has steadily expanded its offerings of premium brands. The explosive growth of single malt Scotches, 100% agave tequilas, small batch bourbons, vintage-dated rums and luxury vodkas has largely taken place over the past two decades. Master mixologists and bar chefs now have access to far more refined and sophisticated spirits and liqueurs than were previously available, which affords those of us today a marked advantage. As has been asserted repeatedly before in this book, the better the spirit, the better the cocktail.

The Modern Classics

It's not the passage of time that makes a cocktail deserving of being labeled a classic. That celebrity status is afforded to drinks with timeless appeal. The Margarita, Old Fashioned, Manhattan, Daiquiri and Martini, among others, all have that certain unquantifiable combination of traits that make them ageless. All things being equal, they will be as favorably received a century from now as they are today, and as they were when first devised.

The recipes portrayed in this chapter are certifiably delicious, contemporary masterpieces with capacity for greatness. Grab your shaker and keep the muddler within reach because here are the best kept secrets of America's greatest modern classics.

• **Creative Spiriting** — One of the cardinal rules about cocktails is to balance all the ingredients such that they become one homogenous taste sensation. Few drinks better illustrate the point than *La Perla Martini*, an award-winning libation and specialty of Tommy's Mexican Restaurant in San Francisco. The drink is the inspired blend of Gran Centenario Reposado Tequila, Domecq Manzanilla Sherry and Mathilde Poire d'Anjou Liqueur. The cocktail has amazing flavor with each constituent element easily perceived.

The creative pairing of spirits and liqueurs is a bona fide art form. For instance, the delectable *Mujer Verde*, a specialty cocktail at Absinthe Brasserie & Bar, marries the savory flavor of Hendrick's Gin with grande dame liqueurs Green and Yellow Chartreuse and fresh lime juice. The Mosaic Restaurant in Scottsdale showcases a drink called the *Nazdarovie*. It combines the fresh,

Patrón® Silver 100% Agave Tequila

Patrón is the bestselling line of super-premium tequilas in the world. These artisan 100% agave tequilas have remained preeminent since they were introduced in America in the mid-1980s. Uncork any of them and the reasons for their phenomenal popularity will be perfectly evident. But from a purist's standpoint, the first spirit to sample is the inimitable *Patrón Silver 100% Agave Tequila*.

Patrón tequilas are made using traditional techniques, including baking, crushing and slow fermenting the mature agaves. They are then double-distilled in copper pot stills, diluted to 80-proof and repeatedly filtered for purity. Aging takes place in small, 180-liter American oak barrels.

Patrón Silver is a rare gem bottled fresh from the still and loaded with the fresh aromas of lemon and white pepper. The supple body delivers on the promise of buttery sweet and peppery flavors. It is a most elegant blanco tequila.

Patrón Añejo 100% Agave Tequila is a masterpiece with an incomparable, satiny smooth body. The tequila has a generous bouquet with light fruity notes and a palate rich with the flavors of caramel, citrus and spice. The finish is long and semisweet.

Patrón Reposado 100% Agave Tequila is aged a minimum of 6 months, during which it picks up a trace of golden color and hint of toasted oak flavor. The tequila is mellow and inviting with a relaxed finish.

vibrant taste of Jewel of Russia Wild Bilberry Infusion Vodka with Grand Marnier and English Breakfast Tea. The resulting cocktail is soothing and delicious.

The *Comfortable Italian Fortress* is constructed slightly differently. A signature cocktail at Rickshaw's Far East Bistro, the drink is made from a base of PAMA Pomegranate Liqueur, which is modified with splashes of Citadelle Gin, Disaronno Amaretto and Southern Comfort, and orange, cranberry and pomegranate juice. It's precisely balanced and a genuine pleasure to drink. A noteworthy spirit combination as well is the *Autumn Apple*, a specialty at Cyrus that pairs Hangar One Vodka with Calvados Apple Brandy.

One of the famed bastions of modern cocktails is Harry Denton's Starlight Room in San Francisco. The *Passion* is a specialty of the house concocted on a base of Plymouth Gin to which a splash of Campari and Mandarine Napoléon Liqueur are added. The cocktail is finished with a measure of passion fruit juice or coulis. The result is marvelously tart and flavorful.

Another legendary specialty at the Starlight Room is appropriately named *Starlight*. The creation of all-world mixologist Tony Abou-Ganim, the cocktail is made with Campari, Cointreau and a shot each of orange juice and fresh lemon sour mix. The ingredients are gently stirred, strained into a chilled cocktail glass and splashed with seltzer. The drink is again gently stirred before floating Hennessey Privilège V.S.O.P. Cognac on top. The effect is dramatic and the cocktail sublime. The Starlight is an excellent example of a drink with timeless appeal.

• **Bar Chef's Garden** — Crisp, lively cocktails are the result of using fresh, high quality ingredients. It is growing increasingly more frequent for mixologists to stray from out behind the bar and into the kitchen in search of bold and exciting flavors. Invariably this leads aspiring bar chefs to begin working with botanicals, popular ingredients such as fennel, rosemary, cilantro, dill, anise and the like. This drive for freshness has lead many bar chefs to start cultivating their own herbs and produce, or scour the local farmer's market for unusual flavors.

Few concoctions better make the case for working with fresh ingredients than the tall masterpiece, *Balmy Spring*. The signature at Cyrus begins with a jigger of altogether sensational Sarticious Gin, a Californian small batch spirit. Into an iced mixing glass along with the gin go 10 spearmint and lemon balm leaves, half a teaspoon of Kaffir lime zest, 10 pieces of cucumber and a half-ounce of cucumber flavored simple syrup. The concoction is shaken, poured into a chilled Collins glass and finished with seltzer. The drink's taste is reminiscent of its name.

Another specialty of Cyrus and resident bar chef Scott Beattie is the *Irin Jaya*, a cocktail featuring Hangar One Straight and Kaffir Lime Vodkas, Kaffir lime leaves, seeded Fresno chili rings, candied lemongrass and lime juice. The ingredients are shaken, strained into a chilled cocktail glass and finished with cold ginger beer. It's a savory, spicy slice of liquid heaven.

- **Sun Drenched Cocktails** — One significant branch of modern mixology are those drinks in their bouquet and flavor that seem to capture the essence of summer nights on the porch. These are special cocktails in anyone's repertoire. They touch something universal in us, the fond memories of summer days gone by.

Denizens of the desert, the Mosaic's staff, Chef Deborah Knight included, has become highly adept at creating delicious cocktails bearing the unmistakable imprint of summer. Examples include the *Kalamansi Breeze*, a tantalizing variation on the Lemon Drop concocted with Charbay Meyer Lemon Vodka, Triple Sec, ginger-infused syrup and Kalamansi juice, and the *Watermelon Gin Fizz*, a drink that tastes like a picnic in a glass. It's made with Tanqueray Gin, Cointreau, watermelon puree and Lorina Sparkling Lemonade.

Another summer themed marvel is the *Watermelon & Raspberry Over Kiwi*, a signature cocktail at Joe's Seafood, Prime Steak & Stone Crab. In addition to being fun and delicious, part of the allure of the drink lies in its layered presentation. Constructed in two stages, the first layer is made with Grey Goose Vodka, fresh kiwi juice and agave nectar. The

Laphroaig® Single Islay Malt Scotch Whisky

Laphroaig is the best known of the Islay single malts. It is an intriguing whisky, whose persona cannot be separated from the island on which it was created. Its international celebrity has everything to do with flavor — powerful, untamed and unabashedly exuberant flavor. While not for the faint at heart, *Laphroaig Single Islay Malt Scotch Whisky* offers aficionados a rare and singular taste experience.

The Laphroaig Distillery was built in the 1820s by the waters edge on the southeast shore of Islay. It is one of only a handful of distilleries that malts its own barley. They use locally grown peat and the water used in production is drawn from the Kilbride River. The whisky is aged in first fill ex-bourbon barrels in warehouses built on the edge of the Atlantic, where the ocean air is allowed to swirl around the aging casks.

The most widely known expression of Laphroaig is the acclaimed 10-year old. This grand malt is brimming with a salty array of aromas with notes of seaweed and peaty smoke. For all of its vigor, the malt is quite accessible, sporting a full body and a palate imbued with smoke, peat, salt and iodine. The finish is supple and dry.

Laphroaig Quarter Cask Malt is first matured in ex-bourbon barrels and then transferred to quarter casks for finishing. This double maturation in a smaller barrel allows for greater contact with the wood.

The famed Laphroaig range also includes a 10-year cask strength, 15-year, 30-year and 40-year malt. Each is an intriguing spirit graced with the flavor of the sea.

ingredients are shaken with ice and poured into a cocktail glass. The second layer is prepared using Bacardi Razz Rum, pureed raspberries and fresh watermelon juice. Those ingredients are shaken with ice and poured over the back of a spoon, resulting in the second drink floating on the first.

Perfectly suited for warm weather are the Yard House Restaurant's *Brazilian Lemonade*, an iced blend of Ketel One Citroen, Cointreau, Mojito mix and fresh lemonade, and the *Crimson Tea Party*, a specialty cocktail of 33 Restaurant in Boston. The drink is skillfully devised from a diverse mix of ingredients, including 42 Below Manuka Honey Vodka, chilled crimson berry tea, lemon juice and muddle mixed berries.

The *Blueberry Ballad*, a specialty cocktail of The Refectory Restaurant that combines cherry vodka, limoncello, and blueberry-pomegranate juice and lemon juice. It's light, well-balanced and thirst quenching. Another of their sublime and refreshing libations is *Summer Twilight*, a cocktail made with Stoli Ohranj, Vox Raspberry, Blue Curaçao and a generous portion of Nantucket Nectar Lemonade.

• **Muddled Gems** — Reliance on muddling fresh ingredients into drinks is gaining broad based acceptance within the mixology community. Factor in the enhanced production value and the technique is a no-lose proposition. Take for example Rickshaw's ultra-popular *Ginger-Apple Mojito*. It's prepared by first muddling together sliced ginger, julienne cut green apples, simple syrup and lime juice before finishing the drink with a jigger of Citadelle Apple Vodka and a splash of club soda.

The Stone Rose Lounge in Manhattan promotes the *Grapefruit Basil Limeade*, a cocktail made with No. TEN by Tanqueray, grapefruit juice and muddled basil leaves, while the P.F. Chang's specialty, *Cantaloupe Chang's*, is an engaging blend of SKYY Melon Vodka, Brizard Watermelon Liqueur with muddled cantaloupe, Thai basil and fresh lemon sour mix.

The *Dark Autumn* features muddled blueberries and Macallan Amber Liqueur. A signature cocktail at 33 Restaurant, the drink also contains Captain Morgan Spiced Rum, lime juice and a dash of cinnamon.

Perhaps the most creative use of muddling is involved in the making of Cyrus' tall, iced libation, *Pelo del Perro* ("Hair of the dog"). Made with Hangar One Straight Vodka, Charbay Ruby Red Grapefruit Vodka, agave nectar, lime and pink grapefruit juices, the specialty also contains the rejuvenating boost of a muddled B-12 pill. Clearly this drink was devised through the benefit of practical experience.

• **Return of Tall Drinks** — Tall drinks enjoy certain advantages over their straight up counterparts, and as a result are making a comeback. The larger capacity glasses afford more creative latitude with respect to ingredients, especially the use of carbonated mixers. In addition, because these drinks are served with ice, maintaining proper serving temperature isn't an issue.

The *Ginger Jimmy* illustrates the point well. It's prepared with muddled mint leaves and sugar, along with crushed ice, a jigger of luscious Jim Beam Black Bourbon and a fill of Reed's Premium Ginger Beer. The drink is somewhat spicy and totally refreshing.

The same is undoubtedly true about the Cyrus specialty, *Rhubarbarella*. The tall drink is prepared with Hangar One Straight and "Buddha's Hand" Vodkas, ginger/rhubarb simple syrup, chopped shiso leaves and candied rhubarb pieces. The concoction is shaken and strained into an iced glass and then finished with a fill of Cock 'n' Bull Ginger Beer.

Not Too Far East is a tall specialty drink at P.F. Chang's concocted with Navan Vanille Cognac Liqueur, citrus spice tea, lemon sour mix and a float of Malibu Pineapple Rum. At Bookmarks the tall specialty of the house is the *Inferno*, an effervescent blend of Belvedere Vodka, Campari, Tabasco and chocolate liqueur. The ingredients are shaken, strained and topped off with club soda.

Last, from swank Ibiza Dinner Club in Seattle comes the *Green Tea Cooler*, the uncomplicated, yet delightful combination of muddled orange slices, Charbay Green Tea Vodka, lemon sour mix and seltzer. It's a well-conceived, flawlessly executed modern classic.

Stone Rose Lounge

📖 **Time Warner Building**
10 Columbus Circle
New York, NY 10019
☎ **212.823.9770**
▶▶ **www.gerberbars.com**

R ande Gerber's Stone Rose Lounge is so groovy that it should be reserved for superheroes. It's like a fabulous perch overlooking Gotham. The good news is that with the exception of super villains they let average citizens through their doors. Yeah, this place is really that cool. The only thing better would be if the Rolling Stones were the house band.

The swank Manhattan landmark is located on the 4th floor of the Time Warner Center on Columbus Circle. The building's marble floors and glass walls reverberate with the sounds of people passing through the busy retail complex. The Stone Rose is expansive and teeming with a beautiful, well-heeled clientele, whether they be the

after-work crowd, or the fashionable Lincoln Center set.

The upscale lounge is an architectural masterpiece replete with rosewood and stone design finishes, marble topped tables, plush velvet banquettes, leather couches and chairs. A large painting of a nude adorns the sleek, classically styled bar. The back wall of the lounge is comprised entirely of floor to ceiling windows offering a breathtaking vista of Central Park and the Manhattan skyline. The overall effect is mesmerizing.

Eventually thoughts return to the order of the day, which is sampling Stone Rose's hors d'ouvres and renowned signature cocktails. The appetizer menu lists delectable, lounge appropriate snacks such as Tuna Wasabi Tartar served on crisp wonton crackers and a Caviar-Filled Beggar's Purses.

The Stone Rose is known for their cocktails and complete mastery of Martinis, Manhattans, Margaritas and Mojitos. Signature drinks include the *Flirtini*, which pairs Grey Goose L'Orange Vodka, pineapple juice and Champagne, and the *Grapefruit Basil Limeade*, a cocktail made with No. TEN by Tanqueray, grapefruit juice and muddled basil leaves.

This is one New York destination not to be missed. —RP

Flirtini
Drink recipe on pg 239

Apple Blossom

Specialty of Shanghai 1930
Created by Shanghai's staff
Cocktail glass, chilled
Pour ingredients into an iced mixing glass
1 1/2 oz. Canadian Whiskey
1 1/2 oz. DeKuyper Pucker Sour Apple Schnapps
1/2 oz. Cherry Brandy
Splash cranberry juice
Shake and strain
Garnish with a thinly sliced green apple
Pour ingredients into the iced mixing glass. Shake thoroughly and strain contents into a chilled cocktail glass. Garnish with a thinly sliced green apple.

Autumn Apple

Specialty of Cyrus
Created by Scott Beattie
Cocktail glass, chilled
Pour ingredients into an iced mixing glass
1 oz. Hangar One Straight Vodka
1/2 oz. Calvados Apple Brandy
1/2 oz. fresh lemon juice
1 oz. ginger-apple juice*
Shake and strain
Top with sparkling apple juice
Garnish with a baked apple chip
Pour ingredients into the iced mixing glass. Shake thoroughly and strain contents into a chilled cocktail glass. Top with sparkling apple juice. Garnish with a baked apple chip.
*Enhanced Ginger-Apple
   Juice Recipe - pg 319

"Celebrity status is afforded to drinks with timeless appeal."

Midori® Melon Liqueur

Midori Melon Liqueur burst into the American limelight in the early 1980s and the brand can now be found on every self-respecting back bar in the country, not to mention the world. In fact, its popularity continues to grow as steadily increasing numbers of contemporary mixologists incorporate Midori into their recipes.

This indispensable liqueur is made from a base of neutral spirits and proprietary flavors, the most readily identifiable of which is honeydew melon. Its lustrous, emerald green color is absolutely intriguing, which has certainly played a role in the liqueur's meteoric success.

Midori has a lively bouquet with the engaging aromas of melon, banana and strawberry. Its soft, supple body immediately fills the mouth with the fresh fruit flavors of honeydew, ripe cantaloupe and bananas. The medium-weight body and slightly sweet palate make it ideal for use in mixed drinks. The liqueur has excellent persistence of flavor.

Midori's ascendancy into celebrity status can be attributed to its one of a kind flavor, vivid color and moderate 40-proof, all of which contribute to its exceptionally high mixability quotient. Add to that a distinctively shaped, textured bottle and you've got a modern classic.

It's difficult to imagine operating a popular club without Midori. Like most great supporting actors, it receives little fanfare, but among professionals, it ranks on the short list of "must have" back bar entries. Without it a large segment of popular mixology drops off-line.

Balmy Spring

Specialty of Cyrus
Created Scott Beattie
Collins glass, ice
Pour ingredients into an iced mixing glass
1 1/2 oz. Sarticious Gin
1/2 oz. cucumber simple syrup*
1/2 tsp. Kaffir lime zest
10 spearmint leaves, chiffonade
10 lemon balm leaves, chiffonade
10 pieces cucumber from simple syrup
Shake and strain
Top with club soda
Stir
Pour ingredients, except the club soda, into the iced mixing glass. Shake thoroughly and strain contents into the iced collins glass. Top with club soda and stir gently.
*Cucumber Simple Syrup Recipe - pg 319

Bayard Fizz

Specialty of The Campbell Apartment
Created by Mark Grossich
Cocktail glass, chilled
Pour ingredients into an iced mixing glass
2 oz. Bombay Sapphire Gin
2 tsp. raspberries marinated in
   Stock Maraschino Liqueur
1/4 oz. fresh lemon juice
1/4 oz. simple syrup
Shake and strain
Top with club soda
Garnish with 3 fresh raspberries
Pour ingredients, except the club soda, into the iced mixing glass. Shake thoroughly and strain contents into a chilled cocktail glass. Top with club soda. Garnish with 3 fresh raspberries.

Blarney Stone

Specialty of Dave & Buster's
Created by Barry Carter
Green apple sugar rimmed cocktail glass, chilled
Pour ingredients into an iced mixing glass
1 1/4 oz. Jameson Irish Whiskey
3/4 oz. DeKuyper Pucker Sour Apple Schnapps
2 oz. cranberry juice
Shake and strain
Garnish with a lemon twist
Pour ingredients into the iced mixing glass. Shake thoroughly and strain contents into a green apple sugar rimmed, chilled cocktail glass. Garnish with a lemon twist.

Bleeding Orange

Specialty of Cyrus
Created by Scott Beattie
Cocktail glass, chilled
Pour ingredients into an iced mixing glass
1/2 oz. Charbay Blood Orange Vodka
1/2 oz. Charbay Meyer Lemon Vodka
1/2 oz. Hangar One Straight Vodka
3 dashes Fee's Peach Bitters
1/2 oz. spiced simple syrup*
1/2 oz. fresh Meyer lemon juice
1/2 oz. fresh blood orange juice
Shake and strain
Pour ingredients into the iced mixing glass. Shake thoroughly and strain contents into a chilled cocktail glass.
*Spiced Simple Syrup Recipe - pg 322

Blueberry Ballad

Specialty of The Refectory Restaurant & Bistro
Created by Julie Mulisano
Cocktail glass, chilled
Pour ingredients into an iced mixing glass
1 oz. Three Olives Cherry Vodka
1/2 oz. Caravella Limoncello
1 oz. Pom Blueberry Pomegranate Juice
Splash fresh lemon juice
Splash club soda
Shake and strain
Garnish with a cherry
Pour ingredients into the iced mixing glass. Shake thoroughly and strain contents into a chilled cocktail glass. Garnish with cherry.

Brazilian Lemonade

Specialty of Yard House
Created by Kip Snider
Sugar rimmed pint glass, chilled
Pour ingredients into an iced mixing glass
2 oz. Ketel One Citroen
1/2 oz. Cointreau
1/2 oz. Monin Mojito Mix
2 fresh lemon wedges squeezed into glass
5 oz. fresh lemonade
Shake thoroughly - do not strain
Garnish with two fresh mint leaves
Pour ingredients into the iced mixing glass. Shake thoroughly - do not strain - pour contents into an empty, sugar rimmed, chilled pint glass. Garnish with two fresh mint leaves.

California Dreamin'

Specialty of Rio/All American Bar and Grille
Created by Anthony Alba, Bobby Gleason
Tall house specialty glass, ice
Pour ingredients into an empty mixing glass
2 lemon wedges
2 strawberries
Muddle contents
Add ice
1 oz. Cazadores Reposado Tequila
1 oz. DeKuyper Pucker Watermelon Schnapps
Splash grenadine
1/2 oz. rock candy syrup
2 oz. fresh orange juice
2 oz. fresh lemon sour mix
Shake and strain
Garnish with a fresh strawberry
Place lemon wedges and strawberries into the empty mixing glass. Muddle and add ice. Pour in the remaining ingredients. Shake thoroughly and strain contents into an iced, tall house specialty glass. Garnish with a fresh strawberry.

Ultimat® Chocolate Vanilla Flavored Vodka

Take a moment and consider how brilliant the concept of a chocolate and vanilla flavored vodka is. Who doesn't crave chocolate? And vanilla, well, it's as popular as ever and the foundation of every ice cream sundae ever created. Then these universally appealing flavors are imbued into a classy Polish vodka. It's a no-brainer, right? The proof of just how splendid such a spirit can be is as close as the nearest bottle of super-premium *Ultimat Chocolate Vanilla Flavored*.

This mouth-watering spirit is crafted at the Polmos distillery in Bielsko-Biala, Poland. The base vodka is made from a singular blend of 70% potato and 15% wheat and rye. Each ingredient contributes to the vodka's bouquet and taste profile. All natural chocolate and vanilla flavorings are then added, after which the vodka is meticulously filtered to remove all trace impurities. It is bottled at 80-proof.

Introduced in 2003, this luxurious flavored vodka is a genuine pleasure to drink. It is crystal clear with a generous cocoa and vanilla bean bouquet and a rounded, silky and light-weight body. The vodka has a semisweet palate marked with the pronounced lip smacking flavors of milk chocolate and creamy vanilla, both of which persist throughout the lingering finish. The vodka's ideal balance is perfectly suited for drink making.

The Ultimat Vodka range also includes *Ultimat Black Cherry Flavored Vodka*. It is made from fresh cherries macerated in super-premium Ultimat Vodka. It's clear, medium-weight with a prominent aroma of cherry blossoms and a palate of black cherries and spice.

Cantaloupe Chang's

Specialty of P.F. Chang's China Bistro
Created by P.F. Chang's staff
Cocktail glass, chilled
Pour ingredients into an empty mixing glass
1 oz. fresh cantaloupe juice
3 Thai basil leaves
1 oz. sweet 'n' sour
Muddle contents
Add ice
1 1/2 oz. SKYY Melon Vodka
1 oz. Marie Brizard Watermelon Liqueur
Shake and strain
Garnish with a lemon twist
Pour cantaloupe juice, basil leaves and sweet 'n'
sour into the empty mixing glass. Muddle and
add ice. Pour in the remaining ingredients. Shake
thoroughly and strain contents into a chilled
cocktail glass. Garnish with a lemon twist.

Centaur

Specialty of Stone Rose Lounge
Created by Jeff Isaacson
Rocks glass, chilled
Build in glass
1 tsp. sugar
5 mint leaves
3 drops bitters
Muddle contents
Add ice
1 1/4 oz. Rémy Martin V.S.O.P. Cognac
Fill with ginger ale
Place the sugar, mint and bitters into the empty,
chilled rocks glass. Muddle and add ice. Pour in
the cognac and fill with ginger ale.

Charbay Green Teaze

Specialty of Mosaic Restaurant
Created by Stephanie Kozicki, Deborah Knight
Cocktail glass, chilled
Pour ingredients into an iced mixing glass
2 1/2 oz. Charbay Green Tea Vodka
1/4 oz. Cointreau
1/2 tsp. green tea infused syrup
Shake and strain
Garnish with a lemon twist
Pour ingredients into the iced mixing glass. Shake
thoroughly and strain contents into a chilled
cocktail glass. Garnish with a lemon twist.

Chinatown

Specialty of Indigo Eurasian Cuisine
Created by Jason Castle, Eddie Trongkamsataya
Cocktail glass, chilled
Pour ingredients into an iced mixing glass
3 oz. Yazi Ginger Vodka
1 oz. Hanger One Mandarin Blossom Vodka
Dash vanilla syrup
1 oz. club soda
Shake and strain
Garnish with an orange slice and pickled
    ginger skewered with a wooden stick
    and placed in glass
Pour ingredients into the iced mixing glass.
Shake thoroughly and strain contents into a
chilled cocktail glass. Garnish with an orange
slice and pickled ginger skewered with a wooden
stick and placed in glass.

Comfortable Italian Fortress

Specialty of Rickshaw Far East Bistro & Bambú Lounge
Created by Melvin Espinal
Cocktail glass, chilled
Pour ingredients into an iced mixing glass
1 oz. PAMA Pomegranate Liqueur
1/4 oz. Citadelle Gin
1/4 oz. Amaretto
1/4 oz. Southern Comfort
Splash orange juice
Splash cranberry juice
Shake and strain
Sink a splash of pomegranate juice
Pour ingredients, except the pomegranate juice,
into the iced mixing glass. Shake thoroughly
and strain contents into a chilled cocktail glass.
Carefully sink a splash of pomegranate juice so it
sits in the bottom of the cocktail glass.

Crimson Tea Party

Specialty of 33 Restaurant & Lounge
Created by Jenn Harvey
Cocktail glass, chilled
Pour ingredients into an empty mixing glass
Handful mixed berries
1/2 oz. simple syrup
Muddle contents
Add ice
1 oz. 42 Below Manuka Honey Vodka
1/2 oz. fresh lemon juice
2 oz. crimson berry tea, cooled
Shake and strain
Garnish with a fresh strawberry
Place berries and simple syrup into the empty mixing glass. Muddle and add ice. Pour in the remaining ingredients. Shake thoroughly and strain contents into a chilled cocktail glass. Garnish with a fresh strawberry.

Cure for the Blues

Specialty of Mosaic Restaurant
Created by Stephanie Kozicki, Deborah Knight
Cocktail glass, chilled
Pour ingredients into an iced mixing glass
1 1/2 oz. Absolut Kurant Vodka
1/2 oz. Absolut Vodka
1/4 oz. DeKuyper Blue Curaçao
1/2 oz. G.E. Massenez Crème de Cassis
2 tsp. blueberry puree
Shake and strain
Garnish with 3 fresh blueberries
Pour ingredients into the iced mixing glass. Shake thoroughly and strain contents into a chilled cocktail glass. Garnish with 3 fresh blueberries.

Dark Autumn

Specialty of 33 Restaurant & Lounge
Created by Jenn Harvey
Cocktail glass, chilled
Pour ingredients into an empty mixing glass
Handful blueberries
1/2 oz. Macallan Amber Liqueur
Muddle contents
Add ice
1 oz. Captain Morgan Original Spiced Rum
Splash Rose's Lime Juice
Dash cinnamon
Shake and strain
Garnish with 3 fresh bluberries on a skewer
Place blueberries and Macallan Amber Liqueur into the empty mixing glass. Muddle and add ice. Pour in the remaining ingredients. Shake thoroughly and strain contents into a chilled cocktail glass. Garnish with 3 fresh bluberries on a skewer.

Darkness

Specialty of Rio/ iBaR Lounge
Created by Behnam Gerami
Rocks glass, chilled
Build in glass
8 blackberries
3/4 oz. fresh lime juice
1 oz. rock candy syrup
Muddle contents
Add ice
1 1/2 oz. Effen Black Cherry Vodka
Top with Sprite
Stir gently
Place the blackberries, lime juice and syrup into the empty rocks glass. Muddle and add ice. Pour in the remaining ingredients. Stir gently.

Dixie Swizzle

Specialty of The Campbell Apartment
Created by Mark Grossich
Bucket glass, ice
Build in glass
1 1/4 oz. Jack Daniels Tennessee Whiskey
1 oz. Southern Comfort
1 oz. peach juice
Splash ginger ale
Garnish with an orange twist
Pour ingredients into the iced bucket glass in the order listed. Garnish with an orange twist.

G-spot Tini

Specialty of Bourbon Street & Voodoo Lounge
Created by Matt Spencer
Cocktail glass, chilled
Pour ingredients into an iced mixing glass
1 oz. DeKuyper WilderBerry Schnapps
1 oz. Chambord
3/4 oz. DeKuyper Pucker Grape Schnapps
3/4 oz. DeKuyper Pucker Cheri-Beri Schnapps
Splash cranberry juice
Splash lemon-lime soda
Shake and strain
Garnish with a cherry
Pour ingredients into the iced mixing glass. Shake thoroughly and strain contents into a chilled cocktail glass. Garnish with a cherry dropped into the bottom of the glass.

Tommy's Mexican Restaurant

🏠 **5929 Geary Blvd.**
San Francisco, CA 94121
☎ **415.387.4747**
▶▶ **www.tommysmexican.com**

If you thrive on being in a place filled with people loving the moment, then **Tommy's Mexican Restaurant** is your kind of nightspot. The energy in Tommy's is palpable and absolutely engaging. It's perpetual vibe is a major draw, due in no small measure to the entire Bermejo family. They run Tommy's as if they eat, drink and breathe the place 24/7, which naturally, they lovingly do.

Located in San Francisco's Avenues, Tommy's is a traditionally appointed Mexican restaurant, comfy and brimming with authentic charm. Though the bar only seats seven, the lounge is typically hopping. The back bar is a tiered altar lined with a glorious collection of tequilas, 275 brands and growing. In fact, Tommy's may well be the most respected tequila haunt in the country. Julio Bermejo is a noted authority and an esteemed judge at the San Francisco World Spirits Competition.

Widely unofficially acknowledged as the country's tequila ambassador, Julio has helped put Tommy's Restaurant on the global map.

Another major attraction is the restaurant's sumptuous bill of fare, an offering loaded with favorites like quesadillas, burritos and enchiladas, as well as Yucatan specialties, Ceviche de Tommy and a Bar-B-Q Cheeseburger to die for. Everything is made from scratch, according to family recipes. The service is impeccable, the dining experience memorable.

Tommy's other claim to immortality is the lounge, where the Margarita rules supreme and master mixologist Jacques Bezuidenhout holds court. The bar menu is packed with brilliantly conceived cocktails, signatures such as the *Lilly's Martini*, a specialty crafted with El Tesoro Platinum, Lillet Blanc and muddled grapefruit twists, and the *Besito*, an effervescent quaff of Corazón Tequila Reposado, juices and apricot puree finished with sparkling wine.

It doesn't get more authentic than Tommy's. —RP

Besito
Drink recipe on pg 44

Ginger-Apple Mojito

Specialty of Rickshaw Far East Bistro & Bambú Lounge
Created by Rickshaw's staff
Bucket glass, chilled
Build in glass
2 oz. fresh lime juice
2 oz. simple syrup
1 piece sliced ginger
5 slices green apple, julienne cut
Muddle contents
Add ice
1 1/2 oz. Citadelle Apple Vodka
Top with club soda
Garnish with an apple wheel slice
Pour the lime juice, simple syrup, ginger and apple slices into the empty bucket glass. Muddle and add ice. Pour in the vodka and top with club soda. Garnish with an apple wheel slice.

Ginger Jimmy

Specialty of Mosaic Restaurant
Created by Stephanie Kozicki
Bucket glass, chilled
Build in glass
4 mint leaves
2 tbsp. simple syrup
Muddle contents
Fill with crushed ice
1 1/2 oz. Jim Beam Black Bourbon
2 oz. Reed's Premium Ginger Brew
Garnish with a fresh mint sprig
Place mint leaves and simple syrup into the empty, chilled bucket glass. Muddle and fill with crushed ice. Pour in remaining ingredients. Garnish with a fresh mint sprig.

"The creative pairing of spirits and liqueurs is a bonafide art form."

Navan™ Vanille Cognac Liqueur

Marnier-Lapostolle has mastered the art of infusing aged Fine Champagne cognacs with flavor. In the case of world-class Grand Marnier it is an infusion of Haitian orange peels. Now they've expanded their horizons with the release of ***Navan Vanille Cognac Liqueur***, a sensationally delicious liqueur.

Made in Neauphle-le-Château, Cognac, Navan is crafted from a base of cognacs obtained exclusively from the preeminent Grande and Petite Champagne growing regions. The aged Fine Champagne cognac is then infused with black vanilla from Madagascar, the fruit of the orchid and the rarest, most expensive spice after saffron. The assemblage is then further aged to allow the flavors in the liqueur to fully integrate. It is bottled at 80-proof.

Navan is a magnificent, delicately balanced masterpiece. The liqueur has an amber hue with gold highlights and a smooth, light body. After a few minutes the generous, slightly sweet bouquet brings forth the irresistible aromas of vanilla and spice with subtle notes of brandy. The palate is largely dominated by the flavor of the vanilla, but the alcohol expertly balances its sweetness and the character of the cognac eventually shines through. The finish is long and gloriously flavorful.

Navan is ideally showcased in a heated snifter, or on the rocks. Its balance and expansive flavor though make the classy liqueur a natural for featuring in signature cocktails. Navan is certainly the most impressive palindrome ever concocted.

Grapefruit Basil Limeade

Specialty of Stone Rose Lounge
Created by Jeff Isaacson
Bucket glass, chilled
Build in glass
1/2 oz. simple syrup
3 large basil leaves
Muddle contents
Add ice
2 1/2 oz. No. TEN by Tanqueray
3/4 oz. grapefruit juice
Garnish with cracked basil leaves
Pour simple syrup and basil leaves into the empty bucket glass. Muddle and add ice. Pour in the remaining ingredients. Garnish with cracked basil leaves.

Green Tea Cooler

Specialty of Ibiza Dinner Club
Created by Ibiza's staff
Bucket glass, ice
Pour ingredients into an empty mixing glass
4 orange wedges
Muddle contents
Add ice
1 oz. Charbay Green Tea Vodka
1/2 oz. fresh lemon sour mix
Shake and strain
Top with club soda
Garnish with a lemon wedge
Place the orange wedges into the empty mixing glass. Muddle and add ice. Pour in the vodka and sour mix. Shake thoroughly and strain contents into an iced bucket glass. Top with club soda. Garnish with a lemon wedge.

The Inferno

Specialty of Bookmarks
Created by Jonathan Pogash
Collins glass, ice
Pour ingredients into an iced mixing glass
1 1/2 oz. Belvedere Vodka
1/2 oz. Campari
3/4 oz. White Crème de Cacao
2-3 dashes Tabasco Pepper Sauce
Shake and strain
Top with club soda
Stir gently
Garnish with a cherry
Pour ingredients, except the club soda, into the iced mixing glass. Shake thoroughly and strain contents into an iced collins glass. Top with club soda. Stir gently. Garnish with a cherry.

Irin Jaya

Specialty of Cyrus
Created by Scott Beattie
House specialty glass, chilled
Pour ingredients into an iced mixing glass
3/4 oz. Hangar One Kaffir Lime Vodka
3/4 oz. Hangar One Straight Vodka
4 Kaffir lime leaves, thinly sliced
5 fresh fresno chili rings, seeded
10 pieces candied lemongrass rings*
1/2 oz. fresh lime juice
Shake thoroughly - do not strain
Fill with ginger beer
Pour ingredients, except the ginger beer, into the iced mixing glass. Shake thoroughly - do not strain - pour contents into an empty, chilled house specialty glass. Leave room and add about 3 oz of ginger beer. This is a very spicy drink, adjust chili to taste.
*Candied Lemongrass Recipe - pg 318

J BAR Espana

Specialty of J BAR
Created by Desiree Rios
Cocktail glass, chilled
Pour ingredients into an iced mixing glass
1 1/2 oz. Licor 43 Cuarenta y Tres
3/4 oz. Alizé Red Passion
Splash pineapple juice
Splash orange juice
Shake and strain
Garnish with an orange wheel
Pour ingredients into the iced mixing glass. Shake thoroughly and strain contents into a chilled cocktail glass. Garnish with an orange wheel.

Jelly Drama

Specialty of Indigo Eurasian Cuisine
Created by Jason Castle, Jonathan Schwalbenite
Cocktail glass, chilled
Pour ingredients into an iced mixing glass
3 oz. Absolut Mandarin Vodka
Splash Midori
Splash sweet 'n' sour
Splash club soda
2 tsp. grape jelly
Shake and strain
Garnish with a red grape on a wooden skewer
Pour ingredients into the iced mixing glass. Shake vigorously to thoroughly mix jelly and strain contents into a chilled cocktail glass. Garnish with a red grape on a wooden skewer.

Kalamansi Breeze

Specialty of Mosaic Restaurant
Created by Stephanie Kozicki, Deborah Knight
Cocktail glass, chilled
Pour ingredients into an iced mixing glass
2 oz. Charbay Meyer Lemon Vodka
¹/₄ oz. Triple Sec
2 tsp. ginger infused syrup
1 oz. calamansi juice
Shake and strain
Garnish with a Kaffir lime leaf
Pour ingredients into the iced mixing glass. Shake thoroughly and strain contents into a chilled cocktail glass. Garnish with a Kaffir lime leaf.

"The degree of innovation demonstrated behind bars today rivals the creative output of any previous generation."

Belvedere® Cytrus Vodka

One of the pervasive megatrends pertaining to our drinking habits is that we consumers want cocktails with flavor, loads of fresh, true to fruit flavor. One certain way to satisfy this seemingly insatiable desire is to grab a bottle of *Belvedere Cytrus Vodka* and get pouring. It's a classy example of how much flavor a flavored vodka can wallop.

Super-premium Belvedere Cytrus is made at the Polmos Distillery in Zyrardów, Poland. The vodka is distilled from premium rye and underground spring water first in an alembic still and then triple-distilled in a continuous still. Those spirits are macerated with lemons grown in Murica, Spain and limes cultivated in southeastern Spain. The maceration is distilled using low heat in a small copper pot still. Finally, the flavored vodka is rigorously filtered through a complex of carbon screens rendering it free of any trace congeners, or impurities. It is bottled at 80-proof.

Belvedere Cytrus is a simply sensational. The spirit has crystal clarity, a silky, feather-weight body and a generous, citrus-laced bouquet. Upon entry the vodka generates some heat and fills the mouth with a spry, almost tart set of lemon and lime flavors. The finish is crisp, clean and slightly bitter from the macerated pith.

The popular range also includes *Belvedere Pomarancza Vodka*, a superb flavored spirit distilled with the essential oils of Spanish mandarins and limes and Moroccan oranges. Produced in the same artisan manner as Cytrus, the Pomarancza is a gem quality vodka.

La Dolce Vita

Specialty of Marcus' Martini Heaven
Created by Marcus' Staff
House specialty glass, chilled
Pour ingredients into an iced mixing glass
1 ¹/₂ oz. Campari
1 ¹/₂ oz. Gin
2 oz. fresh orange juice
Shake and strain
Garnish with an orange twist
Pour ingredients into the iced mixing glass. Shake thoroughly and strain contents into a chilled house specialty glass. Garnish with an orange twist.

La Perla

Specialty of Tommy's Mexican Restaurant
Created by Jacques Bezuidenhout
Cocktail glass, chilled
Pour ingredients into an iced mixing glass
1 ¹/₂ oz. Gran Centenario Reposado Tequila
1 ¹/₂ oz. Domecq Manzanilla Sherry
³/₄ oz. Mathilde Poire d'Anjou Liqueur
Shake and strain
Garnish with a lemon twist
Pour ingredients into the iced mixing glass. Shake thoroughly and strain contents into a chilled cocktail glass. Garnish with a lemon twist.

Mango Gem

Specialty of The Carnegie Club
Created by Kenneth McClure
Cocktail glass, chilled
Pour ingredients into an empty mixing glass
2 tsp. cubed mango
1 oz. Mango Liqueur
Muddle contents
Add ice
2 oz. Bombay Sapphire Gin
Shake and strain
Top with lemon-lime soda
Garnish with a mango slice
Pour ingredients into the iced mixing glass. Shake thoroughly and strain contents into a chilled cocktail glass. Garnish with a mango slice.

Melon Bull Martini

Specialty of The Original McCormick & Schmick's
Created by Geoff V. Helzer
Cocktail glass, chilled
Pour ingredients into an iced mixing glass
1 ¹/₄ oz. Smirnoff Vodka
¹/₄ oz. DeKuyper Pucker Watermelon Schnapps
3-4 oz. Red Bull Energy Drink
Shake and strain
Garnish with a lime twist
Pour ingredients into the iced mixing glass. Shake thoroughly and strain contents into a chilled cocktail glass. Garnish with a lime twist.

Meyer Beautiful

Specialty of Cyrus
Created by Scott Beattie
Lemon zest and sugar rimmed
    cocktail glass, chilled
Pour ingredients into an iced mixing glass
³/₄ oz. Hangar One Straight Vodka
³/₄ oz. Charbay Meyer Lemon Vodka
¹/₂ oz. Elderflower syrup
1 ¹/₂ oz. fresh Meyer lemon juice
Shake and strain
Pour ingredients into the iced mixing glass. Shake thoroughly and strain contents into a lemon zest and sugar rimmed, chilled cocktail glass.

Miami Ice

Specialty of Yard House
Created by Kip Snider, Tracey Carlyle
Oversized cocktail glass, chilled
Pour ingredients into an iced mixing glass
1 ¹/₂ oz. Stoli Persik Vodka
³/₄ oz. Malibu Pineapple Rum
³/₄ oz. DeKuyper Peachtree Schnapps
Splash sweet 'n' sour
Splash Sprite
Shake and strain
Sink ¹/₂ oz. DeKuyper Pucker
    Island Blue Schnapps
Pour ingredients, except the Pucker, into the iced mixing glass. Shake thoroughly and strain contents into a chilled, oversized cocktail glass. Sink DeKuyper Pucker Island Blue Schnapps into the bottom of the glass.

Mujer Verde

Specialty of Absinthe Brasserie & Bar
Created by Raul Tamayo
Cocktail glass, chilled
Pour ingredients into an iced mixing glass
1 1/2 oz. Hendrick's Gin
1/2 oz. Green Chartreuse
1/4 oz. Yellow Chartreuse
1/2 oz. fresh lime juice
Shake and strain
Garnish with a long lime twist
Pour ingredients into the iced mixing glass. Shake thoroughly and strain contents into a chilled cocktail glass. Garnish with a long lime twist.

Nazdarovie

Specialty of Mosaic Restaurant
Created by Stephanie Kozicki, Matt Rinn
Cocktail glass, chilled
Pour ingredients into an iced mixing glass
2 oz. Jewel of Russia Wild Bilberry
    Infusion Vodka
1/2 oz. Grand Marnier
1 oz. English breakfast tea, cooled
Shake and strain
Garnish with a lemon twist
Pour ingredients into the iced mixing glass. Shake thoroughly and strain contents into a chilled cocktail glass. Garnish with a lemon twist.

Not Too Far East

Specialty of P.F. Chang's China Bistro
Created by P.F. Chang's staff
House specialty glass, ice
Build in glass
1 1/2 oz. Navan Vanille Cognac Liqueur
1 oz. sweet 'n' sour
3 oz. citrus spice tea, cooled
Stir gently
Float 3/4 oz. Malibu Pineapple Rum
Garnish with a lemon twist and fresh berries
Pour ingredients, except the Malibu Pineapple, into the iced house specialty glass in the order listed. Stir gently. Float with Malibu Pineapple. Garnish with a lemon twist and fresh berries.

Olallie Golightly

Specialty of Cyrus
Created by Scott Beattie
Collins glass, chilled
Pour ingredients into an empty mixing glass
3-4 Anise Hyssop leaves, chiffonade
5 Olallieberries
Muddle contents
Add ice
3/4 oz. Hangar One Fraser River
    Raspberry Vodka
3/4 oz. Hangar One Straight Vodka
3/4 oz. fresh lemon juice
3/4 oz. Hyssop simple syrup*
Shake thoroughly - do not strain
5-10 borage flowers
1 oz. club soda
Stir
Place the chiffonade and berries into the empty mixing glass. Muddle and add ice. Shake thoroughly - do not strain - add flowers and club soda. Stir gently. Pour contents into an empty, chilled collins glass.
*Hyssop Simple Syrup Recipe
    Combine 1 quart simple syrup with 6 drops Hyssop essential oil. Shake well.

Orange Crush

Specialty of J BAR
Created by Stephen Cutler
Cocktail glass, chilled
Pour ingredients into an iced mixing glass
1 1/2 oz. Charbay Blood Orange Vodka
1/2 oz. Alizé Red Passion
1 oz. fresh orange juice
Shake and strain
Garnish with an orange slice
Pour ingredients into the iced mixing glass. Shake thoroughly and strain contents into a chilled cocktail glass. Garnish with an orange slice.

P.I.A.

Specialty of Rickshaw Far East Bistro & Bambú Lounge
Created by Melvin Espinal, Jessica Bradshaw
Cocktail glass, chilled
Pour ingredients into an iced mixing glass
1 1/2 oz. Charbay Blood Orange Vodka
1 oz. Godiva White Chocolate Liqueur
10-12 melted milk chocolate chips
Splash orange blossom water
Shake and strain
Garnish with a chocolate dipped
    orange segment
Pour ingredients into the iced mixing glass. Shake thoroughly and strain contents into a chilled cocktail glass. Garnish with a chocolate dipped orange segment.

The World Bar

The Trump World Tower
845 United Nations Plaza
New York, NY 10017
☎ **212.935.9361**
▶▶◀ **www.hospitalityholdings.com**
✉ **info@hospitalityholdings.com**

Located on the ground floor of the Trump World Tower, the tallest and among the most expensive residential buildings in the world, The World Bar redefines posh and cosmopolitan sophistication. Like a place featured on the pages of *Architectural Digest*, the cocktail lounge is so magnificently elegant, the natural inclination is to slip off your shoes before entering.

The World Bar features design elements such as 35-foot ceilings, wood paneled walls, towering curtained windows and a floating interior mezzanine that overlooks the United Nations and its beautifully manicured gardens. The understated decor

in the two level room is done in a gold tone color scheme with brass Giacometti-style cocktail tables, banquettes with matching ottomans, dramatic custom lighting fixtures, sleek, modernistic chairs and low upholstered sofas. The overall effect is striking.

The East Side landmark is a popular nightlife destination, due in no small part to its ultra-luxurious, cocktail party atmosphere. The clientele makes for a beautiful crowd, a shifting mix of foreign diplomats and ambassadors, building residents, celebrities and upwardly mobile New Yorkers.

The World Bar offers an extensive selection of vintage wines, Champagnes, spirits and cigars. The bar's repertoire of cocktail specialties is equally impressive. The magnificent *World Cocktail* is concocted with Rémy Martin XO Cognac, white grape juice, bitters and Pineau des Charentes and a fill of Veuve Cliquot Champagne. Other creatively inspired signatures include *The Ambassador*, an elegant blend of Stoli Razberi, Grand Marnier, Blue Curaçao and fresh citrus, and the *Sake Blossom*, which combines lychee puree and Gekkeikan Sparkling Sake.

The World Bar is a superlative cocktail lounge and registered hangout for international jet setters. If you're looking for a memorable evening with the rich and famous, this is the place. —RP

The Ambassador

Drink recipe on pg 44

The Page Turner

Specialty of Bookmarks
Created by Kenneth McClure
Sugar rimmed cocktail glass, chilled
Pour ingredients into an iced mixing glass
2 oz. Beefeater Gin
1/2 oz. Triple Sec
Splash lime juice
1 oz. lychee puree
Shake and strain
Garnish with a lime wedge
Pour ingredients into the iced mixing glass. Shake thoroughly and strain contents into a sugar rimmed, chilled cocktail glass. Garnish with a lime wedge.

Passion

Specialty of Harry Denton's Starlight Room
Created by Jacques Bezuidenhout
Cocktail glass, chilled
Pour ingredients into an iced mixing glass
1 3/4 oz. Plymouth Gin
1/4 oz. Campari
1/4 oz. Mandarine Napoléon
1 3/4 oz. passion fruit juice or coulis
Garnish with peel of a whole lime cut
    into a horse's neck
Pour ingredients into the iced mixing glass. Shake thoroughly and strain contents into a chilled cocktail glass. Garnish with a peel of a whole lime cut in a horse's neck.
NOTE: If using passion fruit coulis taste for tartness and add simple syrup to taste.

> "Quality is the factor that decidedly favors today's drinks."

Pyrat® XO Reserve Rum

Located five miles north of St. Maarten, Anguilla is a scant 35-square miles in area. The tiny island is the home of Anguilla Rums, Ltd., maker of renowned alembic spirits, including *Pyrat XO Reserve Rum*, one of the best kept secrets in the Caribbean.

Introduced in 1998, Pyrat XO Reserve is a blend of nine pot-distilled rums aged in French oak barrels according to the Solera aging system. The blend ranges in age from 8 to 40 years. After aging, the rum is reduced in proof using coral-filtered spring water and bottled at 80-proof.

Pyrat XO Reserve is a genuine treat from start to finish. The rum has a lustrous amber color and a soft, medium-weight body. The broad, expansive bouquet is enticing, offering the comforting aromas of vanilla, allspice and molasses. The XO Reserve is exceptionally smooth upon entry and then builds in intensity, quickly filling the mouth with a warming palate and an array of savory flavors, including cinnamon, vanilla, caramel and a hint of honey. The finish is long, warm and sophisticated.

Introduced in 1998, *Pyrat Pistol Rum* is made from the same nine, barrel-aged alembic rums used to make XO Reserve, however, the proportion of each rum is different. Pyrat Pistol is purposely blended to be lighter than either the XO Reserve or Cask 1623.

The crown jewel of the line is the limited release *Pyrat Cask 1623 Rum*, an assertive rum, brimming with high ester character and taste. This luxurious and sophisticated rum has a palate and finish similar to that of an upper echelon cognac.

Peach Fuzz
Specialty of Backstreet Café
Created by Sean Black
Cocktail glass, chilled
Pour ingredients into an iced mixing glass
1 1/2 oz. Absolut Apeach Vodka
1/3 oz. Campari
1/4 oz. Cointreau
Splash club soda
Splash simple syrup
1 1/2 oz. fresh orange juice
Garnish with an orange slice
Pour ingredients into the iced mixing glass. Shake thoroughly and strain contents into a chilled cocktail glass. Garnish with an orange slice.

Pelo del Perro
Specialty of Cyrus
Created by Scott Beattie
Tall house specialty glass, ice
Pour ingredients into an empty mixing glass
500mg B-12 pill, crushed
Add ice
3/4 oz. Hangar One Straight Vodka
3/4 oz. Charbay Ruby Red Grapefruit Vodka
1/2 oz. agave nectar
1/2 oz. fresh lime juice
1/2 oz. fresh pink grapefruit juice
Shake and strain
Crush the 500mg B-12 vitamin capsule or pill in the bottom of the empty mixing glass. Add ice. Pour in the remaining ingredients. Shake thoroughly and strain contents into an iced, tall house specialty glass.

Perfect 10 Martini
Specialty of Backstreet Café
Created by Sean Beck
Cocktail glass, chilled
Pour ingredients into an iced mixing glass
2 oz. No. TEN by Tanqueray Gin
1/4 oz. Cointreau
1/4 oz. orange juice
1/4 oz. Santa Cruz Wild Berry Juice
1 oz. POM Pomegranate Juice
Shake and strain
Garnish with pomegranate seeds
    and an orange twist
Pour ingredients into the iced mixing glass. Shake thoroughly and strain contents into a chilled cocktail glass. Garnish with pomegranate seeds in the bottom of the glass and an orange twist.

Plum Dandy
Specialty of Cyrus
Created by Scott Beattie
Collins glass, chilled
Pour ingredients into an empty mixing glass
5 peppermint leaves
Muddle lightly
Add ice
3/4 oz. Hangar One Mandarin Blossom Vodka
3/4 oz. Hangar One Straight Vodka
3/4 oz. Choya Plum Wine with Ume Fruit
Splash Chinese five-spiced honey*
Splash lemongrass simple syrup*
3/4 oz. fresh lemon juice
5 pieces preserved cherry
Shake and strain
Garnish with 10 star jasmine flowers
Place the mint leaves into the empty mixing glass. Muddle lightly and add ice. Pour in the remaining ingredients. Shake thoroughly and strain contents into an iced collins glass. Garnish with 10 star jasmine flowers.
*Lemongrass Simple Syrup Recipe - pg 321
*Chinese Five-Spiced Honey Recipe - pg 318

Puebla Peach
Specialty of The Spanish Kitchen
Created by Kanani Kroll
Sugar rimmed cocktail glass, chilled
Pour ingredients into an iced mixing glass
1 1/2 oz. Stoli Persik Vodka
Splash sweet 'n' sour
2 oz. mango puree
2 oz. Sprite
Shake and strain
Garnish with a peach slice
Pour ingredients into the iced mixing glass. Shake thoroughly and strain contents into a sugar rimmed, chilled cocktail glass. Garnish with a peach slice.

Purple People Eater

Specialty of Dave & Buster's
Created by D & B Mixologists in Providence, RI
Blue raspberry sugar rimmed
    cocktail glass, chilled
Pour ingredients into an iced mixing glass
1 oz. Stoli Ohranj Vodka
1/2 oz. HPNOTIQ
1/2 oz. DeKuyper Pucker Island
    Blue Schnapps
1/4 oz. sweet 'n' sour
1 oz. cranberry juice
Shake and strain
Sink 1/4 oz. HPNOTIQ
Garnish with a cherry
Pour ingredients, except the HPNOTIQ, into the iced mixing glass. Shake thoroughly and strain contents into a blue raspberry sugar rimmed, chilled cocktail glass. Sink the HPNOTIQ. Garnish with a cherry.

Rhubarbarella

Specialty of Cyrus
Created by Scott Beattie
Collins glass, chilled
Pour ingredients into an iced mixing glass
3/4 oz. Hangar One Citron
    "Buddha's Hand" Vodka
3/4 oz. Hangar One Straight Vodka
1/2 oz. fresh lemon juice
1/2 oz. ginger/rhubarb simple syrup*
5 shiso leaves, chiffonade
10 candied rhubarb pieces,
    from the simple syrup
Shake thoroughly - do not strain
Fill with Cock 'n Bull Ginger Beer
Stir
Pour ingredients, except the ginger beer, into the iced mixing glass. Shake thoroughly - do not strain - pour contents into an empty, chilled collins glass. Top with ginger beer. Stir gently.
*Ginger/Rhubarb Simple
    Syrup Recipe - pg 319

Rusty Ale

Specialty of Savoy
Created by Eric Scheffer, Ricky Shriner
Cocktail glass, chilled
Pour ingredients into an iced mixing glass
2 1/2 oz. Maker's Mark Bourbon
1/2 oz. Drambuie
1/2 oz. ginger ale
Shake and strain
Garnish with an orange twist
Pour ingredients into the iced mixing glass. Shake thoroughly and strain contents into a chilled cocktail glass. Garnish with an orange twist.

Southwest Seasons

Specialty of Jade Bar
Created by Justin Reed
Cocktail glass, chilled
Pour ingredients into an iced mixing glass
3 oz. Hangar One Kaffir Lime Vodka
2 stalks cilantro
Three dashes lemongrass simple syrup*
Splash cranberry juice
1/2 oz. fresh lime juice
Shake and strain
Garnish with a lime wedge
Pour ingredients into the iced mixing glass. Shake thoroughly and strain contents into a chilled cocktail glass. Garnish with a lime wedge.
*Lemongrass Simple Syrup Recipe - pg 321

Starlight

Specialty of Harry Denton's Starlight Room
Created by Tony Abou-Ganim
Cocktail glass, chilled
Pour ingredients into an iced mixing glass
1 1/2 oz. Campari
3/4 oz. Cointreau
1 oz. fresh orange juice
1 oz. fresh lemon sour mix
Shake and strain
Fill with club soda
Stir
Float with Hennessey Privilège V.S.O.P. Cognac
Garnish with a lemon and lime wheel
Pour ingredients, except the club soda and cognac, into the iced mixing glass. Shake thoroughly and strain contents into a chilled cocktail glass. Top with club soda and stir gently. Float the cognac. Garnish with a lemon and lime wheel.

Summer Twilight

Specialty of The Refectory Restaurant & Bistro
Created by Julie Mulisano, Paula Meyers
Cocktail glass, chilled
Pour ingredients into an iced mixing glass
1 oz. Stoli Ohranj Vodka
1 oz. Vox Raspberry Vodka
1/4 oz. Blue Curaçao
3 oz. Nantucket Nectar Lemonade
Shake and strain
Garnish with a lemon wheel
Pour ingredients into the iced mixing glass. Shake thoroughly and strain contents into a chilled cocktail glass. Garnish with a lemon wheel.

Sunsplash

Specialty of Harry Denton's Starlight Room
Created by Tony Abou-Ganim
House specialty glass, ice
Pour ingredients into an iced mixing glass
1 1/2 oz. Belvedere Pomarancza Vodka
1/2 oz. Cointreau
1 oz. fresh lemon sour mix
1 1/2 oz. fresh orange juice
1 1/2 oz. cranberry juice
Shake and strain
Garnish with an orange slice
    and lemon spiral twist
Pour ingredients into the iced mixing glass. Shake thoroughly and strain contents into an iced house specialty glass. Garnish with an orange slice and lemon spiral twist.

Tartini

Specialty of Brûlée the Dessert Experience
Created by Peter Van Thiel
Cocktail glass, chilled
Pour ingredients into an iced mixing glass
1 1/4 oz. Chambord
1 1/4 oz. Stoli Razberi Vodka
1 1/4 oz. cranberry juice
Handful fresh raspberries
1 tsp. sugar
Shake and strain
Garnish with a lime wedge
    and fresh raspberry
Pour ingredients into the iced mixing glass. Shake thoroughly and strain contents into a chilled cocktail glass. Garnish with a lime wedge and fresh raspberry.

Thai Bojito

Specialty of 33 Restaurant & Lounge
Created by Jenn Harvey
Bucket glass, chilled
Build in glass
3-4 basil leaves
1/2 oz. simple syrup
Muddle contents
Add ice
1 1/2 oz. Hanger One Kaffir Lime Vodka
1/2 oz. coconut milk
Fill with club soda
Garnish with a Kaffir lime wedge
Place the basil leaves and simple syrup into the empty, chilled bucket glass. Muddle and add ice. Pour in the remaining ingredients. Garnish with a Kaffir lime wedge.

Tony Soprano

Specialty of Indigo Eurasian Cuisine
Created by Tim Skelton, Jason Castle
Bucket glass, ice
Build in glass
2 oz. Tuaca Liquore Italiano
1 oz. Disaronno Amaretto
2 oz. pineapple juice
1 oz. sweet 'n' sour
Pour ingredients into the iced bucket glass in the order listed.

Tuaca Berry Blast

Specialty of Yard House
Created by Kip Snider
Pint glass, ice
Pour ingredients into an iced mixing glass
1 oz. Finlandia Wild Berry Fusion Vodka
3/4 oz. Tuaca Liquore Italiano
3/4 oz. Midori
1 oz. Sprite
2 oz. cranberry juice
2 oz. fresh lemon sour mix
Shake and strain
Garnish with a cherry
Pour ingredients into the iced mixing glass. Shake thoroughly and strain contents into an iced pint glass. Garnish with a cherry.

Tupelo Tea

Specialty of Mosaic Restaurant
Created by Stephanie Kozicki
Cocktail glass, chilled
Pour ingredients into an iced mixing glass
1 1/2 oz. Hanger One Straight Vodka
1/4 oz. DeKuyper Peachtree Schnapps
1 tsp. Tupelo honey
1/2 oz. cranberry juice
1 oz. ginger peach tea, cooled
Shake and strain
Garnish with a lemon twist
Pour ingredients into the iced mixing glass. Shake thoroughly and strain contents into a chilled cocktail glass. Garnish with a lemon twist.

Vanilla Rum Crusta

Specialty of Absinthe Brasserie & Bar
Created by Jonny Raglin
Sugar rimmed wine glass, chilled
Pour ingredients into an iced mixing glass
2 oz. Charbay Tahitian Vanilla Bean Rum
1/2 oz. Cointreau
1/2 oz. Luxardo Maraschino Liqueur
1/4 oz. simple syrup
3/4 oz. fresh lemon juice
Shake and strain
Garnish with a horse's neck lemon twist*
    made from a whole lemon
Pour ingredients into the iced mixing glass. Shake thoroughly and strain contents into a sugar rimmed, chilled wine glass. Garnish with a horse's neck lemon twist made from a whole lemon.
*Horse's Neck Lemon Twist
Twist the entire lemon over the cocktail and drape the twist so it is hanging out the cocktail on two ends.

Voo-Ju

Specialty of Savoy
Created by Judy Mann
Cocktail glass, chilled
Pour ingredients into an iced mixing glass
1 1/2 oz. Malibu Rum
1 1/2 oz. Stoli Vanil Vodka
Splash fresh lime juice
1/2 oz. pineapple juice
Shake and strain
Garnish with a drop of Midori in center
    of the glass
Pour ingredients into the iced mixing glass. Shake thoroughly and strain contents into a chilled cocktail glass. Garnish with a drop of Midori in the center of the glass.

W.H. Taft Apple-tini

Specialty of The Mission Inn Hotel & Spa
Created by Alan Lee
Cocktail glass, chilled
Pour ingredients into an iced mixing glass
1 3/4 oz. DeKuyper Pucker Sour Apple Schnapps
1 1/4 oz. Vox Green Apple Vodka
1/2 oz. lemon-lime soda
3/4 oz. fresh lime sour mix
Shake and strain
Pour ingredients into the iced mixing glass. Shake thoroughly and strain contents into a chilled cocktail glass.

Wandering Poet

Specialty of Mosaic Restaurant
Created by Stephanie Kozicki, Deborah Knight
Cocktail glass, chilled
Pour ingredients into an iced mixing glass
1 1/2 oz. Hanger One Citron
    "Buddha's Hand" Vodka
1 1/2 oz. Rihaku Wandering Poet
    Junmai Ginjo Sake
1 oz. DeKuyper Triple Sec
1/4 oz. yuzu juice
Shake and strain
Garnish with a lemon twist
Pour ingredients into the iced mixing glass. Shake thoroughly and strain contents into a chilled cocktail glass. Garnish with a lemon twist.

Watermelon Gin Fizz

Specialty of Mosaic Restaurant
Created by Stephanie Kozicki
Cocktail glass, chilled
Pour ingredients into an iced mixing glass
2 oz. Tanqueray Gin
1/2 oz. Cointreau
1/2 oz. Lorina Sparkling Pink Lemonade
1 oz. watermelon puree
Shake and strain
Garnish with a fresh watermelon wedge
Pour ingredients into the iced mixing glass. Shake thoroughly and strain contents into a chilled cocktail glass. Garnish with a fresh watermelon wedge.

Yard House

Irvine Spectrum
71 Fortune Dr.
Irvine, CA 92618
☎ **949.753.9373**
▶▶ **www.yardhouse.com**

Many places profess to have something for everyone, only to fall far short of the claim. The Yard House, on the other hand, makes no such claims, but does have something cool and delicious that would satisfy the wants of any American with a pulse.

The upscale, casual restaurant features an open design with a contrasting mix of warm woods, stainless steel accents, original artwork, plush booths and ample seating. The space is dominated by a large, wooden, oval-shaped bar sporting an

amazing array of draft beer tap handles, which depending on the location can easily reach 250 different brands. There are even windows into the restaurant's massive keg room and its 400+ barrels and fittings.

The Yard House food menu pays homage to America's favorite foods, including individual size pizzas, seafood, steaks, ribs, chops and pastas. Among the house specialties is the comfort classic (Mac & Cheese)[2], a tempting dish made with roasted chicken breast, bacon, wild mushrooms, cheddar and Parmesan cheese with castellane pasta. It's a soul satisfying dish.

The draft menu at the Yard House reads like a Who's Who of the beer world. For guests looking to try something new, the restaurant offers a six-pack flight of beers presented in smaller glassware to facilitate responsible sampling. In addition, the bar promotes draft beer floats, divinely inspired concoctions such as Lindeman's Framboise with vanilla ice cream.

The bar is also known for their stellar drink specialties, including the popular favorite *Bikini Tini*, a fanciful cocktail starring Cruzan Banana and Malibu Pineapple rums and RémyRed Red Berry Infusion.

Seriously great food, lively atmosphere, scores of flat screen TVs, a nearly unlimited selection of the world's finest beers, and an extensive offering of groovy drinks make the Yard House an unpretentious, national treasure. —RP

Bikini Tini
Drink recipe on pg 124

Watermelon & Raspberry Over Kiwi

Specialty of Joe's Seafood, Prime Steak & Stone Crab
Created by Dan Barringer
Cocktail glass, chilled
Pour ingredients into an iced mixing glass
Step 1.
Bottom layer
3/4 oz. Grey Goose Vodka
1/2 oz. agave nectar
2 oz. fresh kiwi juice
Shake and strain
Step 2.
Top Layer
1 oz. Bacardi Razz Rum
1 1/2 oz. fresh pureed raspberries, strained
3 oz. fresh watermelon juice
Shake and strain
Garnish with a fresh cut watermelon slice
"Step 1." Pour the vodka, agave nectar and kiwi juice into the iced mixing glass. Shake thoroughly and strain contents into a chilled cocktail glass. "Step 2." Pour the rum, raspberries and watermelon juice into an iced mixing glass. Shake thoroughly and add to the prepared drink, pouring the contents over the back of a bar spoon, to create a separate layer. Garnish with a fresh watermelon slice.

Waverly Street Echo

Specialty of Cyrus
Created by Scott Beattie
Collins glass, ice
Pour ingredients into an empty mixing glass
1/2 oz. Chinese five-spiced honey*
1/2 oz. Meyer lemon juice
1/2 oz. pixie mandarin juice
1 tsp. lavender flowers
Muddle contents
Add ice
3/4 oz. Hangar One Mandarin Blossom Vodka
3/4 oz. Hangar One Straight Vodka
Shake and strain
Fill with club soda
Pour the honey, lemon and mandarine juices, and lavender flowers into the empty mixing glass. Muddle and add ice. Pour in the remaining ingredients. Shake thoroughly and strain contents into an iced collins glass. Top with club soda.
*Chinese Five-Spiced Honey Recipe - pg 318

Agave Simple Syrup Recipe

$1/3$ part agave nectar
$1/3$ part bottled water
$1/3$ part simple syrup

Combine ingredients and bring to a slow heat as you would to make simple syrup. Once the liquids have combined, leave to cool. Do not bring to a boil. Agave nectar can be found in any Whole Foods or quality food store. Refrigerate in a glass container.

Ancho Caramel Sauce Recipe

2 cups sugar
$1/3$ cup water
$1/4$ cup light corn syrup
1 pint heavy cream
1 ancho chili, seeded and chopped
Chopped ancho to taste

Cook sugar, corn syrup and water in large, stainless steal, heavy bottom pot. Wash down sides with cold water often. Do not stir. Cook until sugar caramelizes and is light golden brown. Meanwhile, heat cream and chopped ancho to boil. Shock sugar mixture in an ice bath until it stops bubbling. VERY SLOWLY add cream and stir to dissolve. Return to heat and reduce until caramel coats the back of a spoon. Cool in a bath. When cool, strain out the chopped ancho.

Anjou Pear Puree Recipe

6 Anjou pears
2 oz. fresh lime juice
2 oz. simple syrup
Splash Calvados

Peel, core and cut the 6 pears into slices. Place in a blender with 2 oz. fresh lime juice, 2 oz. simple syrup and a splash of Calvados. Blend thoroughly. Store in a glass container and keep refrigerated.

Apple Simple Syrup Recipe

2-4 Rome Delight apples, peeled and cored
12 oz. prepared simple syrup

Steep apple skins and cores in simple syrup for an hour. Leave to cool and then strain. Store in a sealed glass container.

Apricot-Infused Bombay Gin Recipe

1 liter Bombay Gin
1 lb. apricots

Steep apricots in gin for at least three days in a sealed glass container.

Apricot Nectar Puree Recipe

Juice of two lemons
Juice of four limes
4 oz. rock candy syrup
30 oz. The Perfect Puree Apricot Puree,
   Napa Valley
2 egg whites (pasteurized)

Combine ingredients, stir thoroughly and strain though a cheese cloth. Keep refrigerated.

Armagnac Infusion Recipe

1 bottle 1979 Chateau de Ravignan
   Bas Armagnac
2 cups black raisins
Peel of a whole orange
One Madagascar vanilla bean

Infuse in a sealed glass jar for one week or to taste to get a careful balance of Armagnac, raisins, orange, and a hint of vanilla. Keep refrigerated.

Basil Syrup

6 oz. basil leaves
4 oz. corn syrup

Blanch the basil quickly in boiling, salted water and shock in ice water. Squeeze out all excess water. Thoroughly puree the basil with corn syrup and strain through a fine mesh strainer or cheese cloth. Store in a glass container and refrigerate.

Berry Mix and Juice Recipe

2 oz. strawberries
2 oz. raspberries
2 oz. blackberries
2 oz. blueberries
2 oz. simple syrup
8 oz. fresh lime juice
13 oz. Santa Cruz Wild Berry Juice
Puree 1 oz. of each berry in a blender. Mix in the lime juice, Santa Cruz Wild Berry Juice and simple syrup. Once mixed, run the juice through a fine mesh strainer to remove excess pulp. Add in remaining whole berries and combine.

Bittersweet Chocolate Milk Recipe

1/2 oz. cocoa powder
2 oz. crumbled bittersweet dark chocolate
4-6 oz. steamed milk
Steam milk and chocolates using a cappuccino steamer until chocolate is melted and the milk thoroughly heated.

Bloody Mary Mix Recipe

46 oz. tomato juice
2 oz. Worcestershire Sauce
6 dashes Tabasco Pepper Sauce
2 tbsp. celery salt
1 tbsp. black pepper
1/2 tbsp. salt
2 Dashes Angostura Aromatic Bitters
In a large covered jar, thoroughly mix ingredients and taste-test over ice. Keep refrigerated.

Brugal/Pineapple Simple Syrup Recipe

2 pineapples peeled, cored, cut into 1 inch cubes
24 oz. sugar
2 liters Brugal Añejo Rum
Put sugar and pineapple into a 10 quart pot. Add the rum and simmer over low heat for 1 hour, stirring occasionally. Do not let mixture boil. Cool and strain the syrup through a cheese cloth or sieve.

Candied Lemongrass Recipe

3 stalks lemongrass
A few Kaffir lime leaves
2 cups sugar
2 cups water
Cut the whitish parts of the lemongrass stalks into thin rings. Discard remainder. Combine all ingredients, bring to a boil and simmer for about 15 minutes. Let cool. Do not remove lemongrass. Store in a glass container.

Chinese Five-Spiced Honey Recipe

1 tbsp. dried star anise
1 tbsp. dried fennel seed
1 tbsp. cinnamon
1 tbsp. cloves
1 tbsp. Szechwan peppercorns
3 tbsp. honey
2 cups simple syrup
Coarsely grind spices in a coffee grinder and pour into a stainless steel pan. Toast the spices briefly before carefully adding simple syrup and honey. Bring to a boil and simmer for 15 minutes. Strain out spices and let cool before using.

Clove Studded Orange Peel

Slice orange down side carefully removing the rind. Insert 3 or 4 cloves into the pith side of the rind. Carefully squeeze the orange peel over the cocktail with a flame between the peel and the cocktail releasing the orange oils. Drop the clove studded rind in the cocktail, pith side up.

Coriander Simple Syrup Recipe

2 cups coriander seeds
Prepare a simple syrup using
    equal portions of sugar and water.
Add 2 cups of coriander seeds and
    let simmer for 20 minutes or to taste.
Cool then strain syrup though a tea strainer.

Cucumber Simple Syrup Recipe

2 English cucumbers
1 $^1/_2$ pints simple syrup
Chop 1 cucumber into pieces and add to simple syrup. Let sit for a day then strain out the pieces. Take the other cucumber and cut it in half diagonally. Scoop out seeds and flesh with a spoon, then slice it into thin half moons. Add to simple syrup.

Dark Chocolate Jalapeño Ice Cream Recipe

1 $^1/_2$ quarts half and half
2 jalapeño peppers, julienne cut
1 $^1/_3$ bars bittersweet chocolate,
   broken into pieces
5 whole eggs
1 $^1/_2$ cups sugar
15 oz. heavy cream
Bring the half and half to a boil with the jalapeños. Remove from heat and melt the chocolate in the half and half. Let cool and refrigerate overnight. The next day strain the jalapeño from the base and discard. Make ice cream using the refrigerated base and remaining ingredients. Yields 1 Gallon.

Enhanced Ginger-Apple Juice Recipe

32 oz. bottle Gravenstein Apple Juice
5 drops ginger essential oil
Add the ginger oil to the apple juice and mix well.

Enhanced Pomegranate Juice

32 oz. bottle fresh pomegranate juice
5 drops cardamom essential oil
5 drops nutmeg essential oil
5 drops Red Mandarin essential oil
5 drops black pepper essential oil
Combine ingredients and store in a sealed glass container.

Fig and Almond-Infused Jim Beam Black Bourbon Recipe

1 liter Jim Beam Black Bourbon
$^1/_2$ lb. figs
$^1/_2$ lb. blanched almonds
Steep the figs and blanched almonds in a liter of Jim Beam Black Bourbon for 2-3 days in a sealed glass container.

Fresh Pear Mix Recipe

3 oz. eau de vie de Poire Williams
1 tbsp. Elderflower syrup
1 tbsp. fresh ground pepper
2 oz. fresh lemon juice
32 oz. pear puree
Mix ingredients
Refrigerate and store in a glass jar.

Fresno Chili Rings Preparation

Hollow out the chili (by cutting a circle around the stem, then carefully pulling out the stem and ribs). Remove the remaining seeds by using a spoon and scraping. Slice the bottom of the chili off and cut the chili into thin rings.

Fruit-Infused Sauza Extra Gold Tequila Recipe

Fill jar $^1/_5$ full with pineapples
Fill jar $^1/_5$ full with cantaloupe
Fill jar $^1/_5$ full with strawberries
Fill jar $^1/_5$ full with peaches
1 liter Sauza Extra Gold Tequila
1 liter Midori
10 oz. Blue Curaçao
Core, peel and slice pineapples into rings. Peel, de-seed and cube cantaloupe. Wash and remove leaves from strawberries. Wash, cut and pit peaches. Cover with blue curaçao, tequila and Midori. Let steep for 4-5 days.

Ginger/Rhubarb Simple Syrup Recipe

1 $^1/_2$ pints simple syrup
5 stalks thinly sliced fresh rhubarb
1 red beet, sliced
5 drops ginger essential oil
5 drops galangal essential oil
Combine ingredients and stir. Let set for 2 days for color.

Ginger Simple Syrup Recipe

$1/3$ part water
$1/3$ part sugar
$1/3$ part pieces sliced ginger
Boil the water and add the ginger. Steep for a few minutes. Add the sugar and stir until dissolved. Remove from heat and let cool. Strain with a cheesecloth. Refrigerate in a glass jar.

Green Tea Simple Syrup Recipe

$1/2$ cup water
2 bags green tea
2 tbsp. honey
Boil the water and steep the tea bags for 5-10 minutes. Stir in the honey until dissolved. Refrigerate in a glass container.

Green Tomato Juice Recipe

2 lbs. Green Zebra tomatoes
1 cup water
In a large pot of boiling water, drop in the tomatoes for 5 minutes. Remove from heat and discard water. Peel, seed, dice and puree them in a blender with one cup of water. Return to pot and cook for 15 minutes. Let cool. Puree again and strain. Add enough water to give it the consistency of traditional canned tomato juice.

Heirloom Tomato Juice Recipe

5 lbs. Heirloom tomatoes
1 clove garlic, peeled
1 red bell pepper, peeled and quartered
1 yellow bell pepper, peeled and quartered
1 jalapeño pepper, seeded and hollowed
Bake 5 lbs. of tomatoes on low heat for 10 minutes. Peel, remove the seeds and chop into small pieces. Puree the tomatoes with 1 peeled garlic clove, 1 red bell pepper and 1 yellow bell pepper, and 1 jalapeño pepper. Let stand for 30 minutes before using. Refrigerate in a glass container. Lasts for 2-3 weeks.

Hibiscus-Infusion Recipe

1 gallon water
1 cup packed dried Hibiscus flowers
2 $1/2$ cups sugar
Heat the ingredients and simmer until the mixture is reduced to $2/3$ gallon.

Homemade Maraschino Cherry Recipe

Fill a glass jar with pitted, organic sour black cherries (fresh or frozen). Fill to cover with equal parts simple syrup and Luxardo Maraschino Liqueur. For every cup of cherries, squeeze in half of a lime. Refrigerate up to 2 months.

Hot Buttered Rum Batter Recipe (Cyrus)

1 lb. unsalted butter
4 cups manufacturing cream
1 pint vanilla bean ice cream
$1/2$ cup granulated sugar
$1/2$ cup brown sugar
1 tsp. ground cinnamon
1 tsp. ground allspice
1 tbsp. ground nutmeg
Add all ingredients to a pan and bring to a boil, stirring frequently with a whisk. Simmer for 5 minutes while continuing to stir. Let cool. Batter can be frozen and thawed for use by reheating in a pan.

Hot Buttered Rum Batter Recipe (Joe's)

1 cup unsalted butter
2 cups light brown sugar
1 qt. vanilla ice cream, softened
1 tsp. ground nutmeg
1 tsp. cardamom powder
1 tsp. ground cassia bud
1 tsp. vanilla extract
Place all ingredients into a bowl and whisk thoroughly.

Huckleberry Simple Syrup Recipe

1 lb. huckleberries
$1/2$ cup sugar
1 cup Verjus (unripe grape juice)
Combine ingredients and bring to a boil, stirring occasionally. Reduce heat to a simmer for 15 minutes. The berries should burst. Strain out the solid bits using a fine mesh-strainer.

J BAR Cranberry Habanero Chutney Recipe

1 1/4 oz. frozen cranberries
1/4 cup fresh pineapple, finely chopped
1/4 cinnamon stick, finely chopped
1/3 habanero chili, seeded and minced
1/4 oz. ginger, finely chopped
1/4 cup granulated sugar
1 tbsp. apple cider vinegar
Combine all ingredients in a saucepan and bring to a slow simmer for about one hour over low heat until flavors are married and well balanced. Yields 1/2 cup

Lemon/Mint Simple Syrup Recipe

4 cups water
4 cups sugar
6 lemons, sliced
Zest of 3 lemons
1 1/2 oz. fresh mint
Bring to a boil and simmer until reduced by one quarter. Cool and strain. Store in a sealed glass container.

Lemongrass Simple Syrup Recipe

1/3 part water
1/3 part sugar
1/3 part lemongrass
Bring water to a boil. Add lemongrass and let steep for a few minutes. Add sugar and stir till dissolved. Once sugar is completely dissolved remove from heat and let cool. Blend and strain through a cheesecloth. Refrigerate in a glass container.

Nutmeg, Cassia Bud and Cardamom Sugar Rim Recipe

1 tbsp. ground nutmeg
1 tbsp. ground cassia bud
1 tbsp. cardamom powder
1/2 cup Sugar in the Raw
1/2 cup sugar
Stir ingredients until well mixed

Pepper-Infused Frïs Vodka Recipe

Cocktail onions
Grilled onions
Pimento-stuffed olives
Caper berries
Chili peppers
Cherry peppers
Roasted peppers
Combine equal amounts of the above and cover completely with Frïs Vodka. Steep for a minimum of one week in an airtight glass jar.

Pepper-Infused Silver Tequila Recipe

2 liters Silver Tequila
4-6 jalapeño peppers
Fill jar 1/4 with green bell peppers
Fill jar 1/4 with red bell peppers
Fill jar 1/4 with yellow bell peppers
Place washed and quartered bell peppers into jar. Lance jalapeño peppers and place in jar. Add tequila. Test after 2-3 days.

Pineapple-Infused Tequila Recipe

750ml Gold Tequila
1 fresh pineapple, peeled, cored and sliced
1-2 vanilla beans
Place the pineapple and vanilla beans in a glass container. Cover completely with tequila and seal the container. Test after 3-5 days.

Pumpkin/Chai Mix Recipe

1 cup pumpkin pie filling
1 1/2 cups Voyant Chai Cream Liqueur
Cook over low heat until it comes to a slow boil. Remove from heat and chill over night.

Raspberry/Shiso Puree Recipe

1 pint raspberries
5 tsp. sugar
4 shiso leaves, ice cubes
5 oz. water
Muddle the fresh raspberries and sugar. Set aside. In an empty mixing glass, rip the shiso leaves, add a few ice cubes and water and shake thoroughly. Combine all of the ingredients and strain through a fine mesh strainer, allowing the puree to strain through, but not the raspberry seeds. Store in a glass container. Keep refrigerated.

Red Indian Peach Puree Recipe

2 lbs. Red Indian peaches, peeled and pitted
2 cups water
2 cups simple syrup
Combine ingredients in a blender, puree and strain.

Rose Flower Simple Syrup Recipe

1 oz. Rose Flower Water
4 cups water
2 cups sugar
Bring water to a slow boil. Add the sugar and stir until dissolved. Stir in the Rose flower water. Let cool. Store in a glass container.

Rosemary's Bloody Mary Mix Recipe

Makes one gallon
1 #10 can Roma tomatoes
2 cups oven roasted tomatoes
1 green bell pepper, cut and seeded
1/2 white onion, peeled and chopped
4 garlic cloves, peeled and chopped
3 serano chilis, seeded and hollowed
4 fresh basil leaves
2 bay leaves
1 tbsp. black pepper
1 tbsp. celery seed
1 1/2 tsp. cayenne pepper
1 tsp. kosher salt
4 oz. fresh lime juice
4 oz. fresh lemon juice
6 tbsp. Worcestershire Sauce
2 tbsp. Crystal Hot Sauce
Marinate for 3 days
Blend ingredients thoroughly and strain. Add tomato juice as needed to thin. Refrigerate in a glass container.

Rosemary's Infused SKYY Vodka Recipe

1 medium sprig of fresh rosemary
1 liter bottle SKYY Vodka
Refrigerate and allow to infuse for 15-20 hours. Strain vodka with cheesecloth. Keep refrigerated.

Sangrita Bloody Maria Mix Recipe

Tomato juice
Orange juice
Grapefruit juice
Lime juice
Cholula Hot Sauce
Salt and fresh ground pepper
Fresh jalepeño
Combine ingredients to taste.

Spiced Simple Syrup Recipe

1 tbsp. crushed cinnamon stick
1 tbsp. crushed nutmeg
1 tbsp. whole cloves
1 cup sugar
1 cup water
Combine ingredients and bring to a boil. Let simmer for 15 minutes. Strain with a fine mesh strainer and let cool. Refrigerate and store in a glass container.

Steamed Coconut Milk Mixture Recipe

3 oz. whole milk
6 oz. Goya Coconut Milk
Steam and froth using a cappuccino steamer until well heated and frothed.

Vanilla Bean & Citrus Peel-Infused Bourbon Recipe

150ml bourbon
1 vanilla bean stick, split in half lengthwise
Zest of lemon
Zest of orange
Let sit for one month.

Vanilla Simple Syrup Recipe

1/2 cup water
1/2 cup sugar
2 oz. vanilla extract
Bring water to a slow boil, then stir in sugar to melt. Add vanilla extract. Mix thoroughly, cool and refrigerate.

Drink Index